Walking Poets

# WORDSWORTH AND BASHŌ: WALKING POETS

**Art Editions North**

First published in 2014 by Art Editions North on the occasion of the exhibition
*Wordsworth and Bashō: Walking Poets*
At Dove Cottage & the Wordsworth Museum
24 May to 2 November 2014

Art Editions North is an imprint of the University of Sunderland
Co-published with the Wordsworth Trust

Production, design and curation of catalogue by Manny Ling
Edited by Mike Collier and Janet Ross
Catalogue entries by Carol McKay

The exhibition *Wordsworth and Bashō: Walking Poets* has been curated by Mike Collier and Janet Ross of WALK (Walking, Art, Landskip and Knowledge) at the University of Sunderland

Exhibition organized by Mike Collier and Janet Ross assisted by Ayako Tani and Christopher McHugh

Exhibition and technical design by Arnaud Moinet

Printed by W M Print Limited, Walsall



All photography unless otherwise started by Colin Davison—Rosella Studios.



Contact: aen@sunderland.ac.uk

A British Library CIP record is available
ISBN: 978-1-906832-20-9

Distributed by Cornerhouse Publications
70 Oxford Street, Manchester M1 5NH, England
tel: +44 (0) 161 200 1503
fax: + 44 (0) 161 200 1504
email: publications@cornerhouse.org
www.cornerhouse.org/publications

*Walking Poets*

# WORDSWORTH AND BASHŌ: WALKING POETS

Mike Collier

Art Editions North

The Wordsworth Trust

2014

# CONTENTS

# FOREWORD

**MICHAEL McGREGOR**

*The Robert Woof Director of the Wordsworth Trust*

'Wordsworth and Bashō: Walking Poets' is a splendid example of the importance of collaboration and the value of a creative dialogue between present and past. The exhibition builds on momentum developed through previous collaborations between the Wordsworth Trust, the University of Sunderland and Bath Spa University, in which a range of contemporary artists created fresh and challenging perspectives on Wordsworth's poetry.

I am grateful for this opportunity to thank a number of people who have made this exhibition possible. Mike Collier has been an incredible driving force, his resourcefulness and positive outlook a constant source of inspiration. Janet Ross has effectively and efficiently organised a very complex project and kept it all on track. Brian Thompson has played a key role in the shaping of the exhibition. He is also one of a number of artists that have responded so imaginatively to the work of Wordsworth and Bashō. Their contributions add a wonderfully rich dimension to this exhibition.

Among my colleagues in Grasmere, I would like to thank in particular Jeff Cowton and his curatorial team for all of their hard work.

An exhibition of this scope would not be possible without contributions from a number of funders. I am very grateful to the University of Sunderland, Bath Spa University, the Heritage Lottery Fund, Arts Council England, the John Ellerman Foundation, the Daiwa Anglo-Japanese Foundation and the Great Britain Sasakawa Foundation for their generous support.

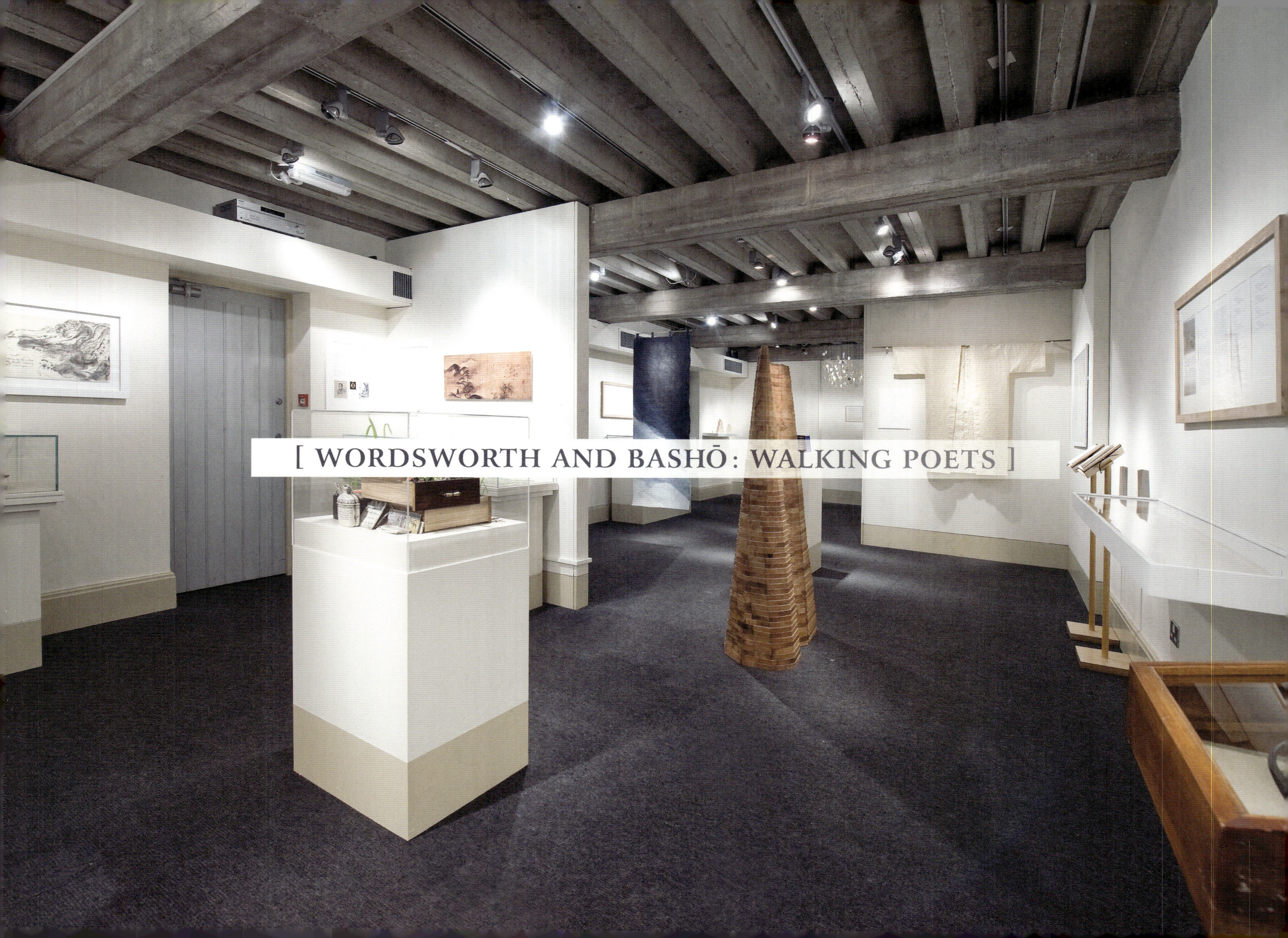

# [ WORDSWORTH AND BASHŌ: WALKING POETS ]

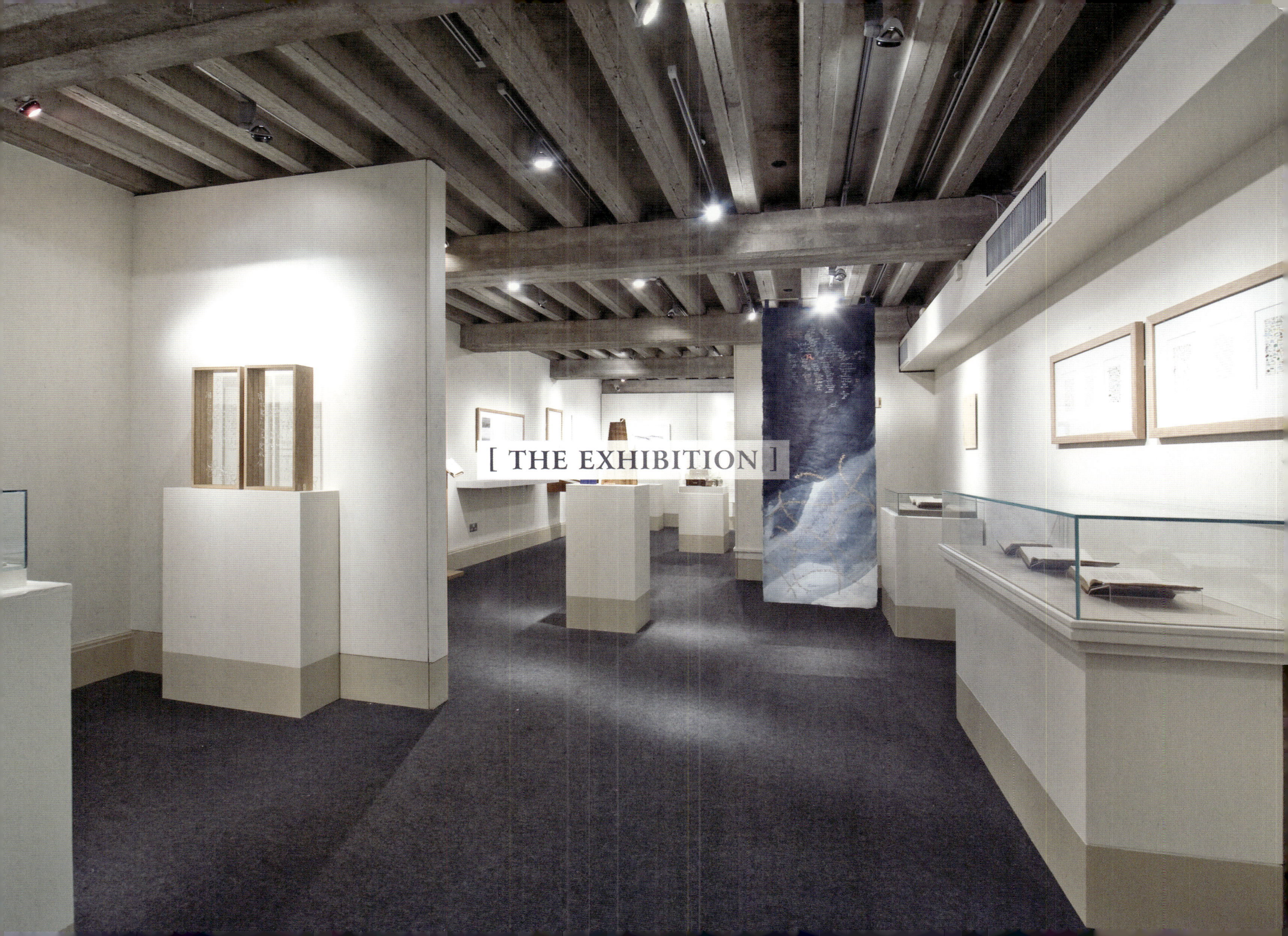
[ THE EXHIBITION ]

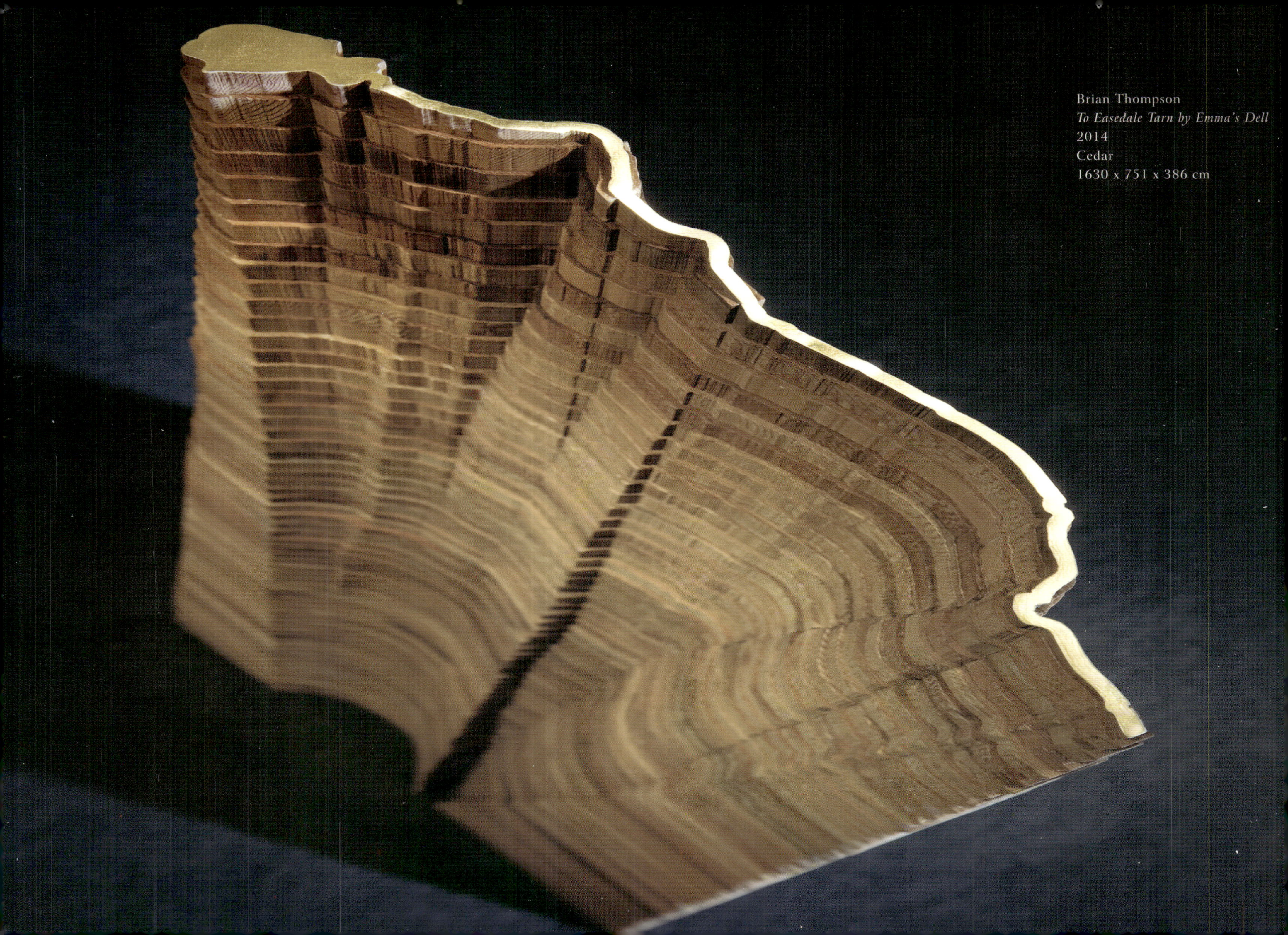

Brian Thompson
*To Easedale Tarn by Emma's Dell*
2014
Cedar
1630 x 751 x 386 cm

# INTRODUCTION

**MIKE COLLIER**

In the exhibition *Wordsworth and Bashō: Walking Poets*, we present the poems and manuscripts (original and facsimile copies) of William and Dorothy Wordsworth and Matsuo Bashō. We wish to explore the subjects of their writings, looking at how each writer created their work and how a close examination of their manuscripts can add further to our appreciation and understanding of their poetry and prose. Contemporary artists from the UK and Japan were asked to consider and interpret these themes and artefacts through specially commissioned work, thereby bringing us closer to the older writing and manuscripts.

The idea for this exhibition arose from a conference and study produced by the Wordsworth Trust (with support from Arts Council England) in 2012 called *Beyond Words: Understanding and Sharing the Meaning of Manuscripts*. In the conference, Jeff Cowton, Curator at the Wordsworth Trust, described how manuscripts had meanings beyond the words themselves and how, for example, handwriting is a visual form which can 'mimic the texture of thought', revealing valuable clues as to the state of mind of the creator. The study recommended that the Trust consider working with contemporary artists to further explore and share these meanings.

In this introduction I aim to explain the background to the exhibition, comparing the work of three poets and writers whose worlds (and poetry), some suggest, could not be further apart, and in this I am greatly indebted to John Elder who has undertaken the only (to my knowledge) serious comparative and sustained study of the two poets and whose support and contribution to this project has been enormously encouraging.[1] I also describe how the project began, and the process behind the commissioning of new work for the show. My colleague, Carol McKay, will discuss elsewhere in this publication the work of each artist and link it to the themes outlined in this introduction, showing how their work has been influenced by the poetry and prose of either Dorothy and William Wordsworth or Matsuo Bashō, or all three.

The first question readers of this essay and visitors to the exhibition might ask is; how can we compare the work of three writers who lived a century apart, in two very different cultures, at opposite ends of the globe?

And the second question that may be asked is: why have we chosen to commission contemporary artists to highlight the work of poets and writers who lived a long time ago?

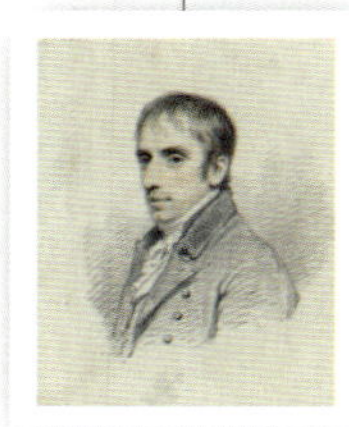

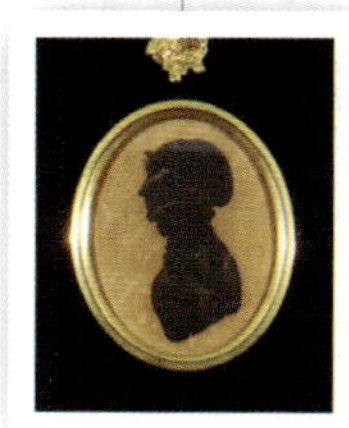

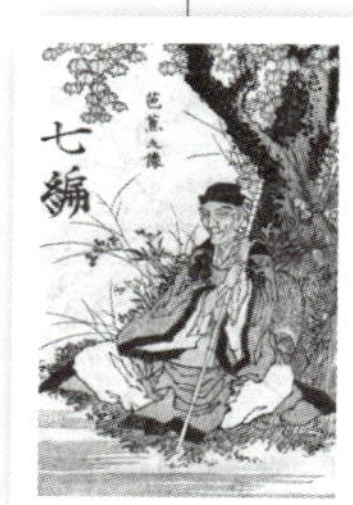

*Portrait of William Wordsworth 1806, Henry Eldridge (1768–1821), pencil and watercolour 15.5 x 12.5 cm, courtesy of the Wordsworth Trust*
*Image of Dorothy Wordsworth, courtesy of the Wordsworth Trust*
*Portrait of Matsuo Bashō, by Hokusai, courtesy of Bloodaxe Books*

I hope, in this introduction, to answer these questions, and in doing so, enable the manuscripts of Dorothy and William Wordsworth and Bashō presented here to be seen in a fresh and exciting light. In the remainder of this essay, I have compared their writing and poetry under a series of generic headings that also form the narrative of the exhibition.

**Background: three poets and writers; two cultures**

Matsuo Bashō was born in Ueno (near Kyoto) in 1644 in a Neo Confucian Japan ruled centrally by the Tokugawa shogunate who cut the country off from the rest of the world for the next two hundred years. This period was characterized by economic growth, strict social order and isolationist foreign policies.

William Wordsworth was born just over a century later in 1770 in Cockermouth, Cumbria; Dorothy, in 1771. In stark contrast to Japan, Britain at this time was undergoing an industrial revolution, forging the beginnings of an expanding empire and encountering fierce debates in radical politics, economics and political philosophy.

The first free inflow of Western civilization to Japan took place toward the end of the nineteenth century, providing the Japanese with a chance to reconsider their traditional, social, intellectual and literary values. Japanese poets of this period were revolutionaries in their own right. They were influenced by Western Romantic poets such as Wordsworth and they saw in Bashō, a poet whose influence on Japanese poets had waned since his death in 1694, a Japanese version of these Western models.[2] As a result, Bashō's fame grew again and there was renewed interest in his poetry and prose in Japan.

Conversely, as Japanese culture travelled across the world to the West, it influenced not only the art of the Post Impressionist painters, but also early twentieth century Western poets such as Ezra Pound and the Imagists, many of whom were interested in Japan and Japanese arts; a second generation of twentieth century poets (the Beat Poets —Gary Snyder, Jack Kerouac and Allen Ginsberg on the West Coast of America) experimented with the *haiku* form, influenced greatly by the poetry of Bashō.[3]

**Walking Poets**

The most obvious 'similarity' between the Wordsworths and Bashō is that they were inveterate walker–poets. Wordsworth's contemporary Thomas De Quincey reckoned that Wordsworth walked a distance of 175,000 to 180,000 miles in his lifetime and it could be argued that walking creates one of the main themes around which *The Prelude* is constructed.

Two of the most important experiences related in *The Prelude*, for example, found their origins in mountain walks (when Wordsworth was overawed by the Ravine of Gondo, the 'Gloomy Pass', or during a night walk to the top of Snowdon). Walking was important to Wordsworth because it created *an interaction* between the traveller and the landscape.[4]

It was similarly important to Dorothy, who walked incessantly throughout much of her life, both on her own and with companions, recording her observations and encounters in the pages of her *Grasmere and Alfoxden Journals* (see figure 1).

The same rationale for walking and writing could equally apply to Bashō who made not one but several journeys in Japan. 'He sought to experience first hand beautiful scenes such as Mount Yoshino, Sarashina, and the pine-clad islands of Matsushima.'[5] His first journey in 1684 was described in *Nozarashi Kikō* ('A Weather Beaten Journey'). Other journeys and journals followed (including, in 1687, *Oi no Kobumi*, 'The Records of a Travel-Worn Satchel' and, in 1688, *Sarashina Kikō*, 'A Visit to Sarashina Village'—a copy of this particular journal is on display in the exhibition; see figure 2). His art reached its greatest form in 1689 in his masterpiece *Oku no Hosomichi*, 'The

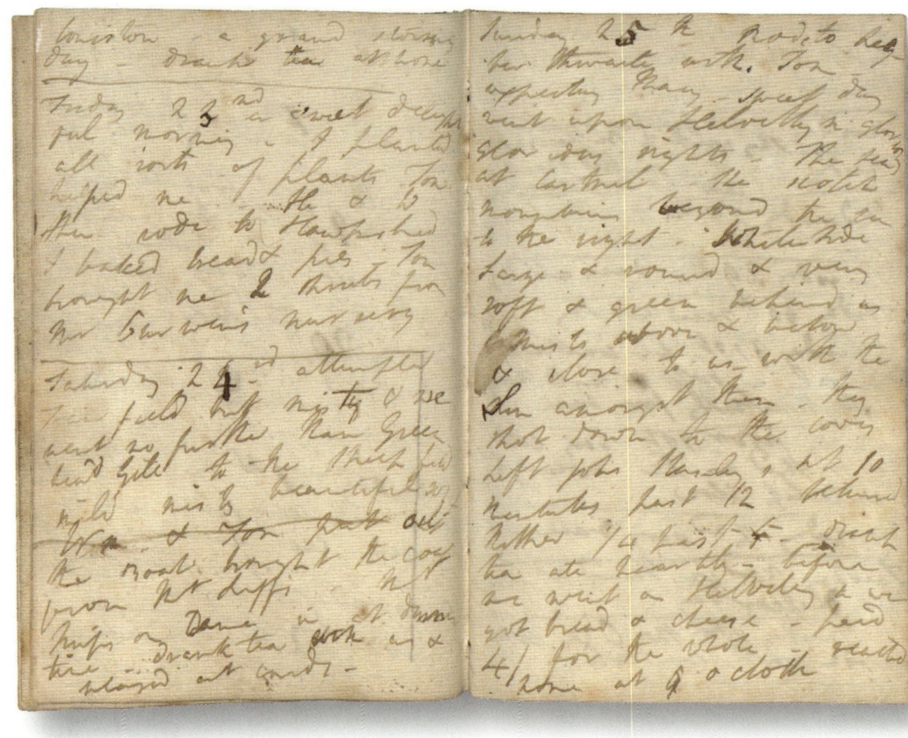

Figure 1
Dorothy Wordsworth
*Grasmere Journal*
Entry for 24 and 25 October 1801

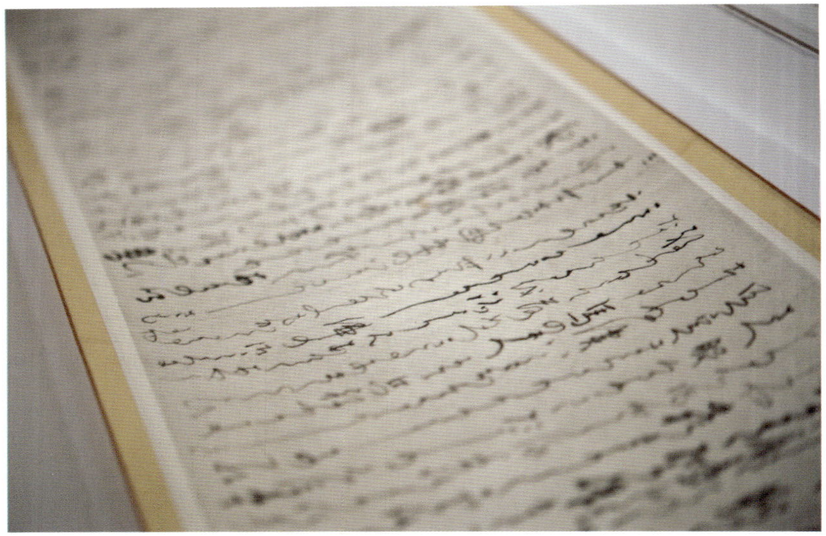

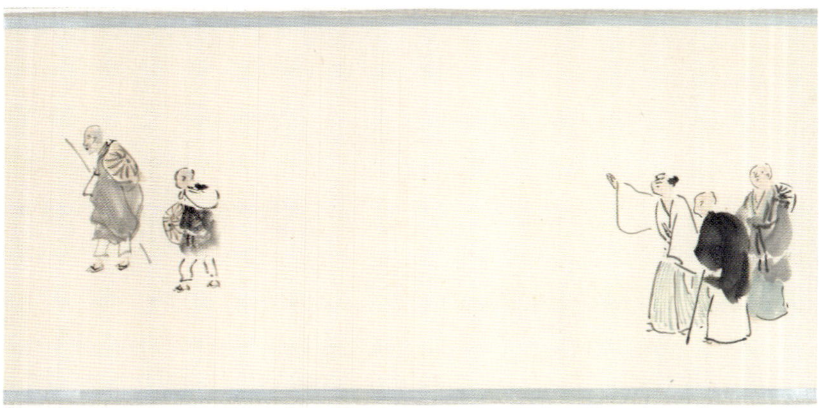

Figure 2, Matsuo Bashō, *Sarashina Kikō* draft, c.1688, paper, sumi ink, 20 x 1380 cm Replica borrowed from Iga City Bashō Memorial Museum (copyright holder could not be contacted)

Figure 3, Matsuo Bashō (text), Yosa Buson (drawing and writing), *Narrow Road to the Deep North; Scroll 1*, 1778, paper, sumi ink, colour, 20 x 450 cm (detail), courtesy of Kyoto National Museum

Narrow Road to the Deep North'. In this poem/travel book, he recounts his last long walk, completed with his disciple Sora, some 1,200 miles covered over five months beginning in May 1689. The Japanese term *oku* refers to the northern backcountry of the main Japanese island of Honshū, and it also means 'deep' in the sense of interior, such as the depths of a mountain and spiritual depths.[6] We are delighted to be able to show not one, but two versions of this journal. The first is a reproduction in Bashō's own hand; the second is a transcription by Yosa Buson (1716–1784), written and illustrated over a century later in 1778 (see figure 3). Buson was a poet and painter of the Edo period who revered Bashō. As well as making this copy of Bashō's seminal work, Buson was inspired to embark on his own wanderings to the 'deep north', following in the master's footsteps.

It is interesting to note, within the context of this exhibition, that recent studies have shown what the Wordsworths and Bashō recognised intuitively; namely that walking boosts creative inspiration. Stanford researchers examined the creativity levels of people while they walked versus while they sat and found that a person's creative output increased by an average of 60 percent when walking.[7]

**Wordsworth and Bashō: environmental pioneers?**

For both Bashō and Wordsworth, 'man' and nature were intertwined in a great oneness with the earth—and with the heavens, too. In Wordsworth's writing, there are elements of pantheism; in Bashō, Zen. In our exhibition at Dove Cottage we have shown two relevant passages (one from Wordsworth—an excerpt from his account of an ascent of Snowdon from Book XIV of *The Prelude*—and one from Bashō with an account of his ascent of Mount Gassan) that illustrate well this sense of man being subsumed within the power of nature (see figure 4):

> The Moon stood naked in the Heavens, at height
> Immense above my head, and on the shore
> I found myself of a huge sea of mist,
> Which, meek and silent, rested at my feet:
> A hundred hills their dusky backs upheaved
> All over this still Ocean, and beyond,
> Far, far beyond, the vapours shot themselves,
> In headlands, tongues and promontory shapes,
> Into the Sea, the real Sea, that seemed
> To dwindle, and give up its majesty,
> Usurp'd upon as far as sight could reach.[8]

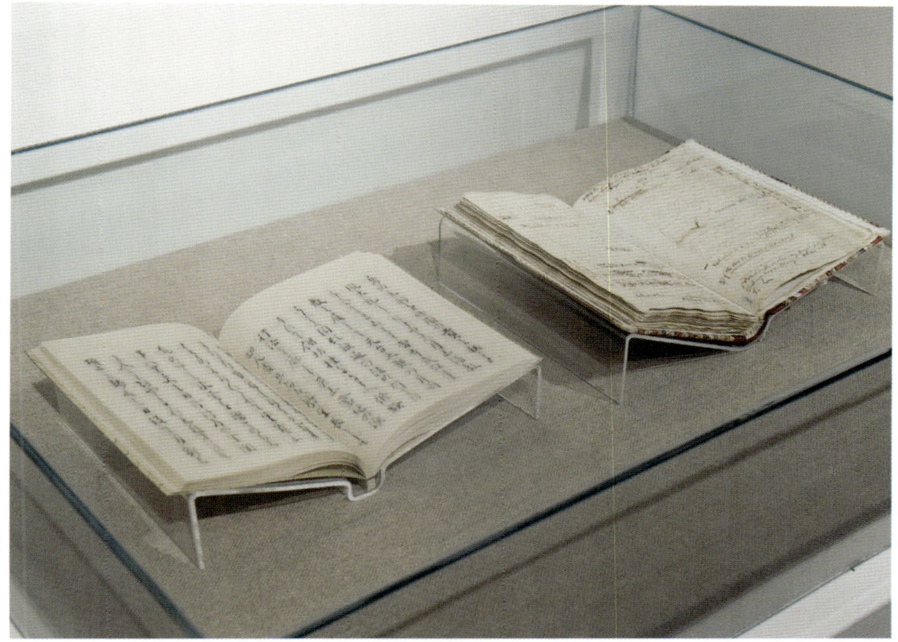

Figure 4, Installation shot of display case showing the copy by Soryū of Matsuo Bashō's *Narrow Read to the Deep North* open at the ascent of Mount Gassan (courtesy of Iga City Bashō Memorial Museum) and William Wordsworth, *The Prelude*, fair copy (with revisions), 1805, in the hand of Mary Wordsworth with later revision, open to show Book XIII, Wordsworth's ascent of Mount Snowdon (courtesy of the Wordsworth Trust)

And the second from Bashō's *The Narrow Road to the Deep North:*

> I climbed Mount Gassan on the eighth ... I walked through mists and clouds, breathing the thin air of high altitudes and stepping on slippery ice and snow, till at last through a gateway of clouds, as it seemed, to the very paths of the sun and the moon, I reached the summit, completely out of breath and nearly frozen to death. Presently the sun went down and the moon rose glistening in the sky. I spread some leaves on the ground and went to sleep resting my head on pliant bamboo branches. When, on the following morning, the sun rose again and dispersed the clouds, I went down towards Mount Yudono.'[9]

However, the poetry and prose of both the Wordsworths and Bashō was underpinned by more than just an *observation* of nature. The Japanese writer Hakutani wrote: 'Bashō carried nature within him and brought himself to the deepest level of nature, where all sounds lapse into the world of silence and infinity.'[10] Both William and Dorothy Wordsworth, too, perceived and understood landscape to be 'beyond anything simply visible' compressed 'into its elements, earth, air and water'.[11] Dorothy's prose, for instance, is illuminated by many moments of extraordinary emotional sharpness—as when she talks, on 15 April 1802, about how 'the wind seized our breath',[12] and later in her Journal she says that the evening of the 7th May 1802 presented 'a terrible kind of threatening brightness at sunset above Easedale'.[13]

The poetry and prose of Dorothy and William Wordsworth and Bashō emphasize the importance of a direct, unmediated experience of nature—an experience developed through our active imagination. The work of the Romantic poets argued, I think, for a rebalancing of a view of the world that had, since the Enlightenment, placed a greater importance on measuring and recording experience, whilst devaluing our emotional and creative responses to the natural world. Their approach, it could be said, is even more relevant for us today as our contemporary world is facing the twin evils of pollution and climate change.

**People in the poetry and prose of the Wordsworths and Bashō**

Although both the Wordsworths and Bashō have been labelled 'nature poets', this could be, perhaps, a little misleading, because they were also very much concerned with people or some form of 'cultured nature'.[14] In Bashō's prose, for instance, we encounter a wide variety of people he met 'on the road'—each different and individual. A glance at the subjects of some of Wordsworth's poems ('The Sailor's Mother', 'Beggars', 'The Discharged Soldier' and 'The Leech Gatherer') reveal *his* interest, too, in the people of the road he met when walking. Similarly, we find frequent observations of local friends, acquaintances and literary colleagues in the pages of Dorothy's journals.

## The continuity of the past into the present

The work of Wordsworth and Bashō is part of an ongoing continuum of creative reflection and activity that stretches both back in time and through to the present. The poetry of the Romantics was radical and different. It often used conversational English and a direct observation of nature. Wordsworth 'quarried the past'[15]—folk literature and ballads—in seeking this more direct form of verse that could be understood by everyone; hence the *Lyrical Ballads*.

Bashō's writing (both his poetry and prose) was 'deeply imbued with a sense of the passage of time and the impermanence of all things (and) he wrote often of the continuity of the past into the present'.[16] Like the Romantics, his writing was completely different from those of his immediate poetic predecessors, relying not on the false wit of sophisticated court life, but on his knowledge of, and reflection on, everyday life and the natural world, as well as an understanding of classical Chinese poetry (which he studied in Kyoto for five years early in his life).

Bashō developed a simple but profound and serious style of composing poetry. He admired the 'wandering poets' Li Po and Tu Fu of China as well as Sōgi and Saigyō of Japan. Nothing is contrived. There are no puns or attempts at urbane sophistication. Like Dorothy and William Wordsworth, Bashō writes of a direct and deep engagement with nature. In this exhibition, we have three key illustrated *haiku* by Bashō that emphasize this approach:

A crow
has settled on a bare branch
autumn evening[17]

The old pond
a frog jumps in
sound of water[18] (see figure 5)

A wild sea—
and flowing out towards Sado Island,
the Milky Way[19]

We hope, too, that the wide range of new work on display in this publication and in the exhibition will give readers and visitors new ways of seeing the manuscripts afresh; to see them as exciting, living documents, part of a creative continuum that stretches from the past through to the present.

## A collaborative practice

It may come as a surprise to realize that Wordsworth was a creative collaborator rather than the solitary genius often portrayed. It is true that the title of his most famous poem, 'I wandered lonely as a Cloud', encourages this popular reading of Wordsworth. However,

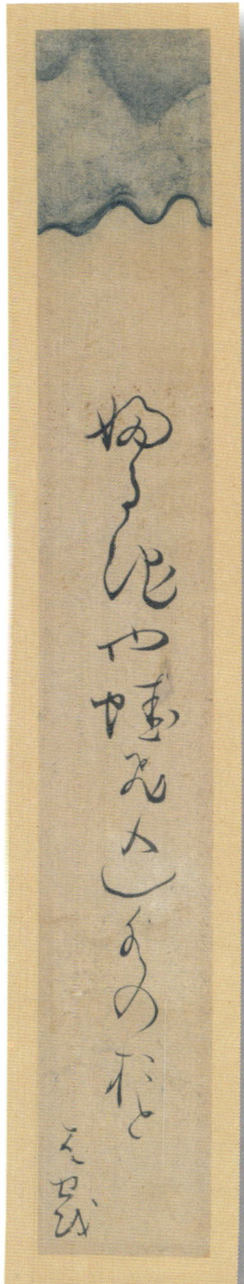

Figure 5, Matsuo Bashō,
*Furuikeya*
Tanzaku-strip, paper, sumi ink
36 x 5 cm
Facsimile courtesy of
Kakimori Bunko

he collaborated closely with Coleridge on his (their) first major important publication—the *Lyrical Ballads*—whilst his other work owed much to Dorothy: their sharing of experiences that would become the subject of his poems, her recording of them in a journal to which he could turn as an aid to memory, and in the physical creation and copying of verse with which she could be occupied for several hours in a day.

Bashō also benefited from creative collaboration, undertaking his journeys with companions; *The Narrow Road to the Deep North* (for instance) is punctuated by references (and occasional contributions) from his companion, Sora.

It is in this spirit of collaboration that we invited a number of the artists in this exhibition to work collaboratively—and, in the spirit of cultural exchange, to encourage artists from the UK and Japan to work together.

**Letter writing and correspondence**

Some two hundred letters are known to have been written by Bashō—many of them similar in style to his published prose, and some including *haiku*. The Wordsworths wrote thousands of letters. The letter can be the purest and most direct form of writing—a place where feelings are often exposed. Whilst there is, of course, no direct display of temper in any of Bashō's prose or poetry, it does fleetingly arise in his letter writing—for instance, in the letter Bashō wrote to a student named Shudo who was trying to set up a branch school in Osaka after hearing he had fallen out with fellow students. 'You suffer from a somewhat selfish disposition. If you do not do as I tell you, I intend to sever my relations with you', Bashō says in the letter.

For the Wordsworths, the sending and receiving of letters was an important part of everyday life (see figures 6 & 7). It provided the only means of keeping in touch with family and friends; the receipt of a letter from Coleridge, for example, could greatly affect the Wordsworth household's spirits. The cost of paper and postage was expensive, with the recipient expected to pay for delivery. Often every inch of the paper was written upon to save the expense of using a second sheet. The handwriting, number of deletions and layout of a letter can tell us much about the formality or otherwise of the relationship between sender and recipient.

**Framing the scripts**

In this exhibition, some of the artists explore the idea developed by writers such as Coleridge and Wordsworth that there is a specific relationship between the word used to describe an object or thing and the object itself—a poetic, embodied relationship. Coleridge, writing in a letter to William Godwin[20] suggested that 'words can embody and not just stand for thoughts and things' and he 'puts his linguistic faith in words as "living things"—as plants, as live bodies'.[21]

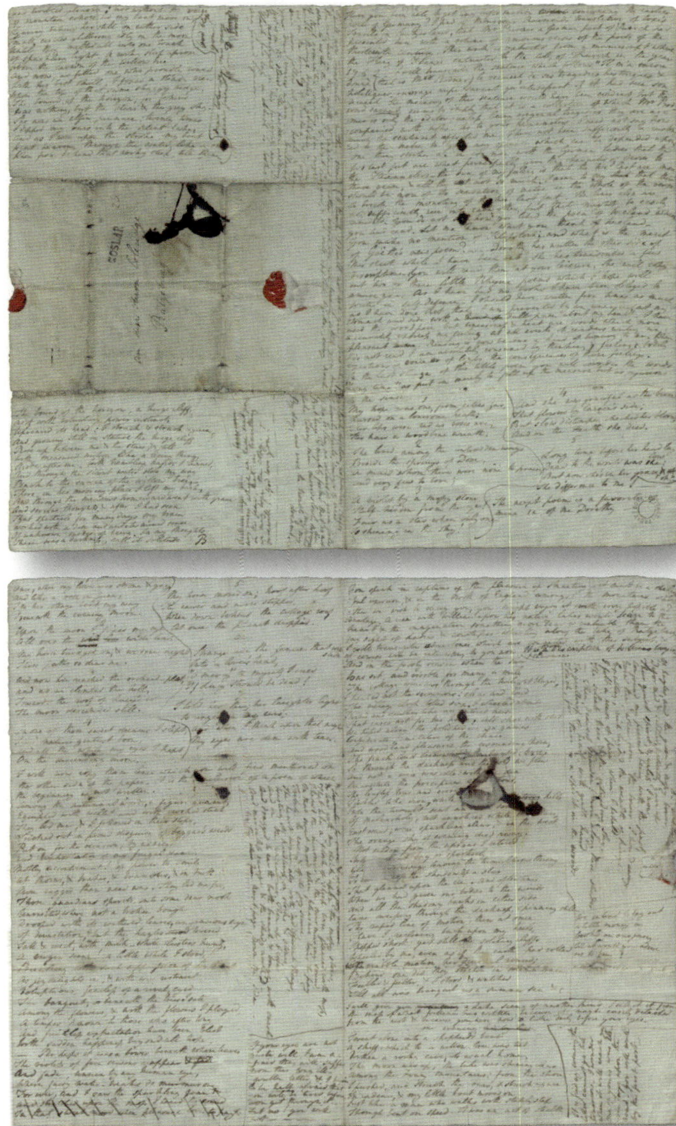

Figures 6 & 7, William Wordsworth and Dorothy Wordsworth
*Letter to Samuel Taylor Coleridge*, 14 Dec or 21 Dec 1798
'The Goslar letter', including early versions of lines towards
*The Prelude*, and other poems (front and back)

He continued:

> Is *thinking* impossible without arbitrary signs? &—how far is the word "arbitrary" a misnomer? Are words &c parts & germinations of the Plant? And what is the Law of their growth?—In something of this order I would endeavour to destroy the old antithesis of *Words & Things,* elevating, as it were, words into Things, & living Things too. [22]

A number of the artists in this exhibition have focused not just on the printed page, but also the handwritten texts of both Wordsworth and Bashō (and his follower, Buson). The personally expressive power of the Romantic poets *is* of course clearly evident in the printed word, yet it is strengthened enormously in the handwritten manuscripts on display here. Similarly, our understanding of the *haiku* poetry of Bashō has largely come down to us in a highly aesthetic, pared down, modernist form (the *haiku*, typeset, on the page), whereas in fact Bashō's and Buson's calligraphy, whilst still beautifully restrained and spare, is actually so much more personally, and wonderfully, expressive than this.

In seeing together here the handwritten texts of William and Dorothy Wordsworth and the calligraphy of Bashō and Buson, we might imagine again that these poets are not as far apart as we may have originally thought. It is precisely this expressive approach that some of the contemporary artists in this exhibition have developed (see figures 8 & 9), whilst others have focused on the ego-less typeset poetry, influenced by twentieth century Western poets who themselves drew extensively on the work of Bashō.

**The Wordsworths, Bashō and Zen: the journey into wisdom**

So far in this introduction, I have looked at straightforward and relatively uncontroversial comparisons between the work of the Wordsworths and Bashō. However, there was another key area in particular that I *felt*, intuitively, was worthy of exploration when beginning this project, and that was the deeper 'spiritual' association between the writers. Was this, perhaps, another connection between the Wordsworths and Bashō—or, if not, what did any differences between the approach of the three writers say about them and the respective cultures out of which their work emerged?

Despite the 'self-focus' that Keats for one attributed to Wordsworth, I sensed that there were many passages in Wordsworth's writing when the poet's ego seemed to me to become subsumed *within* the world—a sense that was corroborated by my reading of a fascinating book by John G. Rudy called *Wordsworth and the Zen Mind*. In his introduction, Rudy suggests that 'Throughout his poetry, Wordsworth chronicles moments of self-forgetting extraordinarily similar in course and profile to the Zen experience of the cosmic influx resulting from its formal procedures of self-emptying. As with Zennists, these occasions of self-forgetting form the spiritual basis of

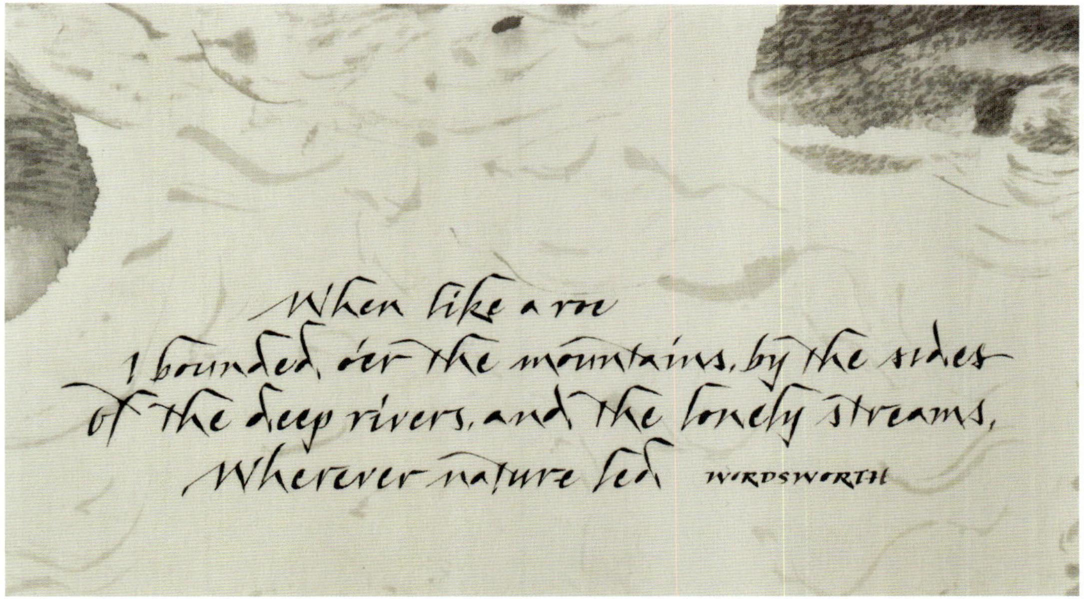


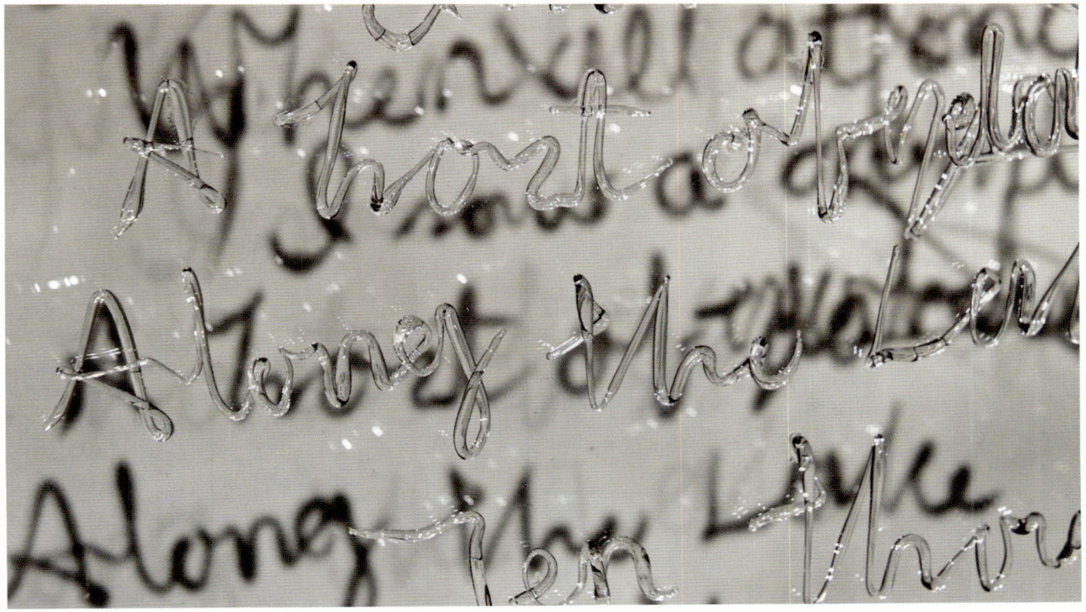

Figure 8
Manny Ling and Christine Flint-Sato
*Water Lines* (detail)
2014
Sumi ink on paper
46 x 106 cm

Figure 9
Ayako Tani
*Drafting* (detail)
2014
Handmade oak frames, lampworked borosilicate glass, soda glass
30 x 60 x 12 cm

his art and the driving force behind his creativity.'[23]

And I have felt
A presence that disturbs me with the joy
Of elevated thoughts; a sense sublime
Of something far more deeply interfused
Whose dwelling is the light of the setting suns,
And the round ocean and the living air,
And the blue sky, and in the mind of man. ...[24]

Rudy continues: 'A comparison of selected poems in the Wordsworth canon with some of the leading documents in Zen literature and philosophy establishes a less self-conscious, less egotistical strain in Wordsworth's art, refines our understanding of the poet's engagement with the *unio mystica*, and creates for his work a less ideological, more universal context.'[25]

I look'd for universal things; perused
The common countenance of earth and heaven;
And, turning the mind in upon itself,
Pored, watch'd, expected, listen'd; spread my thoughts
And spread them with a wider creeping; felt
Incumbences more awful, visitings
Of the Upholder of the tranquil Soul,
Which underneath all passion lives secure
A steadfast life ...[26]

And, perhaps most interesting of all to me (since I rate the work of Dorothy Wordsworth very highly), Rudy says of *her* writing in this 'area' that it was a substantial influence on Wordsworth's thinking: 'her acceptance of the mystery of things, her ability to see, hear and feel without necessarily seeking for an intellectual principle behind things, for a separate logos, as it were, is the measure of her identity with the universe.'[27] Dorothy's writing retains, he says;

> not a mind that seeks for anything beyond itself, but one that accepts freely, that pens to the impulses of nature—to the shining of the moon, to the play of 'misty mountain winds'.[28] ... Being the eyes of nature itself, Dorothy reads only what is there and seeks nothing beyond the surface of things.[29]

This reading of the Wordsworths and Bashō is, I realise, a somewhat speculative comparison (indeed a colleague called it, not unreasonably, a perilous one). However, it is one that has, for me, driven this project forward—and it is one I believe many of the artists in this exhibition have subconsciously tackled in their work. I leave it up to you, the reader, and the visitor to the exhibition, to make your own decision here about any deeper relationship between the work of Dorothy and William Wordsworth and Bashō when reading the passages of poetry and manuscript copies of their work represented here or when looking at the work of the contemporary artists in the show.

**Preparing the exhibition**

As a 'Prelude' to the exhibition, the Wordsworth Trust hosted a Symposium at the Jerwood Centre, Dove Cottage in January 2014 —an event which was attended by the artists in the exhibition (see figures 10–17). This afforded all involved a unique opportunity to meet and exchange ideas with the added privilege of being able to work with original Wordsworth poetical manuscripts (ninety per cent of which belong to the Trust) and facsimile manuscript copies of Bashō's work kindly lent to us by the Kyoto National Museum and the Waseda University Library. Access of this sort to these manuscripts is, of course, rare; and so it was wonderful to be able to handle material of such enormous cultural value, as well as being inspired by the landscape of the 'Wordsworth's Lake District' in winter. Workshops on sumi ink painting and Japanese book binding using traditional Japanese paper by Manny Ling, Christine Flint-Sato, Nao Sakamoto and Ewan Clayton illuminated the symposium, and a number of artists walked up Easedale, led by sculptor Brian Thompson.

Our aim over the three days (from 20–22 January 2014) was to generate ideas for a visually stunning exhibition, bringing out the beauty and power of the original manuscripts, and to look at ways in which the contemporary artwork might give visitors new ways of seeing the manuscripts afresh. Thus the handling of the documents during the symposium formed a crucial part of the process of the creation of the new work for the exhibition.

This was a very productive and intense few days. All the artists stayed together at the Thorney How Youth Hostel in Grasmere, working during the day in the Trust's extensive library of texts and manuscripts and sharing ideas over an evening meal. The Symposium was a great success and has subsequently resulted in the work represented here in this catalogue and exhibition.

I am enormously grateful to the artists in this exhibition—Ewan Clayton; Ken Cockburn; Alec Finlay; Christine Flint-Sato; Zaffar Kunial (Poet in Residence at the Wordsworth Trust, 2014); Eiichi Kono; Manny Ling; Christopher McHugh; Nobuya Monta; Inge Panneels; Andrew Richardson; Autumn Richardson; Nao Sakamoto; Minako Shirakura; Richard Skelton; Ayako Tani and Brian Thompson. They have risen to the challenge presented by this project and produced an extraordinarily varied range of work (poetry, glass, calligraphy, sculpture, painting, design, ceramics and music) of the highest quality.

And finally—by way of a caveat—I should say that I am primarily an artist and occasional curator and not an academic with an in-depth knowledge of the work of either the Wordsworths or Bashō. Sometimes this can be useful, but such enthusiasm will only go so

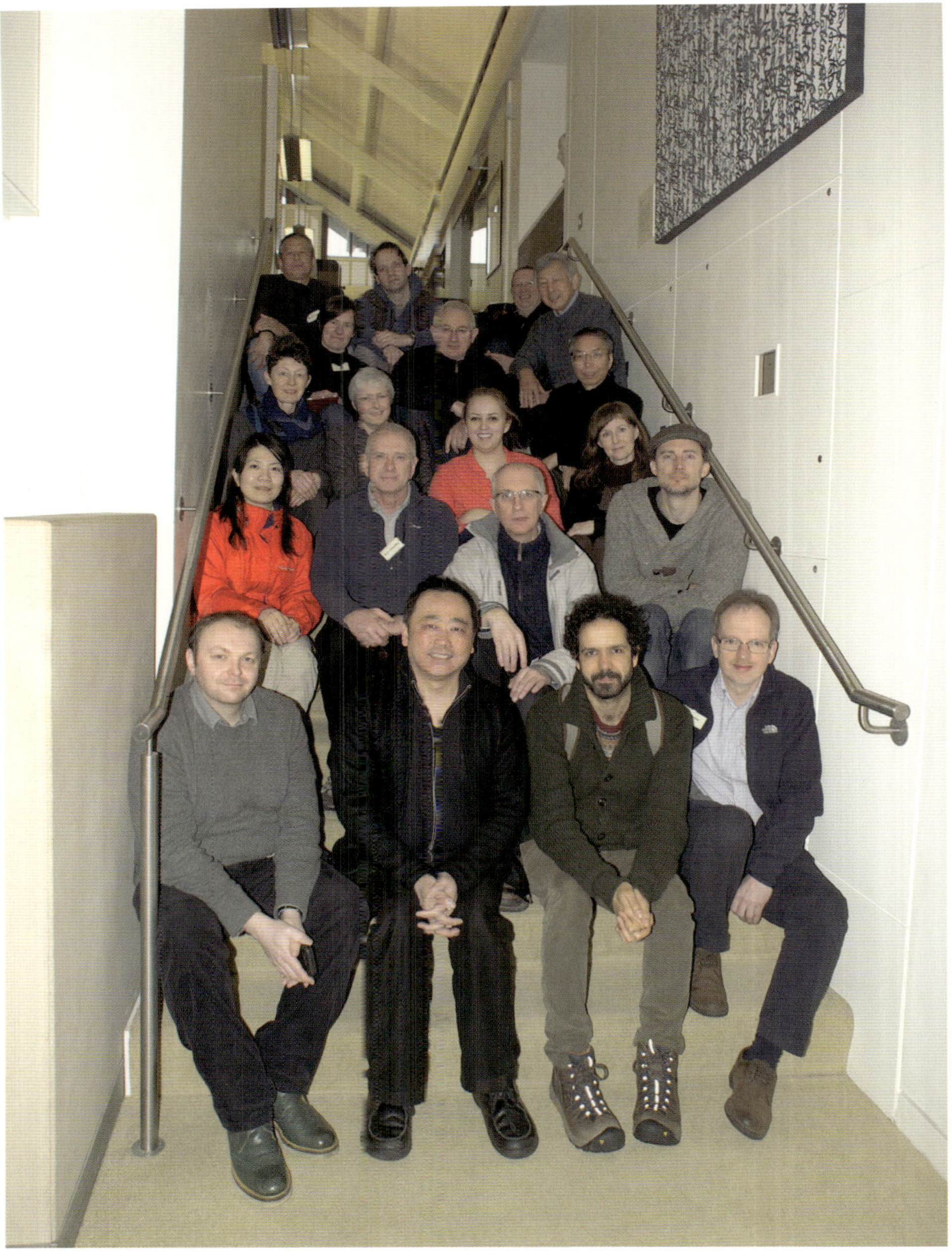

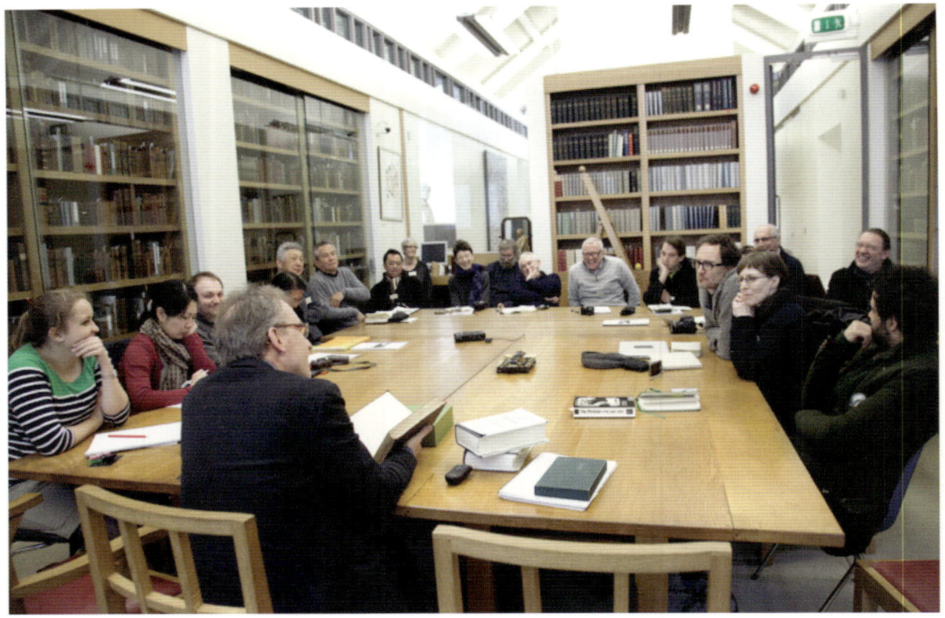

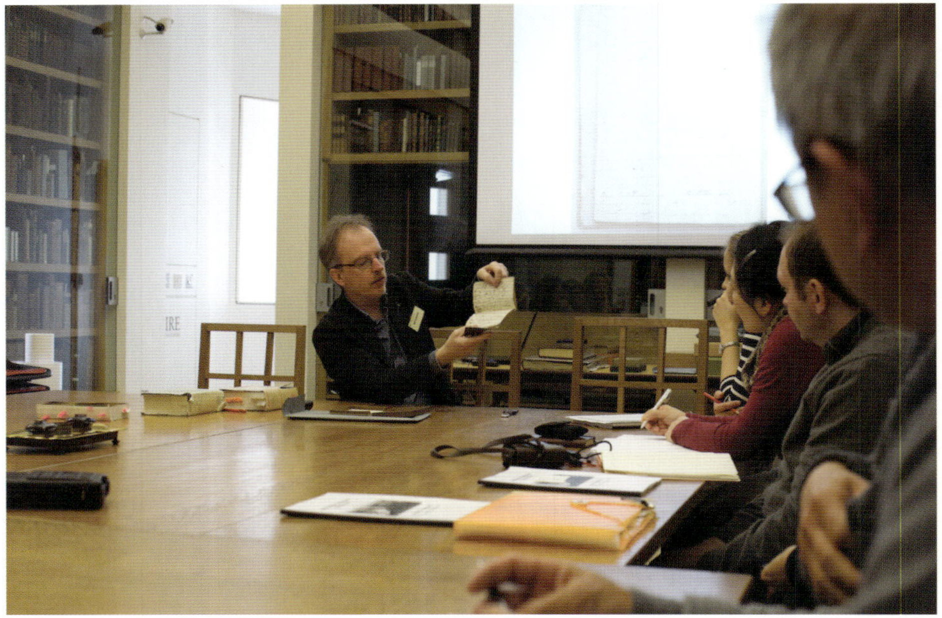

Figures 10 to 12
Artists' Symposium at the Jerwood Centre, the Wordsworth Trust, January 2014
Photography by David Unsworth

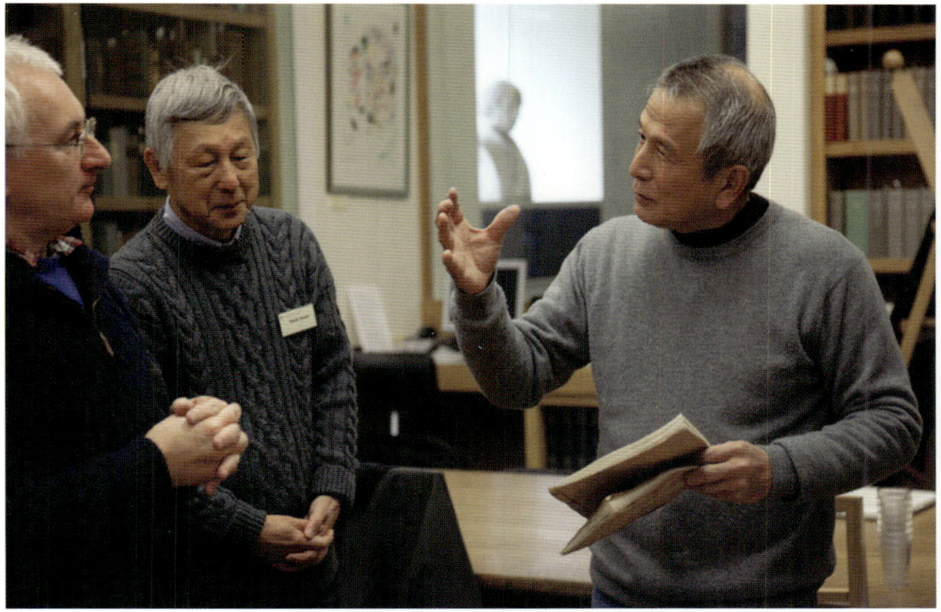

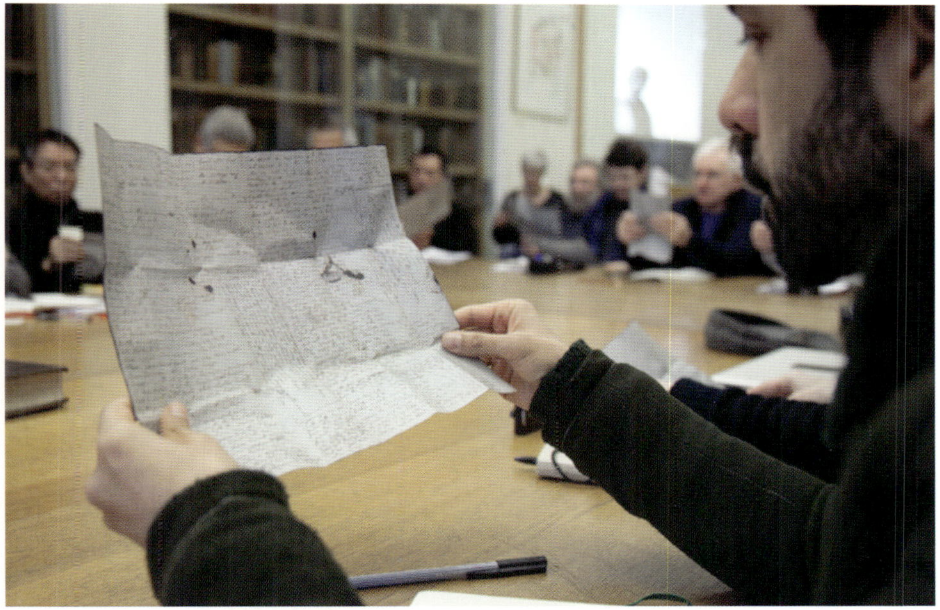

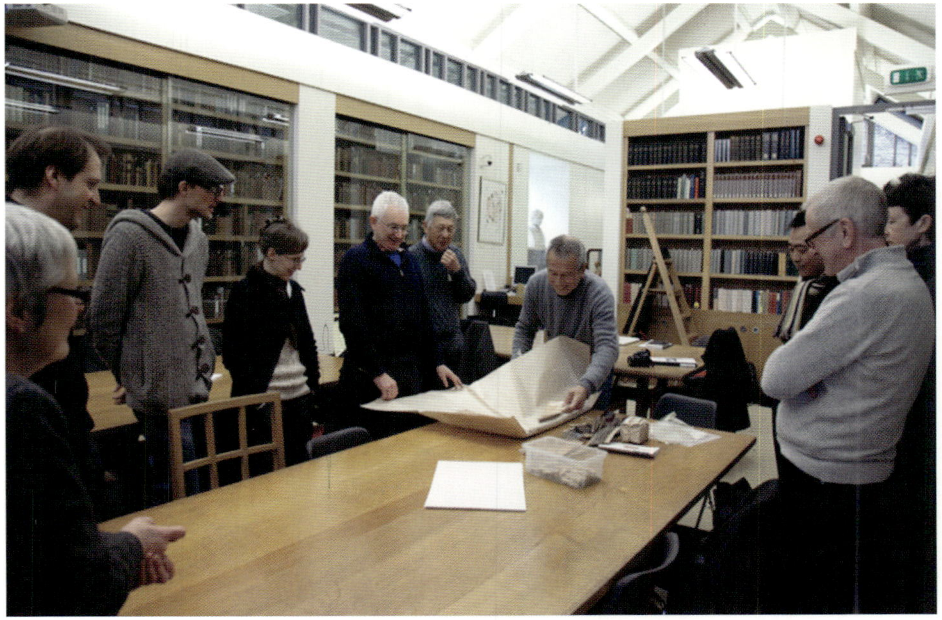

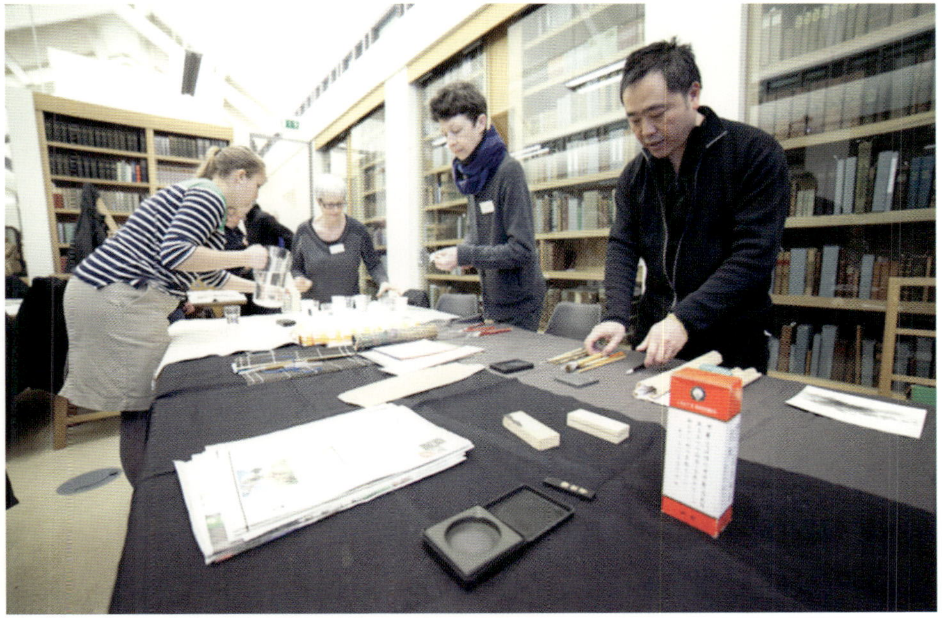

Figures 13 to 16, Workshops and discussions
Artists' Symposium at the Jerwood Centre, the Wordsworth Trust, January 2014
Photography by David Unsworth

far—and so I am hugely indebted to Jeff Cowton, Curator of the Wordsworth Trust, whose support, advice and enthusiasm throughout this project have been immense, and to the writers who kindly responded to my request to write a series of more informed essays for this publication: **Professor John Elder (Emeritus):** Middlebury College, US; **Professor Shōko Azuma**: Jumonji University, Tokyo; **Dr. Kaz Oishi:** University of Tokyo; **Professor Ewan Clayton:** University of Sunderland; **Pamela Woof**: President of the Wordsworth Trust; **Dr. Carol McKay:** University of Sunderland.

I approached each with some trepidation and asked them, frankly, an almost impossible task—to write about the work of Wordsworth and Bashō in just 1000 words. They, too, have risen magnificently to this, different, and tough, challenge. I hope that, together, they will give you, the reader, a much deeper insight into the work of the Wordsworths and Bashō and, in the case of Carol McKay's texts, a clearer picture as to how the new work in this exhibition and catalogue can help us all see the work of the Wordsworths and Bashō anew. I am also grateful to Geoffrey Wilkinson for his kind and valuable support at different stages in this project. Geoffrey has recently written a fascinating essay 'The Narrow Road to the Western Isles—if Keats had journeyed with Bashō'.[30]

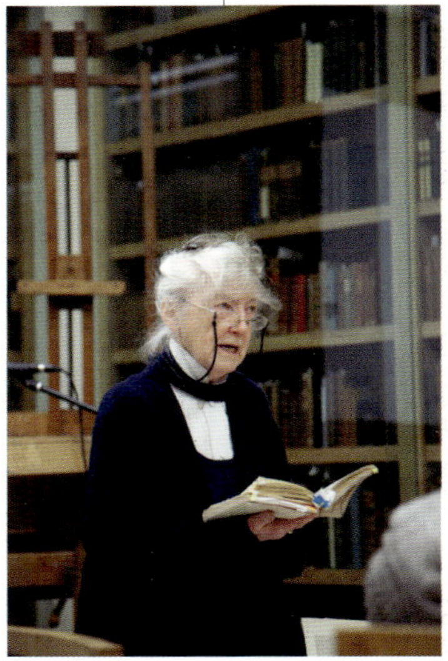

Figure 17,
Pamela Woof talking at the Artists' Symposium, January 2014

But *why* is this show timely? The poetry and prose of William and Dorothy Wordsworth, and that of Bashō, urge us, I think, to value nature for what it is—and not (as we politically do in the twenty-first century) to re-frame the argument and adopt the language of the economic rationalists. The cognitive linguist Lakov says 'if you adopt the language and values of your opponents, you lose because you are reinforcing their frame'.[31] Costing nature (says George Monbiot), 'tells us that it possesses no inherent value; that it is worthy of protection only when it performs a service for us; that it is replaceable. You demoralize and alienate those who love the natural world while reinforcing the values of those who don't'.[32] Those who believe that they can protect nature by adopting this 'frame' of economic rationalism are stepping into a trap their opponents have set. The strongest arguments (says Monbiot) that opponents can deploy—arguments based on values—cannot, just now, be heard. That is why it is more important than ever that the poetry and prose of Dorothy and William Wordsworth and Bashō ***is*** heard and understood and why, too, we have much to learn from the Japanese and Eastern approaches to nature.

**Endnotes**

1. John Elder, *Imagining the Earth: Poetry and the Vision of Nature,* Urbana, IL: University of Illinois Press, 1985, pp.93–115 (Chapter 4, 'The Footpath of Tradition').

2. Makoto Ueda, *Matsuo Bashō; The Master Haiku Poet*, Tokyo: Kodansha International, 1982, pp.176–7.

3. Jeffrey Johnson, *Haiku Poetics in Twentieth-Century Avant-Garde Poetry,* Lanham, MD: Lexington Books, 2011, pp.61–3.

4. David McCracken, *Wordsworth and the Lake District: A Guide to the Poems and their Places*, Oxford: Oxford University Press, 1988, p.3.

5. David Landis Barnhill (trans.), *Bashō's Journey,* Albany, NY: SUNY Press, 2005, p.5.

6. *Ibid*. p.4.

7. May Wong, 'Stanford study finds walking improves creativity', *Stanford News,* 24 April 2014.

8. *The Prelude* (1805), XIII. 40–49.

9. Matsuo Bashō, *The Narrow Road to the Deep North and Other Travel Sketches,* London: Penguin, 1996, trans. N. Yuasa, p.125.

10. Yoshinobu Hakutani, *Haiku and Modernist Poetics,* New York: Palgrave Macmillan, 2009, p.17.

11. Pamela Woof, 'Wordsworth and Dorothy Wordsworth: Walkers' in Collier, M. (ed.), *Wordsworth and Bashō: Walking Poets*, Sunderland: Art Editions North, 2014.

12. Pamela Woof (ed.), *Dorothy Wordsworth: The Grasmere and Alfoxden Journals,* Oxford: Oxford University Press, 2008, p.85.

13. *Ibid*. p.97.

14. Donald Keene, *Appreciations of Japanese Culture,* Tokyo: Kodansha International, 1982, p.124.

15. Henry Hitchings, *The Secret Life of Words: How English Became English,* London: John Murray, 2008, pp. 265–6.

16. David Landis Barnhill (trans), *Bashō's Journey,* Albany, NY: SUNY Press, 2005, p.5.

17. Robert Hass, *The Essential Haiku,* Tarset: Bloodaxe Books, 2013, p.30.

18. *Ibid*. p.35.

19. *Ibid*. p.53.

20. William Keach, 'Romanticism and Language', in Curran, S. (ed.), *The Cambridge Companion to British Romanticism,* Cambridge: Cambridge University Press, 1993, p.111.

21. *Ibid.*

22. Samuel Taylor Coleridge *Letters—Collected Letters of Samuel Taylor Coleridge.* Griggs, E. L. (ed.), 6 vols., Oxford: Clarendon Press, 1956–71 (Letters I, pp.625–6).

23. John G. Rudy, *Wordsworth and the Zen Mind: The Poetry of Self-Emptying,* Albany, NY: SUNY Press, 1996, p.16.

24. 'Lines written a few miles above Tintern Abbey', 93–99.

25. *Ibid* p.17.

26. *The Prelude* (1805), III. 110–18.

27. *Ibid* p.9.

28. 'Lines written a few miles above Tintern Abbey', 134–36.

29 *Ibid.*

30. Geoffrey Wilkinson, 'The Narrow Road to the Western Isles – if Keats had journeyed with Bashō' in *The Keats-Shelley Review*, Vol. 28 No. 1, April 2014, 49–57.

31. George Monbiot, 'Can you put a price on the beauty of Smithy Wood?', *Guardian,* 22 April 2014, p.27.

32. *Ibid.*

**Biographical Note**

Mike Collier is a lecturer, writer, curator and artist. He studied Fine Art at Goldsmiths College before being appointed Gallery Manager at the ICA in London. He subsequently became a freelance curator and arts organiser, working extensively in the UK and abroad. In 1985 he moved to Newcastle to run the Arts Development Strategy at the Laing Art Gallery, where he initiated the Tyne International Exhibition of Contemporary Art. Since 2004 he has worked at the University of Sunderland where he is a Reader in Fine Art. Throughout his career, Collier has maintained his artistic practice and much of his work is based around walking. He completed his practice-led PhD at the University of Sunderland in 2010, and subsequently co-founded WALK (Walking, Art, Landskip and Knowledge), a research centre looking at how cultural practitioners engage with the world through walking.

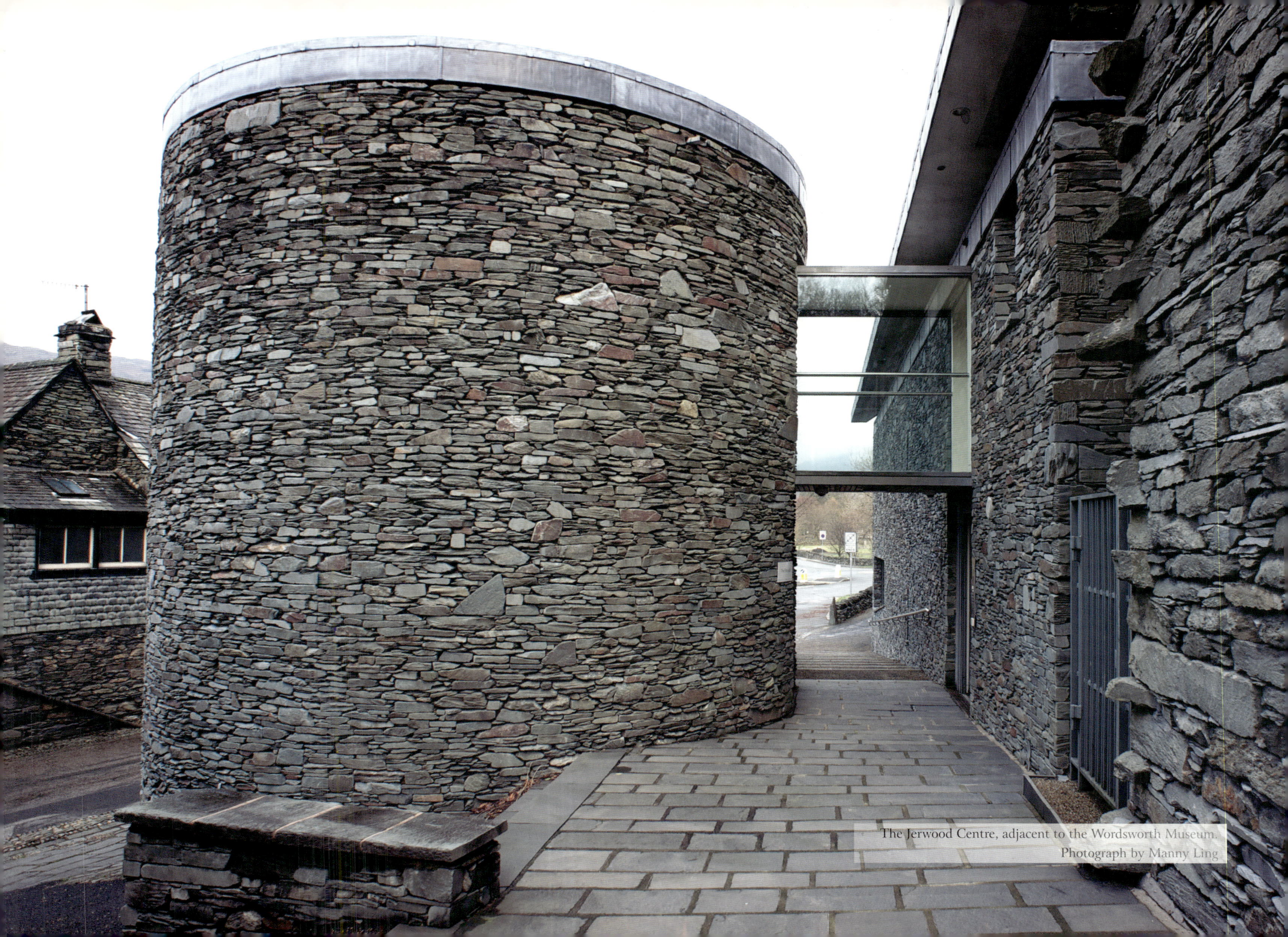

The Jerwood Centre, adjacent to the Wordsworth Museum.
Photograph by Manny Ling

# [ ESSAYS ]

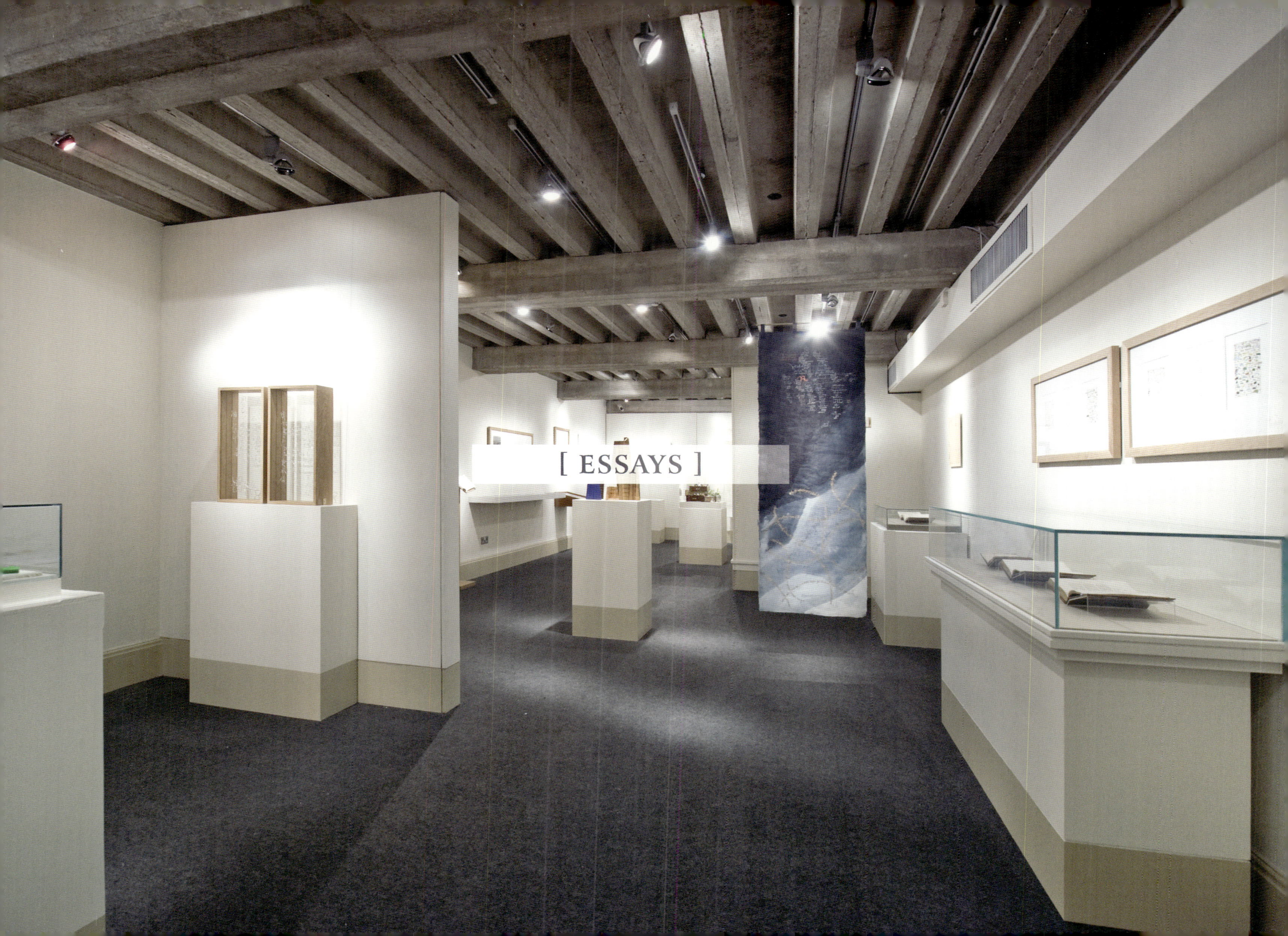

# BORDERERS

## JOHN ELDER

Biologists refer to the boundary-zone between two ecosystems as an ecotone, or edge. 'Edge-effect' often lends a special richness to such border-regions. They may well harbour species from each adjacent habitat, as well as some that are unique to the ecotone, and they typically possess an unusually high density of biomass. Edges often shift too, whether in the fluctuation of a tidal zone or at the successional line where woods advance into an abandoned meadow. Alertness is thus at a special premium for creatures drawn to the abundant resources of a moving edge. Seeking nourishment, they may simply end up being what's for lunch.

The artists and writers contributing to this exhibition have themselves ventured into a precarious but promising edge; precarious, because there are dramatic gaps between the poetic worlds of Wordsworth and Bashō. Neither of them ever visited the other's country and Wordsworth never heard of, much less read, his Japanese predecessor's writing. Beyond the fact that one of them was trained in the Zen Buddhist tradition and the other had a Christian background, they also wouldn't have had the slightest exposure to what the other was reading. Bashō was inspired by the lineage of Tu Fu and Saigyō, Wordsworth by Shakespeare, Spenser and Milton. All the more impressive, then, are the deep resonances between these poets that have contributed to making Bashō such an important influence on western poets today, Wordsworth so beloved in Japan.

In creating his own work for the present show Ken Cockburn found himself drawn to a passage from Book II of *The Prelude* referring to the 'observation of affinities / In objects where no brotherhood exists / To passive minds'. In investigating the affinities between Bashō and Wordsworth it's pertinent to note that word's origin in the Latin *affinis* (*ad* + *finis*): 'bordering on'. They are kindred writers in part through their shared calling to the margins of their societies, the shifting edges between nature and culture where insight may germinate. Bashō's narrow path to the interior, *Oku no Hosomichi*, anticipates Wordsworth's choice, at the beginning of 'Michael' and elsewhere, to depart 'from the public way'.

Wordsworth and Bashō alike desired spiritual as well as physical separation from the social mainstream. Bashō's challenging path led him to a remote field where women were singing at their work, a zone where poetry could be regrounded in the ancient communal rhythms of agriculture: *fūryū no / hajime ya oku no / ta ue uta*, 'Culture's beginnings / here in the interior / rice-planting songs' (adapted from Sam Hamill's translation). He turned away from the artificially ruralized tea huts of wealthy connoisseurs to seek true simplicity in the heart of the land. Wordsworth similarly rejected the 'gaudiness and inane phraseology of many modern writers' out of a hunger for '[h]umble and rustic life' where 'the essential passions of the heart find a better soil in which they can attain their maturity … '. (This language comes from the poet's 1800 preface to the second edition of *Lyrical Ballads*.)

Just as Bashō had been inspired by the women's rice-planting song, Wordsworth's imagination was stimulated, his heart stirred, by hearing the song of the Solitary Reaper at another sort of edge. The speaker's question 'Will no one tell me what she sings?' indicates that not only her isolated labour but even her language—Scots Gaelic—feels ancient and remote to him. In part because of such a gap, this encounter remains a wellspring for the poet's memory and imagination: 'The music in my heart I bore, / Long after it was heard no more.'

In the choice to turn away from the conventional, materialistic expectations of their societies, Bashō and Wordsworth were both motivated by the desire for a deeper quality of awareness. One of the first scholars to point out this essential similarity was R. H. Blyth, who lived, taught English and studied Zen and *haiku* in Japan from 1936 until his death in 1964. His teaching and study continued there even when he was interned during the war. Among his many brilliant, quirky books are *Zen and English Literature* and the four-volume, lavishly illustrated study called simply *Haiku*. In the first volume of that latter masterpiece (published in 1949) he wrote, 'Haiku record what Wordsworth calls those "spots of time", those moments which for some quite mysterious reason have a peculiar significance—a kind of satori, or enlightenment, in which we see into the life of things'.

Blyth's sense of such a parallel is especially striking when *Oku no Hosomichi* is compared with *The Prelude*. Once more, it's important to acknowledge significant differences at the outset. Bashō's work is a considerably shorter one, its voice less overtly autobiographical than is the case in Wordsworth's narrative. It also has no equivalent to *The Prelude*'s lengthy passages about residence in Cambridge and London or to his politically charged descriptions of travel through Revolutionary France. Having said this, though, one can affirm that these are two of world literature's most resonant accounts of walking, and that both works also find their sharpest focus at sudden moments of intensified awareness.

Bashō often describes a phenomenon or event along the path, then pauses to distill that moment's meaning in a *haiku*. One example comes in the poet's account of a visit to Yamagata Province. Bashō writes, 'The temple doors, built on rocks, were bolted. I crawled among boulders to make my bows at shrines. The silence was profound. I sat, feeling my heart begin to open'. Then comes the *haiku*: 'Lonely stillness— / a single cicada's cry / sinking into stone' (Hamill's translation).

A similar shift of diction and intensity happens again and again in *The Prelude*, though in Wordsworth's case this is as often a recoil from previous experience as a distillation of it. In Book VI, when the speaker realizes that he has already, unwittingly, crossed the Alps, a 'melancholy slackening' ensues. But that mood in its turn suddenly gives way to a visionary experience of 'The torrents shooting from the clear blue sky, / The rocks that muttered close upon our ears, / Black drizzling crags that spake by the way-side / As if a voice were in them ... '. Wordsworth's surrounding medium is blank-verse rather than prose, while his galvanizing experiences are less separate and compact than Bashō's *haiku*. Nevertheless, the two poems share the same essential rhythm in which the narrative voice is arrested and illuminated by flashes of insight. At such moments their readers too may be released from society's expectations and inflections into an experience of immediate awareness at a vital edge.

**Biographical note**

Following his studies at Pomona College and Yale University, John Elder taught English and Environmental Studies at Vermont's Middlebury College for thirty seven years. Among his chief interests as a teacher were English Romanticism, American nature writing, and Japan's *haiku* tradition. His three latest books—*Reading the Mountains of Home, The Frog Run,* and *Pilgrimage to Vallombrosa*—all combined discussions of literature, descriptions of the Vermont landscape and memoir. He has just published another memoir, entitled *Picking up the Flute*, which takes the form of a website where reflections about playing Irish traditional music on the wooden flute are complemented by recordings of pertinent tunes.

John and Rita Elder live in the Green Mountain town of Bristol and produce maple syrup with their two sons at a nearby sugarbush. They are active in statewide conservation and climate-work and entertain themselves in the evening playing music together on the flute and concertina.

Seawaithe Valley, Borrowdale
Photograph by David Unsworth

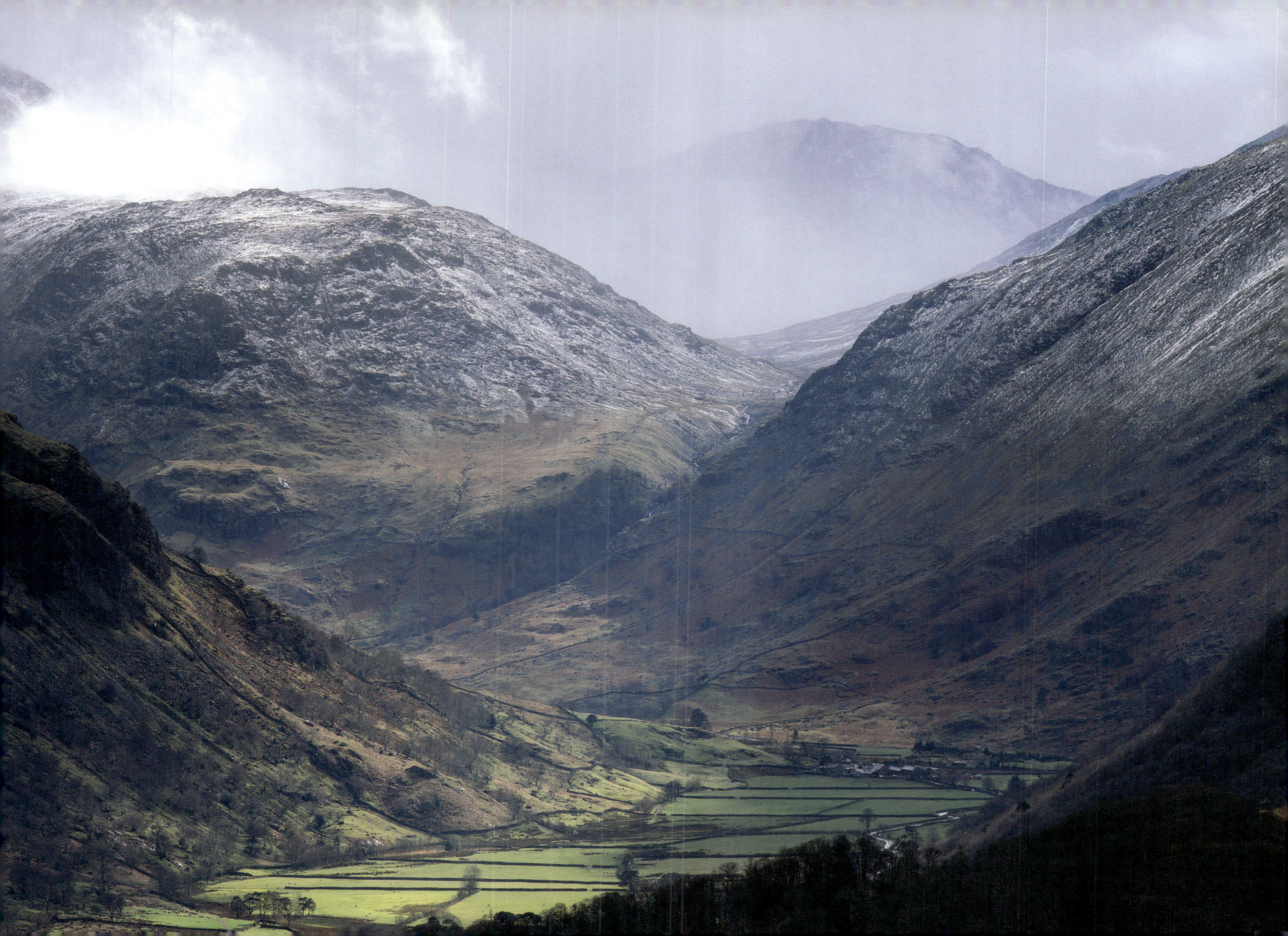

# WORDSWORTH AND DOROTHY WORDSWORTH, WALKERS

**PAMELA WOOF**

I would walk alone
In storm and tempest, or in starlight nights
Beneath the quiet Heavens ... and I would stand
Beneath some rock, listening to sounds that are
The ghostly language of the ancient earth
Or make their dim abode in distant winds.[1]

Wordsworth in his late twenties was remembering himself as a boy of thirteen or fourteen years, a teenager still at school. Sometimes he took walking with him the household dog, and the dog would become 'Tired, and uneasy at the halts I made'.[2] For the young Wordsworth was 'busy with the toil of verse', his dog receiving great caresses when an image came out right, and giving 'timely notice' to the composing poet when strangers approached. Wordsworth was developing the habit, which he kept all his life, of saying his lines out loud as he walked, so that he might hear and possibly refine the music of his words. He would sometimes on summer mornings walk with 'a friend / Then passionately loved , and the two of them would stroll along,

By the still borders of the misty lake
Repeating favourite verses with one voice,
Or conning more, as happy as the birds
That round us chaunted.[3]

These walks would be at dawn, well before 6.30am when classes began at Hawkshead school.

So Wordsworth learnt early to be a versatile and creative walker: he could be solitary and he could enjoy companionship; he walked by night, and by day, and in all weathers; he liked both to move and to stand still; he listened as earth's sounds spoke to him and his own voice spoke out rhythmically as he moved. All this was before he met again the sister who would become his closest and most sympathetic walking companion and friend through the greatest part of his adult life.

Dorothy Wordsworth had been separated from her four brothers when she was six, shortly after the death of their mother. By the time she met the boys again their father too had died, Wordsworth was seventeen and Dorothy fifteen. They met, after more than nine years, at their grand-parents' in Penrith and were immediately at home with each other but had little sustained time together until Dorothy was twenty-three.

Wordsworth had early come to enjoy walking and the vital thinking that went with it, and he continued to make long walking excursions by rivers and through mountain ranges as a student and young man. How had Dorothy fared in distant Yorkshire? Had she walked? She had loved her childhood life in Halifax, loved her mother's kind cousin who brought her up, her local friends, her local school. Torn from Halifax at fifteen, she corresponded with her friend there and captured in words some of the pleasures she was missing:

> Oh! how I long to burst into your parlour … Oh! how often has that Fire-place been surrounded by a Party of happy children … Do you think you should know me in crossing the Top of the Back-lane from the shop …[4]

She had played with her friends in the Back-Kitchen, the Croft, and 'other of our favourite Haunts'; she hopes again to 'wander' with Jane Pollard 'along the pleasant Banks of the Calder'. She pictures Jane:

> In Whiteley wood? the old lane or Birkswood? thinking upon our past pleasures, when we used to roam in search of *bilberries* with our black porringers in our hands?[5]

She slept well after such active days and is reminded of them in her early thirties after 'a long and toilsome walk' with her brother to reach Loch Ketterine in 1803:

> I slept as soundly on my chaff bed as ever I have done in childhood after the long day's playing of a summer holiday.[6]

We, most of us, can attest to similar experiences; but they are far from the intensity of Wordsworth's mountain boyhood, his hearing

> among the solitary hills
> Low breathings coming after me, and sounds
> Of undistinguishable motion, steps
> Almost as silent as the turf they trod.[7]

Or consider the terrifying blankness that invaded both his sleeping and waking hours when, in a boat taken without leave, the boy had rowed in moonlight upon a mountain lake, and found that

> huge and mighty forms that do not live
> Like living men moved slowly through my mind
> By day, and were the trouble of my dreams.[8]

Dorothy had yet to discover such power in the hills, and perhaps, again like most of us, she came to realise that power mainly through her imagination and from Wordsworth's own poetry; from this she understood the forces he had known and felt in the solitary rambles of his youth.

Yet Dorothy herself was an unusual young woman. From age seventeen to twenty-two she lived with her Uncle William and his young family in his rectory at Forncett in the flat countryside of Norfolk. There she learnt something of the value of walking. The first kind of walking was that with her brother when he stayed for six weeks at his uncle's over Christmas 1790–91. He had been walking in the summer, almost marching, with an undergraduate friend through exciting revolutionary France and through the Alpine sublimities of Switzerland and Italy. He was now in an English rectory getting to know more of his sister who explained their routine to Jane:

> We used to walk every morning about two hours, and every evening we went into the garden at four or half past four and used to pace backwards and forwards 'till six.[9]

Such regular pacing backwards and forwards, over a limited distance on path, field, road or terrace where the walking was easy and there was no stumbling, gave Wordsworth the perfect context for thinking, conversation and, more particularly, for composition. The continuous rhythm of the body's walking could help the flow of blank verse lines, could let the thinking have uninterrupted movement for as long as it needed, for the length of a page or a paragraph. Later, Wordsworth built terraces in his hilly Lake District gardens, made level paths that, like medieval cloisters, encouraged meditation. In Grasmere, with the beauties of the fells, the woods, and the valley about him, Wordsworth often walked backwards and forwards, sometimes alone, sometimes with Dorothy.

The second way of walking that Dorothy learnt at Forncett was solitary, long and alone. As a young lady of nineteen, the Rector's niece, it would be thought not quite proper for her to walk to her friends, 'the Miss Burroughses ... sweet girls',[10] though they and their village were only three miles distant: 'I go alone, am not I daring?',[11] she confided to her Halifax friend Jane. And then she would walk back. Certainly, such a character as Miss Bingley from the contemporary novel, Jane Austen's *Pride and Prejudice*, would have judged Dorothy indecorous.

Yet it meant that by the end of 1799 when she and Wordsworth set up house in Grasmere she was for the poet a perfect walking companion. The brother and sister enjoyed each other's company, talking or silent, composing or noticing, walking backwards and forwards, or walking over a distance everywhere about the valley; walking together, with friends, or alone, walking at all times of day or night and in all seasons. They made Grasmere and the Lake District their own by walking in it and by writing about their experience.

Living in one place year by year, changing in themselves and seeing the valley change, meant that they were not just walking through space and place; they were walking through time as well. Levels of meaning began to cling, for example, to a wood that was by the road walked on locally most days. Their younger, sea-faring visiting brother had made for himself a path through the wood's dense trees in 1800; the older poet brother later discovered the pathway, walked on it and wrote about his younger brother, his boyhood, his life at sea, his mind's range as he would pace his 'Vessel's deck / In some far region', conjuring up as he walked 'undying recollections' of his native hills and his brother's verse about those hills, even as that brother, composing, walked on 'his' path through the grove that murmured 'with a sea-like sound'.[12] Their sister, adding to the already rich association writes in her journal about one of many visits to 'John's grove' and describes

> A sweet sea-like sound in the trees above our heads, we walked backwards & forwards some time for dear John's sake.[13]

Here, nature, the sea and the love of the three siblings come together across space and time as thought, feeling and language are shared.

Why was the Grasmere walking so special? Wordsworth had walked before: France and the Alps of course; North Wales and the climbing of Snowdon to see the dawn but catch the moon; across Salisbury Plain alone and up the Wye Valley to North Wales; from Kendal to Keswick with Dorothy, eighteen miles to Grasmere, then staying one night there and another fifteen, says Dorothy with pride but incorrectly, to Keswick in 1794; about Racedown in Dorset with Dorothy; on the Quantocks in Somerset with Coleridge and Dorothy; in Goslar, Germany with Dorothy, both of them wrapped in furs against the cold; from Sockburn-on-Tees in the North East to and then through the Lake District with Coleridge and with John back from a sea voyage; and finally, from Sockburn again, across Yorkshire, into Westmorland and on to Grasmere with Dorothy over three cold snowy days in late December 1799. At the end of this last walk was Dove Cottage, and out of all the walks there came poetry.

Yet Grasmere intensified the walking and intensified the poetry. Wordsworth and his sister were living there; it was home. They did not simply walk through it; they walked into it, deeply into it, so that they knew it, permanently. Their writing showed a richness of response to walking that was in the place that was home. It was more than immediate; feelings, images and words became lasting memories.

Images and observations are generally more quickly put down on paper by a journal-writer than by a poet; Wordsworth certainly composed out of doors and in his head, sometimes quickly, but not always immediately seizing on an idea; and after that he needed time for revision on paper. It could be a slow process.

Dorothy could write her account of a day that same night, though often she had to catch up on omitted days. She looked about her,

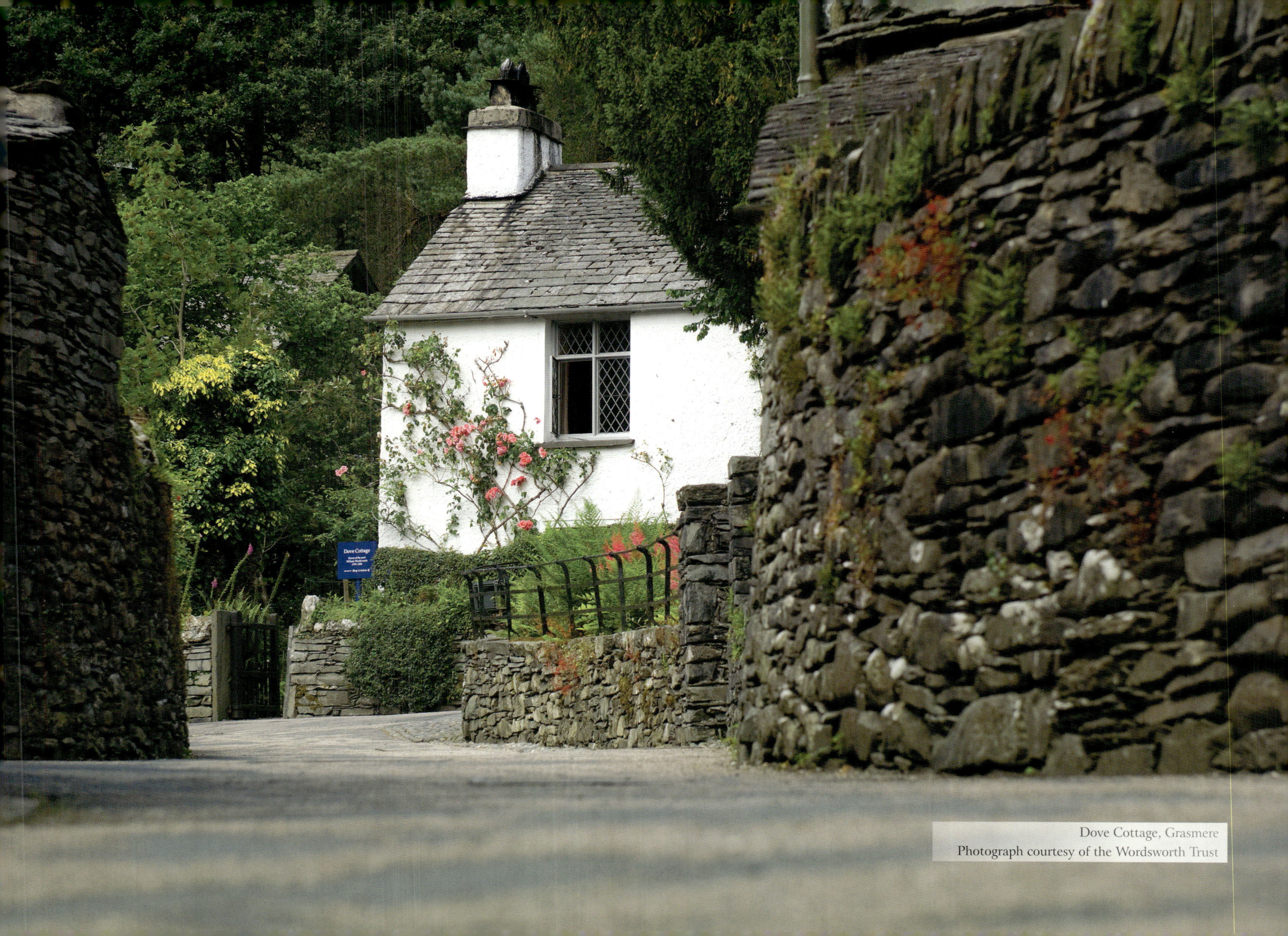


Dove Cottage, Grasmere
Photograph courtesy of the Wordsworth Trust

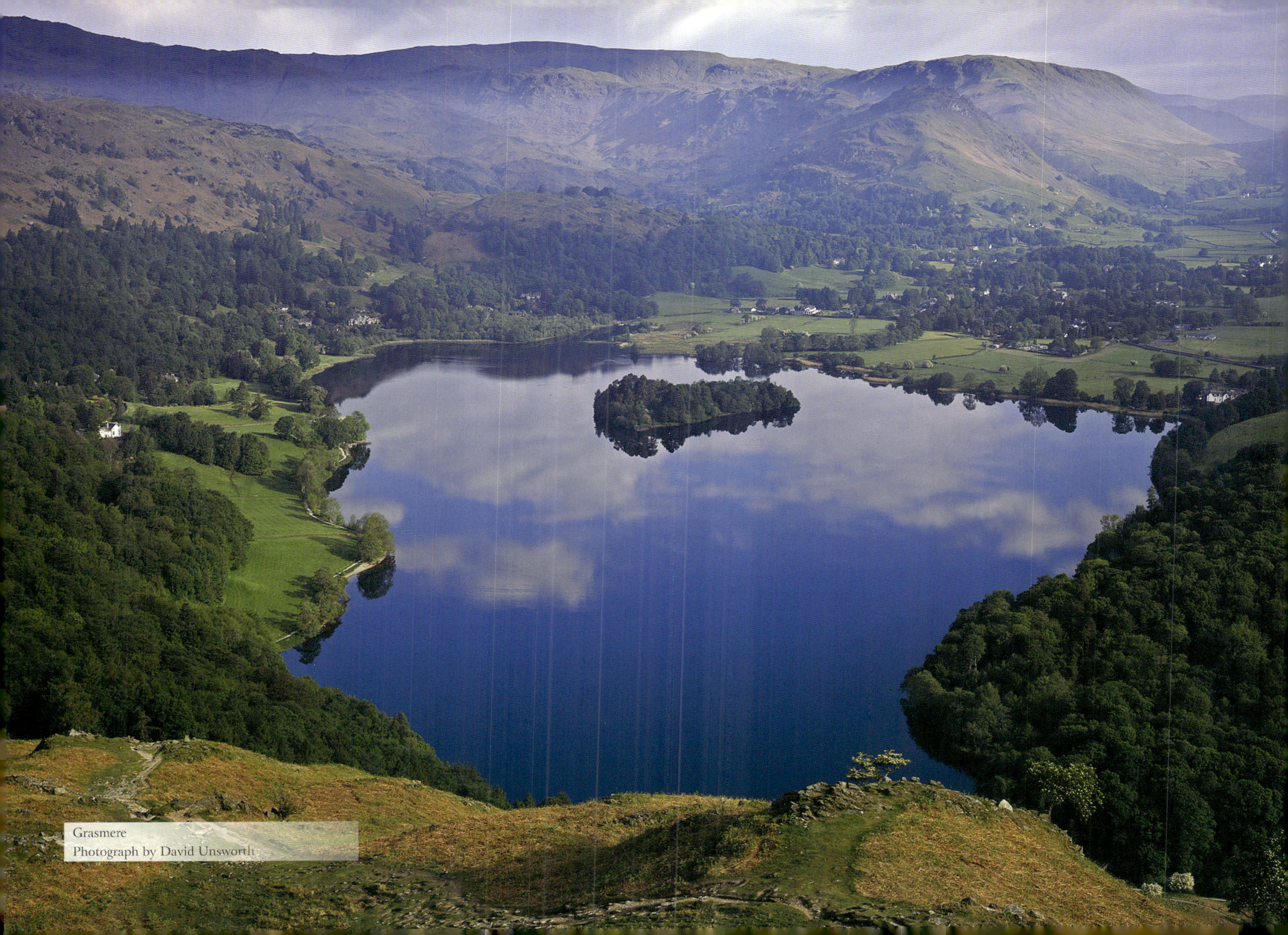

Grasmere
Photograph by David Unsworth

at sky and earth. She walked. Soon after coming to the Lakes, Wordsworth away, she was walking one night the four miles from Ambleside back to Grasmere and was accompanied part of the way by Mrs Nicholson, the postmistress. Dorothy wrote:

> This was very kind, but God be thanked I want not society by a moonlight lake – [14]

Nor did she; she could see 'moonshine like herrings in the water'.[15] Or, in a different season, reluctant to set off till after tea in 'a soaking all-day Rain' she saw 'hawthorns on the mountain sides like orchards in blossom',[16] thus giving to an ordinary wet day the sudden surprising presence on a bleak mountainside of intense freshness, colour and scent, such as a spring orchard has in sunshine. But along with the delicate beauty of her image is the sadness of its transience; only a week later, she notes realistically, no longer offering a joyous comparison but simply the fact:

> The lower hawthorn blossoms passed away, those on the hills a faint white.

Fifty springs indeed are little room, as Housman would say a hundred or so years later, to see the cherry hung with snow.

The house, of course, had its domestic imperatives: dealing with quantities of rhubarb, baking bread, mending clothes, reading, visitors calling, drinking tea, ironing, writing letters, copying poems, gardening. In walking out of the house, absorbing through frequent noticings details in the changing appearances of the valley, Dorothy was often stimulated to use imagery. Not written for publication, the journals have a lovely freedom and they mix particular realistic details with leaps far beyond the specific; the hawthorns as orchards in blossom are an example. Or, Wordsworth and Dorothy's walking out to John's grove, sitting for a while and listening, then lying down 'unseen by one another' and listening to 'the peaceful sounds of the earth', hearing not only the birds but the waterfalls:

There was no one waterfall above another—it was a sound of waters in the air—the voice of the air.[17]

Lying on the earth, hearing waters in air. This is a perception beyond anything simply visible; Wordsworth in fact had his eyes shut. There is here a compression of landscape into its elements, earth, air and water; its power is of the most basic and the notion of the 'voice of the air' is magical.

Even walking can be too fast; the Wordsworths often stopped in their walks, sat, lay down, listened and looked.

> We rested a long time under a wall. Sheep & lambs were in the field—cottages smoking. As I lay down on the grass, I observed the glittering silver line on the ridges of the Backs

of the sheep, owing to their situations respecting the Sun —which made them look beautiful but with something of strangeness, like animals of another kind—as if belonging to a more splendid world.[18]

The alternation of walking with stillness allows in a very natural way for both noticing and letting the mind dwell upon the things seen, moving, as here, even towards fantasy.

Sometimes in their walking the Wordsworths did not themselves choose to be still; they were compelled to stillness by the force of wind and weather. There was a 'furious' wind when they set out from the foot of Ullswater to walk the length of the lake and then over a high pass back to Grasmere. They had to rest twice, once 'in the large Boat-house, then under a furze Bush … The wind seized our breath... —We rested again & again'.

This enforced resting meant that they not only noticed but remembered. Dorothy, writing her journal two days later, recalled even the variations of colour on twigs; she noted what flowers grew on the lake-shore, recalling more later and then adding these to her list; she remembers their wondering how a few daffodils should come to be growing by the water side, and then sees 'more & yet more & at last— …', and so her passage rises into the triumphant characterisation of 'daffodils so beautiful'. Her sentence lengthens into delight as, unusually for Dorothy, full verb after full verb expresses the exuberance of the celebratory scene:

> they grew among the mossy stones about & about them, some rested their heads upon these stones as on a pillow for weariness & the rest tossed & reeled & danced & seemed as if they verily laughed with the wind that blew upon them over the Lake, they looked so gay, ever glancing, ever changing …[19]

Wordsworth was walking with Dorothy on that April day in 1802. We do not have his reaction at the time; it comes some two years later from a surging movement of memory. That walk of April 1802 was then both remembered and changed; it had, as it were, slept in the poet's mind and of its own accord it surfaced into vividness but a vividness at once softer and more dramatic than in Dorothy's portrayal. Only through time and memory could the experience become perfectly the poet's own. Appropriately therefore he is solitary, not with his sister, in the poem 'I wandered lonely as a Cloud'. The wind is not 'furious' now, but a breeze that sets the flowers more gently 'fluttering and dancing'. The poet does not come upon the flowers in twos and threes gradually, and then 'more & yet more & at last …', as Dorothy had done; his awareness is dramatic, 'all at once I saw a crowd'. After the aimless 'wandering' the poet wants the force of revelation; it hadn't been there, but he creates it. There is no need to say more here about Wordsworth's most recognised poem, but it is important to see that a shared walk affected the two writers differently: for Dorothy, it formed the content of her lively, exhilarated sympathy of the moment for both flowers and furious wind; for Wordsworth, it became the stuff of an imaginative re-creation, a memory reborn as a recurring source of involuntary delight, the richness at last of the dancing daffodils, a richness that was permanent because it was in the mind.

Often in his poetry, though not necessarily in actuality, the poet walked alone; it is the reader who is invited to walk mentally beside him, and accept him as a guide into new territory: here, the world real shepherds, not pastoral fictions, in a real and remote northern valley:

> If from the public way you turn your steps
> Up the tumultuous brook of Green-head Gill,
> You will suppose that with an upright path
> Your feet must struggle...

But alongside the brook is a 'hidden valley'.

> With a few sheep, with rocks and stones, and kites
> That overhead are sailing in the sky.

And the reader is invited to notice that

> Beside the brook
> There is a straggling heap of unhewn stones.

The poem, 'Michael', will be about the significance, the tragic significance, of those stones to an old man, a shepherd who had lived nearby. It is the human association of the valley and its fields, the mountain heights and their winds, the stones of an unfinished sheep-fold by the brook, that interests Wordsworth, not the description of place for its own sake. One fine October day in 1800 Wordsworth and his sister had 'walked up Greenhead Gill in search of a Sheep fold',[20] and Dorothy in her journal describes the place, the orange fern on the mountains, the cattle pasturing on the hill tops, the kites sailing in the sky, the sheep fold falling away, its form nearly that of a 'heart unequally divided', the bright sparkles of the water-breaks and little falls in the brook. Her passage is descriptive of the place as it is.

The same walk for Wordsworth has plunged him into memory, into layers of memory: of himself as a young boy

> Careless of books, yet having felt the power
> Of Nature,

and having felt too the power of a story told to him by his household Dame in Hawkshead about an old Grasmere shepherd. His Dame, Ann Tyson, had heard the story as a girl, and so the shepherd who never finished the sheepfold by the brook was already long dead. The poem 'Michael' is an exploration of great love and loss and the endurance of loss, while inextricable in its telling are the 'many thousand mists', 'these fields, these hills', the storm, the mountains, the

> Feelings and emanations, things which were
> Light to the sun and music to the wind.

Wordsworth could make the passion of the old shepherd real and true because he knew himself what life the hills gave him. He knew the mists and winds, had rambled the fells as a schoolboy, walked them as a young man and now lived daily in their sight, could walk on a fine October morning, and find in his memory and imagination, among these empty hills a celebration of how human love and strength can deal with the eternal onslaught of suffering.[21]

Wordsworth and Dorothy walked the roads as well as the fells of Grasmere valley, and they stopped and talked, or rather listened—Dorothy particularly was good at listening—to the sad stories of the poor, the people on the fringes of society who were forced to walk the roads: the beggars, discharged soldiers, rag men, old sailors, abandoned women, widows, whole families with dog and crying infant. Wordsworth and his sister walked for pleasure, not in the dire need that was the lot of most of the wayfarers they met; they gave bread, small sums of money (Dorothy once gave as much as a shilling and thought afterwards that she could have got away with sixpence), but most of all they gave attention. They listened. Dorothy sometimes wrote down the stories the vagrants told, for, after all, the accounts could have been useful to Wordsworth as a narrative poet. He had been a passionate radical and an idealist, hoping for a more equal society, in the early years of the French Revolution; he had included poems about the pathos and resilience of the poor in that astonishingly original volume shared with Coleridge, *Lyrical Ballads*, 1798. Clearly thinking it might be useful to her brother because he was pondering, they both were pondering, ideas about the uses of poetry (these were to be discussed in the preface to the second edition of *Lyrical Ballads* 1800), Dorothy described an encounter with an old man they had both met during a walk the week before. This old man 'lived by begging' and hoped to buy and sell 'a few godly books'; he had formerly been a leech-gatherer, but 'leeches were very scarce'. Dorothy gives a detailed account of what the man looked like, what he wore, carried and what he told them: deaths of wife and nine children, the entire absence of the one living son, a sailor; seasonal problems and scarcity of leeches, a skull-fracturing accident he had had driving a cart. [22]

Wordsworth in fact made no use of the walk or Dorothy's description of the encounter at the time, but two years later he took another solitary walk as a poet, walking as it were into his own poetry and in that imagined walk he remembered and came upon the old man of two years before. The man now, in the poem, was indeed a leech-gatherer and was actually standing by a 'little pond or moorish flood'. 'Motionless as a Cloud the Old Man stood', and the poet engages him in conversation. We, as readers, have walked with the poet to this point in the poem, enjoying the sun after the night's rain, hearing the birds, breathing the air 'filled with pleasant noise of waters'. Like the sky, the grass, the hare, the woods and distant waters, like the 'Traveller then upon the moor', who is the poet himself conducting us upon his walk, we sense the general rejoicing; the Traveller is 'happy as a Boy'. But the solitary walk of the poet's imagination induces thinking, and the poet's mood changes to worry and gloom, the very opposite of happiness. It is then that, depressed at the despondency that poets suffer, he, our guiding poet, and we with him, see the leech-gatherer. Now, at this moment, Wordsworth could surely have made use, along with his own memory of the encounter, of Dorothy's detailed description of two years before. The old man had struck them both as an example of human strength and endurance in the face of almost overwhelming disasters. And Wordsworth, finishing the first drafts of his poem, did have several verses fully devoted to the old man's direct words, to particular and new details about him and to such specific facts as Dorothy had presented in her journal. This all seemed too much for the first readers, Sara and Mary Hutchinson; indeed, they pronounced the old man's words 'tedious'. At first, Wordsworth felt outraged and misunderstood, but then he destroyed most of that section of the poem and finished it by redirecting the walk that had begun on such a golden morning of the earth's and the poet's happiness; he has the poem move now into the darker spaces of his own mind. The leech-gatherer himself is taken out of his own specific and calamitous history and becomes such a symbol of endurance in an alien world as one of those erratic boulders that are seen up and down the Lake District and have been carried long ages past by glaciers and deposited among rock formations of a different period; or, says Wordsworth, he is like an ancient sea-beast, hardly alive, crawled out of the depths of the sea to repose for a time in the sun. With these comparisons the leech-gatherer has lost most of the specific details of his particular life in history; he is almost mythic, a symbol of astonishing endurance. The poet walks up to the old man stationary by the pond and learns about his 'Employment hazardous and wearisome', about his 'many hardships' and how

> From Pond to Pond he roamed, from moor to moor.

To the poet, remembering his earlier despondency, even fear, and 'mighty Poets in their misery dead', the old man seems like 'one whom I had met with in a dream'. The leech-gatherer patiently goes on with his task; he tells the poet again,

> that, gathering Leeches, far and wide
> He travelled; stirring thus about his feet
> The waters of the Pond where they abide.

The poet began the poem as a 'Traveller then upon the moor', a walker; the leech-gatherer too has travelled, and now, very old he is still walking from pond to pond, stopping, stirring the waters and walking again. The poet's walking and the old man's seem to mingle in the poet's consciousness. The old man's travelling, his continuing endurance into old age, his patient walking as though through life itself has become a powerful image for Wordsworth; it has become part of him:

> In my mind's eye I seemed to see him pace
> About the weary moors continually,
> Wandering about alone and silently.

Wordsworth called the poem 'Resolution and Independence'; the leech-gatherer walks with a purpose, and having met him, so does the poet. Walking in Grasmere valley was part of life; it refreshed body, mind and spirit:

> I am not quite well—we have let the bright sun go down without walking—now a heavy shower comes on & I guess we shall not walk at all,

complained Dorothy to her journal at the end of April 1802. But they did walk, not far, but enough:

> we walked backwards & forwards between our house & Olliffs. We talked … William left me sitting on a stone.

Wordsworth presumably continued his pacing. Dorothy often sat outside. She clearly felt better:

> When we came in we corrected the Chaucers …[23]

In old age and illness, Dorothy had the same desire to be outside and close to the healing (her word) presence of nature; in a period of confinement to the house she wrote:

> The sun shines so bright and the birds sing so sweetly that I have almost a painful longing to go out of doors, and am half tempted to break my bonds and sally forth into the garden …[24]

Wordsworth totally escaped such limitations. By 1804 there was a toddler in the house, a baby expected, and it was perhaps as well, living in a cottage, that he had got into the habit of composing out of doors. Dorothy explained to Catherine Clarkson in February 1804:

> … He walks out every morning, generally alone, and brings us in a large treat almost every time he goes. The weather with all its pleasant mildness, has been very wet in general, he takes out the umbrella, and I daresay, stands stock-still under it, during many a rainy half-hour, in the middle of road or field.[25]

Wordsworth was writing 'the Poem on his own early life' (*The*

*Prelude*), explained Dorothy, and by the end of May he was in the same position and it was still raining. This time Dorothy was writing to her new correspondent Lady Beaumont:

> ... at present he is walking, and has been out of doors these two hours though it has rained heavily all the morning. In wet weather he takes out an umbrella, chuses the most sheltered spot, and there walks backwards and forwards, and though the length of his walk be sometimes a quarter or half a mile, he is as fast bound within the chosen limits as if by prison walls. He generally composes his verses out of doors, and while he is so engaged he seldom knows how the time slips away, or hardly whether it is rain or fair.[26]

The two kinds of walking—this meditative pacing and the walking that covered distance—were constants throughout life for Wordsworth and his sister: for Dorothy, until she became too ill in the early 1830s (she lived until 1855), and for Wordsworth, almost until his death in 1850. This everyday walking in the Lake District—to Ambleside, Keswick, Ullswater, the Langdale valley—was punctuated by some dozen ambitious pedestrian tours, and again, Wordsworth found in these matter for poetry. Walking was in his blood, a need. Wordsworth knew it and discusses his need in *The Prelude* 1805. He could see some virtues in the city, but in his heart he turned

> To you, ye pathways and ye lonely roads,
> Sought you, enriched with everything I prized,
> With human kindness and with nature's joy.

He goes on to speak of the bliss of walking 'Through field or forest with the maid we love' as he had walked with his sister in Grasmere, 'the home of both'. And next to that he placed the 'dear delight'

> of wandering on from day to day
> Where I could meditate in peace, and find
> The knowledge which I love, and teach the sound
> Of Poet's music to strange fields and groves,
> Converse with men, where if we meet a face
> We almost meet a friend ...
>
> I love a public road: few sights there are
> That please me more; such object hath had power
> O'er my imagination since the dawn
> Of childhood, when its disappearing line,
> Seen daily afar off, on one bare steep
> Beyond the limits which my feet had trod,
> Was like a guide into eternity ...
>
> ... the lonely roads
> Were schools to me in which I daily read
> With most delight the passions of mankind,

> There saw into the depth of human souls ...[27]

Wordsworth's poetry bears all this out. Walking the portions of the earth they walked was not trivial to either Wordsworth or his sister Dorothy. It was the context for the creative music of poetry; it was where humans met and sympathised with each other; it was an invitation to discover more, possibly apprehend the infinite; it contained sadness, joy, dignity and beauty as well as misery; it made the walker alive and alert to the unexpected. The known ways of Grasmere had a deep sweetness to the Wordsworths and the unknown ways of the world had a human sweetness too, one that mingled with the poet's thought

> Of travelling through the world that lay
> Before me in my endless way.[28]

**Notes**

For *Prelude* references (*Prel.*), see the 1805 text in *William Wordsworth, The Major Works*, ed. Stephen Gill, Oxford: Oxford University Press, 1984.

Letters can be found by date in *The Letters of William and Dorothy Wordsworth: The Early Years, 1787–1805*, ed. Ernest De Selincourt, rev. Chester L. Shaver, Oxford: rothy Wordsworth's Grasmere Journals are from *The Grasmere and Alfoxden Journals*, ed. Pamela Woof, Oxford: Oxford University Press, 2002, referred to here as GJ, with date.

**Endnotes**

1. See the whole passage, *Prel.*, II, 321–41
2. *Ibid.*, IV, 90–120.
3. *Ibid.*, V, 587–91.
4. *Letter,* 16 June 1793.
5. *Letter,* 10 and 12 July 1793.
6. *Journals*, I, 377–78.
7. *Prel.*, I, 329–32.
8. *Prel.*, I, 424–26.
9. *Letter*, 23 May 1791.
10. *Letter*, 26 June 1791.
11. *Letter*, 5 June 1793.
12. See the poem, 'When first I journeyed hither'.
13. GJ, 23 Feb 1802.
14. GJ, 2 June 1800.
15. GJ, 31 Oct 1800.
16. GJ, 9 June 1802.
17. GJ, 29 April 1802.
18. GJ, 29 April 1802.

19. GJ, 15 April 1802.

20. GJ, 11 Oct 1800.

21. See the poem 'Michael'.

22. GJ, 3 Oct 1800.

23. GJ, 28 April 1802.

24. Letter, 12–17April 1834, in *The Letters of William and Dorothy Wordsworth: The Later Years, 1821–53*, ed. Ernest De Selincourt, rev. Alan G. Hill, 4 vols., Oxford: Oxford University Press, 1978–88.

25. *Letter,* 13 Feb 1804.

26. *Letter,* 25 May 1804.

27. *Prel.*, XII, 126–65.

28. See the poem 'Stepping Westward'.

**Biographical Note**

Pamela Woof is a retired Lecturer in Literature in the Department of Lifelong Learning, Newcastle University. She has been a Trustee of the Wordsworth Trust for many years, and is now Honorary President. Alongside her late husband, Dr Robert Woof, Pamela contributed to exhibitions at the Wordsworth Museum and has published many articles on Wordsworth and the Romantics. In 2013 her exhibition for the Wordsworth Trust *Dorothy Wordsworth: Wonders of the Everyday* was the first exhibition to be specially devoted to Dorothy Wordsworth as a woman and a writer. She also wrote a book by the same title (proceeds to the Wordsworth Trust and available through the Trust) in which she discusses further aspects of Dorothy Wordsworth's marvellous and original writing. Her World's Classics edition, *Dorothy Wordsworth: The Grasmere and Alfoxden Journals*, Oxford 2002, is the standard text.

Dove Cottage, the home of William and
Dorothy Wordsworth from 1799–1808
Photograph courtesy of the Wordsworth Trust

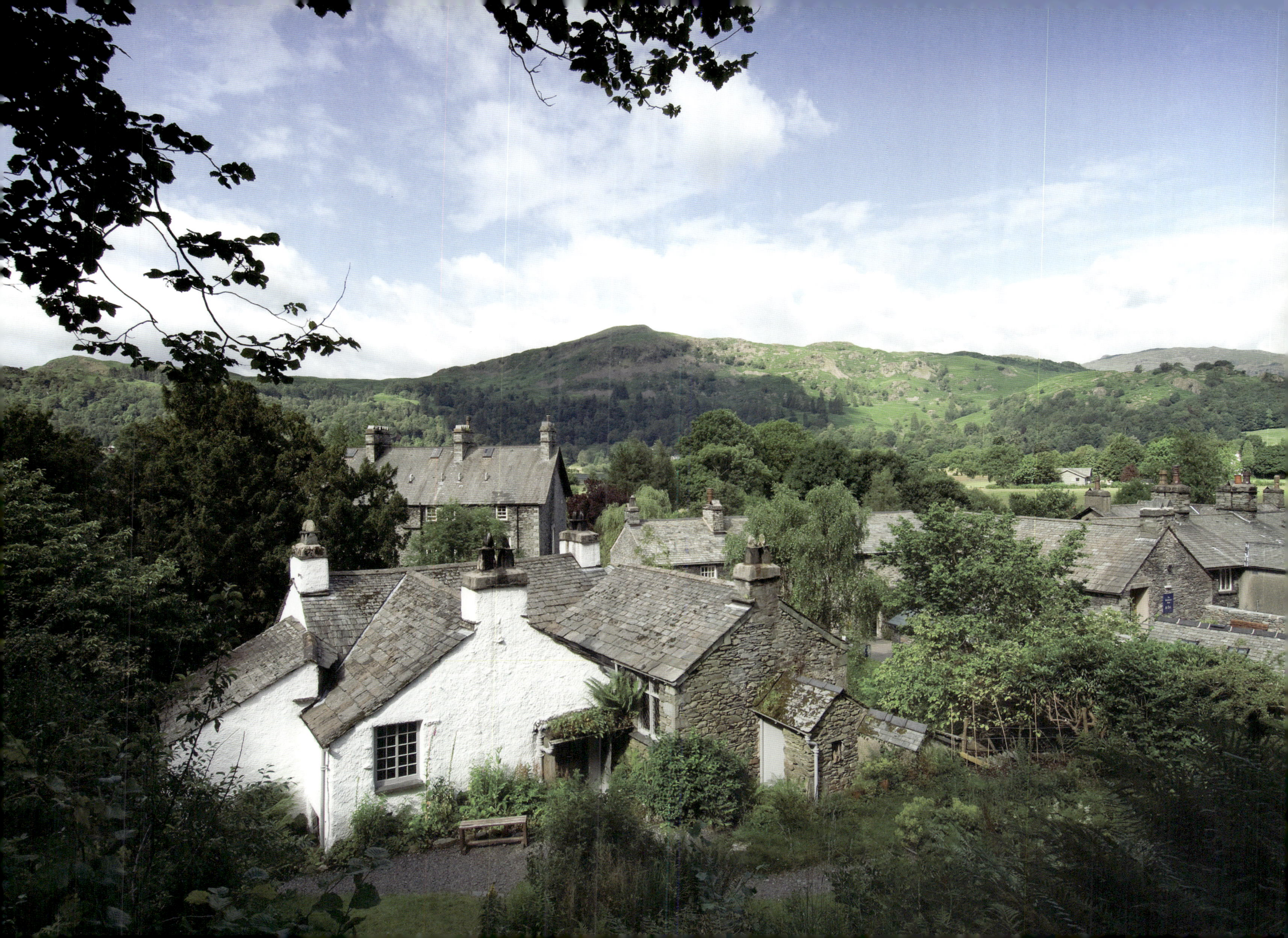

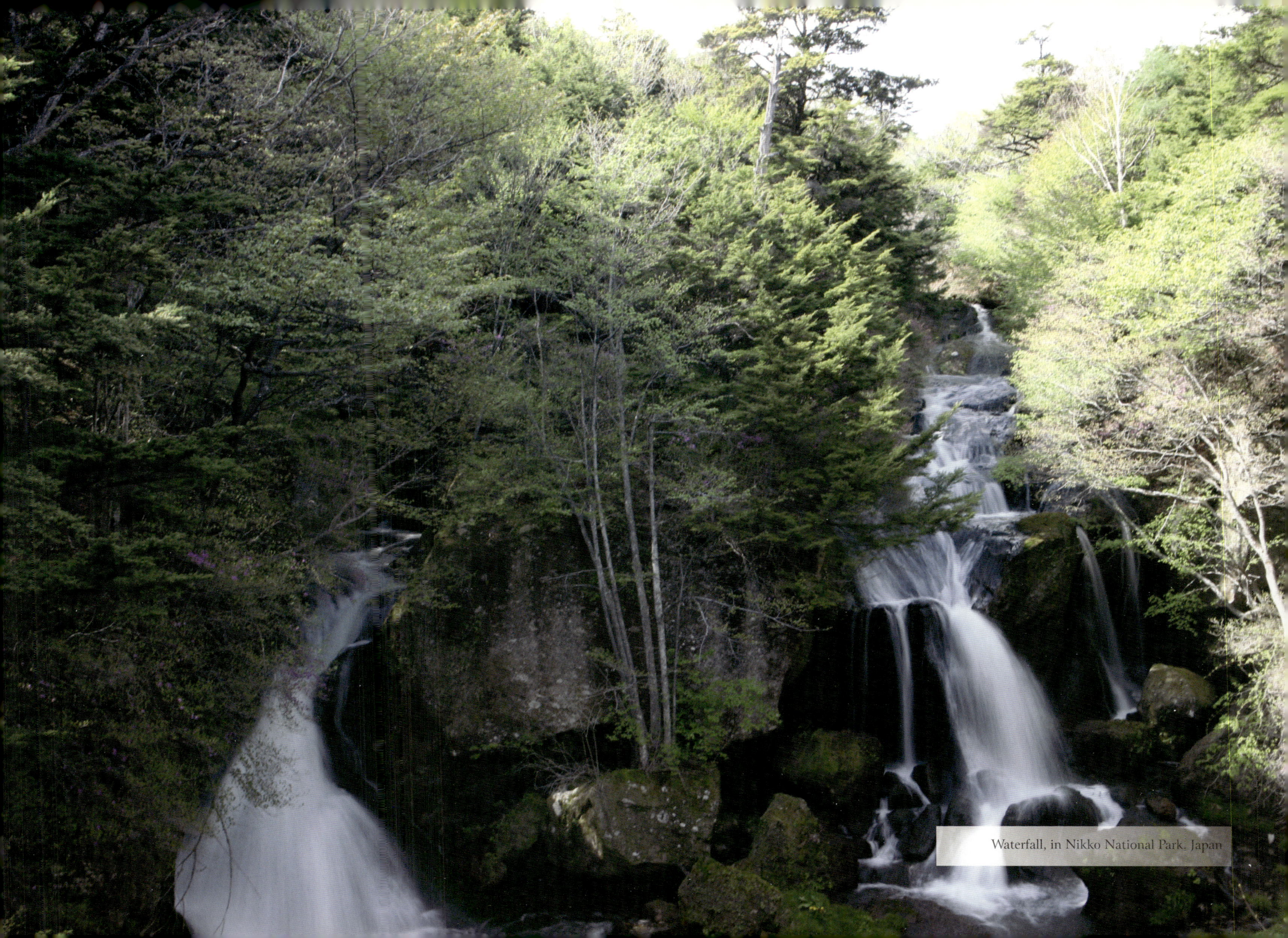

Waterfall, in Nikko National Park, Japan

# TWO RECOLLECTIVE JOURNEYS TO THE NORTH: BASHŌ AND WORDSWORTH

**KAZ OISHI**

On 2nd May 1689, the thirty-sixth day of his peripatetic journey from Edo, Bashō walked into Shinobu, a village near Fukushima, to visit the famous rock which was believed to have been used to dye a kind of cloth known as *shinobu mojizuri*. *Shinobu mojizuri* had been adopted by ancient poets as one of *utamakura*, place names famed and rhetorically used in classical poems, but Bashō found the rock itself half buried in the ground. His journey to the deep north of Japan was a personal pilgrimage to such neglected literary *topoi*. The village name of Shinobu is said to have been derived from a fern called *shinobuso*, but since it is phonetically identical with the verb *shinobu,* meaning 'harbouring secret love or yearning for the past', it had been used in classical poems to imply 'mental distraction by secret love or enchanted recollection' when combined with *mojizuri* denoting 'twisted patterns'. Based on such artistic sentiments, Bashō composed a piece of *haiku* on seeing girls planting rice seedlings in the paddy field:

> The busy hands
> Of rice-planting girls
> Reminiscent somehow
> Of the old dyeing technique.[1]

The swinging movements of the girls' hands evoked the traditional *mojizuri* artisan skills in Bashō's mind, but his imagination also flashed back to the ancient days when people expressed their secret love in verse. The *topos* of *shinobu mojizuri* encapsulates and conjures up such layers of sentiments.

This is almost a *haiku* version of Wordsworth's 'The Solitary Reaper', composed after his 1803 tour to Scotland. The singing voice of a 'solitary Highland Lass' (2) while cutting and binding the grain prompted the poet to envisage 'old, unhappy, far-off things, / And battles long ago', then to think of 'more humble' matters of today and future (19–20, 21).[2] Wordsworth's journey was similar to Bashō's foot journey to the north: it was a process of visiting, imagining and recollecting the immortal voice of the past.[3] Six days after leaving Shinobu, Bashō was enthralled by discovering what he believed to be a stone monument called *Tsubo no ishifumi* on the ancient site of Taga Castle. It was erected during the reign of Emperor Shōmu (CE 724–49) to commemorate the now vanished fortress built in CE 724 and had been celebrated by classical poets as a metaphor for 'something too far or hard to discover'. The inscribed letters were still visible, though covered with thick moss. Bashō rejoiced that it survived a thousand years as 'the living memory of the ancients' in 'this ever-changing world where mountains crumble, rivers change their courses, roads are deserted, rocks are buried'.[4] Standing by the monument, Bashō reassessed and confirmed his own poetical identity within history. His journey was a kind of literary tourism filled with such 'spots of time'—moments of self-examination upon encountering the sites of literary and collective memories.

Just as with Wordsworth, the habit of 'wandering' constituted the crucial part of Bashō's career. Before he followed the footsteps of the twelfth-century itinerant poet Saigyō in the deep north, he had made three long foot journeys to the middle regions of Japan and published travelogues about each. We can find in them beautiful harmony between his poetic consciousness and nature. His scenic descriptions are as picturesque, inspirational and self-reflective as Wordsworth's lines in *Descriptive Sketches* and *The Prelude*. We can see Bashō striving to establish a new poetics then. All his efforts bore fruit in his last travelogue *The Narrow Road to the Deep North*, published posthumously in 1702, which ingeniously unified plain, yet highly aestheticized poems combined with unpretentious prose narratives. 'Days and months are travellers of eternity', he wrote at the very start of the journey (97). With such a sense of mutability, he could clearly discern what remained unchanged in the current of time: places of literary fame repeatedly celebrated by poets from ancient times and the sites of collective memories. By composing poems at each site, he remembered the dead as *genii loci* and aspired to immortalize their histories in a modern poetical language.

Travelling is more often a self-reflective journey to the past in Wordsworth's poems, but his poems on his Scottish tours are comparable to Bashō's journey to the north. They recounted his pilgrimages to literary and historic sites, such as the graves of Burns and Rob Roy, Fingal's Cave and ruined castles. Just as Bashō confirmed his own poetical identity at *Tsubo no ishifumi*, Wordsworth was reassured of his own career when he visited Burns's grave in 1803, who taught him 'How Verse may build a princely throne / On humble truth' ('At the Grave of Burns', 35–36).[5] Though disappointed by the real scenery of the renowned Yarrow in his 1814 trip, 'Yarrow Revisited' composed on his second visit in 1831 is imbued with the sense of time and history. 'Though we were changed and changing', the meandering river united 'Past, present, future, all ... / In harmony' (36, 29–30).[6] It indicates the way in which the picturesque scenery of the river resurrects memories of the dead and the living for the future, '[l]ike guests that meet, and some from far, / By cordial love invited' (31–32). The sense of mutability more distinctly emerges at the ruin of Kilchurn Castle, which is 'softened and subdued / And quieted' by 'the memorial Majesty of Time' ('Address to Kilchurn Castle, Upon Loch Awe',

41–42, 21).[7] Wordsworth also ascertained the collective identity of Scottish people by remembering their heroes, at the grave of Rob Roy in 1803, at Bothwell Castle, and at the Earl of Breadbane's ruined mansion and family tomb in 1831. His other poems—'The Ruined Cottage', for instance—are also concerned with vicissitudes of human life and nature, but poems on his Scottish tours are more seriously engaged in locating and renewing collective memories buried in graves and ruins, just as Bashō's poems are. We can hear such a Wordsworthian voice in Bashō's *haiku* composed for Lord Yoshitsune and his men, who encountered their tragic deaths in 1189 at Hiraizumi:

> A thicket of summer grass
> Is all that remains
> Of the dreams and ambitions
> Of ancient warriors.[8]

The poem represents another 'spot of time', where dead heroes were reassessed and commemorated against the flow of time.

Very curiously, all these poetical recollections by the two poets are constructed by certain fictional manipulations and creative infusions. Just as Wordsworth recast and altered circumstances during his composition, Bashō often changed the chronological order of his journey to enhance the artistic effects of his poems. His meandering handwritings on the manuscripts, occasionally patched up with revised sheets, suggest not only his rambling journey of literary commemorations, but also a reconstructed process of recollection and self-examination as a poet inspired by the vicissitudes of nature and by living in the flow of time and life.[9]

**Endnotes**

1. Matsuo Bashō, *The Narrow Road to the Deep North and Other Travel Sketches*, trans. N. Yuasa, London: Penguin, 1996, p.108.

2. William Wordsworth, *Poems, in Two Volumes, and Other Poems, 1800–1807* , ed. Jared Curtis, Ithaca, NY: Cornell University Press, 1983, pp.184–185.

3. The only study that compares Bashō and Wordsworth is John Elder, *Imagining the Earth: Poetry and the Vision of Nature,* 1985; 2nd edition, Athens, GA: University of Georgia Press, 1996. Elder argues that 'the process of walking serves as a poetic vehicle for [the] unification' of the self and nature, and of past and present both in *The Narrow Road to the Deep North* and in *The Prelude* (p.107). But 'past' is more closely connected to collective memories than to personal ones in their journeys to the north.

4. Bashō, p.113.

5. William Wordsworth, *Last Poems, 1821–1850*, ed. Jared Curtis, Ithaca, NY: Cornell University Press, 1999, p.308.

6. William Wordsworth, *Sonnet Series and Itinerary Poems, 1820–1845*, ed. Geoffrey Jackson, Ithaca, NY: Cornell University Press, 2004, p.491.

7. William Wordsworth, *The Poems of William Wordsworth: Collected Reading Texts from the Cornell Wordsworth Series*, ed. Jared Curtis, 3 vols. Penrith: Humanities-Ebooks, 2009, 3, p.605.

8. Bashō, p.118.

9. There exist a few different versions of manuscripts for *The Narrow Road to the Deep North*. The Yaba version (or the Nakao version) is believed to have been written by Bashō's own hand. It is patched up with around eighty sheets of papers for revisions. The manuscript remained unknown until the end of the last century, but now its photographic reproductions are printed in Ueno Yōzō and Sakurai Takejirō (eds.), *Bashō Jihitsu Oku no Hosomichi,* Tokyo: Iwanami shoten, 1997. See especially pp.23–24, 30–31.

### Biographical Note

Kaz Oishi is Associate Professor in the Department of Language and Information Sciences, University of Tokyo. He graduated from the University of Tokyo and received his MPhil and DPhil from the University of Oxford. After his research fellowship with the Japan Society of Promotion of Science, he taught at the Open University of Japan and Nagoya University. His publications include *Coleridge, Romanticism, and the Orient: Cultural Negotiations*, co-edited with David Vallins and Seamus Perry (2013), *POETICA,* vol.76, Special Issue: 'Cross-Cultural Negotiations: Romanticism, Mobility and the Orient' (co-edited with Felicity James, 2011), 'An Ideological Map of (Mis)reading: William Blake and Yanagi Muneyoshi in Early-Twentieth-Century Japan' in Steve Clark and Masashi Suzuki (eds.), *The Reception of Blake in the Orient* (2006) and various essays on English Romanticism.

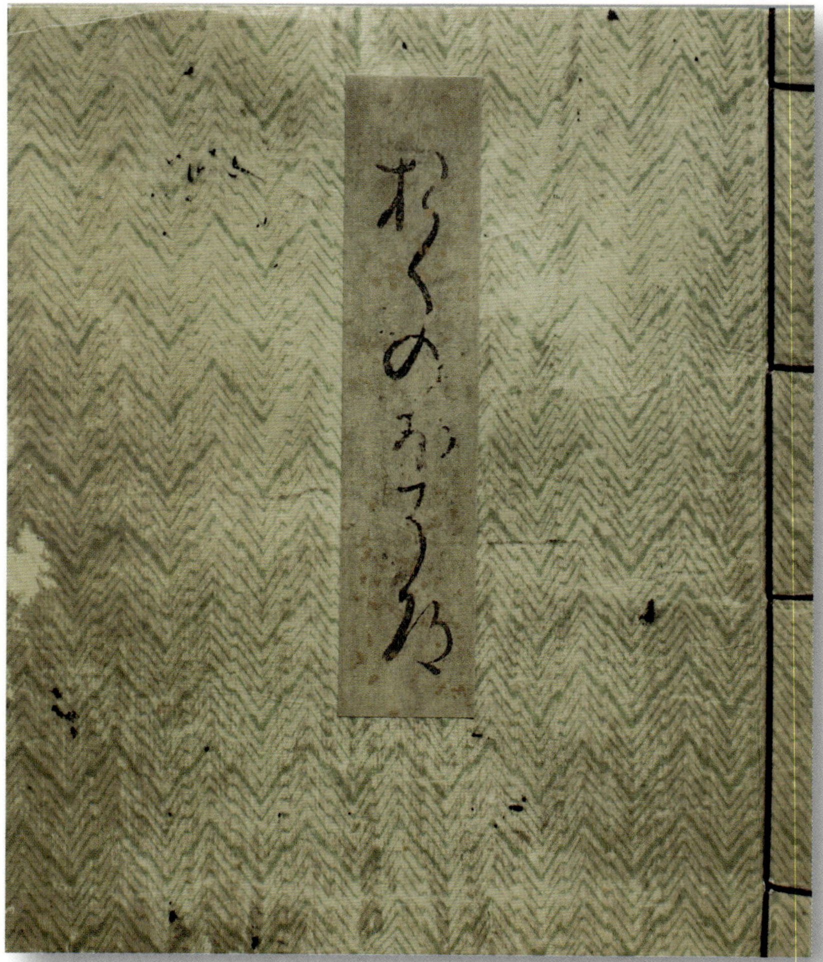

Figure 18, Matsuo Bashō (text and writing of title)
Soryū (writing of all remaining content)
*The Narrow Road to the Deep North,* 1694
paper, sumi ink, 16.7 x 14.2 cm
Replica borrowed from Iga City Bashō Memorial Museum
(copyright holder could not be contacted)

# HANDWRITING AND SCRIPT
# AN EMBEDDED AND EMBODIED RELATIONSHIP TO PLACE AND SOCIETY

**EWAN CLAYTON**

It may seem perverse to compare the sophisticated calligraphy of the Japanese poet Matsuo Bashō (see figure 18) with the tight and restricted handwriting of the British Romantic poet William Wordsworth. Yet the comparison is revealing, not simply of the role writing has played in two contrasting cultures but in highlighting a significant moment in the history of writing in Europe. During Wordsworth's lifetime a shift occurred in the way handwriting was perceived; no longer viewed as a marker of class, gender or occupation, it became understood as a reflection of character and incident. Ultimately this insight led to the incorporation of graphic mark-making within strands of twentieth century art, the rebirth of calligraphy as an art form in the west and an understanding of western writing that brought it closer to the East Asian tradition.

But how to convey these two worlds in a brief space? One must write poetically and allow objects to speak for context.

Two writing tables. Bashō's is low, made for writing whilst seated on the floor. Writing materials are laid across its surface. An ink stone, cool to the touch, drops of water gathered in a pool on its dark surface, will be used to grind the black ink stick lying next to it. The stick is lightly perfumed, made from carbon particles, compacted smoke, the essence of a flame. Nearby lies Bashō's brush. His father, a member of the samurai class, who supplemented his income by giving calligraphy lessons, had taught him how to use this tool. Then, in the court of his young Lord and friend Tōdō Yoshitada, he first employed it for his own poetry.

After Yoshitada's unexpected death at twenty-five Bashō undertook the pilgrimage to the mountain shrine of Kōyasan to entomb a symbolic lock of Yoshitada's hair. Among the tumbled rocks, mists and tall cedar trees he came under the influence of the long-dead patron of the shrine Kūkai or Kōbō-Daishi (774–835), the founder of an esoteric tradition of Buddhism. Kukai was a calligrapher whose influence can be traced in Bashō's early work. Over time Bashō's style changed; reflecting developments in his poetic understanding,[1] he moved towards dry simplicity. He used his calligraphy not only on the solitary road to record his travels but to make inscriptions as presents to friends, patrons and the students who gathered round him. His was an easeful connection to writing.

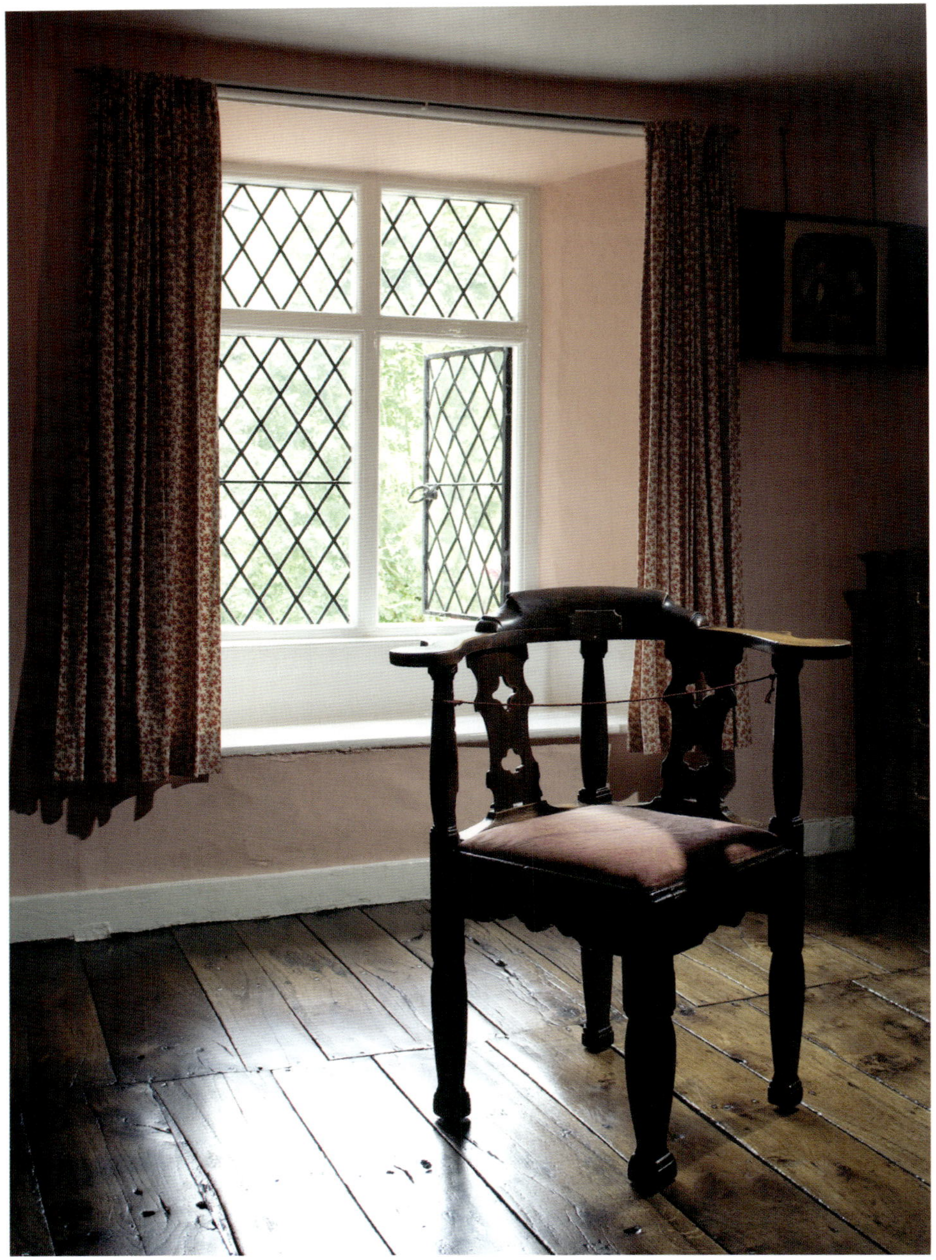

Figure 19, Wordsworth's writing chair, Dove Cottage, Grasmere
Photograph courtesy of the Wordsworth Trust

The symbols Bashō traced went back to distant origins in ceremonies of divination held in late Shang China. The cracks in the bones of ritual burnt offerings were read as signs of emerging forces at work in the Universe. Over the generations soothsayers had come to read the shape of these 'answers' in predictable ways. From the start, characters in East Asian writing systems were likened to symbols of nascent realities. From the first-century CE onwards writing in China had been recognized as an expressive medium and by the eighth century a critical literature around its aesthetics had developed.

On Wordsworth's writing desk lay a writing set, two ornamental glass inkwells on a brass tray to hold quill pens.[2] The shiny nature of the glass and moulded brass contrasted with the pens that lay there. The pens were fashioned from the flight feathers of a goose. They must be cut and split by hand and constantly kept in trim if they were to write. Untrimmed, they scratched, flooded and spluttered on the surface of the papers and notebooks Wordsworth used. Wordsworth shows some connoisseurship in the notebooks he selected, red morocco bound or notebooks bought in Calais covered in blue paper. But the pens are ill-favoured; the ink, thin and bitter, made from iron salts and tannic acid, over time would fade from black to grey, to brown. But in this Wordsworth was not untypical of his time; connoisseurship around writing itself was rare.

Yet by the time Wordsworth was eight years old, south, across the channel, towards the Alps (a route Wordsworth would walk years later) the Swiss cleric Johann Caspar Lavater (1741–1801) had published his widely read *Physiognomic Fragments* [3] (1775–8). In the second edition he added a chapter on 'Character in Handwriting'; Goethe wrote the introduction. Lavater captured something in the *zeitgeist* when he wrote it was 'highly probable that each of us has his own handwriting, individual and inimitable ... is it possible, that this incontestable diversity of writing should not be founded on the real difference of moral character?' [4]

By now printing had spread to provincial towns across Europe. It was familiarity with the uniformities of print that meant handwriting, by contrast, was now recognized as carrying an individual stamp.[5] By the century's end, when Wordsworth was thirty years old, writing had been reconceived as emanating from the natural force and energy of an individual, autographs were soon collected[6] and Lavater's work developed into an articulate awareness of character in handwriting. The foundation of the study of graphology had been laid.[7]

Wordsworth himself may never have known of this work but, ever a bell-weather for developments in the world of the imagination and feeling, by the age of seventeen he had developed a psychosomatic relationship to his script and writing instruments—perhaps the first

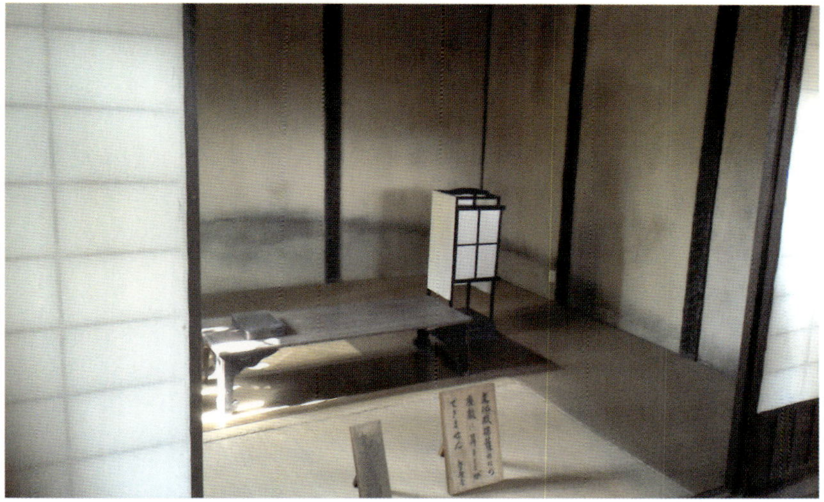

Figure 20, Bashō's study adjacent to his house, Iga City, Japan
Photograph by Ayako Tani (courtesy of Iga City Bashō Memorial Museum)

such case to be documented. In his own obscure imaginings, writing clearly carried a projection of psychological content. When his poetic imagination became engaged, Wordsworth's hand wrestled to express itself, his muscles became bound and pain infused the left side of his body, around his heart. 'I should have written five times as much as I have done but that I am prevented by an uneasiness at my side and with a dull pain about my heart—I have used the word pain, but uneasiness and heat are words which more accurately describe my feeling. At all events it renders writing unpleasant'[8] (from Wordsworth to Coleridge, Goslar: December 1798). This ailment remained with him for the rest of his life.

There is no physical reason, in a right-handed writer, for the left side of the body to become stressed. This is an affliction of feeling. Wordsworth's pain calls attention, both personally and to his times at large, to a disjuncture *and* to new possibilities for connection between hand and heart. Such experiences mark an important turn in the story of western writing: a clear call to authenticity in the activity of writing itself, not simply in letter shape.[9] Here is a potential point for breakthrough into the first western calligraphy of the heart, but one, alas, that it would take several generations to cycle through.

**Endnotes**

1. For further examples of the middle of the three periods of his work that have been identified, see the exhibition catalogue *Bashō: 'Oku no Hosomichi' kara no okurimono*, Tōkyō: Idemitsu Bijutsukan, Heisei 21, 2009.

2. The Wordsworth Trust holds such a pen tray in its archives.

3. Johann Caspar Lavater, *Physiognomische Fragmente zur Beförderung der Menschenkenntnis und Menschenliebe*, Leipzig: 1775–1778.

4. Johann Caspar Lavater, *Essays on Physiognomy*, trans. C. Moore, London: W. Locke, 1797, Vol. 4, p.200.

5. The first time that individual differences in handwriting are acknowledged in a legal context as evidence in Britain is in the writings of the English jurist Geoffrey Gilbert in 1726; see Tamara Plakins Thornton, *Handwriting in America*, New Haven, CT: Yale University Press, 1996, p.35.

6. One of the earliest signs of a growing interest in autographs was the publication of *British Autography, a collection of the Facsimiles of Royal and Illustrious Personages with their Authentic Portraits* in 1788 by John Thane. Thane showed the portraits of 269 persons above examples of their handwriting and signatures, as if this too constituted another aspect of portraiture.

7. When Lavater's work was translated into French in 1806 by Dr Jacques-Louis Moreau, Moreau expanded the section on handwriting. From an English author, John Holt Schooling, *Handwriting and Expression,* London: Kegan Paul, Trench, Trübner & Co., 1892, p.6, we gather 'from M. Moreau's observations that graphology was seriously practiced by a few men, starting from the year 1806'.

8. William Wordsworth, *The Letters of William and Dorothy Wordsworth: The Early Years, 1787–1805,* ed. Ernest de Selincourt, rev. Chester L. Shaver, Oxford: Oxford University Press, 1967, p.236.

9. For a wider discussion of the imaginative symbolism of the heart, see James Hillman, *The Thought of the Heart*, Ascona: Eranos, 1979.

**Biographical Note**

Ewan Clayton is Professor of Design at the University of Sunderland where he collaborates with Manny Ling in running the University's International Research Centre for Calligraphy. Ewan has his own calligraphy workshop in Brighton, Sussex and grew up close by the village of Ditchling, where he, and three generations of his family, worked in a craft Guild established by Eric Gill. For a number of years Ewan worked as a consultant to Xerox's Palo Alto Research Center (PARC) where he researched the use of documents in shaping the patterns of our lives. In 2013 his book *The Golden Thread,* a history of writing, was published by Atlantic Books. He has taught and exhibited work widely in Southern and Central Asia, Africa, Europe and North America. www.ewanclayton.co.uk.

# WANDERER POETS EAST AND WEST: FROM WORDSWORTH AND BASHŌ TO NEW CREATION

**SHŌKO AZUMA**

This year marks the 370th anniversary of Bashō's birth and 320th commemoration of his death. In a year of such great significance, it is a great pleasure to encounter such a creative and thought-provoking exhibition informed by a comparative cultural perspective at the Wordsworth Museum in England's beautiful Lake District.

## 1. Bashō

### What does travel mean to literature and art?

The famous Japanese wandering poet Matsuo Bashō respected the Chinese traveling poet Tu Fu, and admired the Japanese itinerant bard Saigyō. The medieval Japanese author Kenkō writes in his collection of essays *Tsurezuregusa* (Essays in Idleness):

> *Izuku nimo are, shibashi tabidachitaru koso, me samuru kokochi sure.*
>
> No matter what the destination, the act of setting out on even a short journey inspires reawakening.
>
> (Episode 15)

Kenkō's comment is that, wherever the destination, time spent travelling brings a refreshing feeling of new insight. The experience of travel gives us a chance to get away from our day-to-day lives and restore our sensitivity of perception. Indeed, everything we encounter on a trip can seem like an illumination.

This is how Bashō writes of travel:

> *Tōkaidō no hitosuji mo shiranu hito, fūga ni obotsukanashi, tomo ieri*
>
> "Those who do not know of the Tōkaidō have no understanding of *fūga* (artistic expression)," he also said.
>
> Dohō, *Sanzōshi* (Three notebooks)

This is a famous passage where Bashō tells his disciple that unless you have experience of the Tōkaidō, you cannot follow the Path of *haikai*, the historical form of *haiku*. He says that if you aim to create *haikai,* you must at least travel on the Tōkaidō, the most important of the Five Great Routes of Edo-period Japan, a remark that attests to the great importance he put on the experience of travel for the artist.

Bashō made five trips while he was in his forties, and these resulted in his five travel journals. These journeys he undertook—traipsing over the unpaved roads of early modern Japan period on foot, or travelling by palanquin or on horseback—must have involved great hardship. *Nozarashi Kikō* ('Record of a Weatherbeaten Skeleton'), *Kashima Mode* ('Pilgrimage to Kashima'), *Oi no Kobumi* ('Rucksack Notebook'), *Sarashina Kikō* ('Sarashina Travel Journal'), *Oku no Hosomichi* ('Narrow Road to the Interior') ...: Bashō's health was seriously affected by the many days he spent on the road between the ages forty and forty five. When he died at the age of fifty in Osaka, he was travelling to Kyūshū and Shikoku on the journey that was to be his last.

### Nature's Mutability is the Origin of Art

Elsewhere among the teachings that Bashō shared with his disciples we read:

> *Shi no iwaku, "Kenkon no hen wa fūga no tane nari" to ieri.*
>
> The Master said, "The changing nature of the world is the seed of *fūga* (artistic expression)".
>
> Dohō, *Sanzōshi*

The 'master' here is Bashō, saying that all the transformations of the natural world serve as the basis of *haiku*. '*Fūga*' may refer either to art in a broad sense, or to *haikai* in particular. He also said that amid the climate of Japan, with its four seasons, you must closely observe the transformations of nature; and that as soon as you notice something, you must write of it before the spark of inspiration fades. Furthermore, Bashō consistently rejected the old, advising 'seek what is new'; he constantly strove to deepen originality. For him, travel offered the chance to make new discoveries by walking between heaven and earth.

## 2. Wordsworth

### Natsume Sōseki's Theory in 'English Poets' Ideas on Natural Scenery'

Wordsworth is one of the greatest nature poets, an exemplar of nineteenth century Romanticism. In his essay 'English Poets' Ideas on Natural Scenery', Natsume Sōseki, the renowned modern Japanese writer and English literary scholar, explains the naturalism of Wordsworth as something that arises from 'wisdom' and 'philosophical insight', maintaining that he is 'the master of the masters, who integrates with myriad changes and subsumes the universe without insufficiency. That is the naturalism of Wordsworth.'

### Wordsworth and Bashō

Bashō (1644–1694) lived in the early Edo period; the life of Wordsworth (1770–1850) belongs to the latter part of the same era. Both were poets that spoke to their respective nations, both were poets who interacted closely with nature. Both loved travel, and used it as background of their philosophical theories. Both lost their fathers at around the age of thirteen. A difference between them is that while Wordsworth got married and had a family, Bashō remained single, though he associated closely with a network of disciples. Anyhow, one is the Eastern poet in the seventeenth century, and the other is the Western poet of the late eighteenth to early nineteenth century.

### 3. Two Daffodil Poems

Wordsworth's 'Daffodils' (see figure 21) is a deeply affecting masterpiece; Bashō also composed verses on the topic of this flower.

I wandered lonely as a Cloud
That floats on high o'er vales and Hills,
When all at once I saw a crowd,
A host, of golden Daffodils;
Beside the Lake, beneath the trees,
Fluttering and dancing in the breeze.

Continuous as the stars that shine
And twinkle on the milky way,
They stretched in never-ending line
Along the margin of a bay:
Ten thousand saw I at a glance,
Tossing their heads in sprightly dance.

...

And then my heart with pleasure fills,
And dances with the Daffodils.

...

*suisen ya shiroki shoji no tomo utsuri*

narcissus in a vase,
sliding paper door behind—
reflect whiteness of each other

*sono nioi momo yori shiroshi suisenka*

scent of narcissus
          is felt
whiter than peach

Bashō

Because *suisen* (narcissus) is a *kigo* (season word) for winter, Japanese daffodils convey an image of whiteness and cleanliness. It is different from that of Western yellow daffodils. Also, as the pronunciation of the flower's name is derived from the Chinese reading of the

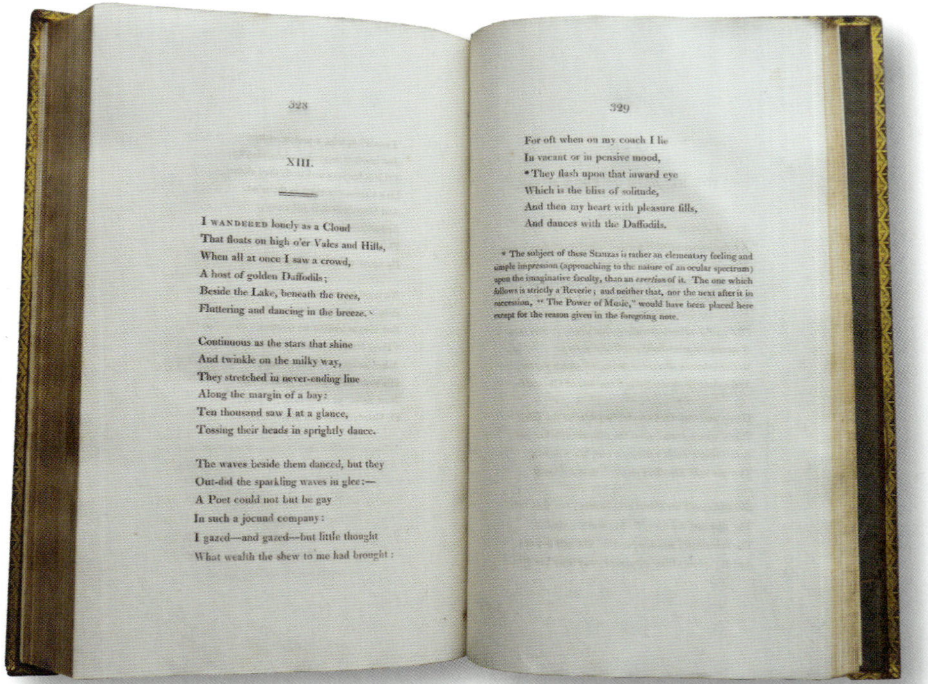


Figure 21
William Wordsworth
*Poems, including Lyrical Ballads*, London, 1815
This copy was presented by Dorothy Wordsworth to John Monkhouse (open to show the second publication of 'I wandered lonely as a Cloud', with the additional second stanza)

characters used to write it, daffodils were never featured in *waka*, 31-syllable courtly verse. The first time daffodils appear in poetry was in Edo-period *haikai*. Bashō was drawn to the beauty of whiteness, and therefore composed exquisite *haiku* on this theme. We also can find daffodils in *ukiyo-e* (coloured woodblock prints), in which the flower is depicted inside a room or by the water. Aside from this, other themes common to both Wordsworth and Bashō are the cuckoo, the butterfly and the daisy.

### 4. Toward a New Challenge

**Walking and Creation/Re-creation from Handwritten Manuscripts**

The concepts of this exhibition are quite unprecedented. In the first place, a consideration of what the act of walking affords to poets, writers and artists is a theme that is extremely simple yet fundamental to humanity. I am sure that it will lead to the opening of new perspectives. In the second place is the idea of the entirely new creative work we attempt in response to our reception of writers' own handwritten manuscripts. This seems to me quite an interesting practice, as long as the manuscripts to which we refer are those inscribed in the poets' own handwriting, even in facsimile form. At all events these two themes are a promising indication of the emergence of creative readers in our own time.

Finally, I would like to mention the fact that International Haiku has proliferated greatly in this age of globalization, and that large numbers of people write *haiku* in their own languages in as many as fifty countries around the world. Here in Britain, the British Haiku Society engages in wonderful activities, many of which I have heard about from its former president, David Cobb. *Haiku* is the shortest poetic form in the world, one that has fascinated poets all over the world by its 'instants of beauty'.

I would like to express my gratitude and good wishes for the future to the Wordsworth Museum for this innovative exhibition in collaboration with the work of Bashō. Also, please let me invite the visitors of this exhibition to come one day to the Bashō Memorial Museums in Japan (one in Kōtō-ku, Tokyo and the other in the city of Iga in Mie Prefecture) and as well as other archives related to Bashō. I wish to express my profound esteem to all the people who have participated in this effort to bring together Wordsworth and Bashō. Last of all, I hope that all of you will enjoy this new creation, and experience the freedom of imagination this exhibition represents.

**Biographical Note**

Shokō Azuma is a professor at Jumonji University, Japan. She graduated with a degree in Japanese literature from Japan Women's University and obtained a doctorate in comparative cultural studies from Ochanomizu University. She specialises in early modern Japanese literature and has written widely on Bashō's poetry. Her study of his use of seasonal language published by Meiji Shoin in 2003 was awarded the Yamamoto Kenichi Literature Prize. She has undertaken comparative research on the representation of journeys in eastern and western literature, taking *The Narrow Road to the Deep North* as a case study.

# [ ARTISTS' WORK ]

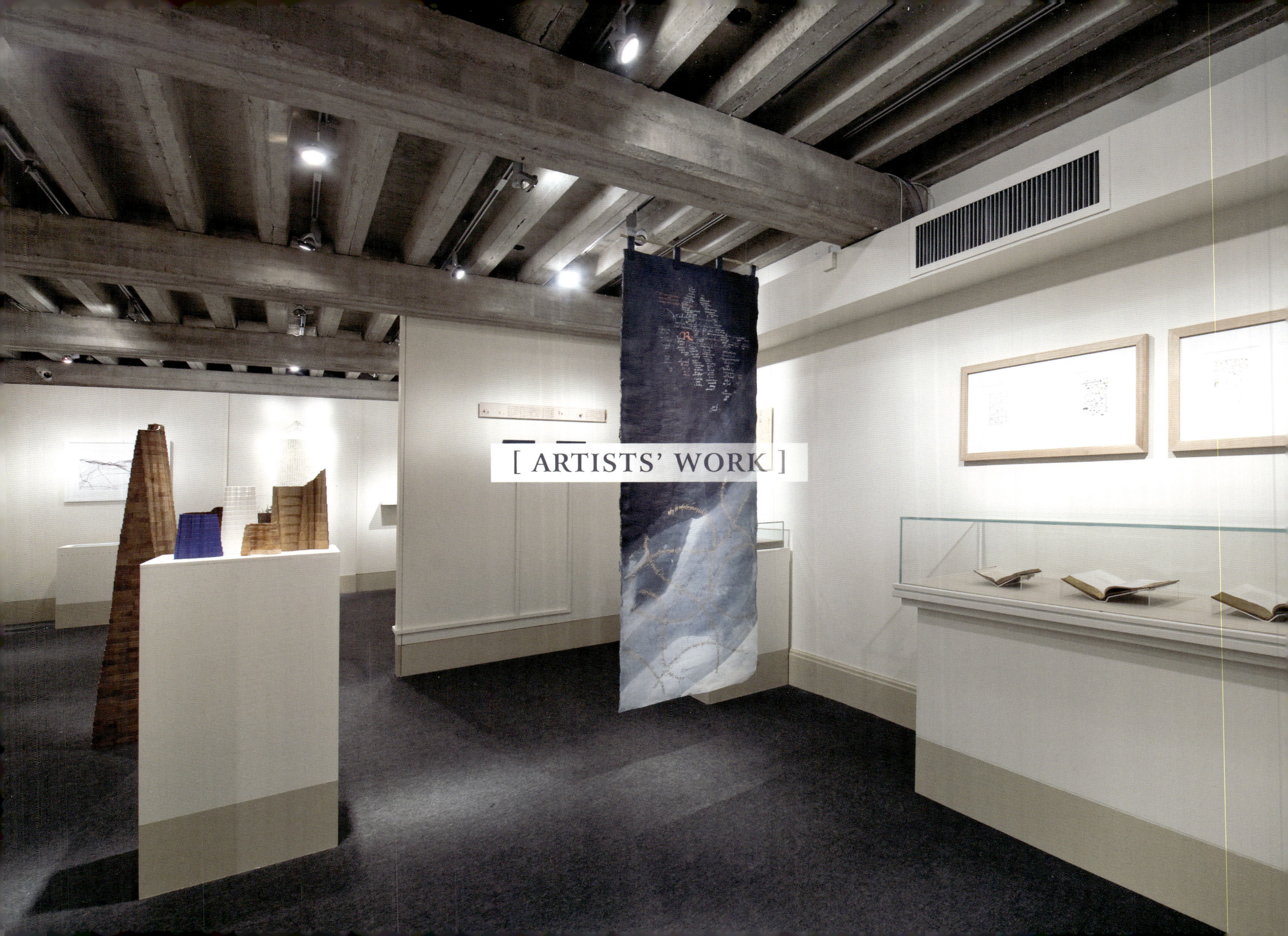

Walking Poets

# WORDSWORTH AND BASHŌ: WALKING POETS

## THE EXHIBITION

**Artists**

Ken Cockburn

Mike Collier

Ewan Clayton and Nao Sakamoto

Alec Finlay

Eiichi Kono

Zaffar Kunial

Manny Ling and Christine Flint-Sato

Christopher McHugh

Nobuya Monta

Inge Panneels and Minako Shirakura

Andrew Richardson

Autumn Richardson

Richard Skelton

Ayako Tani

Brian Thompson

**Manuscripts**

William and Dorothy Wordsworth

Matsuo Bashō

Yosa Buson

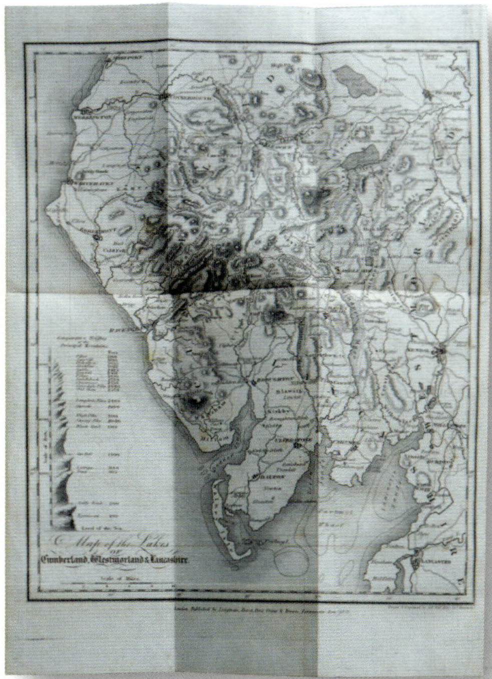

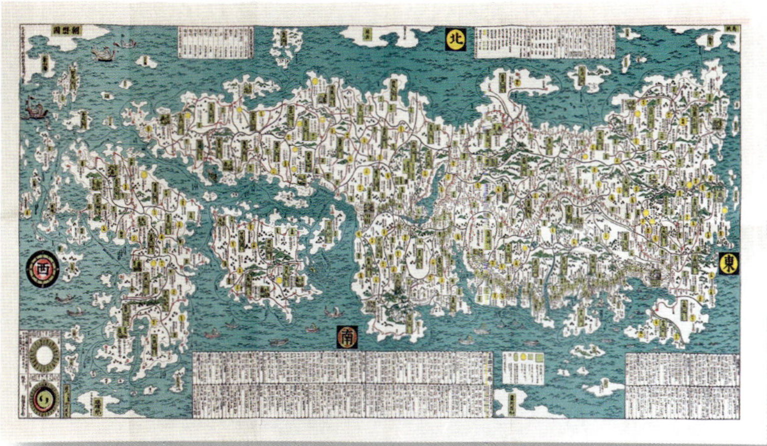

## WILLIAM WORDSWORTH

1. ***Frontispiece, map from a Description of the Scenery of the Lakes in the North of England***
By William Wordsworth, London, 1823
Courtesy of the Wordsworth Trust.

These two maps (which open our exhibition) are very different. The 'Map of Japan' is from the Edo period, and is the sort of map Bashō might have had access to on his travels. It is worth noting that the North of Japan (where Bashō journeyed on the 'Narrow Road to the Deep North') is unrecognisable, geographically, from the north of Japan as we know it today. The map of the Lake District shows the area the Wordsworths explored, often on foot, for much of their life.

## ARTIST UNKNOWN

2. ***Map of Japan in the Genroku period***
Genroko period (1688–1704)
Paper, sumi ink
46 x 90 cm
Courtesy of Kochizu Shiry  Shuppan Co. Ltd.

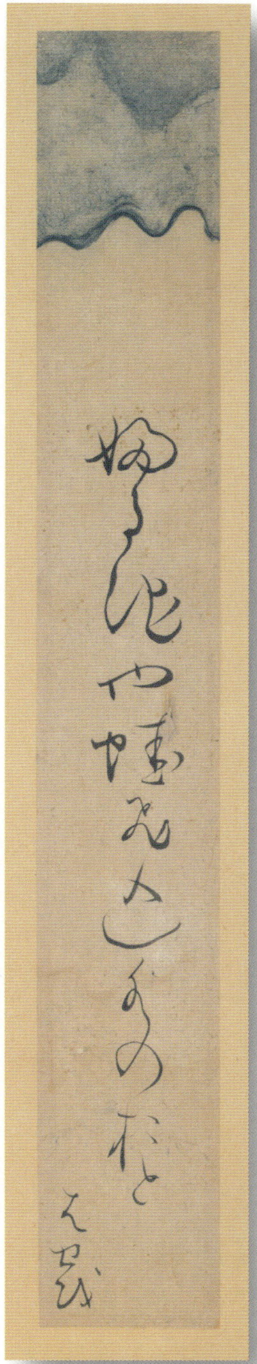

## MATSUO BASHŌ

**3. *Furuikeya***
Tanzaku-strip
1686
Paper, sumi ink
36 x 5 cm
Facsimile produced courtesy of Kakimori Bunko

The old pond
a frog jumps in
sound of water [1]

*Furu ike ya*
*kawazu tobikomu*
*mizu no oto*

This is probably the most famous poem in Japan, and after over three hundred years of repetition, it has, understandably, become a little 'stale' for Japanese people. In the same way, perhaps, poems such as *I Wandered lonely as a Cloud* by Wordsworth have become equally 'stale'. As English readers, we may see this *haiku* differently to a Japanese person—it looks fresh and new. We hope that this exhibition and catalogue will allow UK visitors to similarly look at the poems and manuscripts by William and Dorothy Wordsworth afresh.

A *haiku* is a Japanese poem of seventeen syllables, in three lines of five, seven, and five, traditionally evoking images of the natural world. The name 'haiku' literally translated means 'play verse'.

Endnotes

1. Robert Hass, *The Essential Haiku,* Tarset: Bloodaxe Books, 2013, p.35.

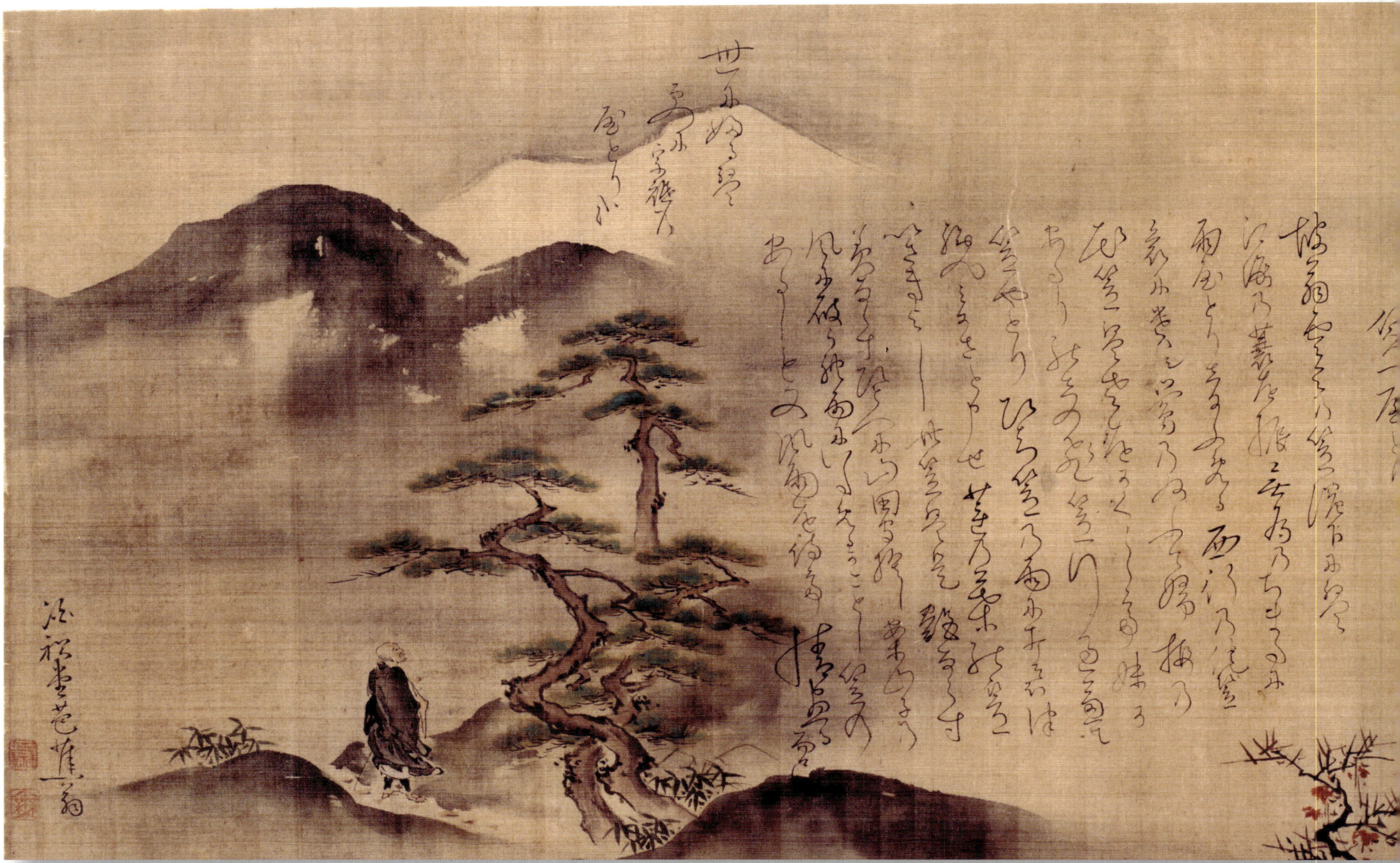

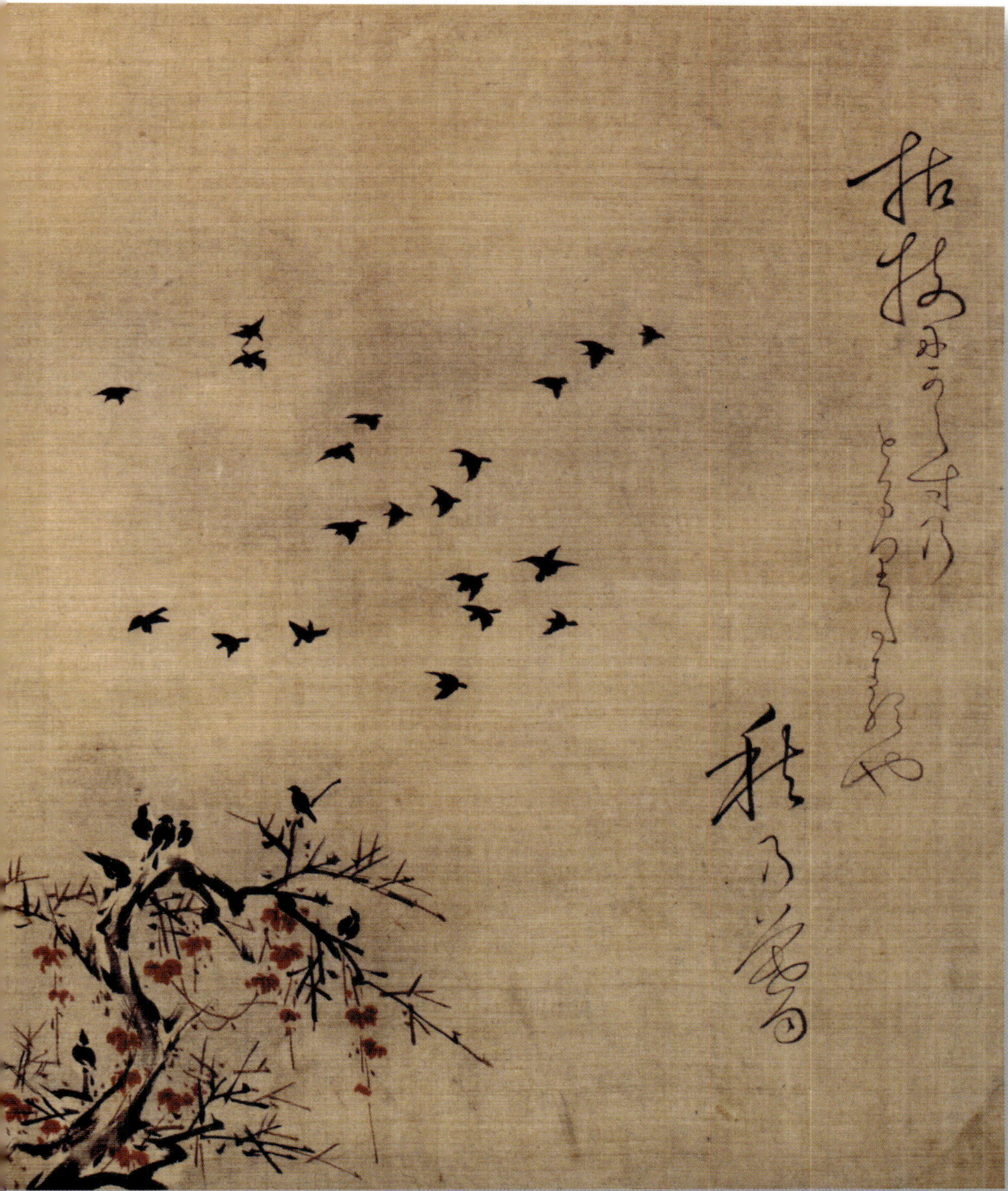

## MATSUO BASHŌ

4. *Kareedani/Kasayadori*
c.1682
Silk, sumi ink, colour
32.9 x 83.2 cm
Facsimile produced courtesy of Waseda University Library

A crow
has settled on a bare branch
autumn evening [1]

Kare eda ni
Karasu no tomari taruya
Aki no kure

Endnotes

1. Robert Hass, *The Essential Haiku,* Tarset: Bloodaxe Books, 2013, p.30.

# KEN COCKBURN

5. ***While yet we may,*** 2014, book, 13 x 18 cm

6. ***While yet we may***, box with cards, 10 x 9 x 3.3 cm, edition of 5

Ken Cockburn works as a freelance writer, translator, editor and writing tutor, based in Edinburgh. He has always been interested in *haiku* and like many previous practitioners of the form, his practice often involves collaborators and other art forms, as in his project with Alec Finlay, *The Road North*, a Scottish version of Bashō's 17th century journey in northern Japan.

Cockburn's new work for this show is deceptively simple in its modes of collaborative composition, bringing together the words of poets separated geographically and historically, yet linked here through poetic reassociation.

The book of verse and box of cards which comprise 'While yet we may' are both composed of seventeen words from Bashō's *Oku no Hosomichi* (*The Narrow Road to the Deep North*) and fifty one extracts from *The Prelude, The Recluse* and 'Lines written a few miles above Tintern Abbey' by William Wordsworth.

The idea for 'While yet we may' came from a 'variable construction' by the poet Gael Turnbull (1928–2004), which consisted of two sets of cards; one of twenty eight cards, each featuring a noun, the other of 112 cards, each featuring a qualifying phrase. As Turnbull explained, 'any one of the one hundred and twelve phrases may relate to any of the twenty-eight nouns'. Of a published version in which each phrase was paired with a noun he wrote, 'this version is no less final than any other'. The same applies to the versions of 'While yet we may' printed and exhibited here.

With thanks to Luke Allan, Alec Finlay, Lorna Irvine, Lila Matsumoto and Angus Reid.

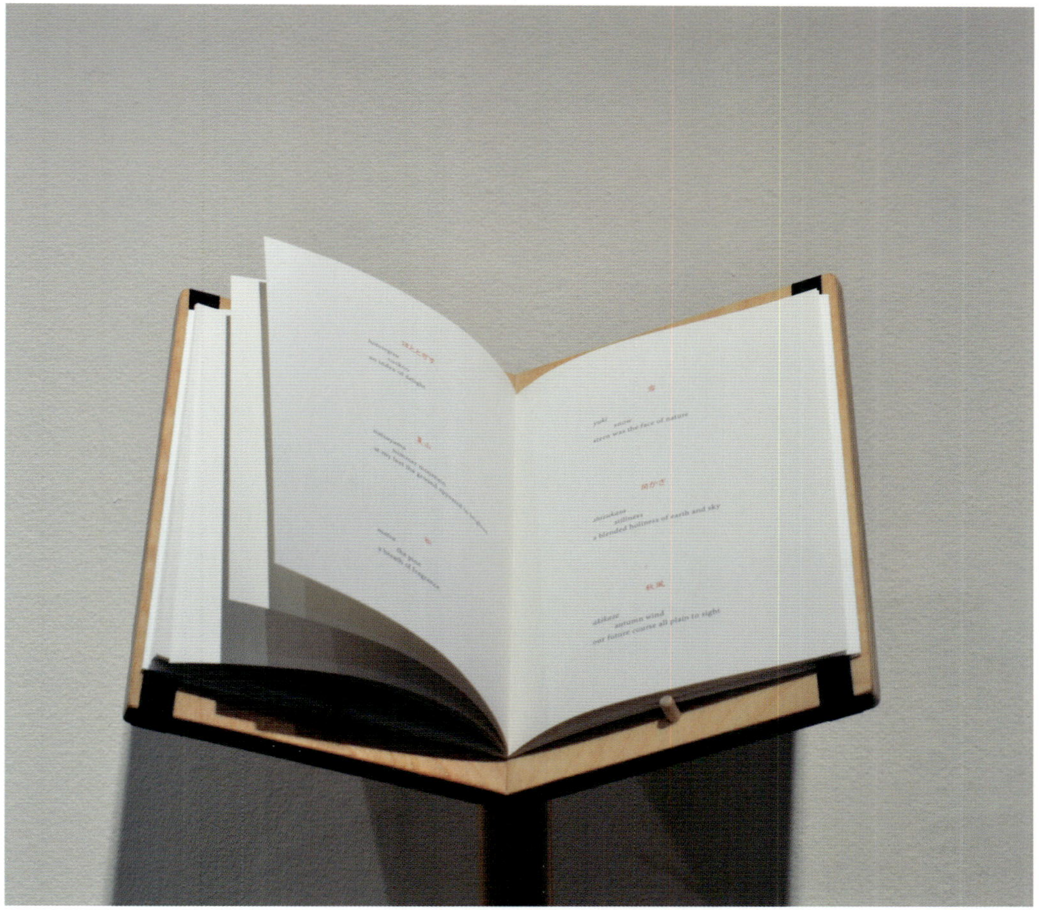

*While yet we may,* book, installation shot

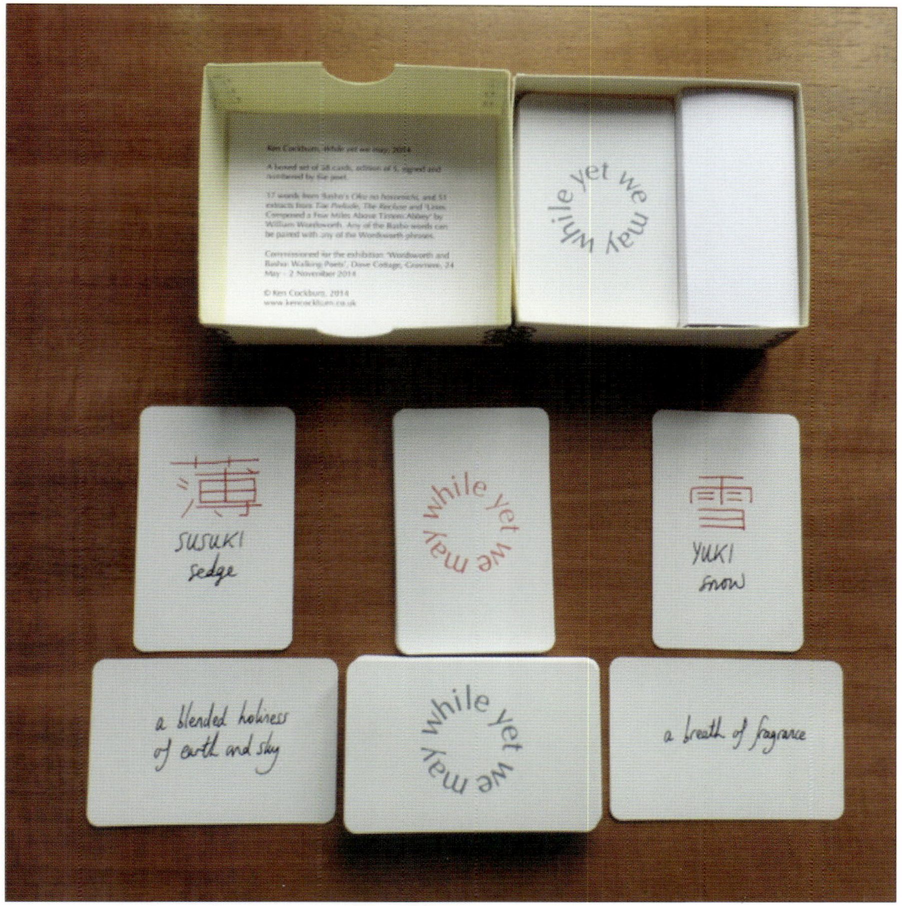


*While yet we may*, box with cards

夢

*yume*
dream
these gleams of past existence

短冊

*tanzaku*
a poem
surpassing grace to me hath been vouchsafed

はやぶさ

*hayabusa*
sweeping falcon
trackless hills by mists bewildered

*While yet we may,* book (detail)

松

*matsu*
the pine
rooted now so deeply in my mind

ほととぎす

*hototogisu*
cuckoo
how fast that length of way was left behind

閑かさ

*shizukasa*
stillness
nor should this, perchance, pass unrecorded

*While yet we may,* book (detail)

ほととぎす

*hototogisu*
cuckoo
an index of delight

夏山

*natsuyama*
summer mountain
at my feet the ground appeared to brighten

松

*matsu*
the pine
a breath of fragrance

*While yet we may,* book (detail)

隻鳧

*sekifu*
a single wild duck
I must tread on shadowy ground

閑かさ

*shizukasa*
stillness
to the brim my heart was full

夏山

*natsuyama*
summer mountain
breath and everlasting motion

*While yet we may,* book (detail)

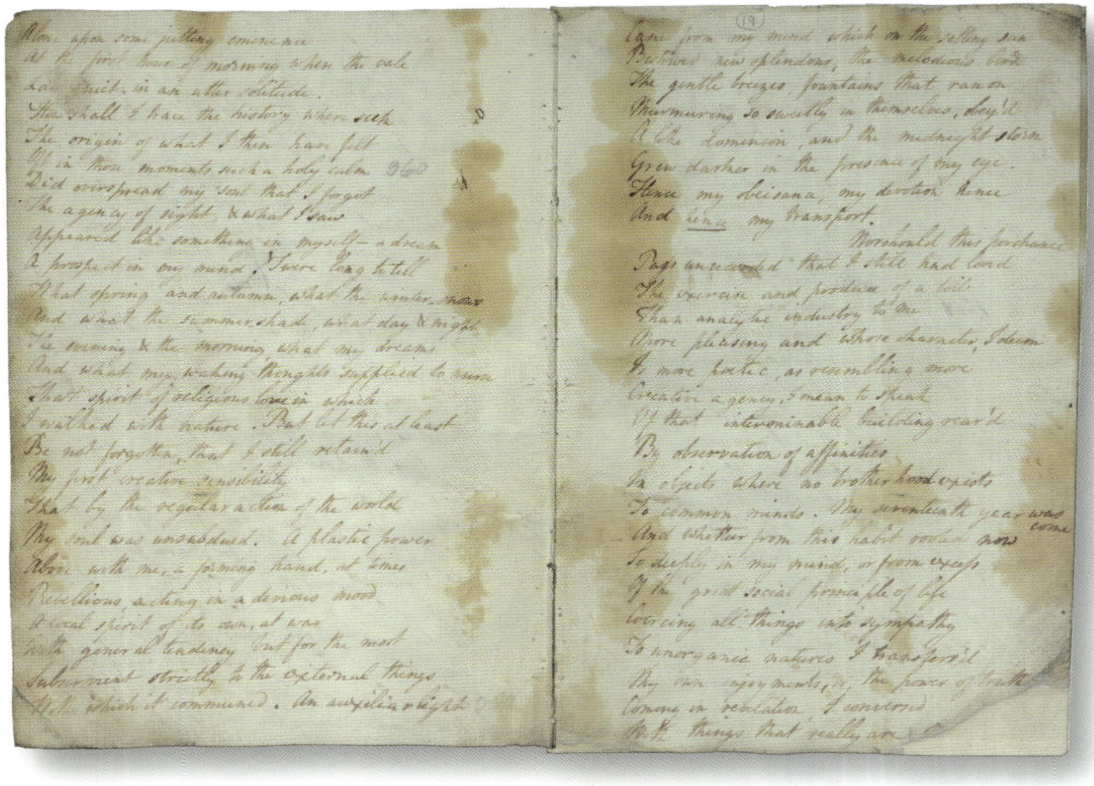

## WILLIAM WORDSWORTH

**7. *The Prelude*, 1799 in the hand of Dorothy Wordsworth**
Open to show 1805 Book II, 381–387
Courtesy of the Wordsworth Trust

This manuscript is a fair copy of lines later published in the full *Prelude*, but which in 1799 comprised only the first two books. As was typical in their way of working, Wordsworth would compose various fragments and then bring them together with either Mary or Dorothy acting as his amanuensis. This is the hand of Dorothy Wordsworth.

Looking north-east from Sour Milk Gill, Easedale, 22 January 2014
Photograph by Ken Cockburn

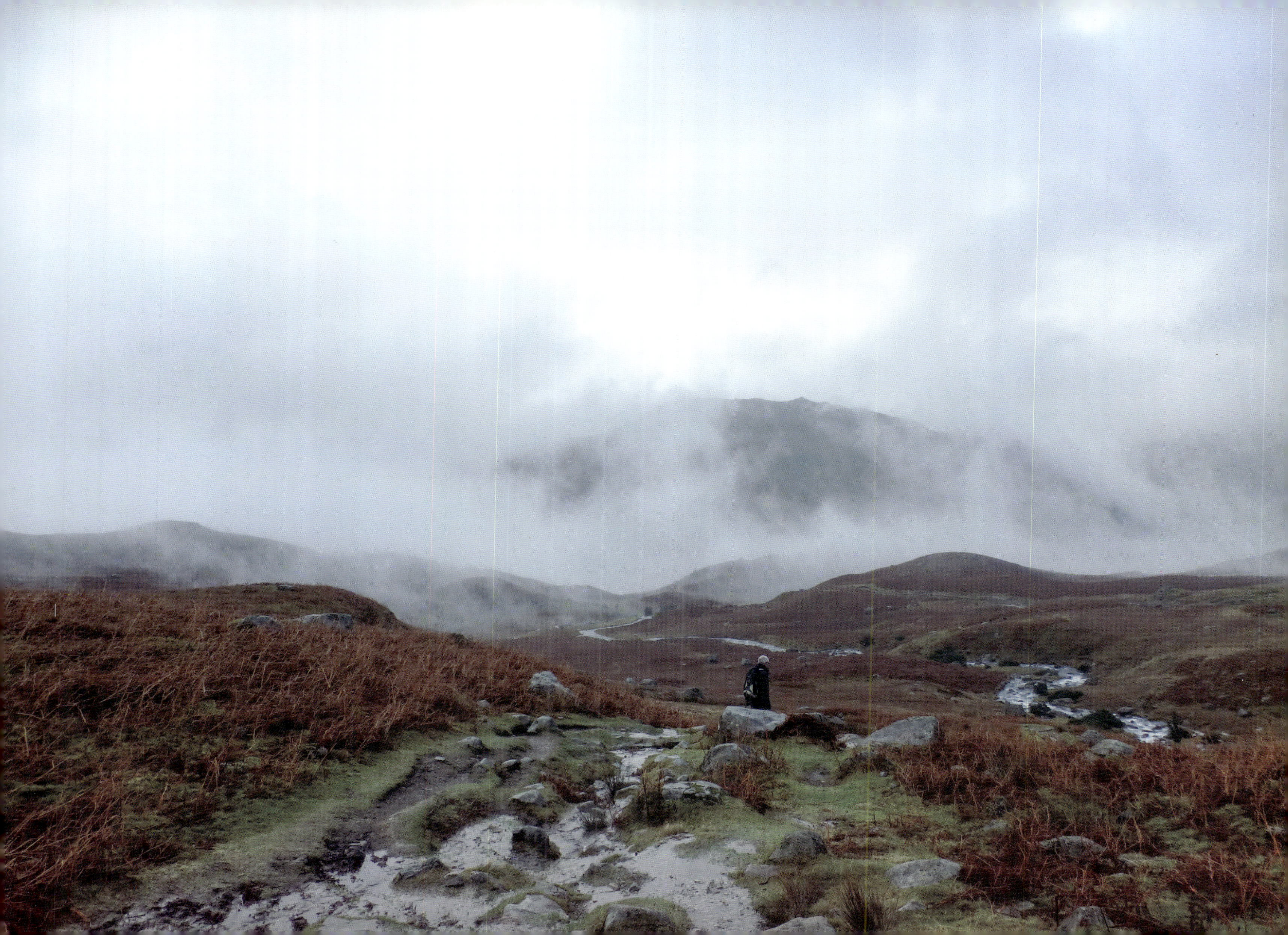

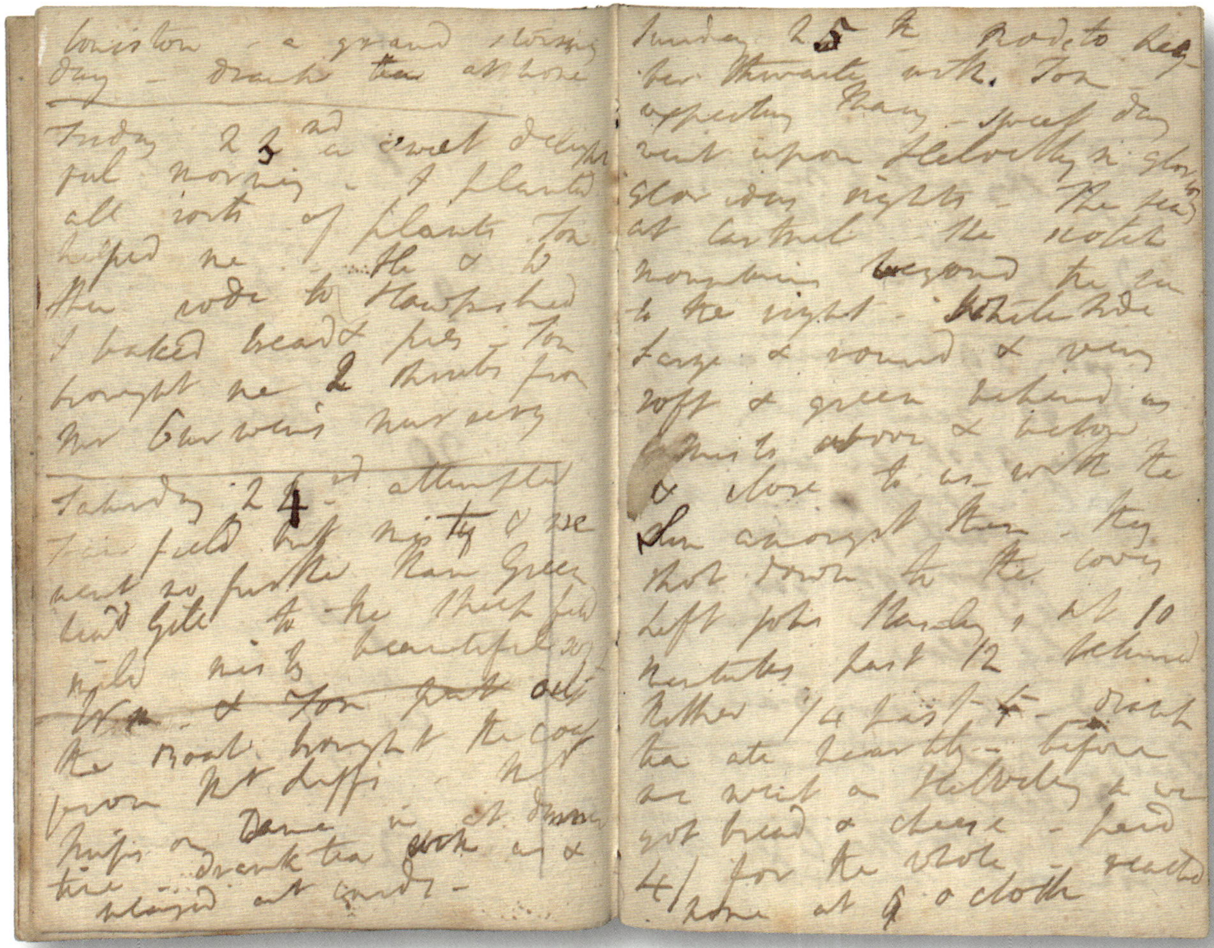
Coniston – a grand stormy day – drank tea at home

Friday 23rd a sweet delightful morning – I planted all sorts of plants Tom helped me. He & W then rode to Hawkshead I baked bread & pies Tom brought me 2 shrubs from Mr Curwen's nursery

Saturday 24th attempted Fairfield but misty & we went no further than Green Head Gill to the sheep fold mild misty beautiful soft. ~~Wm & Tom put out~~ the boat brought the coat from Mr Luffs. Mr Simpson came in at dinner time drank tea with us & played at cards –

Sunday 25th rode to Legberthwaite with Tom expecting Mary – sweet day went upon Helvellyn glorious glorious sights – The sea at Cartmel the Scotch mountains beyond the sea to the right – Whiteside large & round & very soft & green behind us Mists above & below & close to us with the sun amongst them – they shot down to the coves. Left John Stanley's at 10 minutes past 12 returned thither 1/4 past 4 – drank tea ate heartily – before we went on Helvellyn we got bread & cheese – paid 4/ for the whole reached home at 9 o clock

## DOROTHY WORDSWORTH

8. ***Grasmere Journal***
Entry for 24 and 25 October 1801
Courtesy of the Wordsworth Trust

Dorothy Wordsworth wrote a journal of the Wordsworths' lives in Grasmere from May 1800 until the beginning of 1803. Four small notebooks of journal entries survive.

# MIKE COLLIER

**9.** ***The Texture of Thought: Fairfield*** *(From Dorothy Wordsworth's Journal entry, 23rd & 24th October 1801)*
Unison pastel onto digital print
2014
35 x 65 cm

**10.** ***The Texture of Thought: Helvellyn*** *(From Dorothy Wordsworth's Journal entry, 25th October 1801)*
Unison pastel onto digital print
2014
35 x 65 cm

Mike Collier's work often relates directly to walks he has undertaken 'in the footsteps' of others, including Bashō and Wordsworth. He has walked many of the same Lake District routes described by Dorothy in her journals and walking as such is both inspiration and subject matter for a creative practice in which he explores the relationship between artwork and the phenomenological apprehension of specific localities.

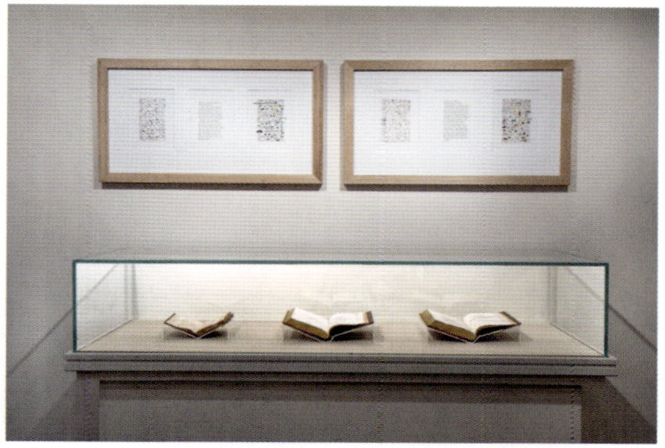

In the pieces included here, Collier colours directly with hand-made Unison pastels over scanned extracts from Dorothy's 1801 Grasmere Journal in which she describes favourite walks made or attempted. Fascinatingly fragile objects, Dorothy's journals bear the physical imprint of their maker, the handwriting both expressive and much laboured over. Often obscured by scoring through and reworking, the legibility of the journals is difficult for contemporary readers more used to words and letters on a screen or on a printed page. Collier's painterly marks add yet another layer of visual intrigue as he responds directly to the content of the journal entries with intuitive colour notations of his own, made quickly in the studio.

In this creative reworking, Collier has deliberately selected journal entries that describe favourite routes Dorothy followed—and ones he has walked a number of times: an ascent of Fairfield foiled by weather, followed two days later by a walk 'upon Helvellyn, glorious, glorious sights'. In the two pieces exhibited here, Collier's interventions draw attention once more to her words and imaginative reveries, to her characteristically fresh powers of natural description.

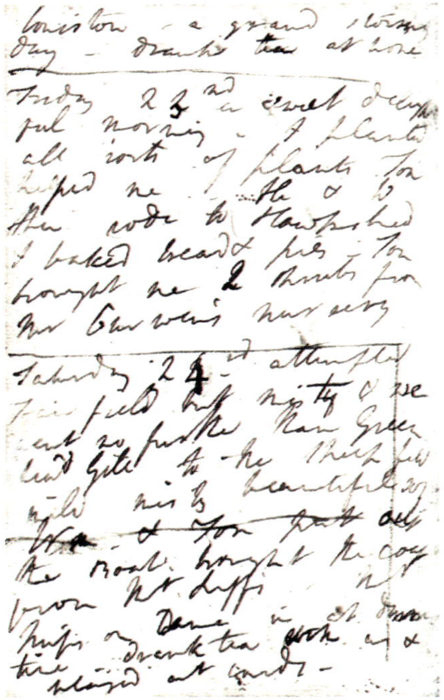

Coniston—a grand stormy day—
drank tea at home.

*Friday 23rd.* A sweet delightful morning. I planted all sorts of plants, Tom helped me. He & W then rode to Hawkshead. I baked bread and pies. Tom brought me 2 shrubs from Mr Curwen's nursery.

*Saturday 24th.* Attempted Fairfield but misty & we went no further than Green Head Gill to the sheepfold—mild misty beautiful soft. Wm and Tom put out the Boat brought the coat from Mr Luff's. Mr Simpson came in at dinner-time—drank tea with us & played at cards.

*The Texture of Thought: Fairfield (From Dorothy Wordsworth's Journal entry, 23rd & 24th October 1801)*

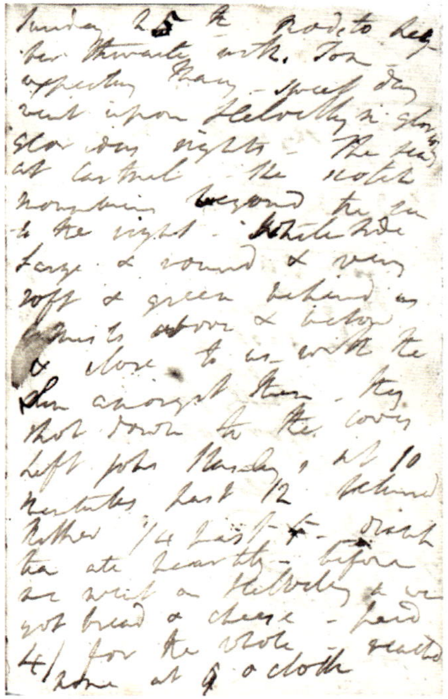

*Sunday 25th.* Rode to Legberthwaite with Tom—expecting Mary—sweet day—went upon Helvellyn, glorious glorious sights—The sea at Cartmel—The Scotch mountains beyond the sea to the right—Whiteside large & round & very soft & green behind us. Mists above & below & close to us, with the Sun amongst them—they shot down to the coves. Left John Stanley's at 10 minutes past 12 returned thither ¼ past 4—drank tea ate heartily—before we went on Helvellyn we got bread and cheese— paid 4/- for the whole—reached home at 9 o clock

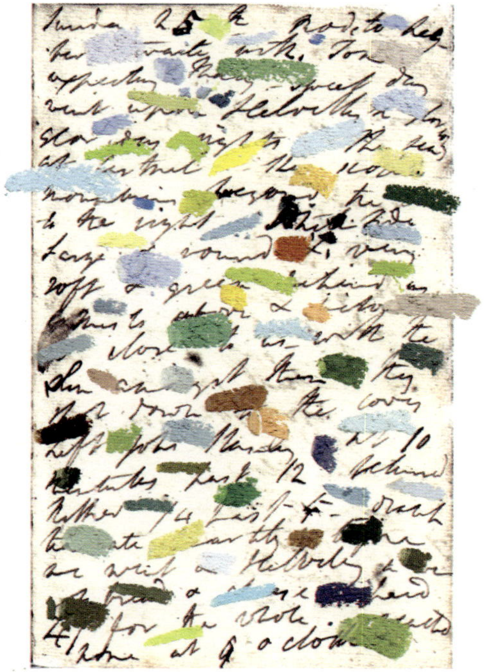

*The Texture of Thought: Helvellyn (From Dorothy Wordsworth's Journal entry, 25th October 1801)*

## **EWAN CLAYTON** (calligraphy) with **NAO SAKAMOTO** (dyed paper)

***11. Infinite Imagination: two poets at night, the moon on Mount Snowdon; the Milky Way over Sado Island***

2014.

Natural indigo dye on kōzo fibre paper with sumi, gold and silver leaf

180 x 66 cm

The collaboration between UK-based calligrapher Ewan Clayton and Japanese paper artist Nao Sakamoto has resulted in a beautifully evocative installation in which the poetic visions of Wordsworth and Bashō are reimagined in echoing layers.

Akin to a hanging scroll and written on both sides, the scale here is intimate yet expansive, the writing visible yet obscured. 'Infinite Imagination' speaks to the fragile materiality of Bashō and Wordsworth's poetry: to the deceptively simple calligraphy of the former as much as the cramped, overlaid scripts of the latter. In their process of writing Wordsworth's and Bashō's words anew, Clayton and Sakamoto draw attention to the aesthetics and physicality of the written word.

Often used in the process of manuscript conservation, Sakamoto's delicate Kozo paper has been coloured with an indigo dye so that it is almost opaque at the top and more transparent at the bottom, becoming in turn the base for Clayton's calligraphic overlay. In this, the almost unrestricted space of the paper becomes a challenge for calligraphic exploration. There is a certain vulnerability in such a collaborative process, a vulnerability that is as much material as ethical, aesthetic as well as philosophical.

Clayton and Sakamoto are equally fascinated by the speculative thought that underpins the writing of Bashō and Wordsworth. The poems selected here imagine moments of moonlit immensity and the infinite ecstasies of the natural world (the famous ascent of Snowdon from Wordsworth's *Prelude* on one side, with Bashō's envisaging of the Milky Way stretching over Sado Island on the other).

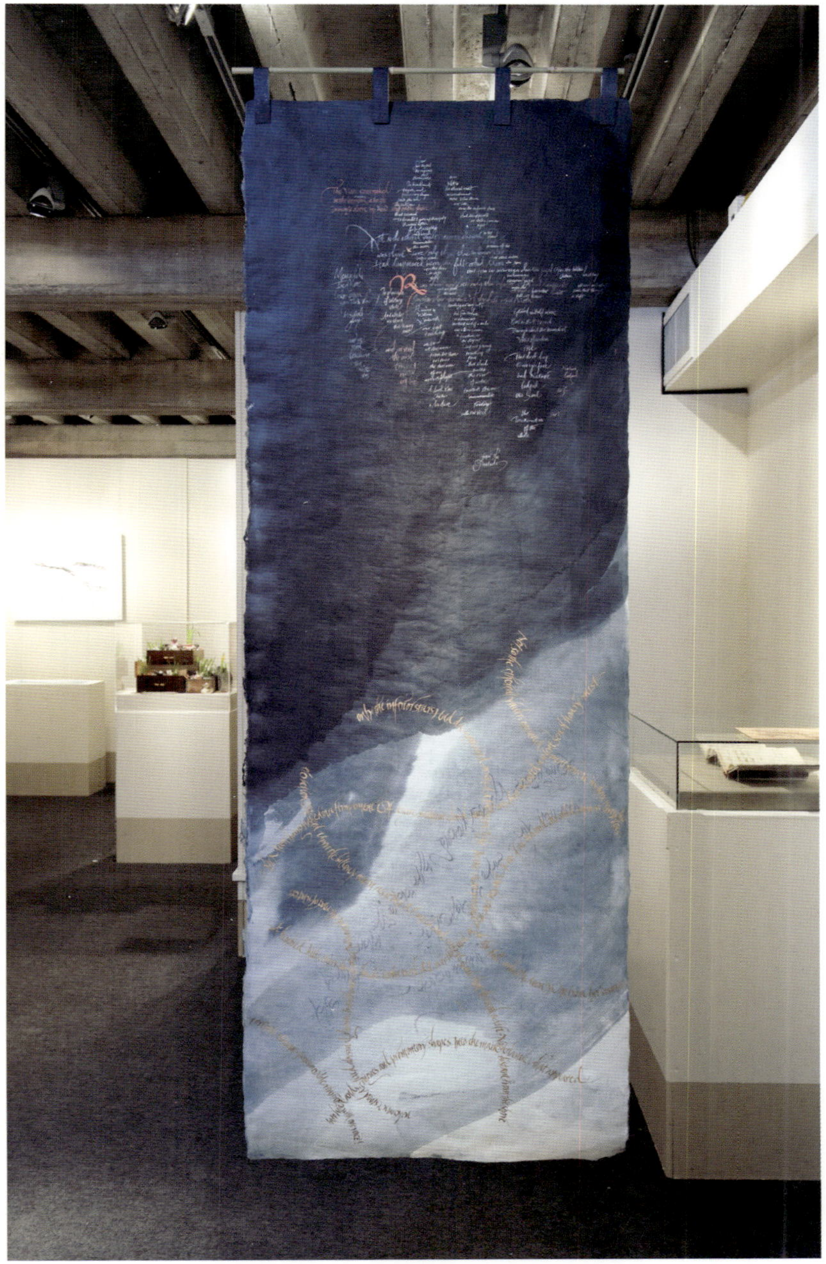

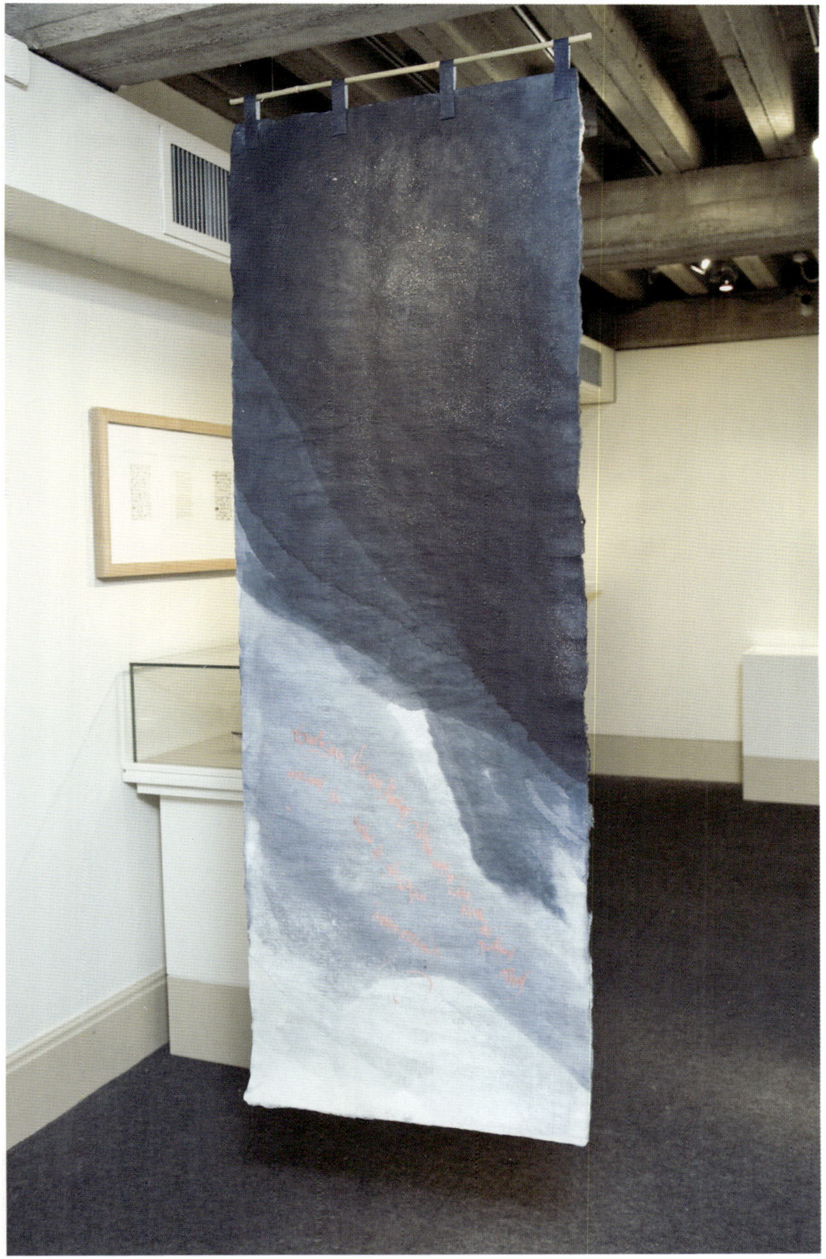

*Infinite Imagination: two poets at night, the moon on Mount Snowdon; the Milky Way over Sado Island, installation shot*

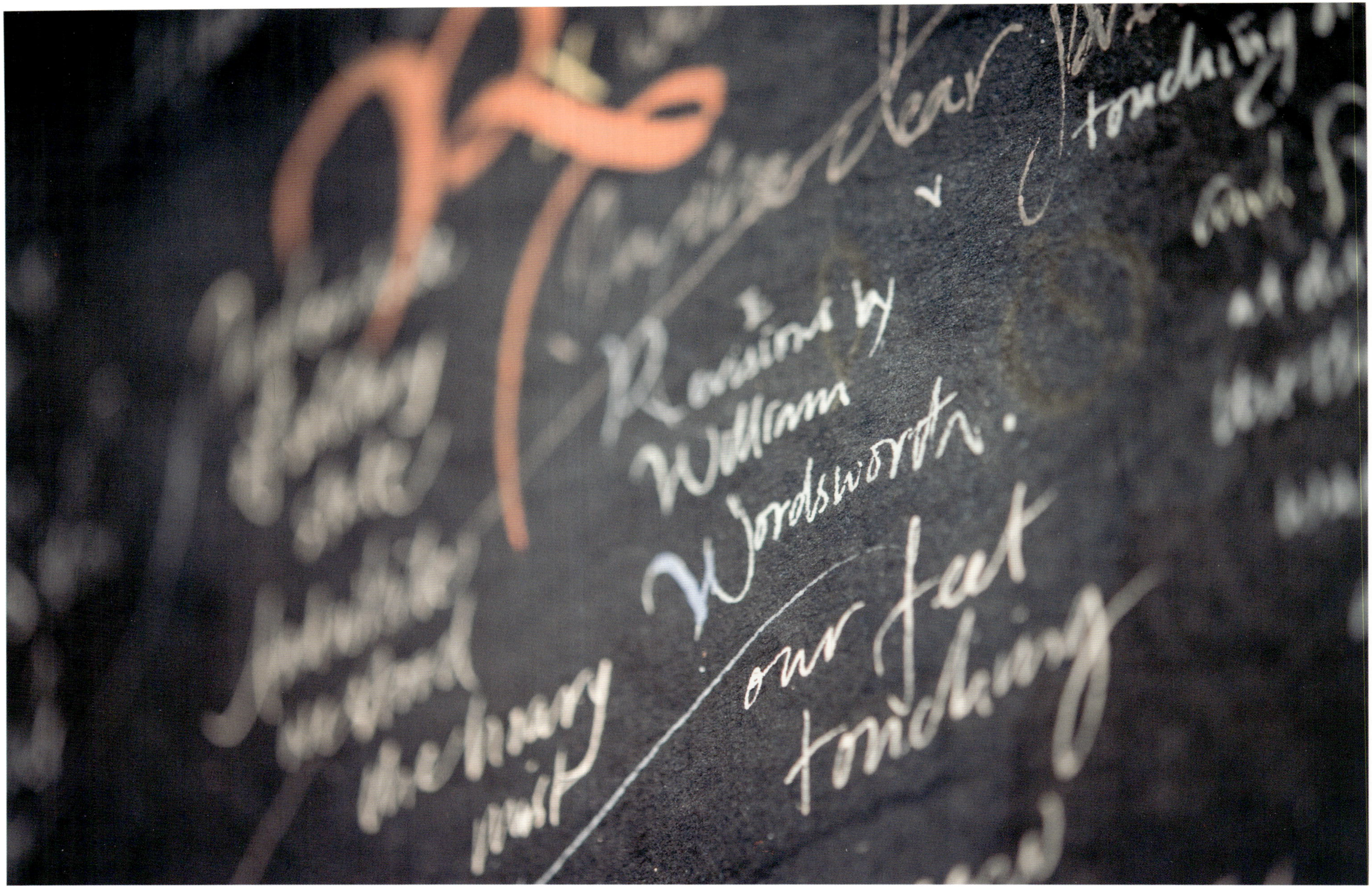


*Infinite Imagination: two poets at night, the moon on Mount Snowdon; the Milky Way over Sado Island* (detail)

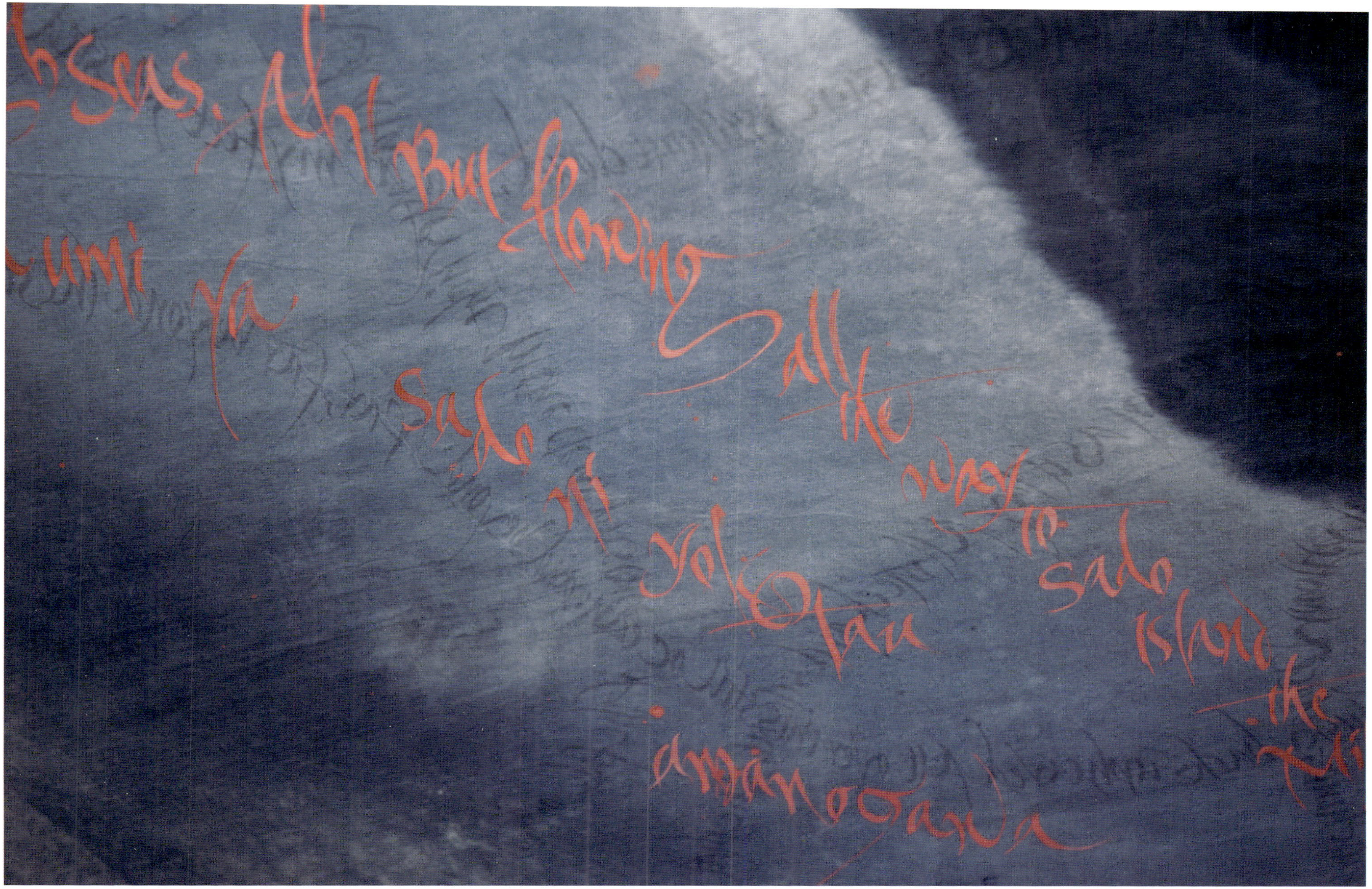


*Infinite Imagination: two poets at night, the moon on Mount Snowdon; the Milky Way over Sado Island* (detail)

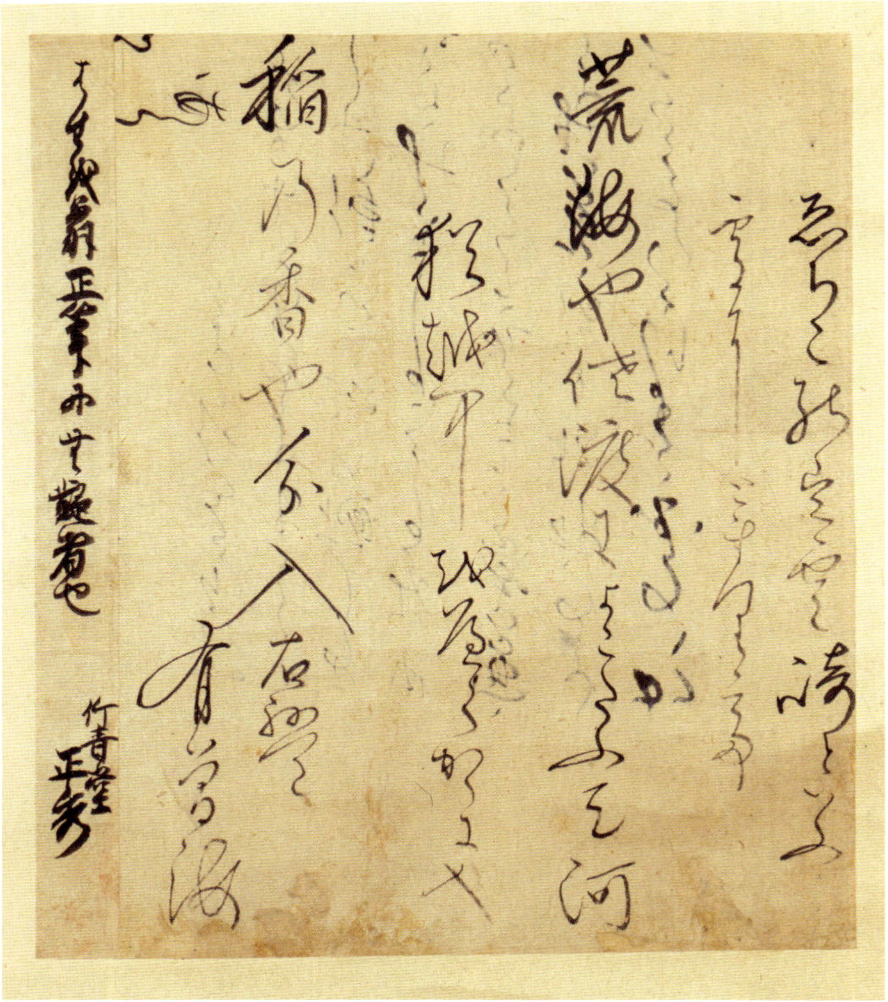

## MATSUO BASHŌ

**12. *Araumiya/Inanokaya*** (draft)
1689
Paper, sumi ink
22.3 x 20.3 cm
Facsimile produced courtesy of Kakimori Bunko

A wild sea –
and flowing out towards Sado Island,
the Milky Way [1]

araumi ya
sado ni yokotau
amanogawa

There are two *haiku* in this image. The 'Milky Way' *haiku,* on the right hand side is one of Bashō's most famous *haiku*. It appears in his travel book of poetry and prose *The Narrow Road to the Deep North* where Bashō, accompanied by his disciple, Sora, first saw the Island of Sado in the distance and could hear the sound of crashing waves.

A number of versions of this *haiku* were produced by Bashō—the one shown in this exhibition is an early draft and includes another *haiku* on the same page. It is interesting to see here Bashō's revisions.

Endnotes

1. Robert Hass, *The Essential Haiku,* Tarset: Bloodaxe Books, 2013, p.53.

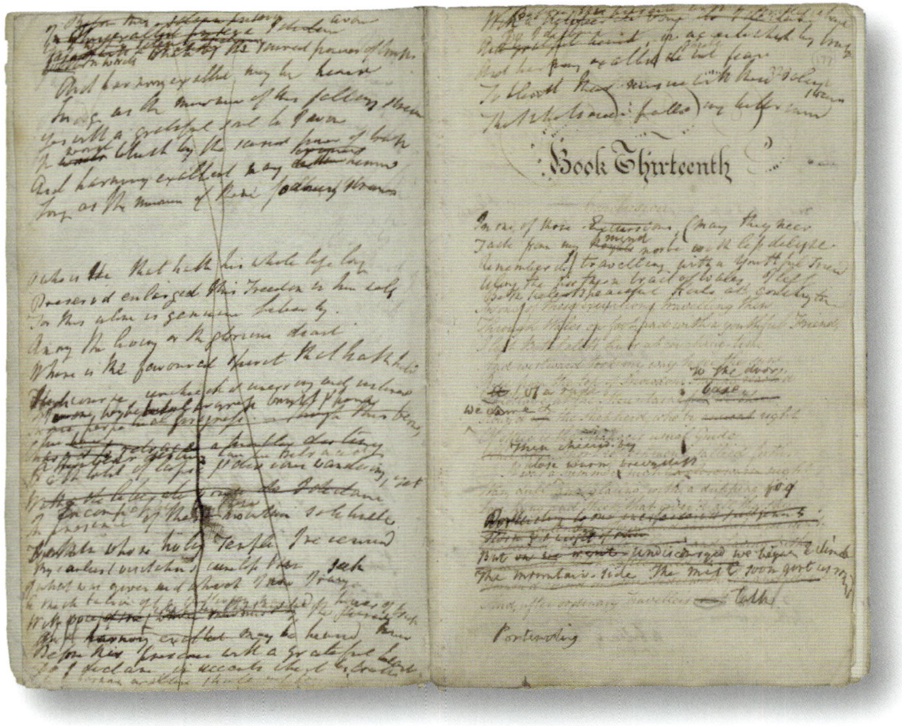


**13. WILLIAM WORDSWORTH**
***The Prelude,*** 1805
Hand of Mary Wordsworth
Open to show Book XIII, climbing of Snowdon
Courtesy of the Wordsworth Trust

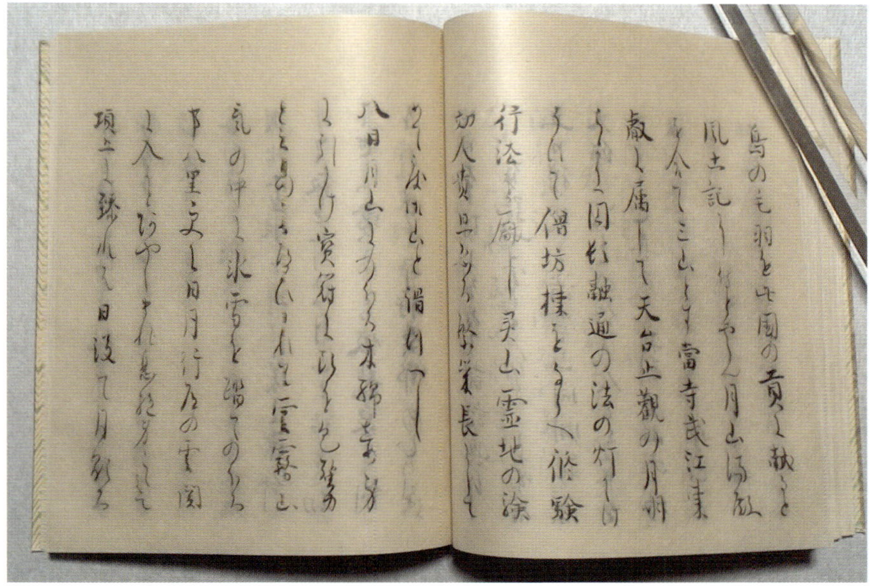

**14. MATSUO BASHŌ** (text and writing of title), 1694
**SORYŪ** (writing of all remaining content)
***The Narrow Road to the Deep North***
Open to show the ascent of Mount Gassan
Paper, sumi ink, 16.7 x 14.2 cm
Replica borrowed from Iga City Bashō Memorial Museum

For both Bashō and Wordsworth, 'man' and nature were intertwined in a great oneness with the earth—and with the heavens, too. In Wordsworth's writing, there are elements of pantheism; in Bashō, Zen. In this exhibition we have shown two relevant passages (one from Wordsworth—an excerpt from his account of an ascent of Snowdon from book XIII of *The Prelude* and one from Bashō with an account of his ascent of Mount Gassan) that illustrate this sense of man being subsumed within the power of nature (see figure 22).

> The Moon stood naked in the Heavens, at height
> Immense above my head, and on the shore
> I found myself of a huge sea of mist,
> Which, meek and silent, rested at my feet:
> A hundred hills their dusky backs upheaved
> All over this still Ocean, and beyond,
> Far, far beyond, the vapours shot themselves,
> In headlands, tongues and promontory shapes,
> Into the Sea, the real Sea, that seemed
> To dwindle, and give up its majesty,
> Usurp'd upon as far as sight could reach.
> (*The Prelude*: 1805, XIII. 40–49)

And the second from Bashō's *The Narrow Road to the Deep North*

> 'I climbed Mount Gassan on the eighth ... I walked through mists and clouds, breathing the thin air of high altitudes and stepping on slippery ice and snow, till at last through a gateway of clouds, as it seemed, to the very paths of the sun and the moon, I reached the summit, completely out of breath and nearly frozen to death. Presently the sun went down and the moon rose glistening in the sky. I spread some leaves on the ground and went to sleep resting my head on pliant bamboo branches. When, on the following morning, the sun rose again and dispersed the clouds, I went down towards mount Yudono.' [1]

Endnotes

1. Bashō; translated by Yuasa N. *The Narrow Road to the Deep North and Other Travel Sketches*, London: Penguin Books, 1996, p.125.

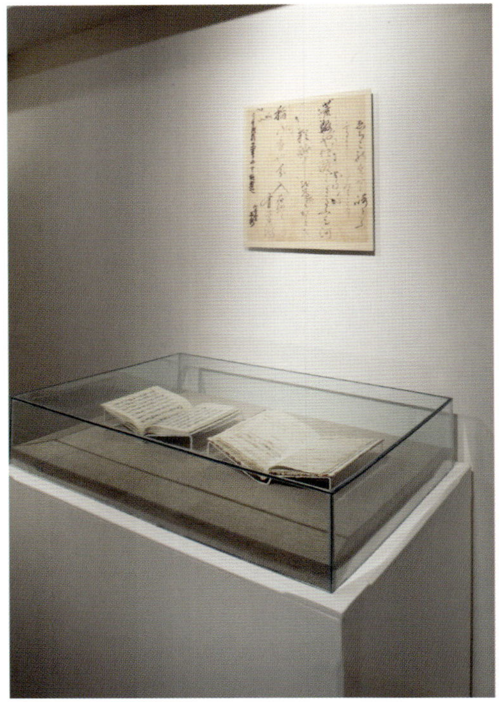

Figure 22, Installation shot of the 'Milky Way' *haiku* on the wall and the 'ascent of Snowdon' and the 'ascent of Mount Gassan' in the display case

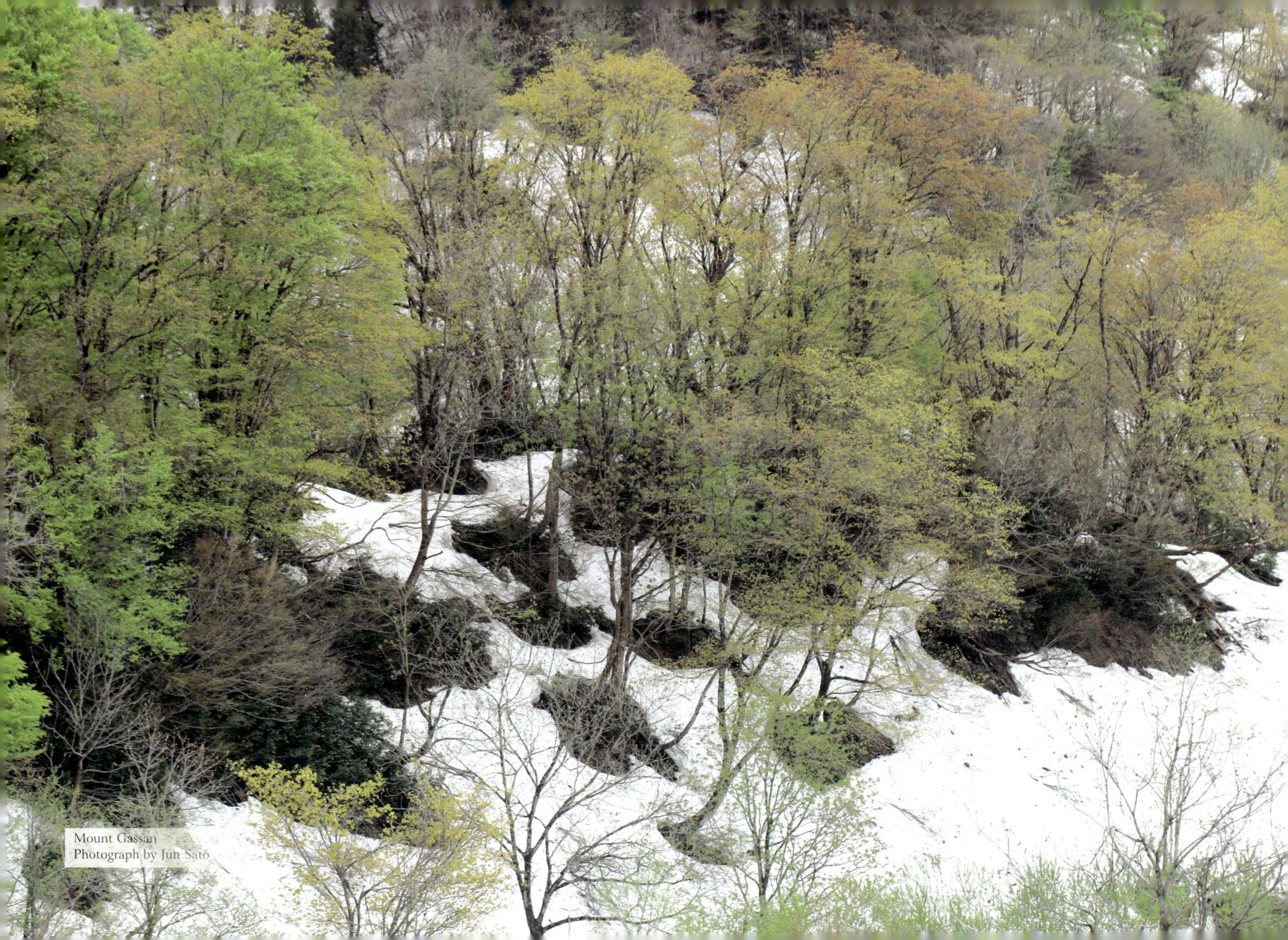
Mount Gassan
Photograph by Jun Satō

# ALEC FINLAY

15. ***word-mntn (Haguroyama)***, 2014, maple cubes, each 4 x 4 cm
16. ***word-mntn (Schiehallion)***, 2014, maple cubes, each 4 x 4 cm
17. ***word-mntn (Slioch)***, 2014, maple cubes, each 4 x 4 cm
18. ***word-mntn (Ogura)***, 2014, maple cubes, each 4 x 4 cm
19. ***word-mntn (Sgùrr nan Gillean)***, 2014, maple cubes, each 4 x 4 cm
20. ***word-mntn (Nikko)***, 2014, maple cubes, each 4 x 4 cm

21. ***a-ga: on mountains,*** 2014, book, 13 x 18 cm

Alec Finlay's beautifully simple 'word mntn' are constructed from wood cubes that, on one level, we may associate with children's building-blocks. Deceptively playful, the 'word-mntn' in fact mask complex layers of literary, artistic, personal and philosophical association. Like much of Finlay's work, they are influenced by Bashō's pared back *haiku* and exemplify the artist's typical concerns with human engagement in landscape. Initially explored as drawings composed from the names of mountains visible on or from Skye, the sculptural 'word mntn' exhibited here are constructed from both Scottish and Japanese mountain names. They typify Finlay's innovative approach to the experiential dimensions of his practice, inviting us as viewers to play imaginatively with the bricks, moving and constructing our own mountains from them.

Working across various media, Finlay's work is often collaborative, socially embedded or digitally shared and as such manifests his belief in the essentially collective nature of creativity. 'Word mntn' extend his interest in our personal and collective senses of mountains, from the etymological roots of their naming through poetry and performative artistic investigation. His collected thoughts on mountain viewing, walking and non-walking appear in the newly published book *a-ga: on mountains* also exhibited here.

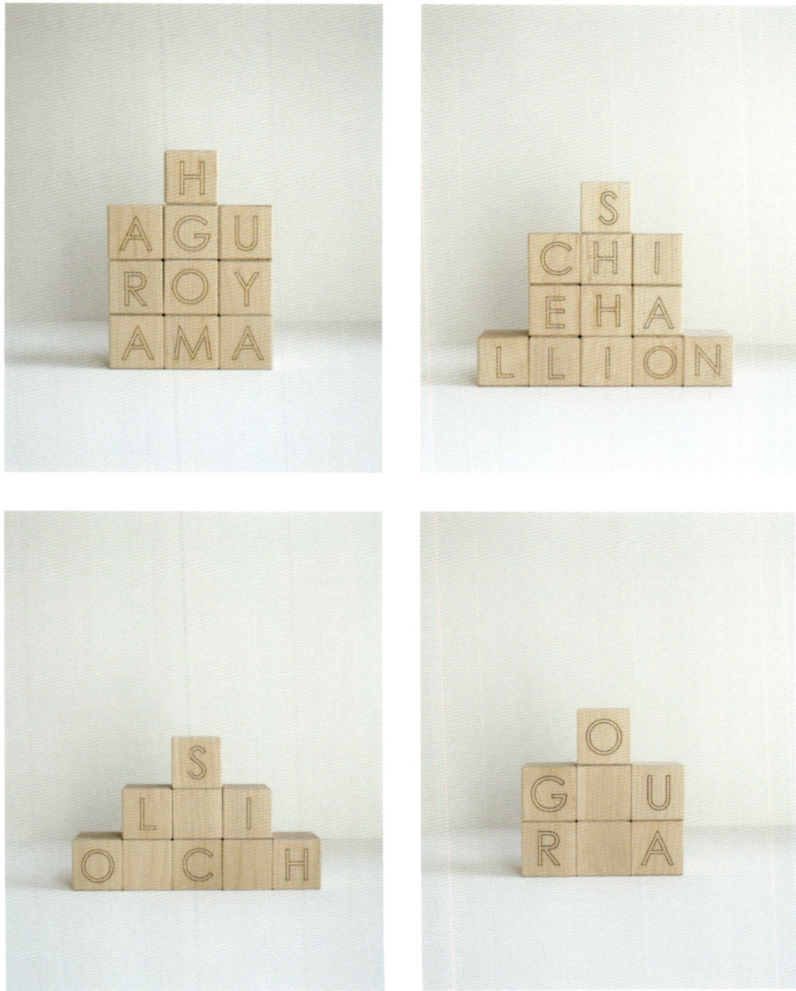


*word-mntn 15, 16, 17 & 18*

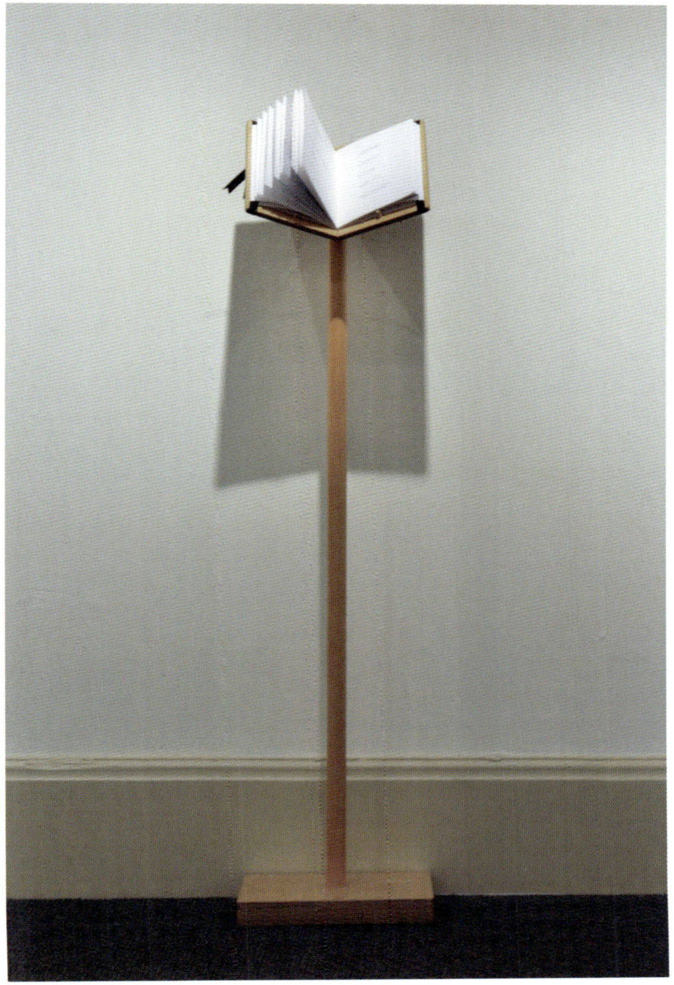

*a-ga: on mountains*, book, installation shot

*selections from a-ga*

the deer's place : *wilderness*

*a-ga* : Sanskrit, 'mountain,
that which does not go'

the mountain is vulnerable :
with one hand
we may blot it out

hills are for daydreamers;
mountains demand vigilance

a mountain can raise itself up
on a fault

without mountains
no tea

war on the lodges
peace to the bothies

place a stone
on the past

Alec Finlay

*a-ga: on mountains,* book (detail)

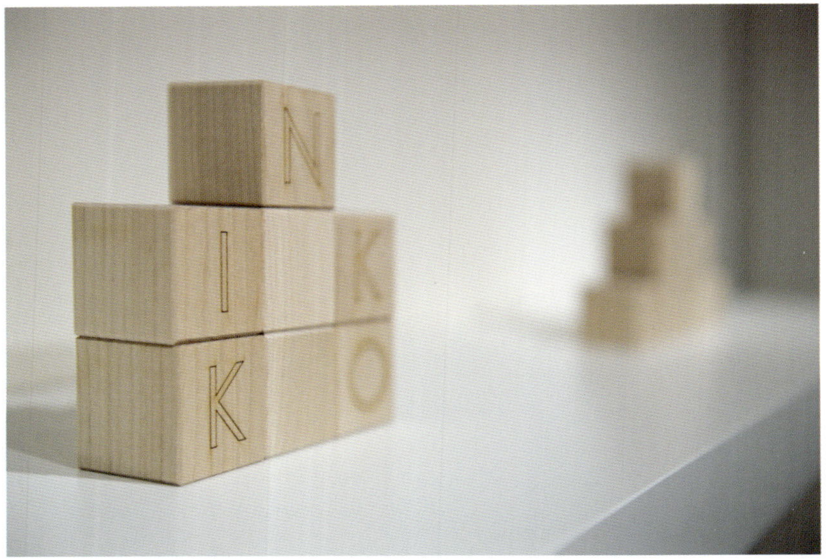


*word-mntn (Nikko),* installation shot

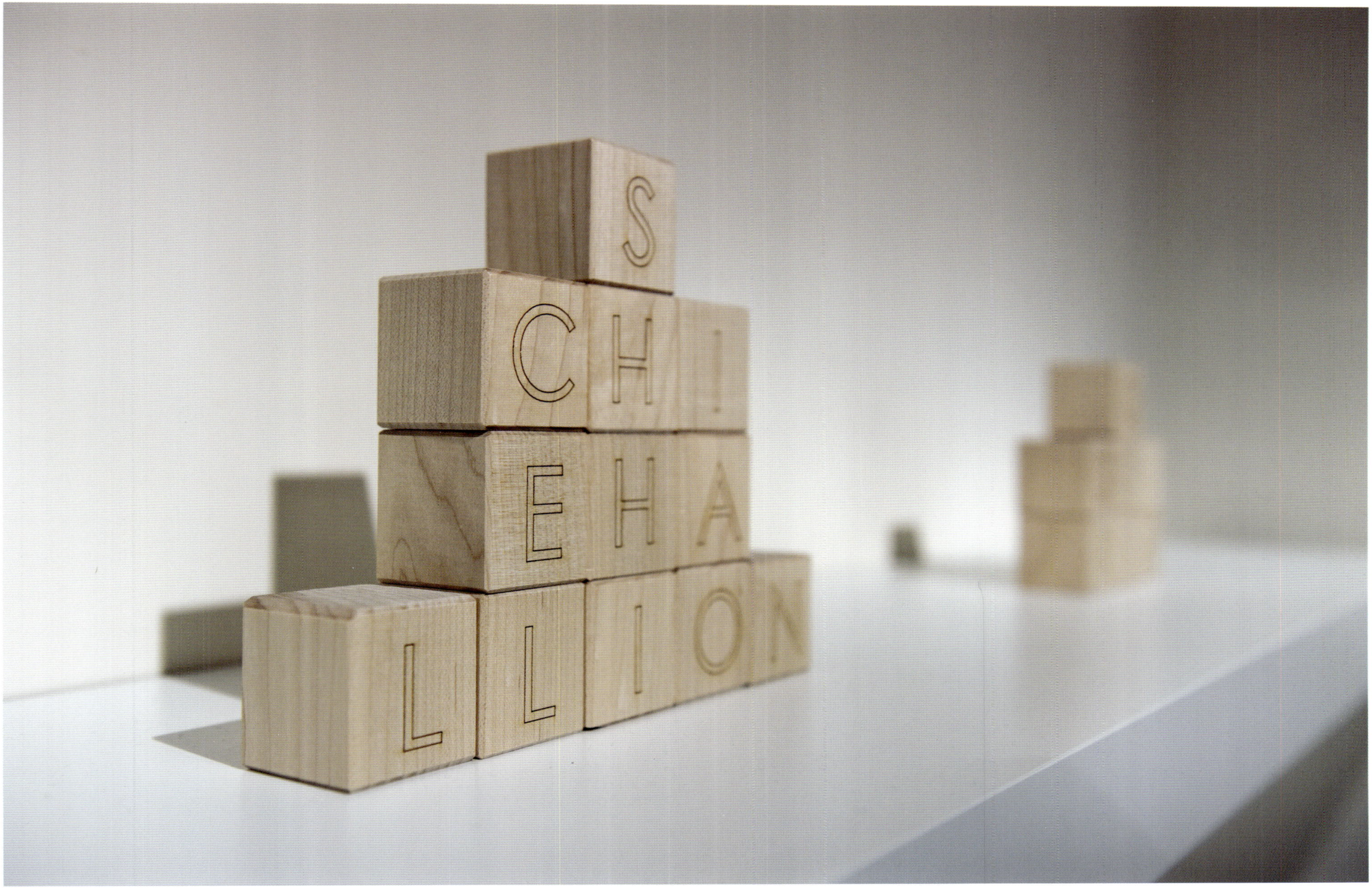


*word-mntn (Schiehallion),* installation shot

# EIICHI KONO

22. ***Homage to Bashō***

2014

Japanese brush writing on both sides of handmade kozo paper (reverse boustrophedon)

140 x 37 cm

In this very personal 'homage', Eiichi Kono looks back to the culture of his youth by way of Bashō. Having spent half of his adult life in Britain, this 'return' to Bashō is also a return to the language and script of his childhood. Performed through the very act of writing, in a gestural tribute that is both familiar and strange, Kono re-presents the entire narrative of Bashō's *Oku no Hosomichi* (*The Narrow Road to the Deep North*) as a singular line progressing from one side of the paper to the other continuously. The structure, without typographic conventions of punctuation, creates what the artist has termed a 'texture of walking narrative'.

Having grown up with an awareness of Bashō as a major Japanese poet and familiar with the concise precision of *haiku*, Kono encountered a different Bashō while reading and then rewriting his great travel diary. In Kono's words, Bashō was suddenly an unfamiliar thing in an unknown place and time, and so the act of writing the characters was enough in itself:

'The writing was arduous, sometimes tedious, sometimes exhilarating, demanding concentration, but regardless of physical discomfort, I was drawn back to the narrative time and again and compelled to continue to the end. As time went on, with the rhythm and sensation of the writing, through my minuscule effort I had a closer sense of Bashō on his journey and felt compassion for his intention.'

*Homage to Bashō,* installation shot

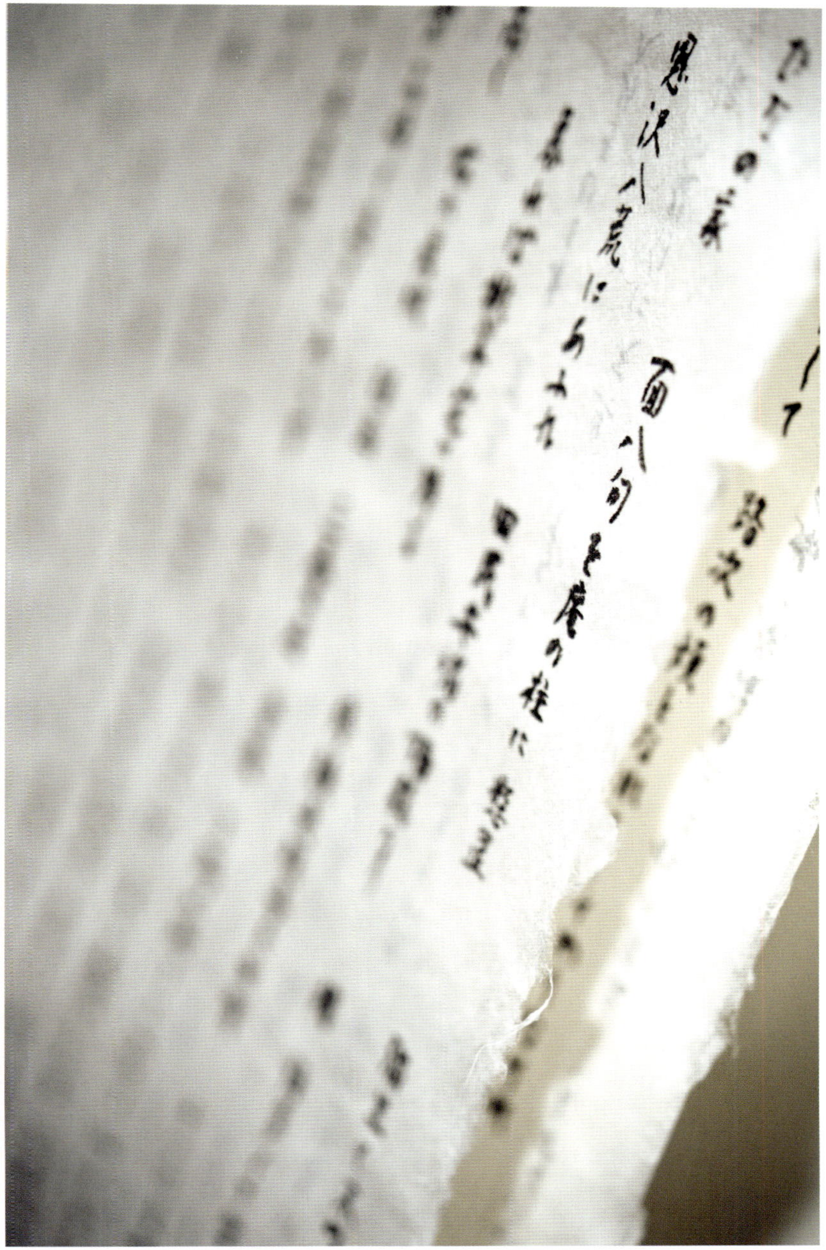

*Homage to Bashō* (detail)

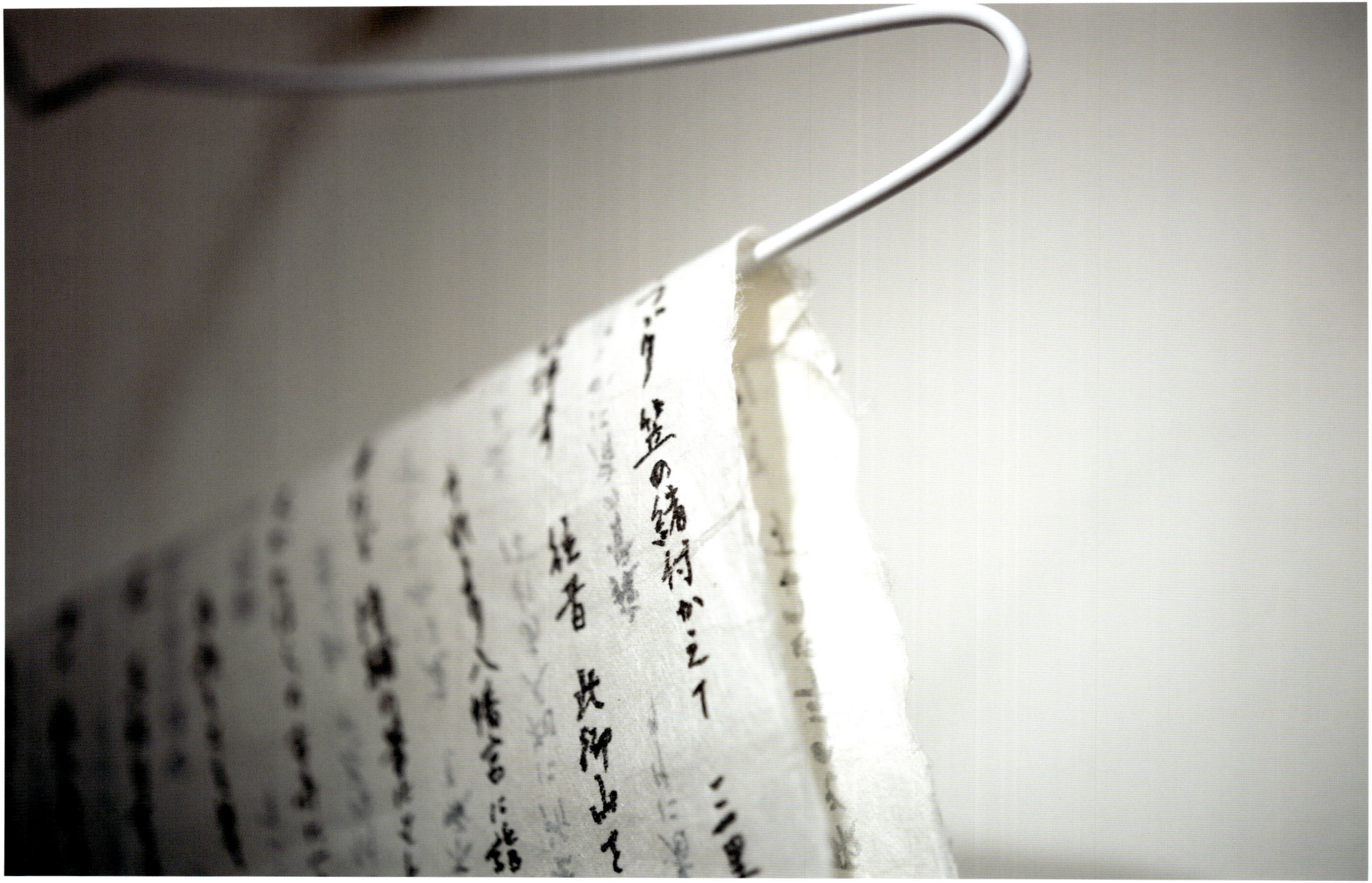


*Homage to Bashō* (detail)

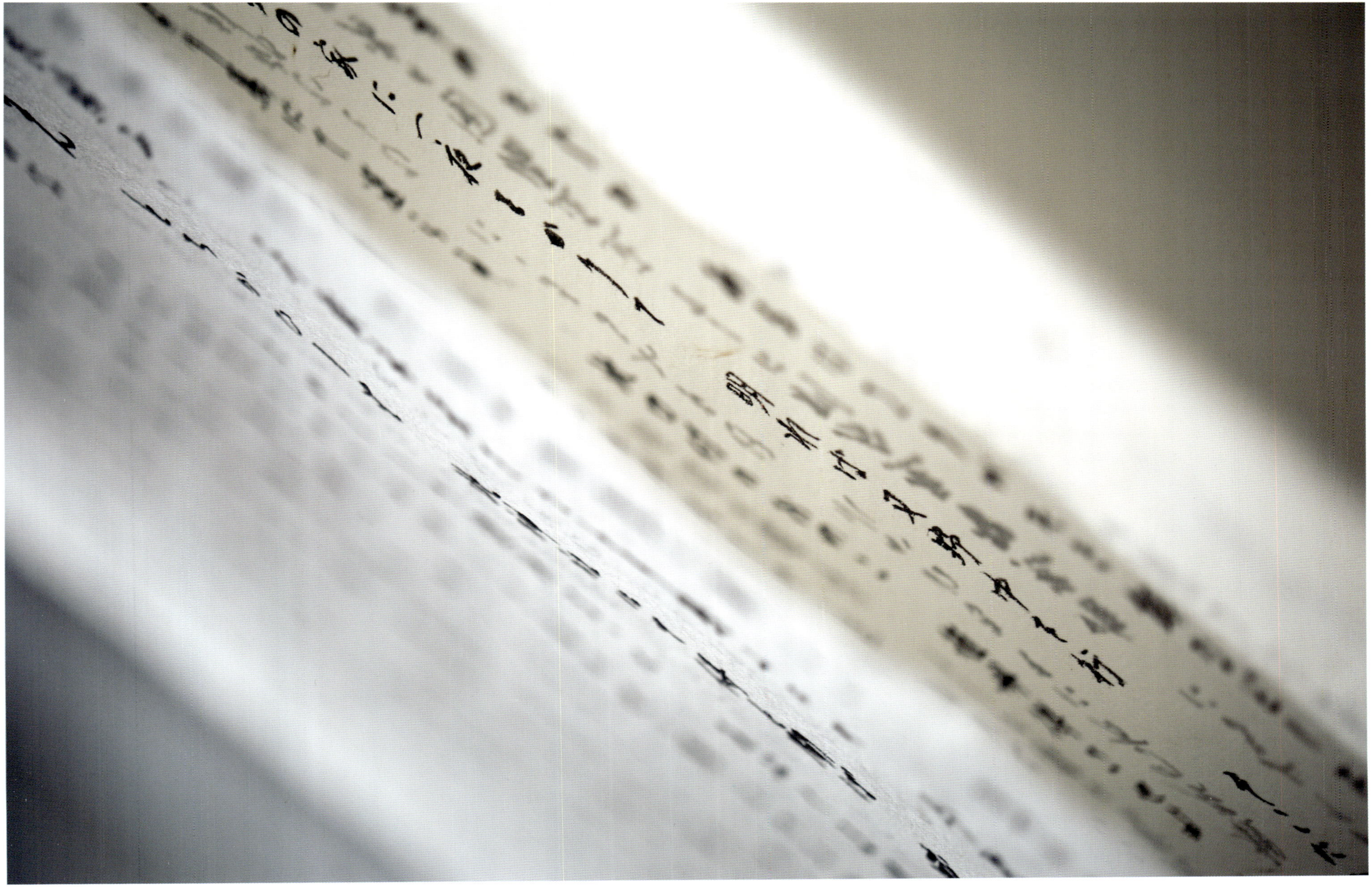

*Homage to Bashō* (detail)

**MATSUO BASHŌ** (text);
**YOSA BUSON** (drawing and writing)
**23.** ***Narrow Road to the Deep North; Scroll 1***
1778
Paper, sumi ink, colour
20 x 450 cm
Courtesy of Kyoto National Museum

**MATSUO BASHŌ** (text);
**YOSA BUSON** (drawing and writing)
**24.** ***Narrow Road to the Deep North; Scroll 2***
1778
Paper, sumi ink, colour
20 x 600 cm
Courtesy of Kyoto National Museum

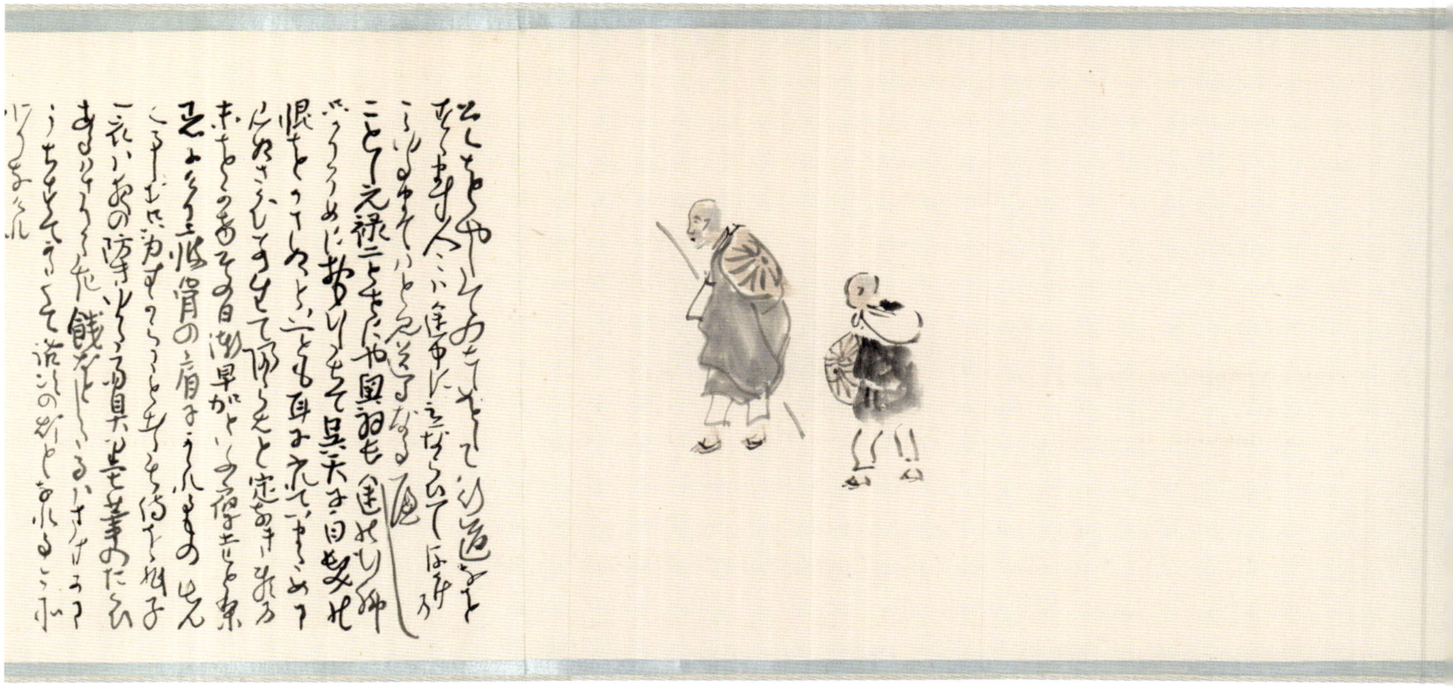

*Narrow Road to the Deep North; Scroll 1* (detail)

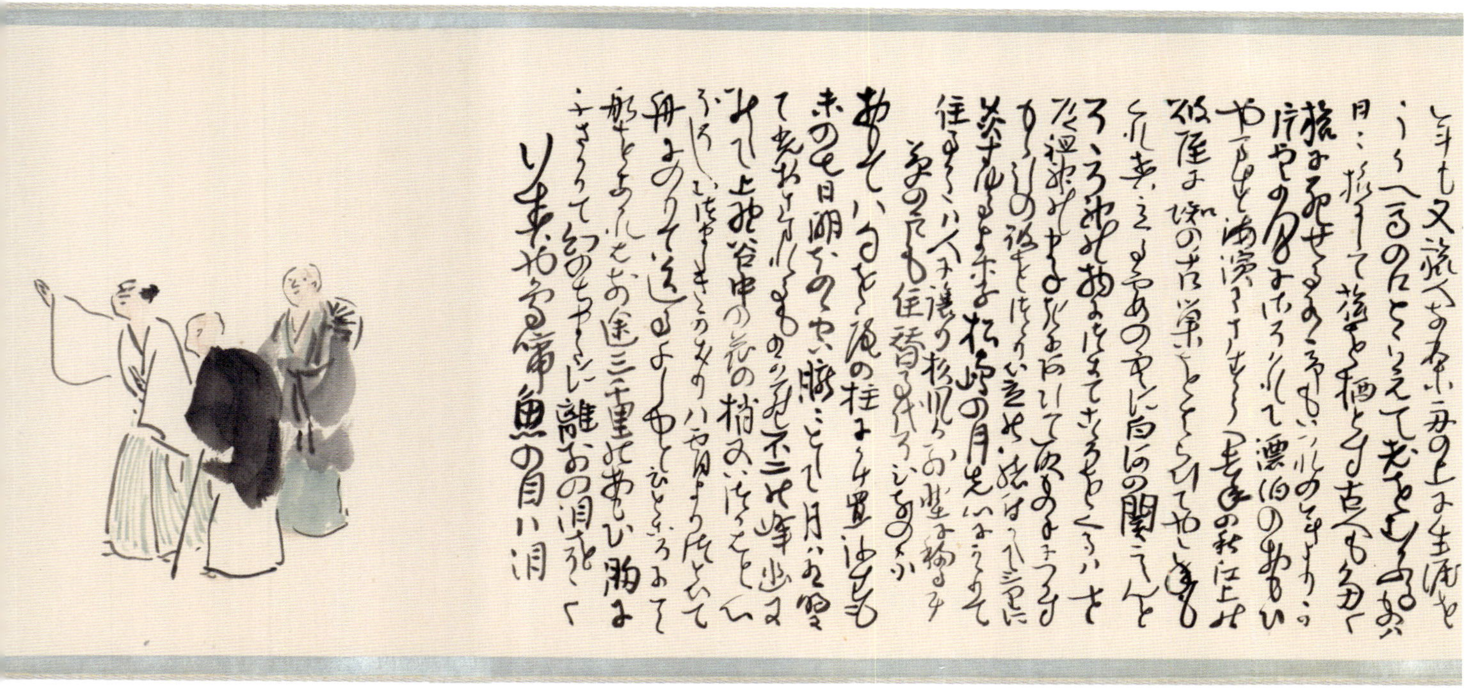

Bashō's art reached its greatest form in 1689 in his masterpiece *Oku no Hosomichi,* 'The Narrow Road to the Deep North'. In this poem/travel book, he recounts his last long walk, completed with his disciple Sora—some 1,200 miles covered over five months beginning in May 1689.

'The Japanese term *oku* refers to the northern backcountry of the main Japanese island of Honshū, and it also means 'deep' in the sense of interior, such as the depths of a mountain and spiritual depths.'[1]

This pair of scrolls is a transcription by Yosa Buson (1716–1784), written and illustrated over a century later in 1778. Buson was a poet and painter of the Edo period who revered Bashō. As well as making this copy of Bashō's seminal work, Buson was inspired to embark on his own wanderings to the 'deep north', following in the master's footsteps.

Endnotes

1. David Landis Barnhill, *Bashō's Journey,* Albany: State of New York Press, 2005, p.4.

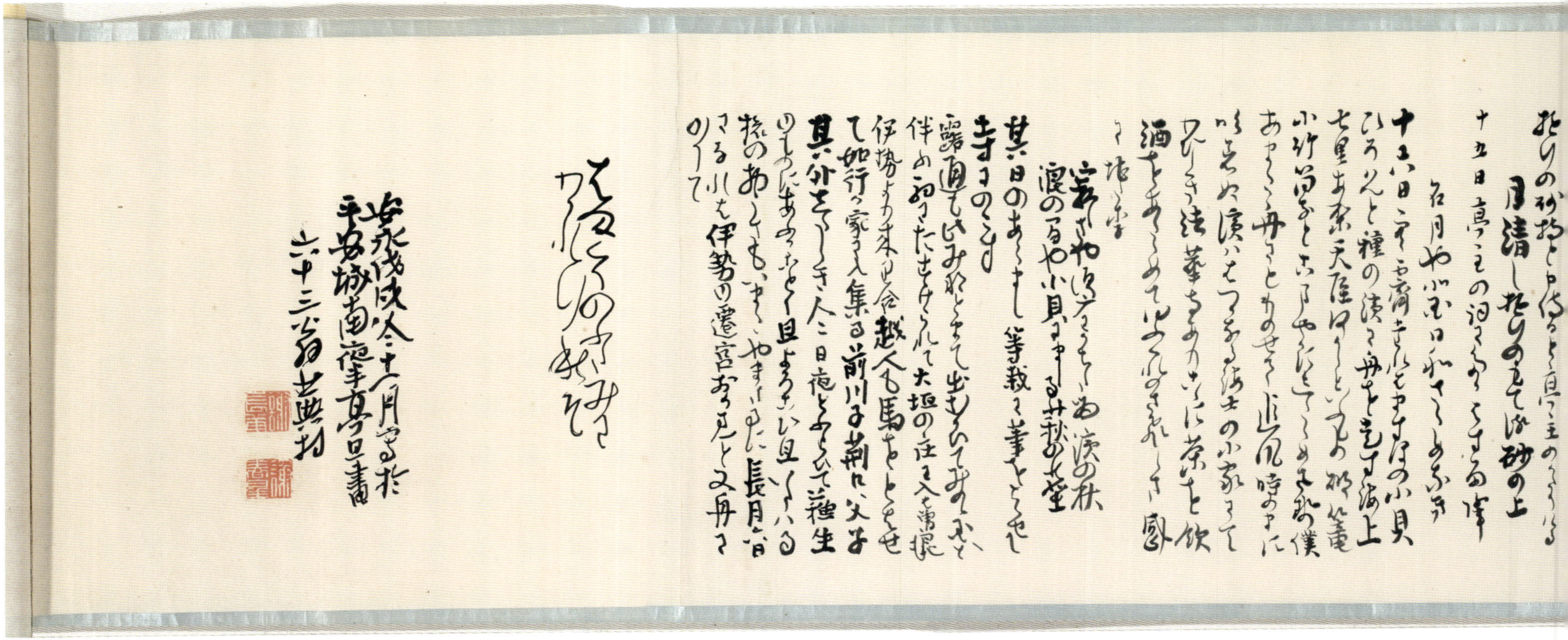

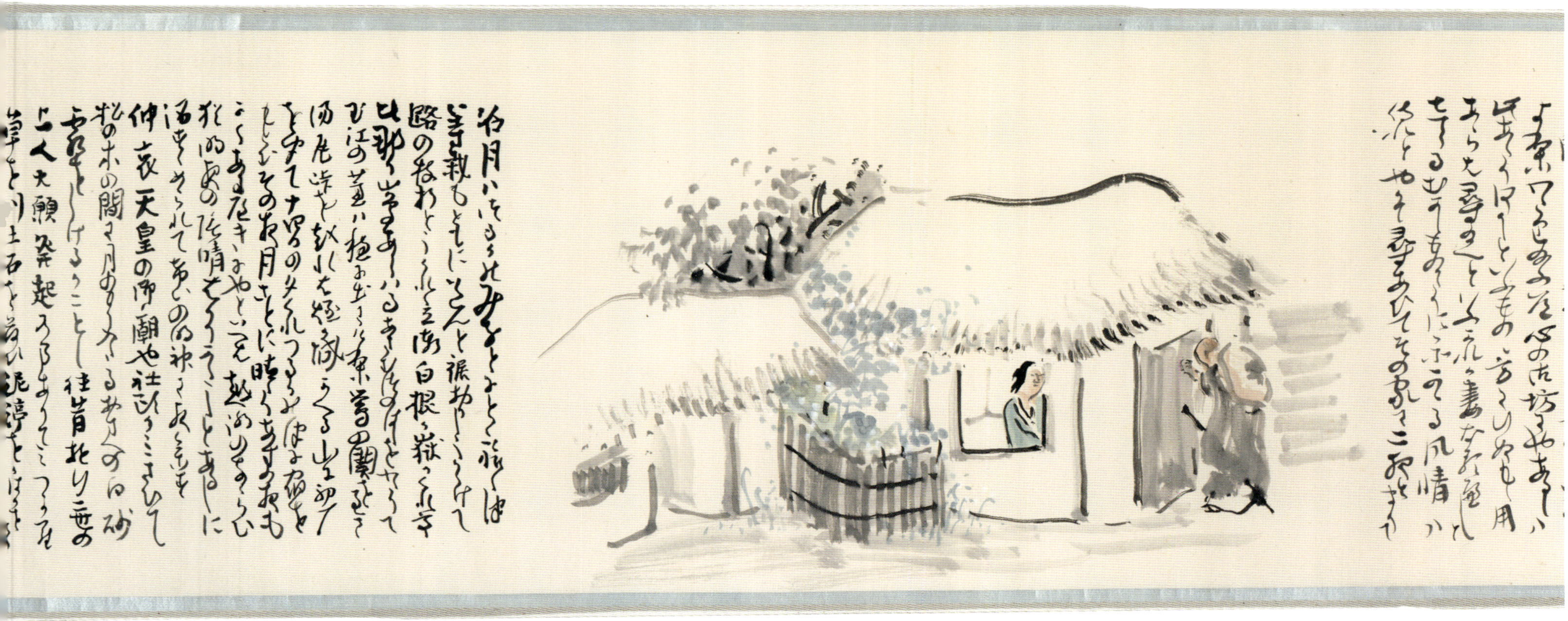

*Narrow Road to the Deep North; Scroll 2* (detail)

# ZAFFAR KUNIAL

25. ***Placeholder***
2014
Digital print
59.4 x 42 cm

*Of all the many places mentioned in poetry, the exact location of most is not known for certain.*

Bashō, *Narrow Road to the Deep North,* 1689

The Wordsworth Trust has hosted a poet's residency for almost twenty years, offering a new writer each year an opportunity to live and work in a cottage in Town End, Grasmere, just around the corner from Dove Cottage, and be inspired by the literary landscape of Wordsworth. Zaffar Kunial is Poet in Residence for 2014 and has produced a new poem especially for the exhibition 'Wordsworth and Bashō—Walking Poets'.

Kunial's 'Placeholder' finely encapsulates the exhibition's theme of artistic legacy: the layered reverberations of previous and other poetic voices from printed page and manuscript. Wordsworth, Seamus Heaney and Kunial exchange a tapestry of words across the centuries, in a poem that is keenly visualized in both its printed and exhibited forms.

In this, 'Placeholder' draws attention to the very material of words and the poetic labour that is involved in their crafting. Kunial's 'scored' space reminds us of the many effacements and rewordings in poetic composition, as we see/hear him dialogue with the words of others. The final line, 'The slide in meaning suits this sliding place', is a gentle answering back to Heaney, whose own words to Wordsworth frame Kunial's own.

Similarly, the great manuscripts in the collection of the Wordsworth Trust, some of which are exhibited here, tell of this struggle for meaning and the slipperiness of such, as poets and readers alike meet with the fabric of text. Heaney himself acknowledged such richness in opening the Trust's Jerwood Centre in 2005.

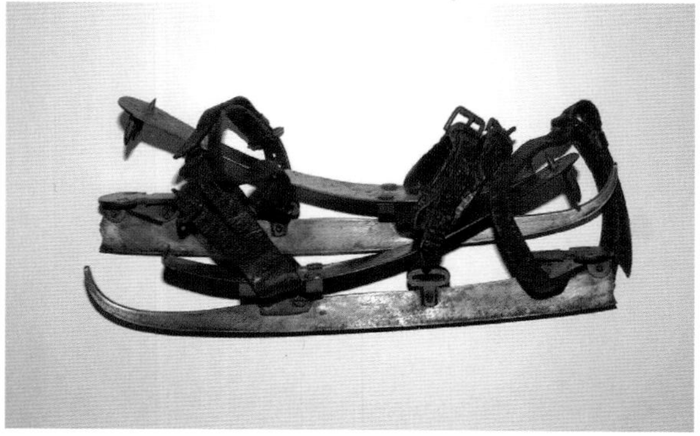

Figure 23, *Wordsworth's Skates,* courtesy of the Wordsworth Trust

# Placeholder

*Not the bootless runners lying toppled*
*In dust in a display case,*
*Their bindings perished,*

*But the reel of them on frozen Windermere*
*As he flashed from the clutch of earth along its curve*
*And left it scored.*
—Seamus Heaney

Those old blades scratched the surface of Esthwaite
and not Windermere, as Heaney had it,
tracing that scrape with a star in *Wordsworth's Skates.*
That the star lay elsewhere sits about right—
I like the mistake. The lake being astray
speaks of dark ice, like Wordsworth's crossings-
out—in the line that lay at the heart of Heaney's
poem in the first place:
                                        *To cut across the* _____
*of a star.* I've scored that space because *shadow*
first held sway. And wrongly, as light can't cast
dark. Next up, the star's *image* would land where
his skate passed. Then, the curt Latin, at last:
*reflex.* Fitting the foot.
                                        And, beyond the grave,
that fixed word's meaning would still change the script.
Cold reflection gave ground to a quick nerve—
till the star touched base, as the steel blade slipped
across that spot of ice—and scored deep space.
The slide in meaning fits this sliding place.

---

*Reflex n. 1508, reflected light … from Latin reflexus … The meaning*
*of involuntary action in response to nerve cell stimulation is first recorded in 1877.*
—Chambers Dictionary of Etymology

*I'll never forget the almost religious thrill I got from seeing the notebook where Wordsworth scribbled the first lines of The Prelude, and seeing also the poet's skate, still trim enough to cut across the reflex of a star.*
—Seamus Heaney, speech on opening the Jerwood Centre, 2005

*Placeholder*

# MANNY LING and CHRISTINE FLINT-SATO

**26. *Mountain Lines, Water Lines***

2014

Sumi ink on Japanese washi paper

46 x 106 cm (each, framed)

The meeting of East and West (Wordsworth and Bashō) is epitomized in the new collaborative work of Manny Ling and Christine Flint-Sato. Flint-Sato is a British sumi ink artist who lives in Japan while Ling, who is from Hong Kong and lives in Britain, also works across Western and Chinese calligraphic traditions.

Central to both calligraphic traditions is the creative repurposing and reinterpretation of existing texts. The combination of image and text is also common in East Asian artistic tradition: Bashō himself often made drawings to go with his poems and diaries. For this collaboration the artists draw on elements of both traditions. Ling initially selected the Wordsworth verses from the poem 'Lines written a few miles above Tintern Abbey,' that would form the basis of their joint reinterpretation. Flint-Sato edited still further, to identify verses related to mountains, water and the liberating potential of nature: elements she could best visualize and express within the East Asian ink painting tradition.

The resulting works manifest a rich layering of process and associations. Wordsworth's verses are re-presented by Ling, written over Flint-Sato's sumi ink painting on Japanese washi paper. Ling's experimental approach to calligraphy, the most traditional of arts, is seen in the lettering he uses, in the strokes and marks that visually echo the movements of plants and other natural elements. Flint-Sato's visualisation of mountains and water in turn is a personal reinterpretation of motifs characteristic in East Asian painting, prioritizing the more abstract elements of the artwork, the washes, lines and dots, that again simultaneously relate tradition and contemporary practice. In this process, the quintessential English poet is refigured through East Asian materials and calligraphic perspectives, as Japanese paper and inks are combined with a distinctly gestural process, one that embraces spontaneity, chance and accident.

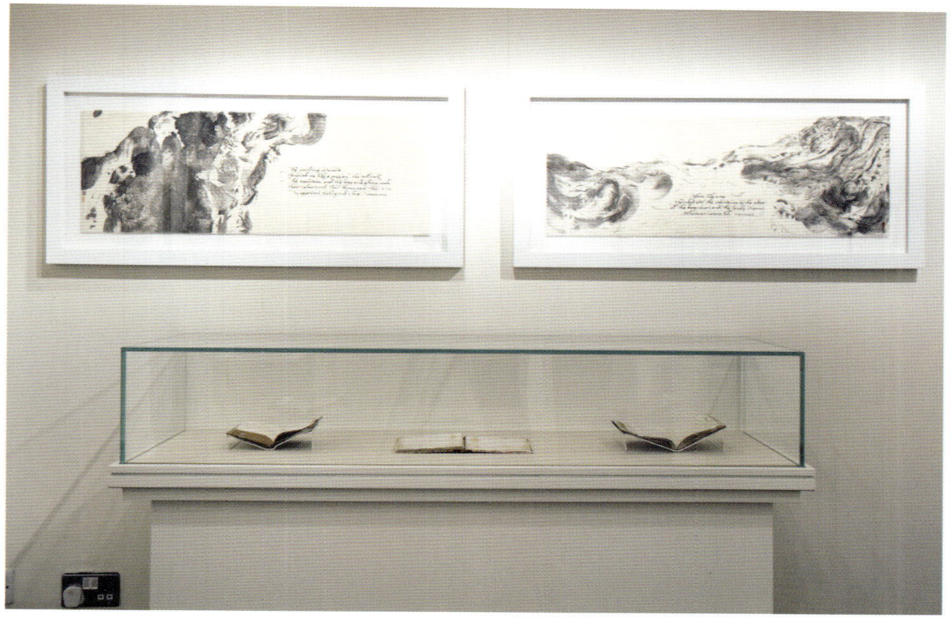

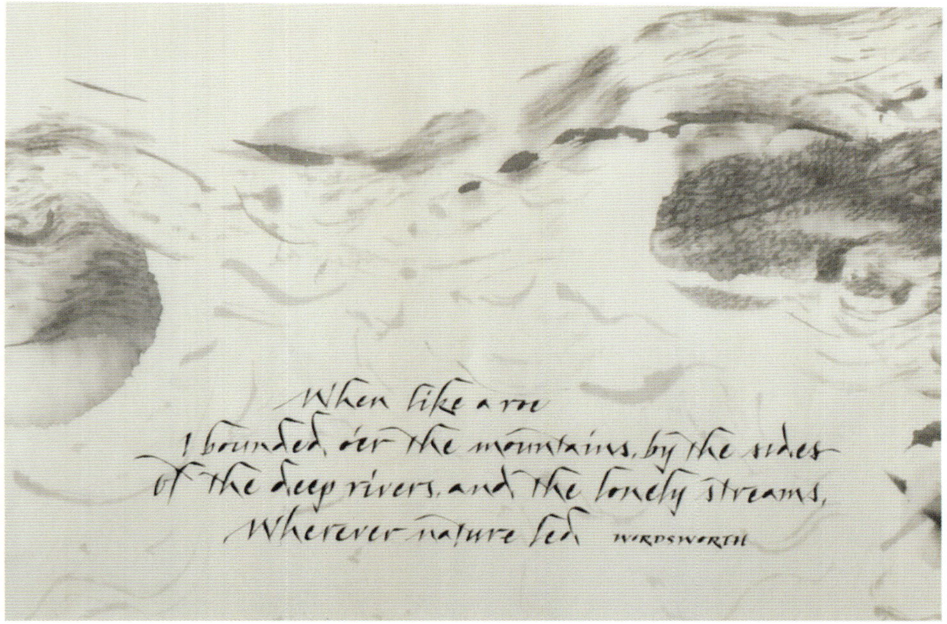


*Mountain Lines, Water Lines,* installation shot
*Water Lines* (detail)

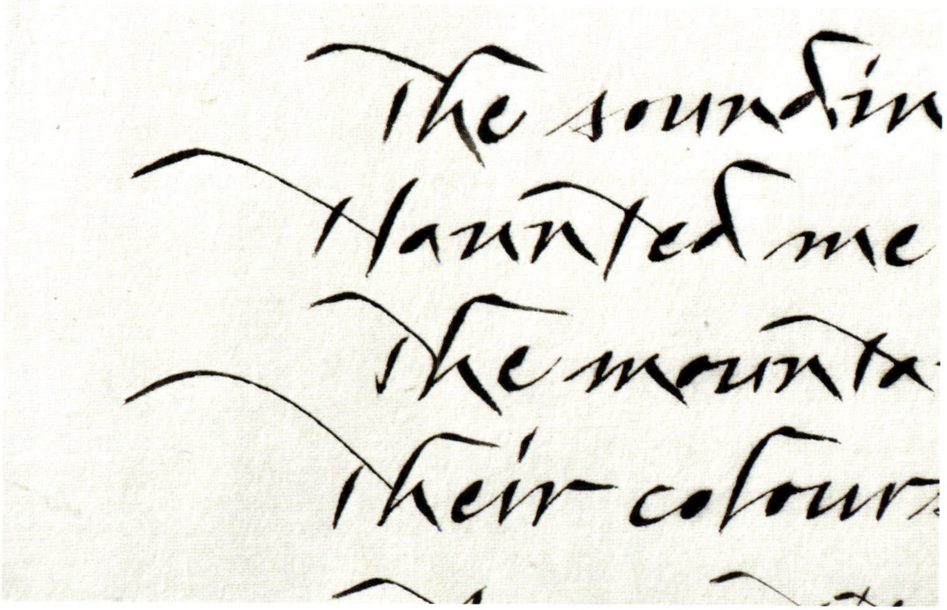


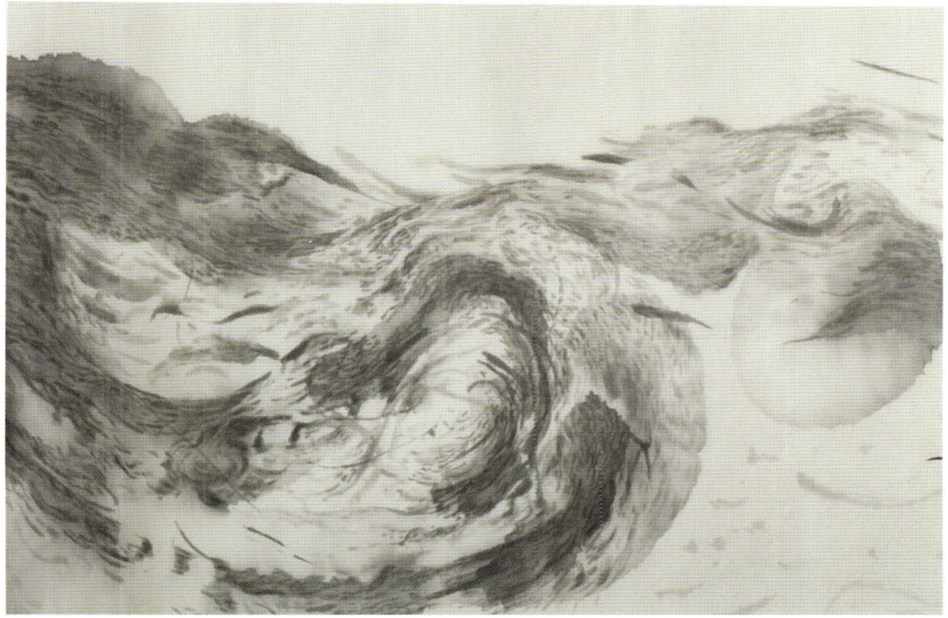

*Mountian Lines* (detail)
*Water Lines* (detail)

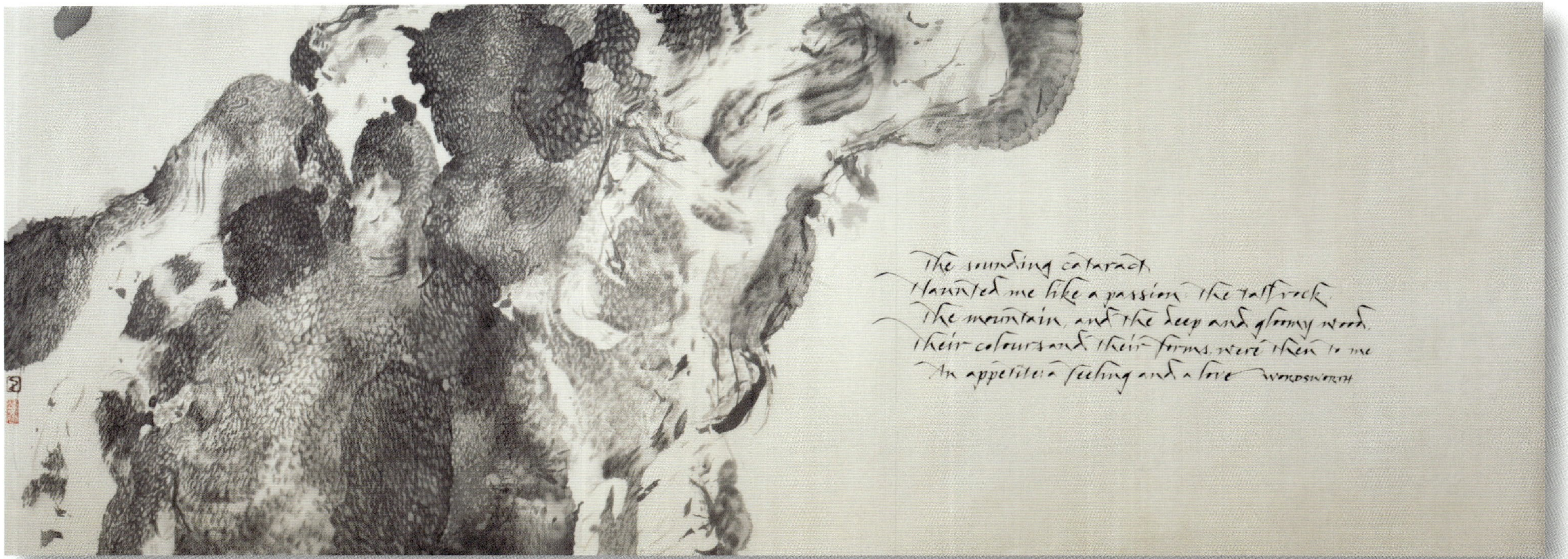


*Mountian Lines*

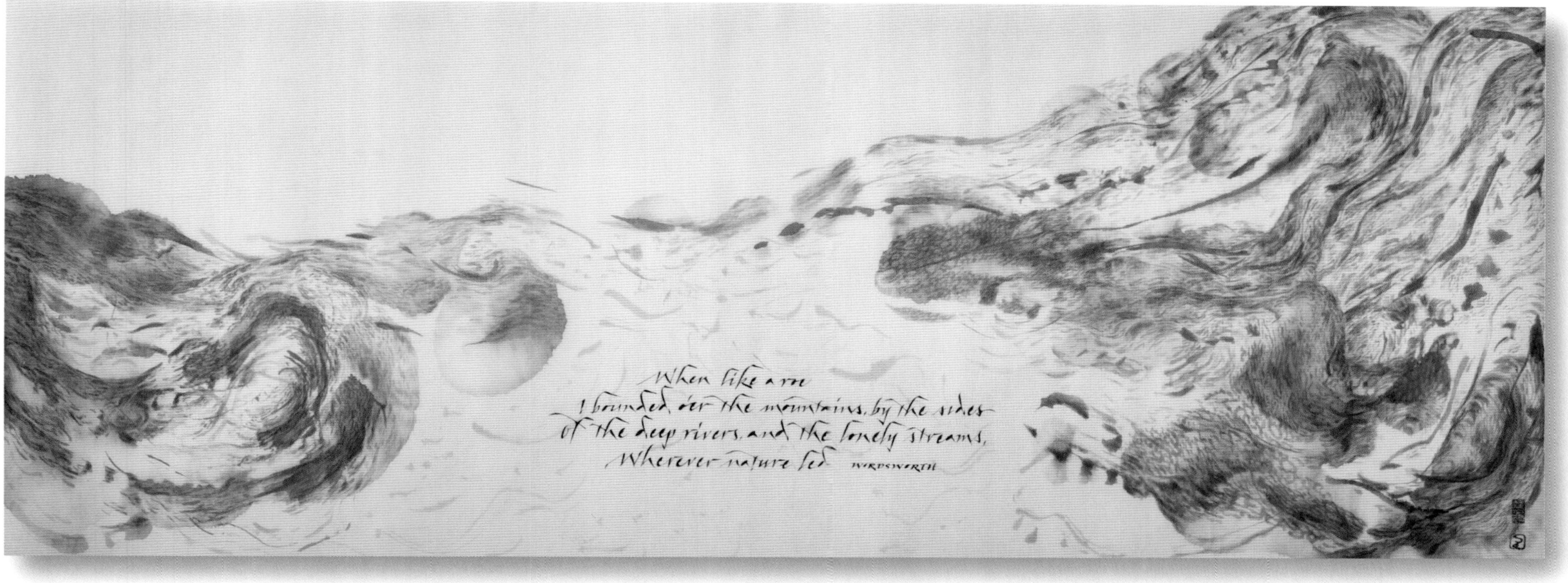
When like a roe
I bounded o'er the mountains, by the sides
of the deep rivers, and the lonely streams,
Wherever nature led
WORDSWORTH

*Water Lines*

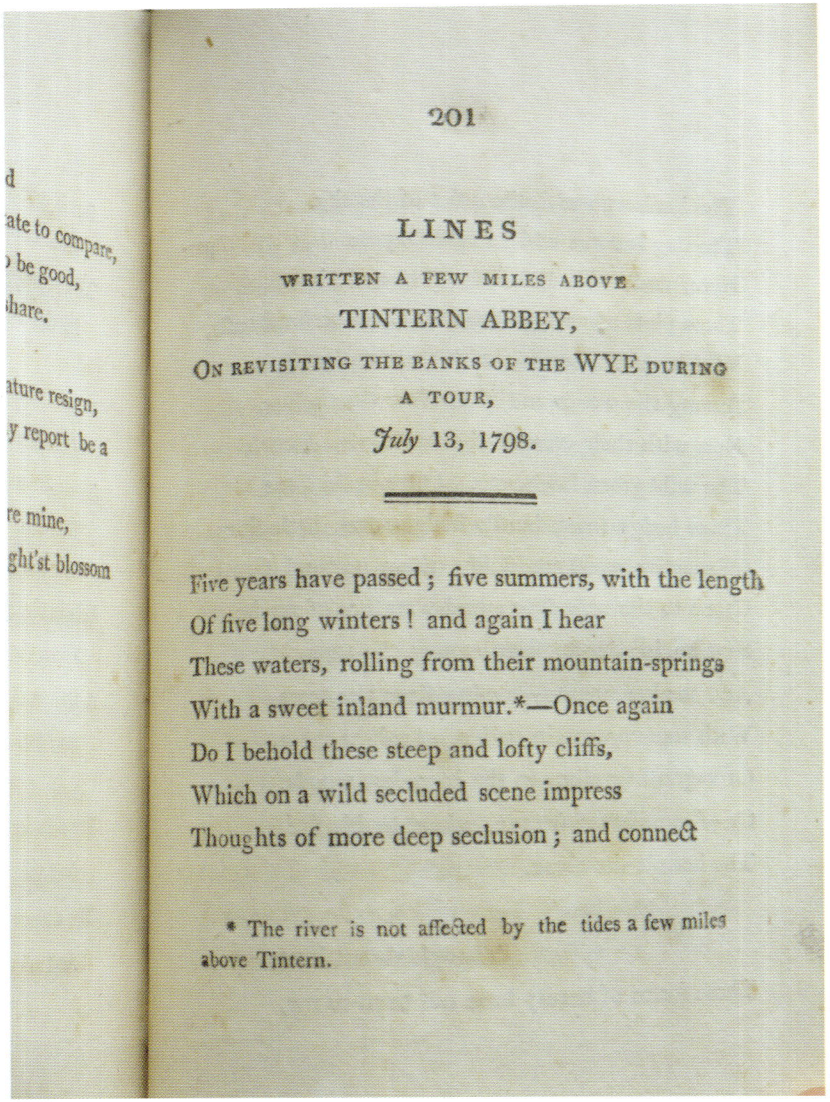
201

LINES

WRITTEN A FEW MILES ABOVE

TINTERN ABBEY,

ON REVISITING THE BANKS OF THE WYE DURING A TOUR,

*July* 13, 1798.

Five years have passed; five summers, with the length
Of five long winters! and again I hear
These waters, rolling from their mountain-springs
With a sweet inland murmur.*—Once again
Do I behold these steep and lofty cliffs,
Which on a wild secluded scene impress
Thoughts of more deep seclusion; and connect

* The river is not affected by the tides a few miles above Tintern.

## WILLIAM WORDSWORTH

**27.** ***Lyrical ballads***
1800
Open to show 'Lines written a few miles above Tintern Abbey'
Courtesy of the Wordsworth Trust

'Tintern Abbey' comes at the end of the first edition of *Lyrical Ballads*, a volume compiled by Wordsworth and Coleridge when they were living in Somerset in 1798. It is a book credited with revolutionising English literature. Five hundred copies were printed and sales were sufficient enough to encourage Wordsworth to publish a second edition two years later, after his move to Grasmere.

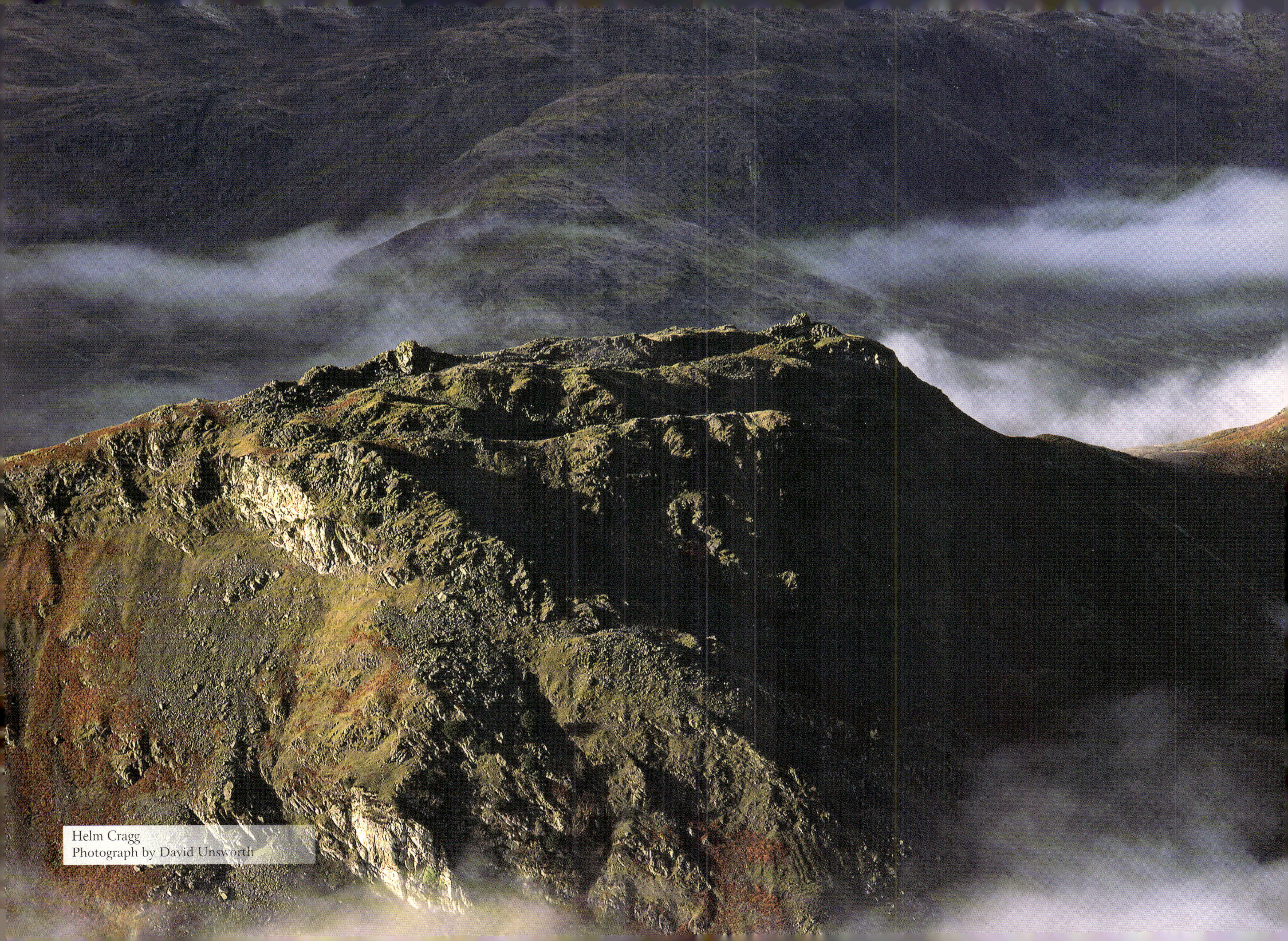

Helm Cragg
Photograph by David Unsworth

# CHRISTOPHER McHUGH

**28. *Flotsam and Jetsam (Portmanteau)***

2014

Porcelain, terracotta, soda glass, mixed media

120 x 60 x 50 cm

McHugh's work responds to themes of memory and the ephemerality of the human condition in the work of both Bashō and Wordsworth. While Bashō often revisited ruins and other sites of communal memory in his poetry, Wordsworth was concerned that human endeavour—both monuments and works of literature—were at risk of destruction through catastrophe and would be outlasted by nature. Both poets were also interested in uncovering for posterity the marginalised histories of everyday folk (the flotsam and jetsam) they met on the road.

Similarly, throughout much of his ceramic work McHugh evokes potentially overlooked narratives and materialises that which otherwise might remain absent. 'Flotsam and Jetsam (Portmanteau)' is an installation piece consisting of hundreds of mainly slipcast and press-moulded ceramic components. By combining durable ceramic elements with an ephemeral, reworkable mode of presentation, the 'scarred' porcelain fragments in the installation occupy an ambivalent position somewhere between absence and presence, manifesting a sense of enduring loss and melancholia. Blades of grass made from soda glass grow through the ceramic assemblage, suggesting the endurance of nature over culture.

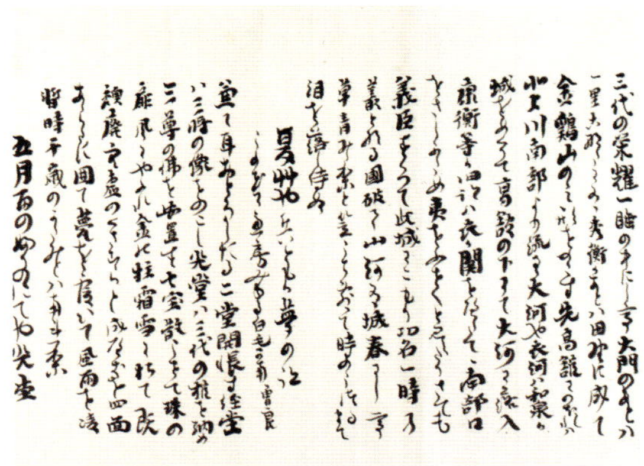

Figure 24, A section of Buson's scroll 1 ('The Narrow Road to the Deep North') containing *The Summer Grass haiku*. Courtesy of Kyoto National Museum

The installation title references Wordsworth's portmanteau suitcase which is on display in Dove Cottage and alludes to Bashō's 'The Records of a Travel-Worn Satchel'. A portmanteau is also a word formed through the combination of two or more other words, resulting in a new meaning. This piece synthesises something of the essence of both poets, repackaging their words into a new object with contemporary resonances. It is inspired by verses 68–92 of Wordsworth's *The Ruined Cottage* and a *haiku* written by Bashō when he visited the abandoned castle at Hiraizumi in 1689 (see figure 24).

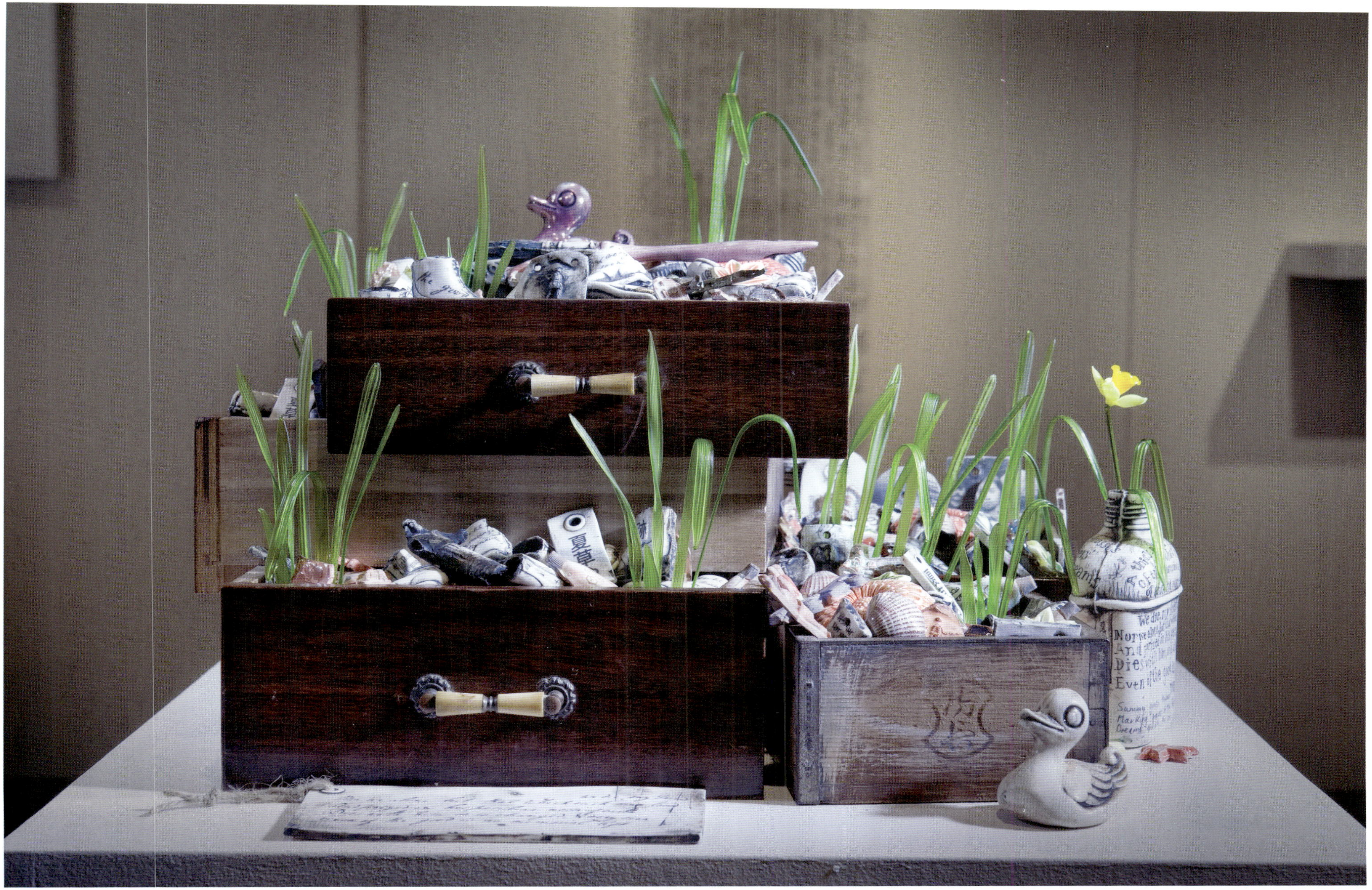

*Flotsam and Jetsam (Portmanteau),* installation shct

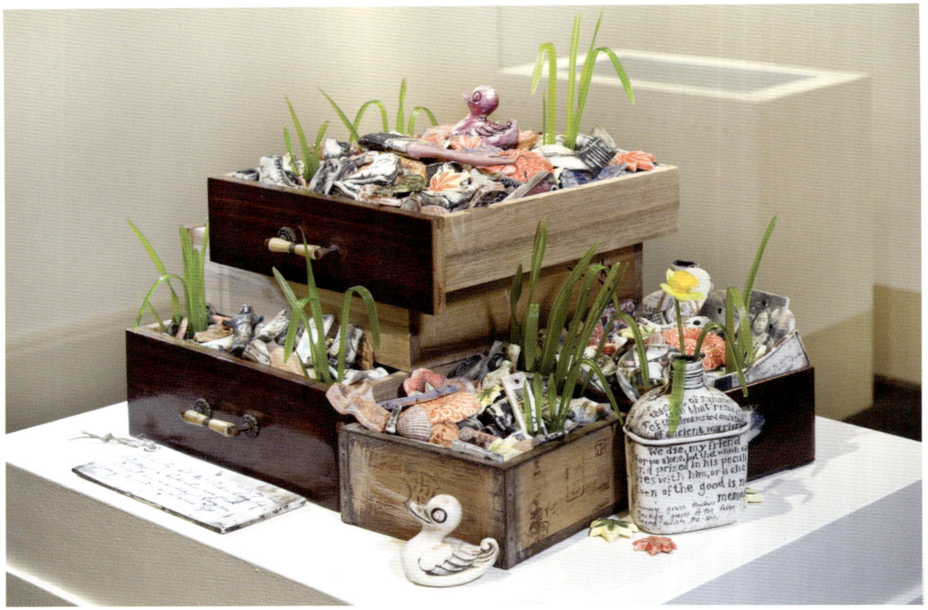

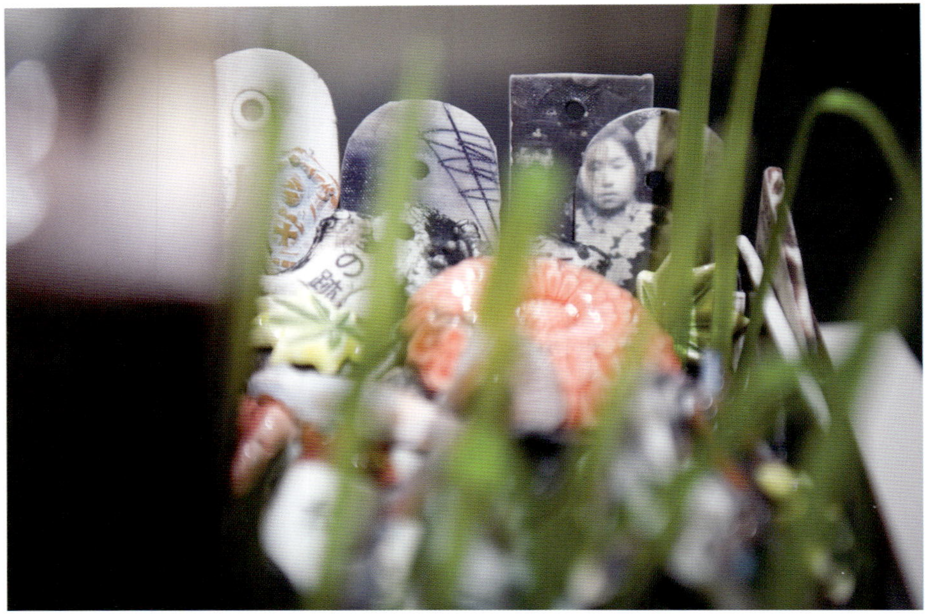

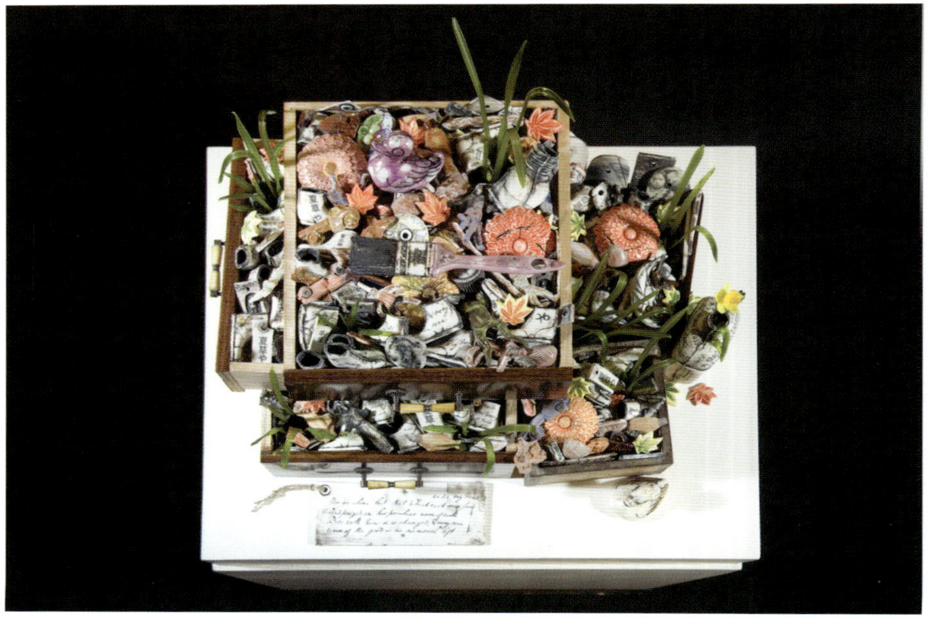

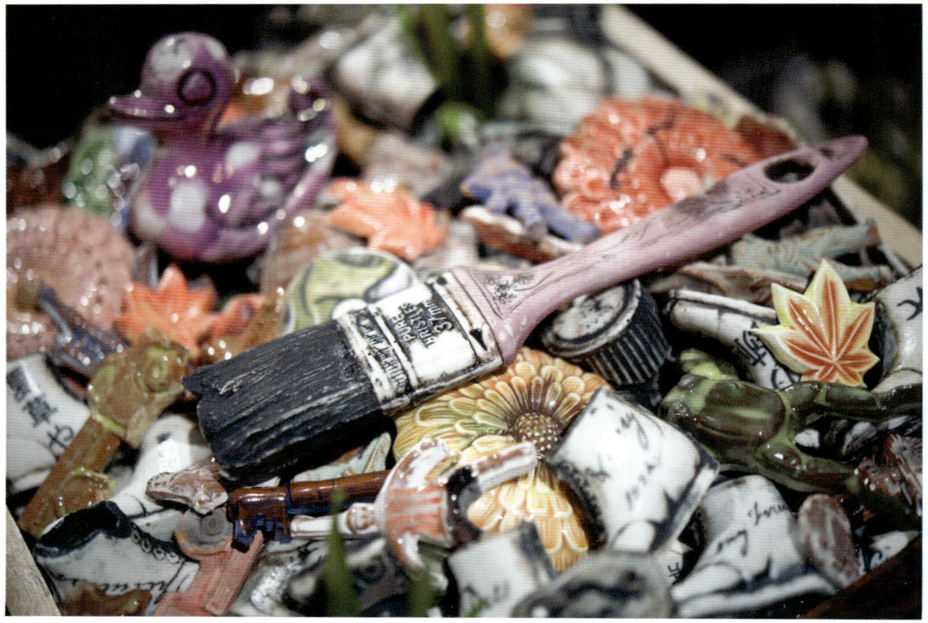

*Flotsam and Jetsam (Portmanteau)*, installation shot

*Flotsam and Jetsam (Portmanteau)* (detail)

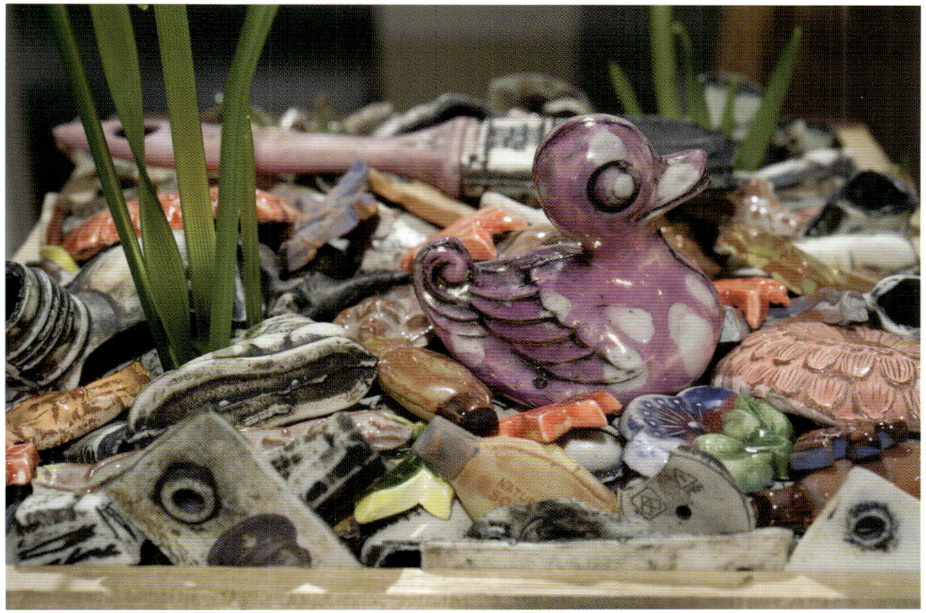

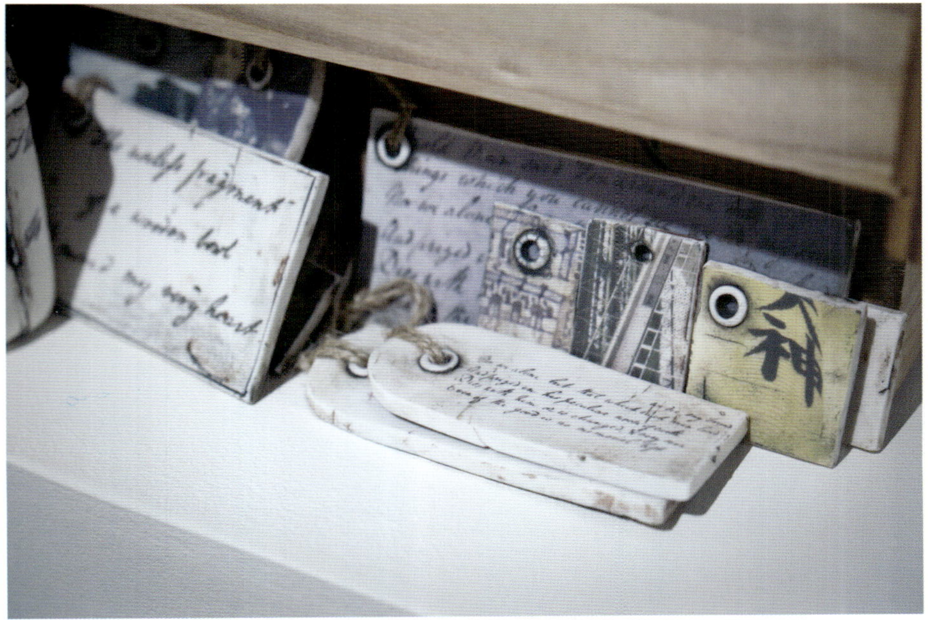

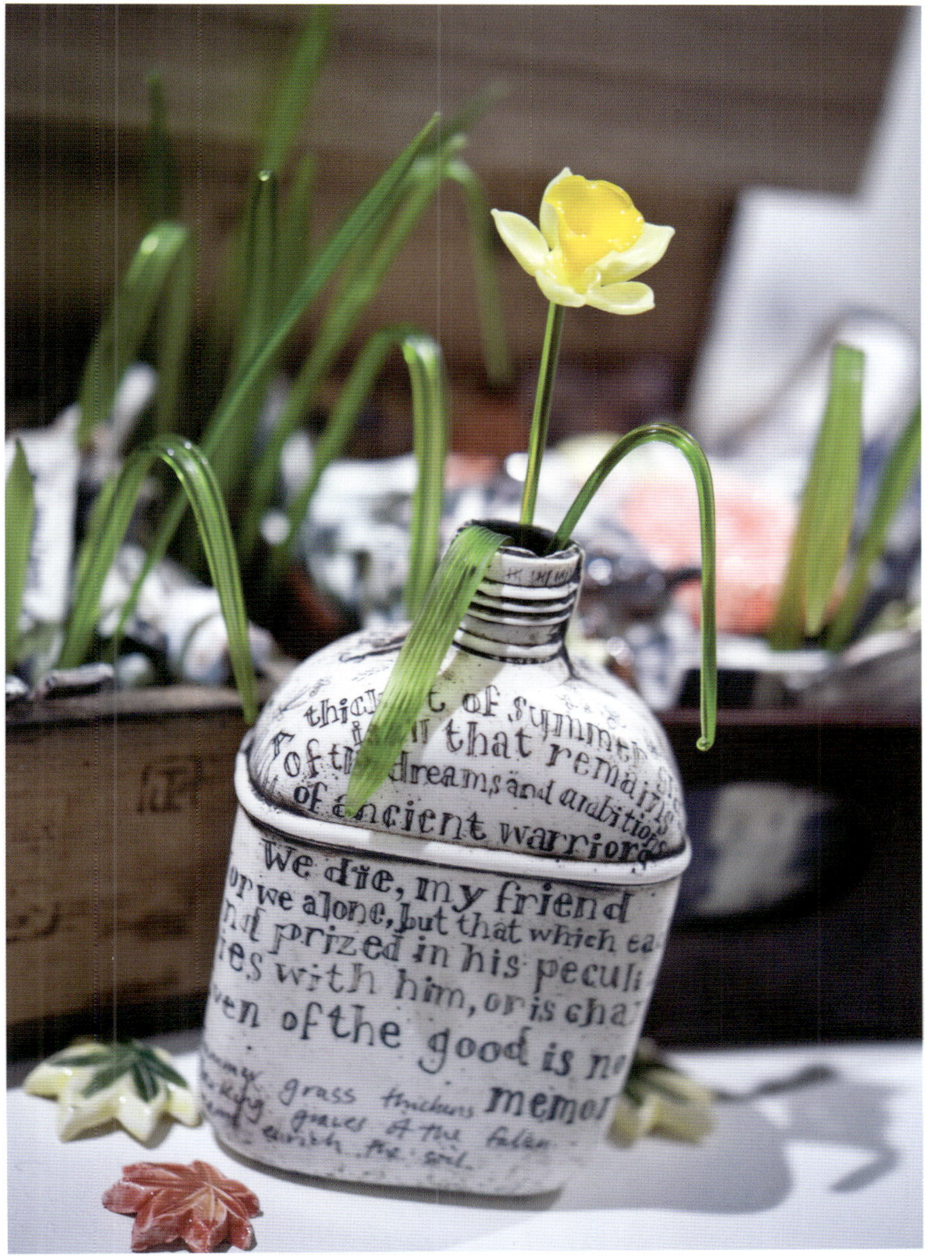


*Flotsam and Jetsam (Portmanteau)* (detail)

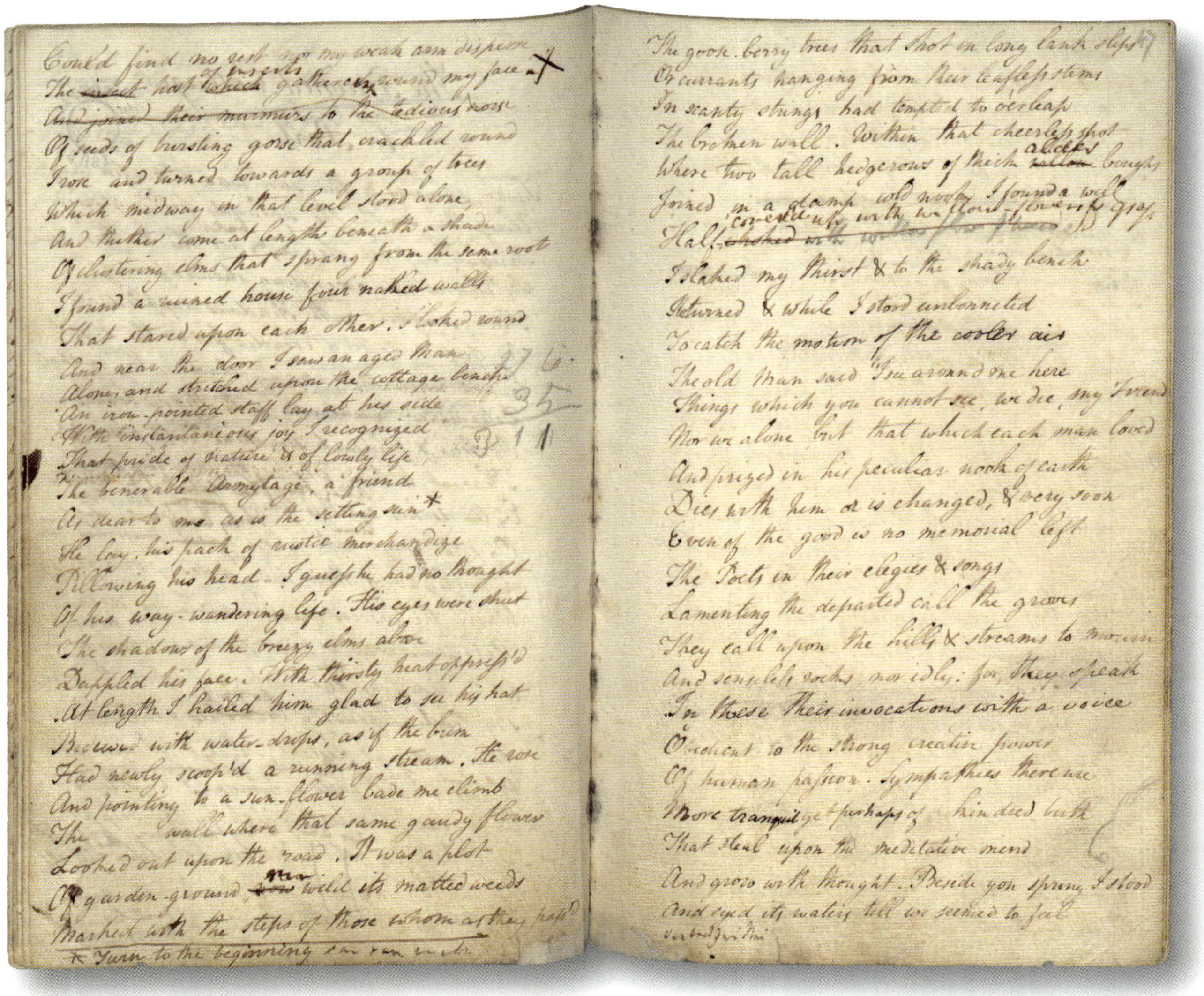

## WILLIAM WORDSWORTH

**29.** ***The Ruined Cottage***
1799 (and later)
Hand of Dorothy Wordsworth
Courtesy of the Wordsworth Trust

This manuscript, one of two red leather bound notebooks used simultaneously in the late 1790s and early 1800s, was used mainly for fair copies of earlier drafts of poems. The earliest drafts of 'The Ruined Cottage' date from 1797 when the Wordsworths were living at Racedown in Dorset; this version was to see further revisions before being published in 1814 as part of Wordsworth's longest poem, *The Excursion*.

Wordsworth's 'Portmanteau' Suitcase, Bedroom, Dove Cottage
Photograph courtesy of the Wordsworth Trust

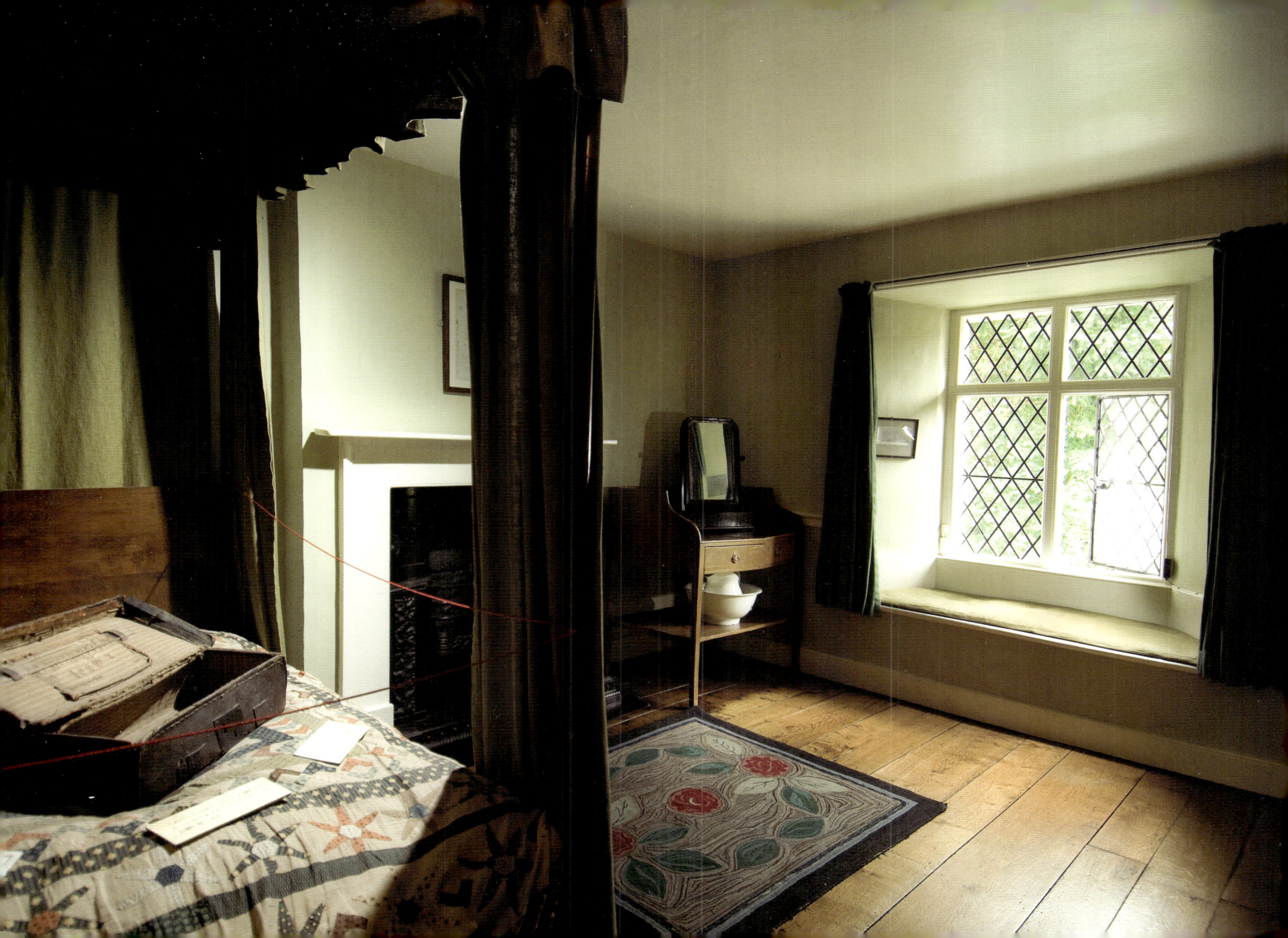

# NOBUYA MONTA

**30.** ***An Imaginary Dialogue***

Suite for viola and guitar

Total duration 19 minutes

With Aki Komi (viola) and Kei Hamada (guitar)

In this suite of four new pieces specially composed for the exhibition, Nobuya Monta imagines what might have been if the two poets, Bashō and Wordsworth, had ever met: what kinds of *haiku* would Bashō create in a visit to the Lake District, and how might Wordsworth have responded whilst walking through the mountains and valleys of Japan? This imaginary dialogue results in a new musical score that echoes with themes of journeying, wandering and longing.

We may speculate further on the many relationships between music and poetry that underpin Monta's work. Both Wordsworth and Bashō were attuned to the sounds of nature; the textual descriptions of landscapes in all Wordsworth's poetry sing with noise, real and imagined, whilst the 'sound of water' in the 'Old Pond' is one of the most recognisable lines from all Bashō's *haiku*. In a more philosophical sense, Wordsworth's poetry is suffused with metaphors of music and

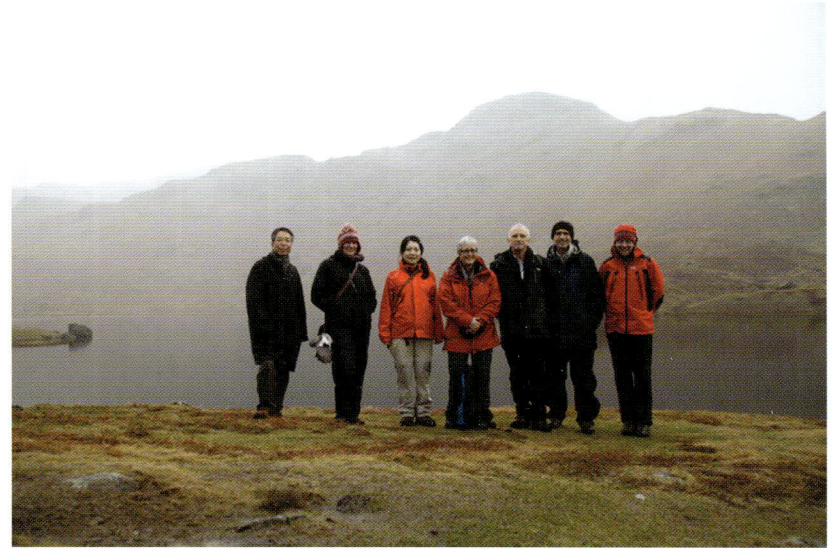

Figure 24, Monta (far left) with fellow artists from the exhibition 'Walking Poets: Wordsworth and Bashō' on a walk up Easedale in the Lake District, January 2014

the 'harmony of music' is a leitmotif, as in Book I of *The Prelude* (1805) where he reflects on the nature of poetic inspiration, 'The mind of man is framed even like the breath / And harmony of music' (351–55). Such connections between music, poetry and aesthetics are of great importance to musician and composer Nobuya Monta, who has done much to promote new international directions in tonal music. Born in Osaka, Monta studied musical composition in both Japan and Europe and continues to perform with leading musicians internationally.

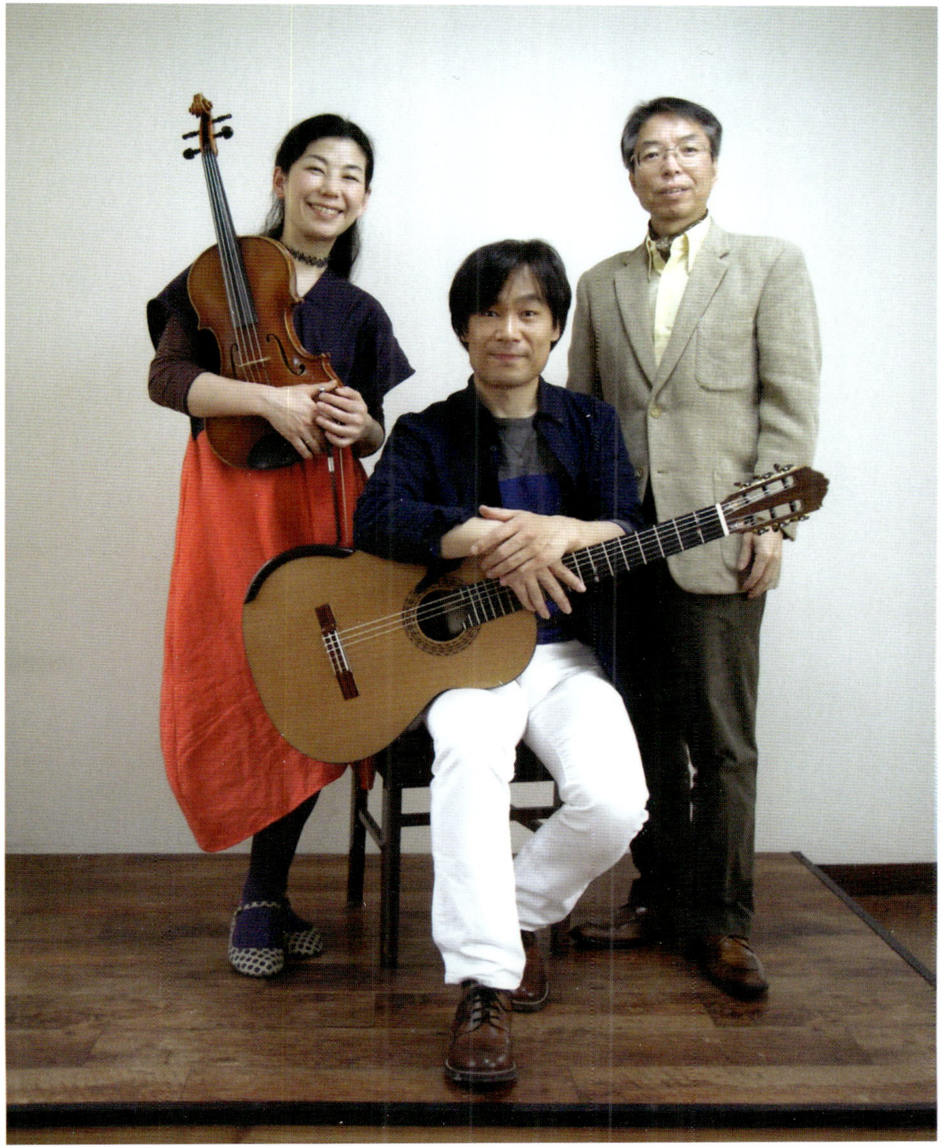

Aki Komi, viola player, and Kei Hamada, guitarist, with Nobuya Monta

# INGE PANNEELS and MINAKO SHIRAKURA

31. ***Wanderers of the Earth: the Milky Way Above***

2014

Glass, paper

Dimension variable (glass map approxiamtely 2 x 2 cm, envelope 11.4 x 16.2 cm, round cards between 4–5cm diameter)

32. ***Wanderers of the Earth: Walk***

2014

Glass

25 x 75 x 4 cm

'Wanderers of the Earth: the Milky Way Above' is a collaboration between artists Inge Panneels and Minako Shirakura. Based respectively in the UK and Japan, their collaboration was made possible by contemporary communications technology (email and Skype) that can bring us closer together even when physically separated.

Aptly, their new work is both a reflection on, and a result of, 'correspondence' and is inspired in part by the poets' original manuscripts and letters that have come down to us over the centuries. Panneels and Shirakura met at the National Glass Centre in Sunderland in 2014 to realise their vision. Taking initial inspiration from Bashō and Wordsworth's poetic referencing of stars and constellations, they created tiny glass world maps as gifts for friends and acquaintances. Wrapped in Japanese paper, these maps were posted out into the world. The envelopes also contained a letter inviting recipients to return their own gift in the form of the word 'star' in their languages written on the enclosed Japanese paper card. These simple exchanged gifts, a world for a star, are part of the installation at Dove Cottage. Accompanying the installation is a glass panel titled 'Wanderers of the Earth: Walk', which bears Wordsworth's and Bashō's poems referring to stars, in Panneels' and Shirakura's handwriting respectively. The panel's colours suggest time change and spatial distance (East and West). The installation, in conjunction with the glass panel, is the artists' attempt to visualise the universe, as a reference to the feelings of immensity and wonder both poets conveyed through their poetry.

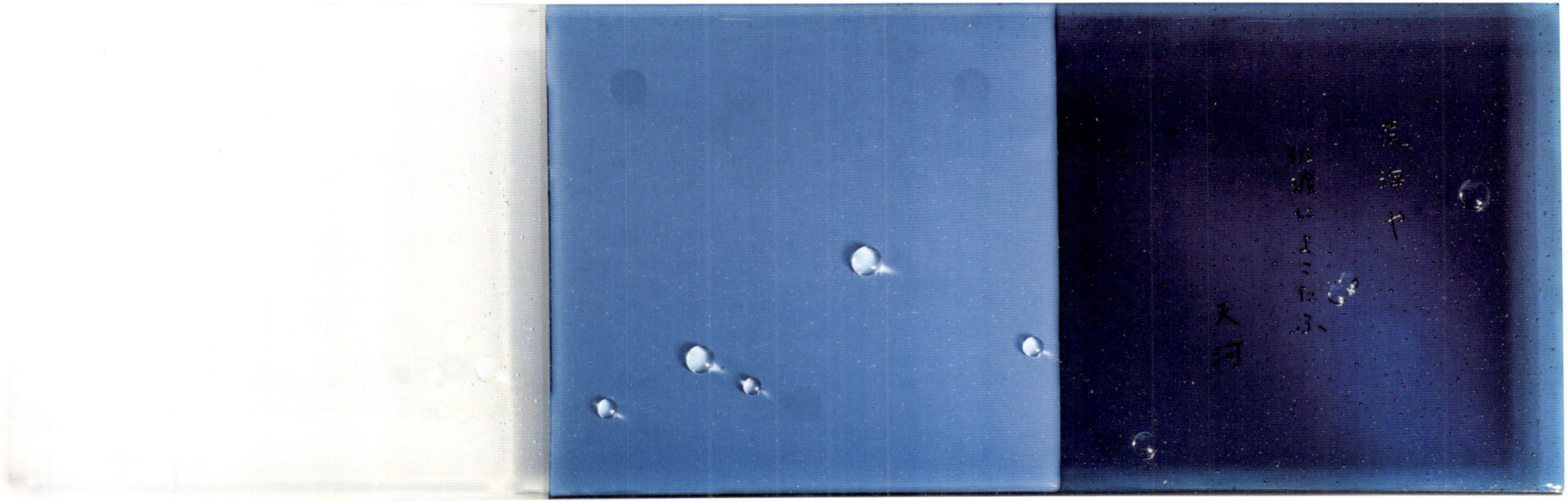


*Wanderers of the Earth: Walk*

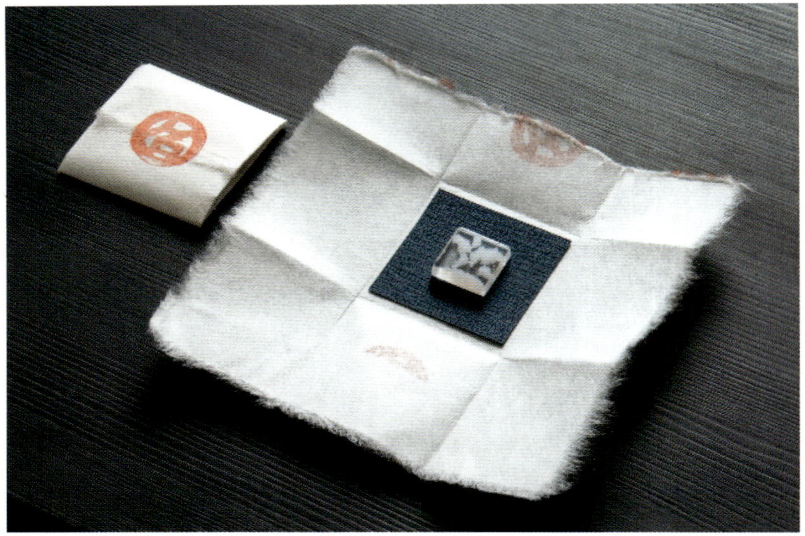

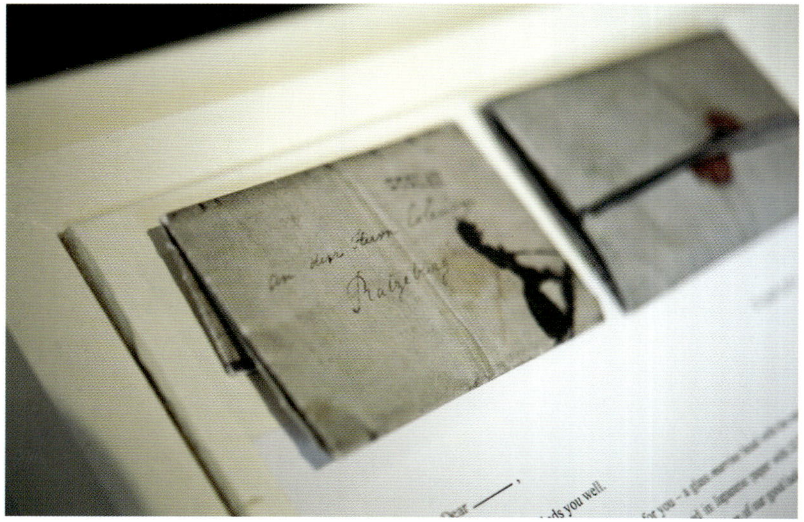

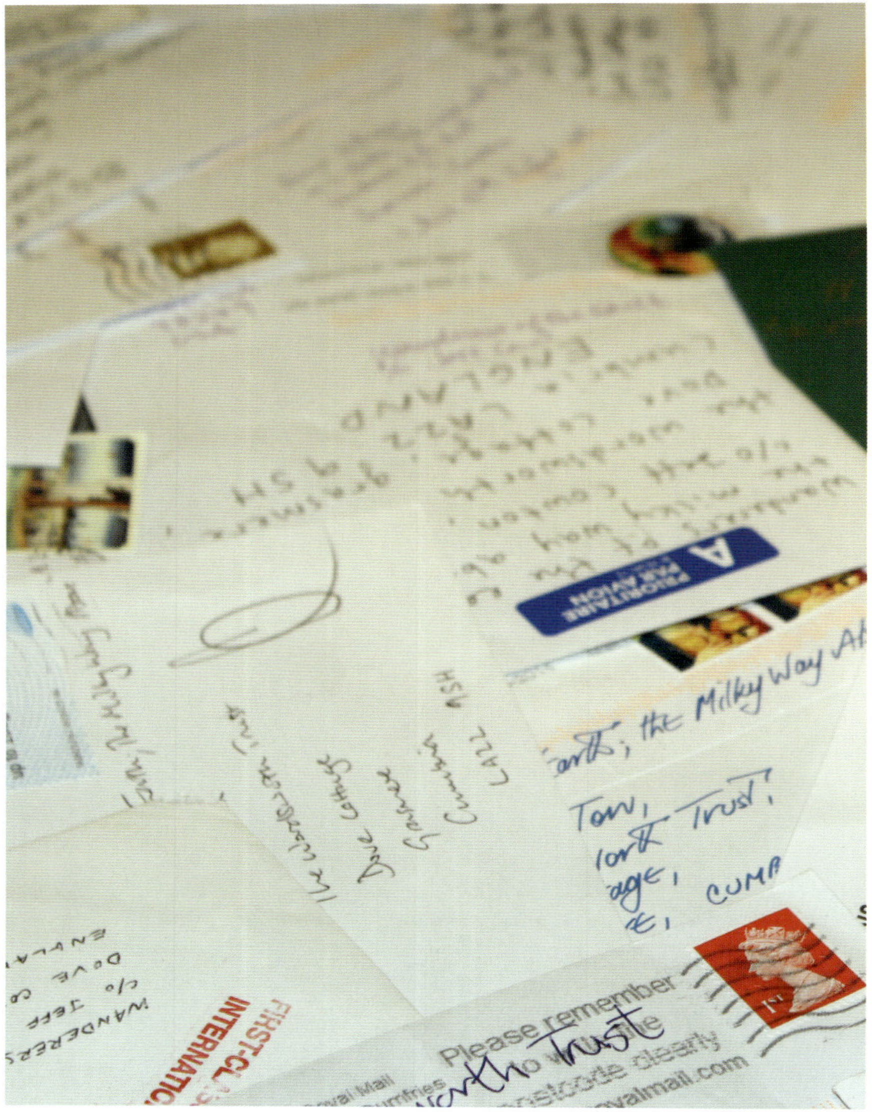


*Wanderers of the Earth: the Milky Way Above.* From the top left clockwise: hand-pulled Murrini slice of world map. Letters received from around the world enclosing stars. William Wordsworth and Dorothy Wordsworth, 'Letter to Samuel Taylor Coleridge', 14 Dec or 21 Dec 1798, 'The Goslar letter', including early versions of lines towards *The Prelude*, and other poems (both sides). Courtesy of the Wordsworth Trust

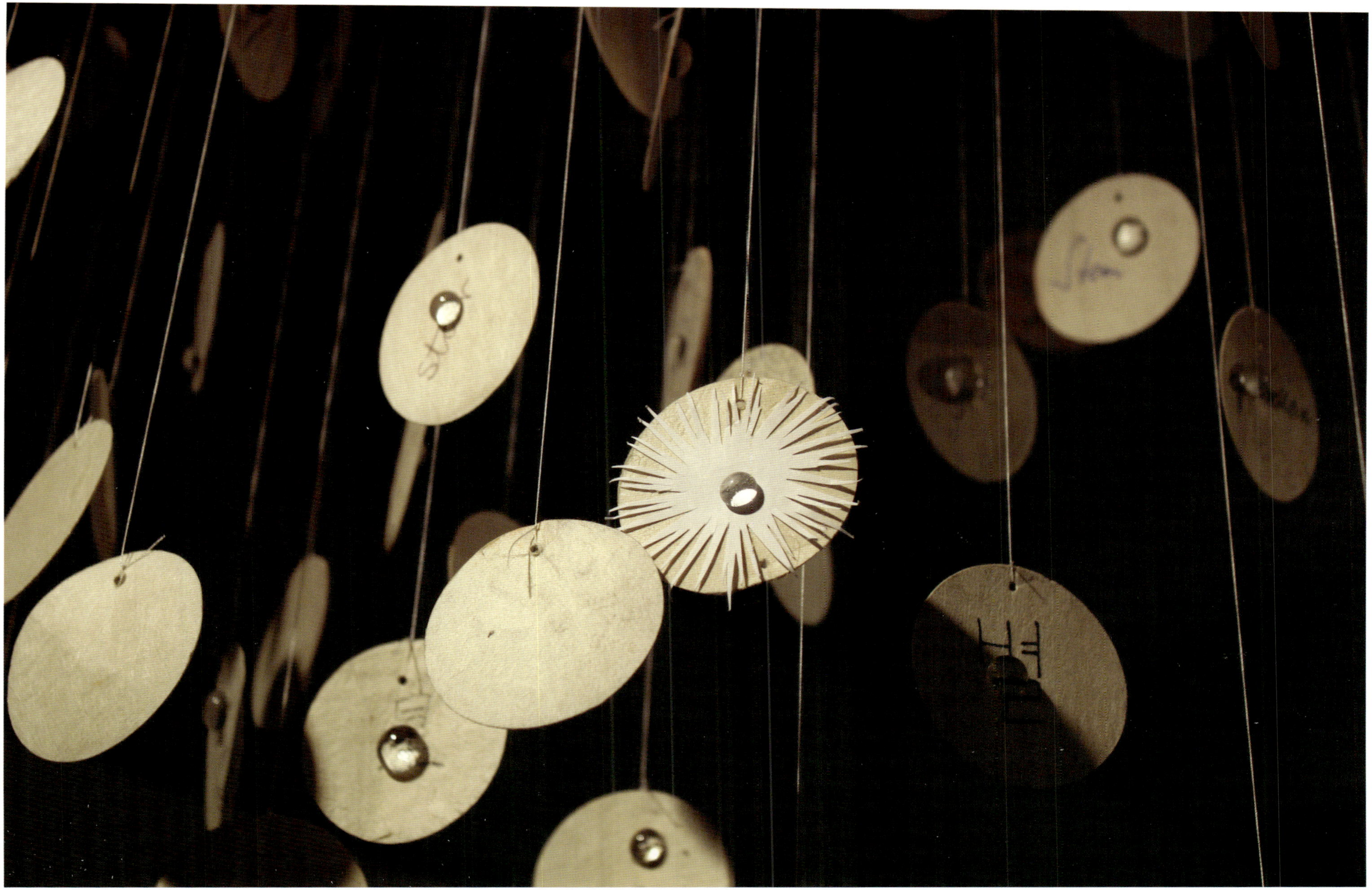

*Wanderers of the Earth: the Milky Way*, installation shot

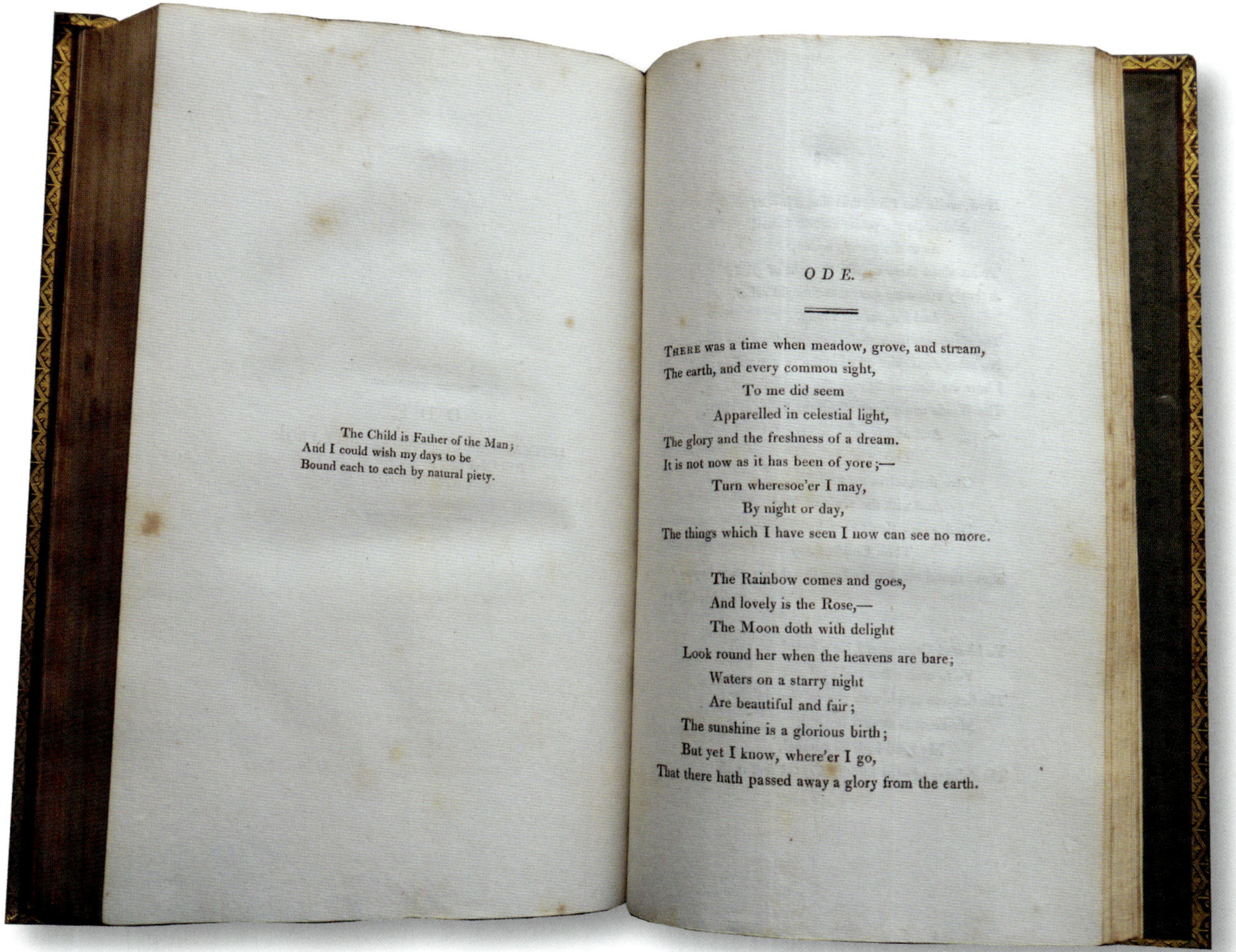


## WILLIAM WORDSWORTH

33. ***Poems, including Lyrical Ballads***
London, 1815
Open to show 'Ode'

The 'Ode' was first published in *Poems, in Two Volumes* and as can be seen here, comes at the end of the second volume. Wordsworth was always concerned about the ordering and appearance of poems within his published works, and it is noteworthy that the 'Ode' should appear with its own title page, separate from any subject or chronological ordering elsewhere.

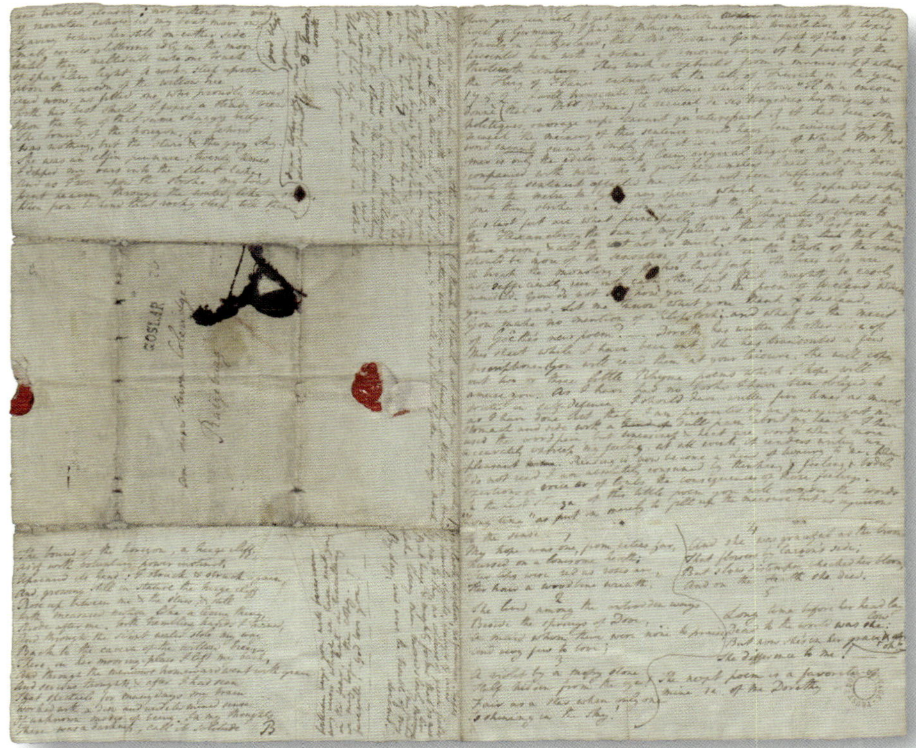 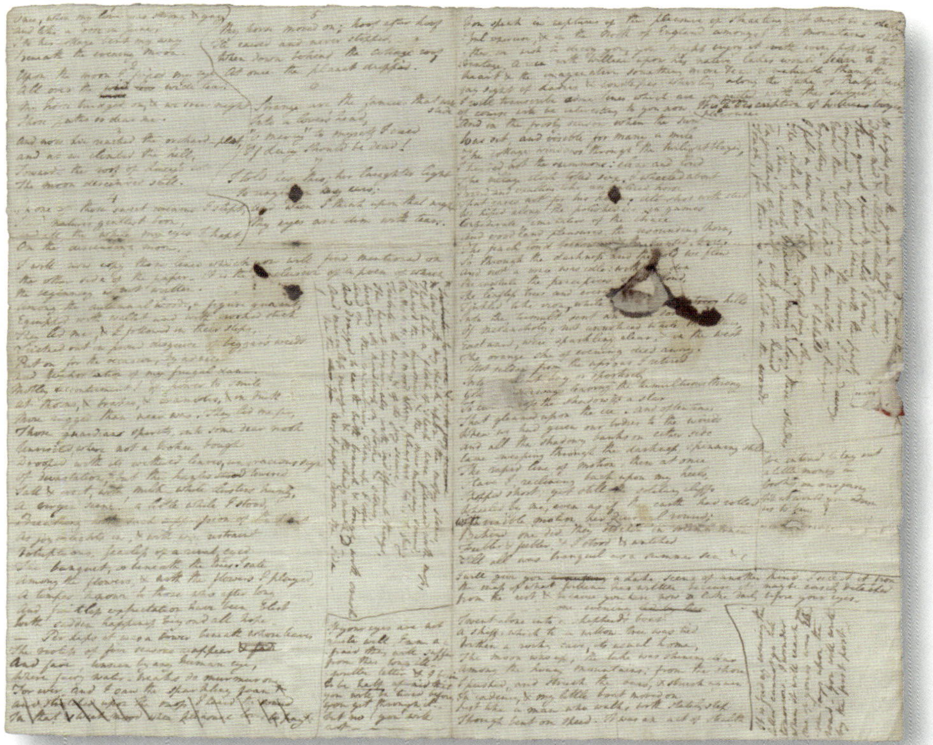

**WILLIAM WORDSWORTH** and **DOROTHY WORDSWORTH** to Samuel Taylor Coleridge, 14 or 21 Dec 1798
**34. 'The Goslar letter including drafts of verse of *The Prelude* and other poems.'**

The letter of December 1798 was written when William and Dorothy were in the small German town of Goslar during its coldest winter for a century. During this time, Wordsworth turned his thoughts to his childhood, recollecting experiences such as skating on Esthwaite and rowing on Ullswater in a boat taken without the owner's permission. This visually striking letter, which includes many of these early drafts, was sent to Coleridge who had travelled with the Wordsworths into Germany and then gone his separate way.

# ANDREW RICHARDSON

**35.** ***The ghostly language of ancient earth***

2014

Interactive map and digital prints

1280 x 720 screen pixels on a 23 inch monitor

**36.** ***The ghostly language of ancient earth***

2014

Map, digital print

Total unfolded size: 100 x 110 cm, folded size: 22 x 13 x 1 cm

Andrew Richardson's work melds old and new modes of landscape representation: extracts from Wordsworth's *The Prelude* are mapped onto a three-dimensional interactive map of the landscape of Grasmere and the surrounding area. The interactive screen version of the map allows viewers to explore the text-landscape, to view it from different angles and perspectives or even to follow a specific 'path' of words. These word paths are directly linked to the shape of Wordsworth's poetry, as the number and length of words in each verse line determine the path's change of direction. In contrast to this interactive exploration, the accompanying digital prints are pauses, quiet hiatuses allowing us a more contemplative viewing experience.

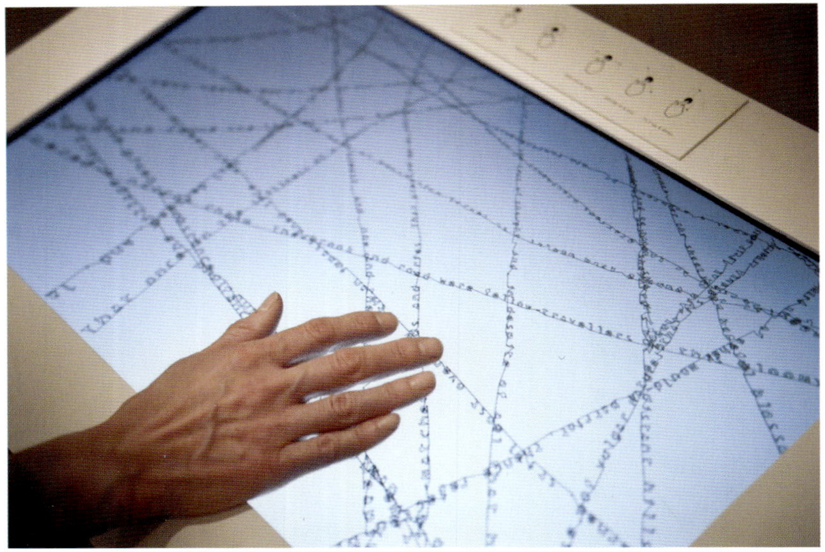

In re-presenting the contours of the landscape Wordsworth wrote about, Richardson returns the poet's words literally and metaphorically to the topography that was so much a part of the poet's life and work. In turn, Richardson allows us to explore the contours of this landscape through touch-screen. We are able to track our own path through the topographical lines of the map, whilst simultaneously following the poetic lines of Wordsworth's most famous literary masterpiece. In so doing, our fingers take us for a walk both literally and imaginatively. As such, Richardson offers a contemporary response to Wordsworth's poetry of place in the context of our digitally connected, screen-based world. Wordsworth's words are digitally scattered on the earth, their legibility actively reformed through each user's hands.

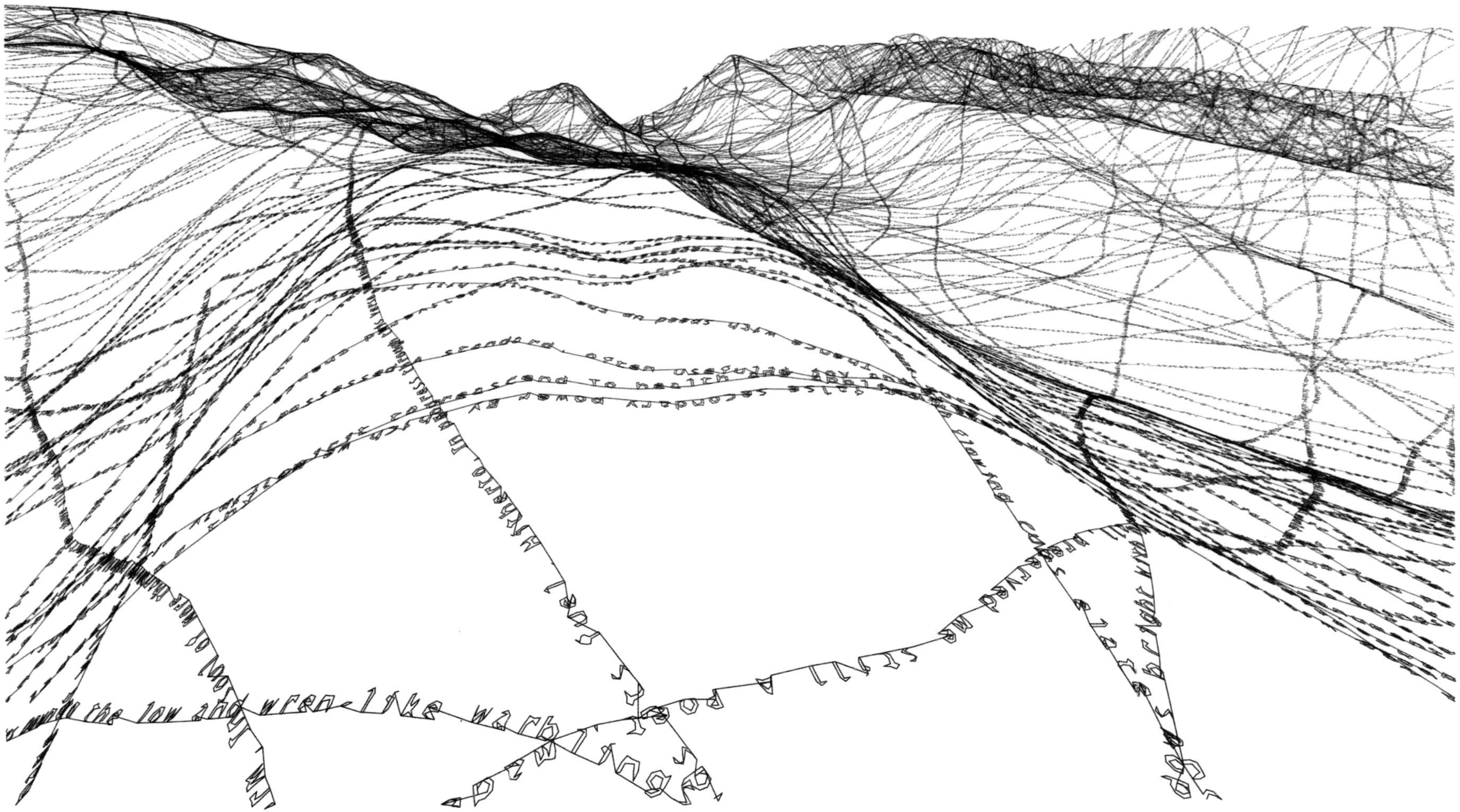


*The ghostly language of ancient earth,* digital image

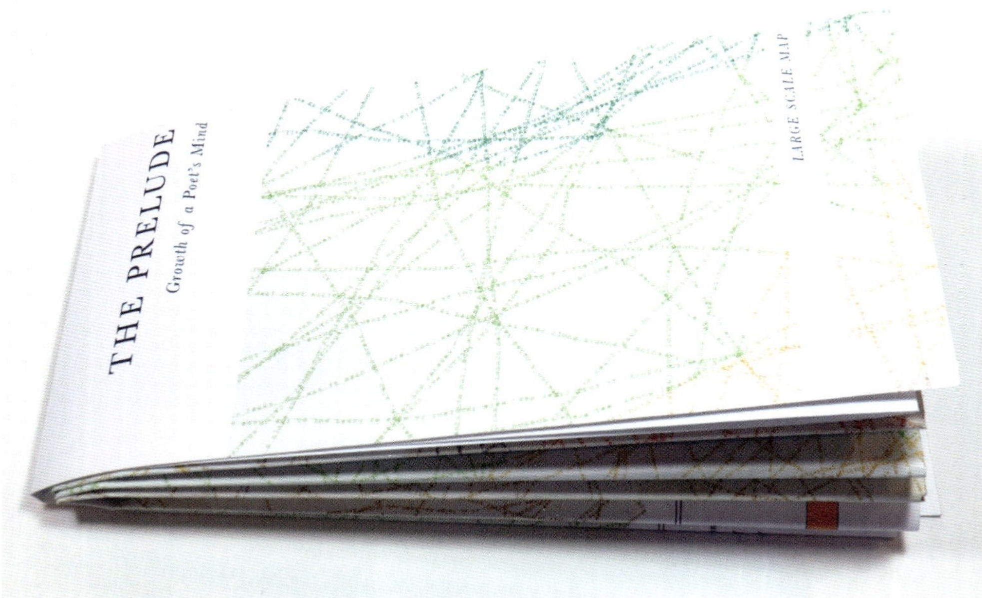


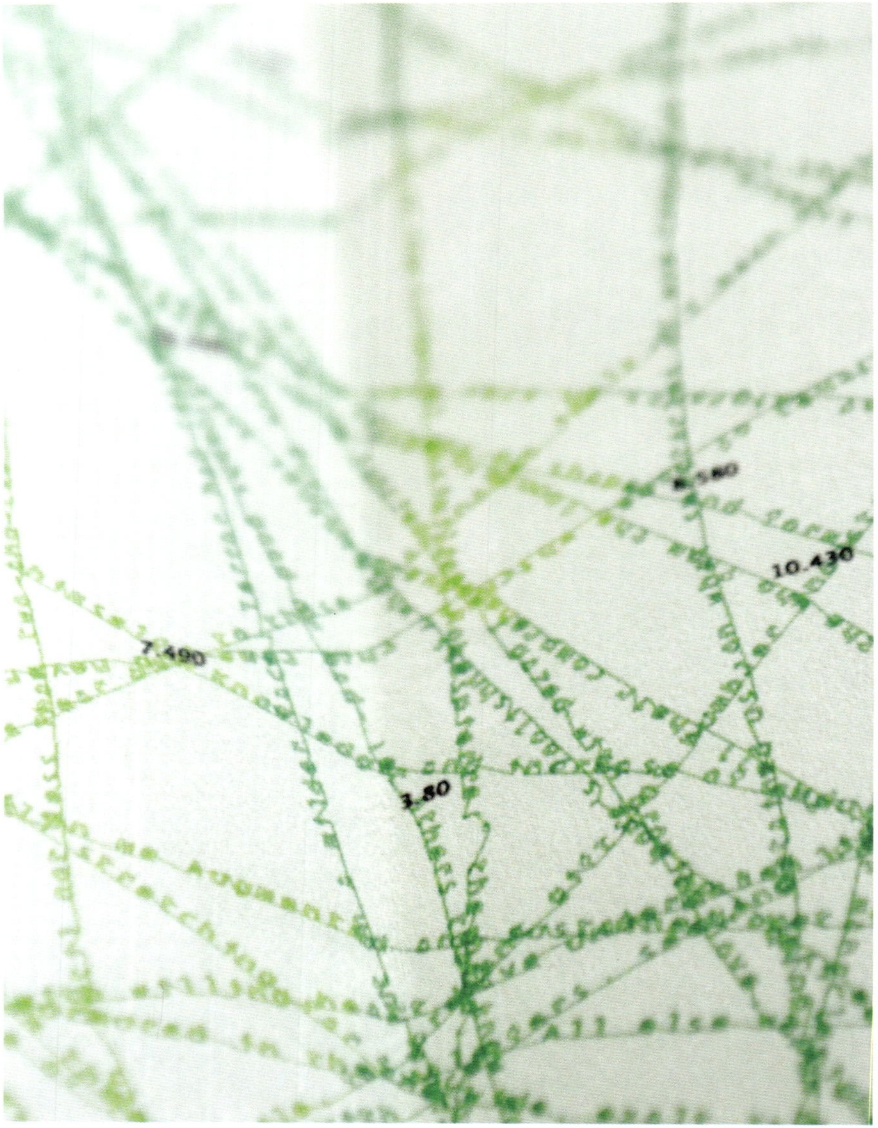


*The ghostly language of ancient earth,* map, digital print

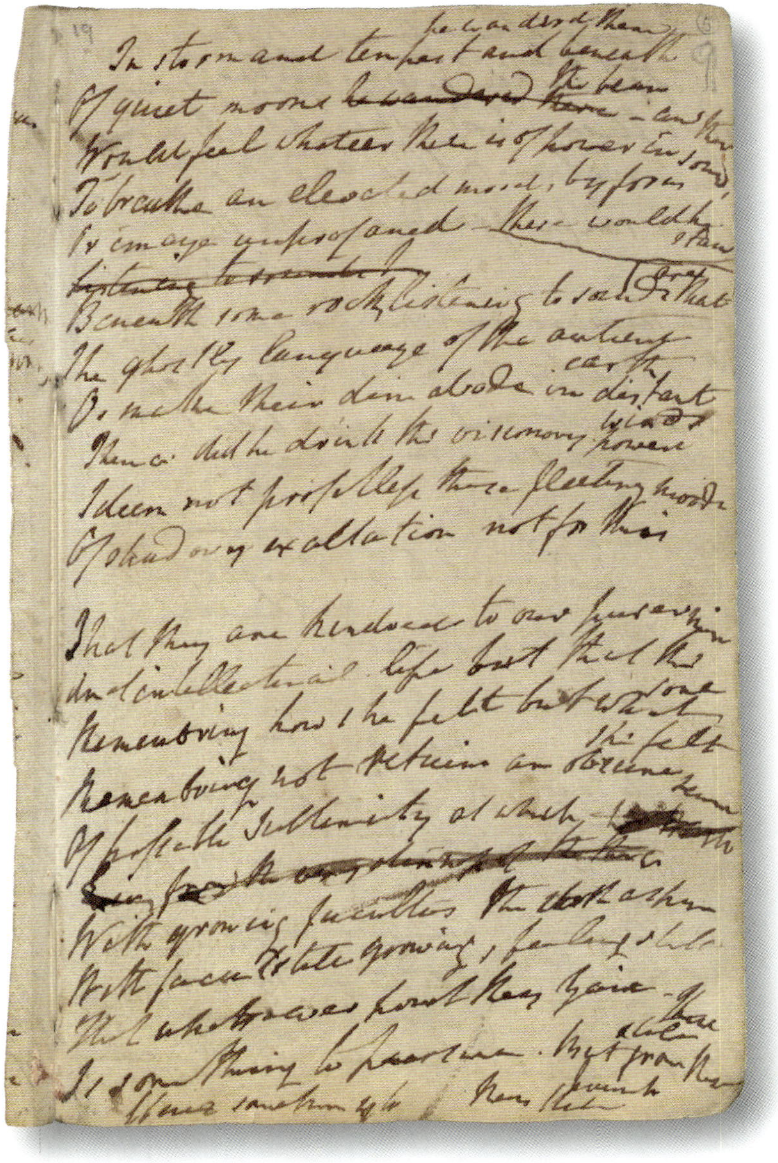

**WILLIAM WORDSWORTH**

***37.** The 'Alfoxden notebook'*

Hand of William Wordsworth,
Open to show *The Prelude,* Book II, 325–360
(the 1805 version numbering)

In storm and tempest or in starlight nights
Beneath the quiet heavens, and at that time
Would feel whate'er there is of power in sound
To breathe an elevated mood by form
Or image unprofaned: and I would stand
Beneath some rock listening to sounds that are
The ghostly language of ancient earth
Or make their dim abode in distant winds.
Thence did I drink the visionary power.
(*The Prelude*, 1805, II. 325–333)

# AUTUMN RICHARDSON

**38. *The Mulberry Coat***

2014

Sewn kōzo paper

123 x 128 cm

**39. *Go To The Pine***

2014

Text on paper

42 x 29.7 cm

Autumn Richardson produces work in a range of media that draws upon the natural landscape, with particular attention given to its ecology and, specifically, botany. Bashō's poetry illuminated even the smallest details of his environment, with much of his writing referencing the plants and trees that surrounded him.

In 'Go To The Pine' the artist plots an imaginary line north, listing each of the plants referenced by Bashō during his final journey, as recorded in two translations: *The Narrow Road to the Deep North* and *Backroads to Far Towns*.

Before setting off on the journeys from which his poetry sprang, Bashō required hand-made coats, hats and shoes, all of which were made from the very plant life that inspired his writing.

'I was living a forlorn life behind the door of my grass hut, feeling more and more lonely with every gust of autumn wind, so I ... took up the skill of the Bamboo-cutter ... declaring myself "the old man who makes his own raincloak."'

'The Mulberry Coat' is an artistic re-imagining of the garment that Bashō might have worn, made from untreated, unsized kōzo (mulberry) paper, and sewn with cotton thread. By focussing on the paper clothing itself, Richardson emphasises the materiality of Bashō's writing process, and the value of paper as a form of protection, a means of recording his thoughts, and a direct form of contact with the landscape itself.

| | |
|---|---|
| bush-clovers | hagi |
| pine | matsu |
| reeds | tamae no ashi |
| goosefoot | hahakigi |
| cockscomb | keito |
| creeping gourds | hechima |
| moonflowers | yugao |
| pine | matsu |
| willow | yanagi |
| bush-clover | hagi |
| chrysanthemums | kiku |
| kaya-thatched | kayabuki |
| pines | matsu |
| pampas | susuki |
| bush-clovers | hagi |
| dwarf pine | komatsu |
| mad-apples | nasubi |
| cucumbers | uri |
| early rice | wase |
| wisteria | fuji |
| bush-clovers | hagi |
| silk-tree | nebu no hana |
| cherry tree | sakura |
| cherry tree | sakura |
| bamboo grass | shino |
| moss | koke |
| pines and oaks | shouhaku |
| rouge-plants | beni |
| shino brush | shino |
| all-devouring grass | kusamura |
| unohana | unohana |
| grass | kusa |
| rice-paddies | denya |
| reed-flats | mano no kayahara |
| pine tree | matsu |
| pines | matsu |
| pines | matsu |
| pine woods | matsu |
| moss | koke |
| sedges | suge |
| iris | ayame |
| dark pine woods | matsu no hayashi |
| white rhododendrons | asebi |
| bush-clover | hagi |
| blue flag | ayame |
| pine | matsu |
| susuki grass | susuki |
| katsumi | katsumi |
| chestnut tree | kuri |
| briars | ibara |
| unohana | unohana |
| rice-fields | ta |
| willow tree | yanagi |
| dripping moss | koke |
| pines | matsu |
| dark cedar | sugi |
| pine-charcoal | matsu no sumi |
| reed-brakes | no |
| double-flowered pink | yae-nadeshiko |
| grass-moor | shinohara |
| plantain tree | basho |
| grass pillow | kusa no makura |
| cherry blossoms | hana |
| grass | kusa |
| artemisia | kyū |

N

*Go to the Pine*

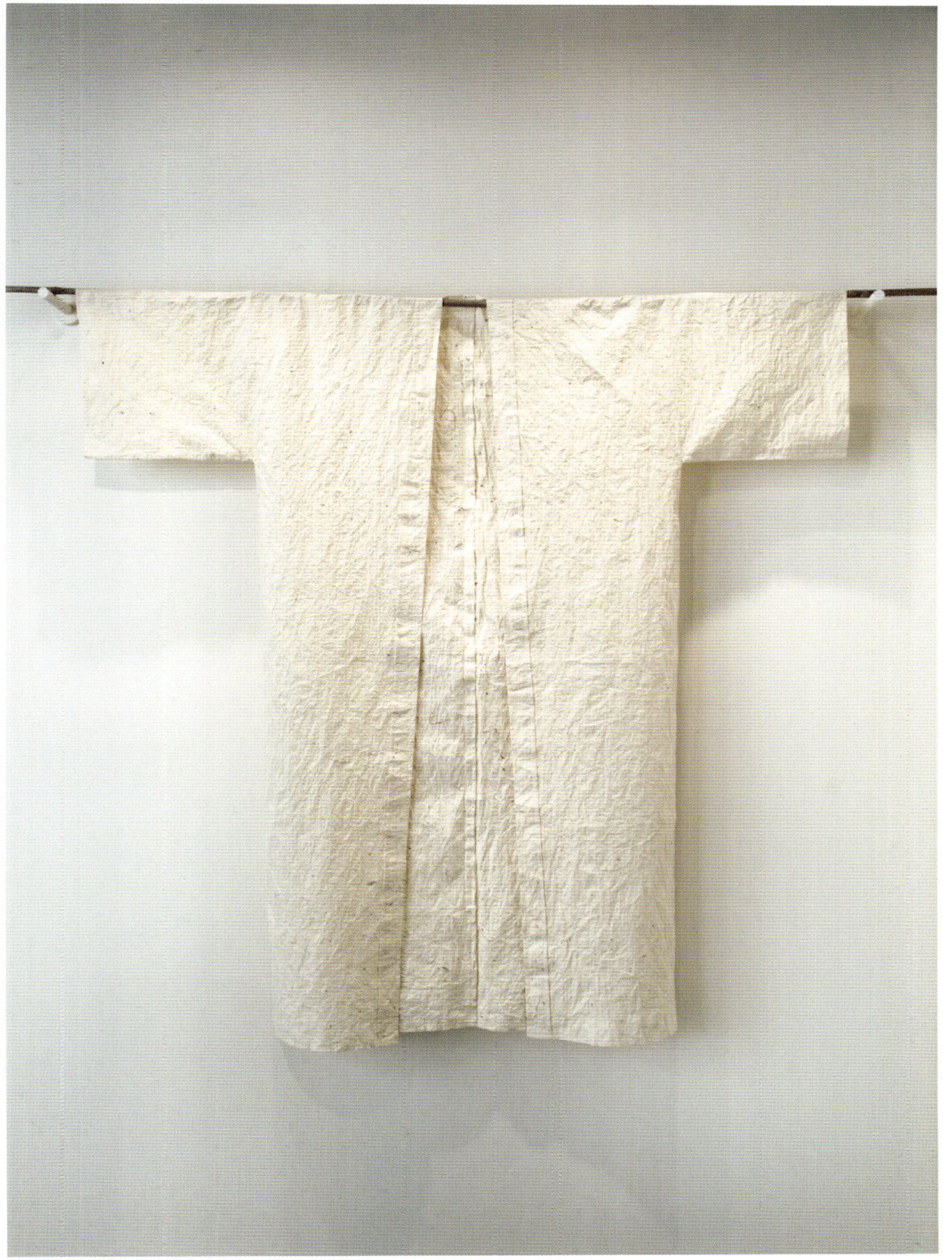

*The Mulberry Coat,* installation shot

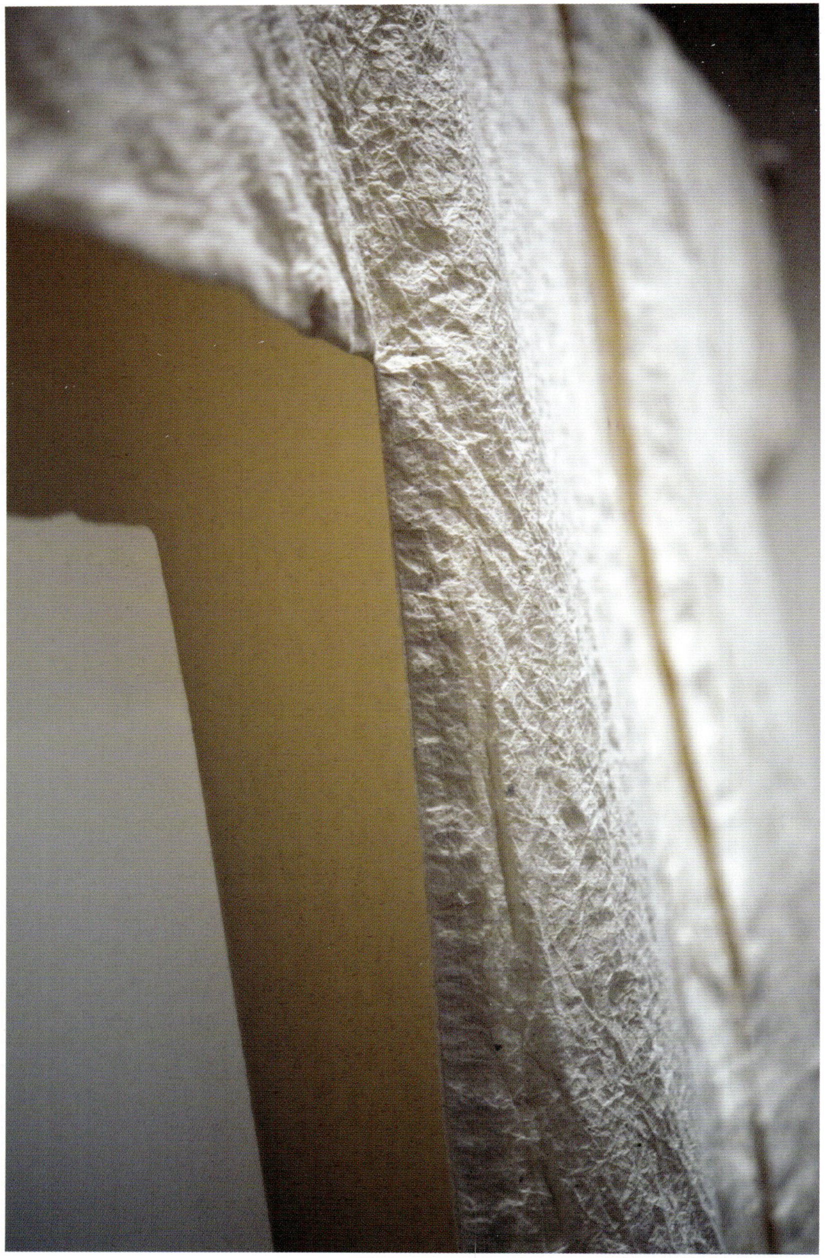

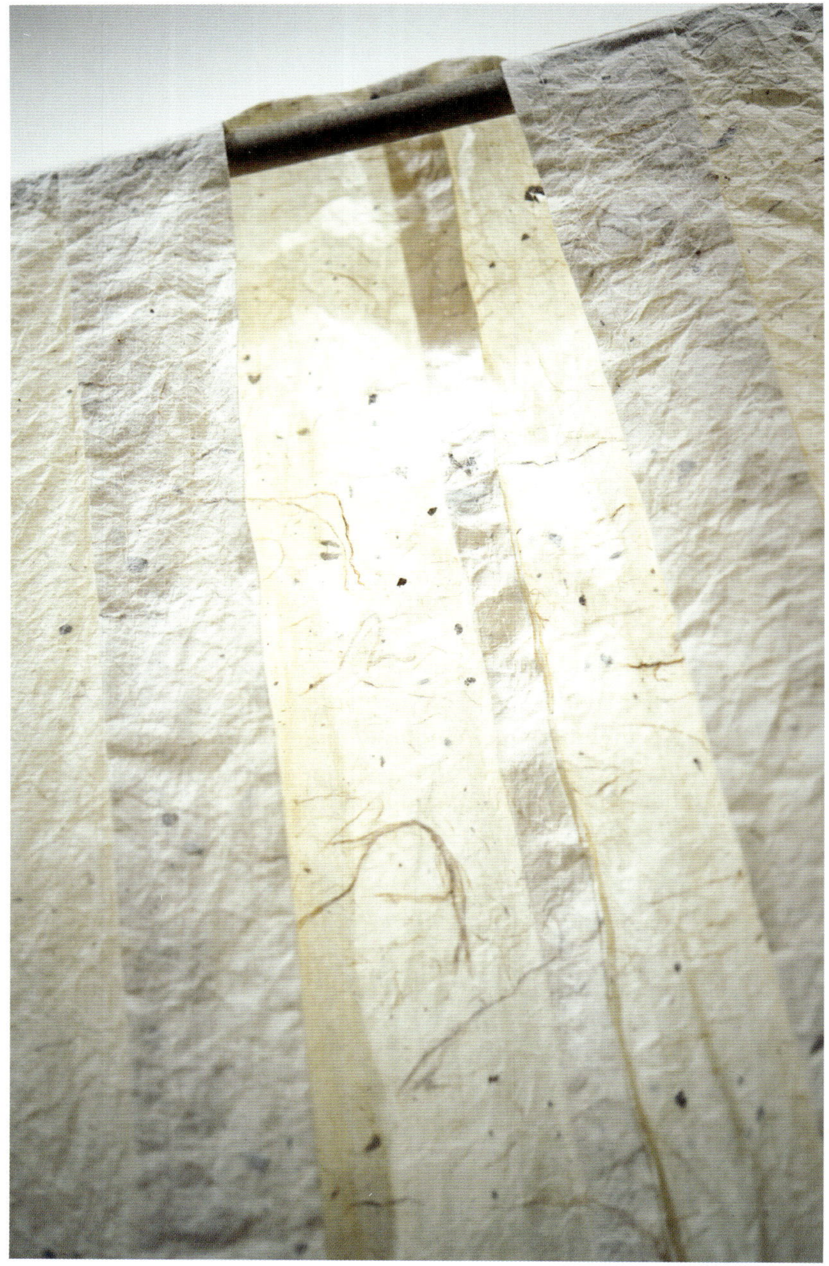

*The Mulberry Coat* (detail)

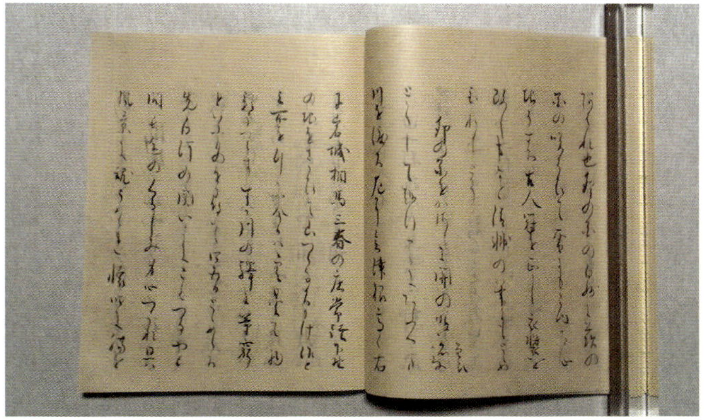

Figure 25, Matsuo Bashō (text and writing of title), 1694
Soryū (writing of all remaining content)
*The Narrow Road to the Deep North*
Open at the page which describes when Bashō travels through the
Shirakawa checkpoint with reference to various flora
Replica borrowed from Iga City Bashō Memorial Museum

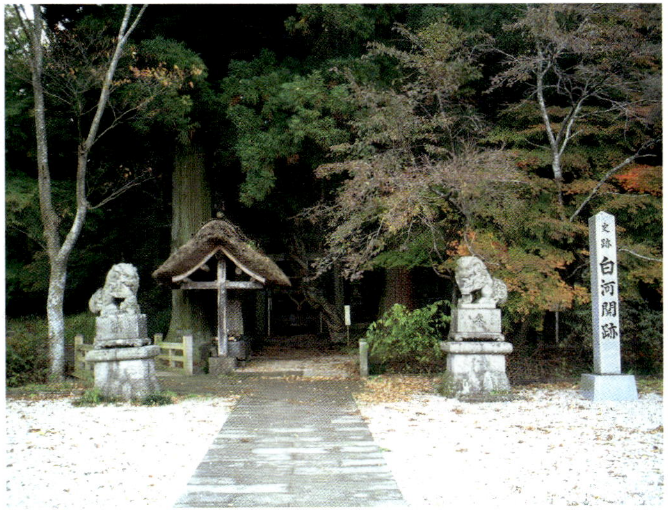


Figure 26, The site of the old Shirakawa checkpoint,
Photograph by Kaneyoshi Urabe

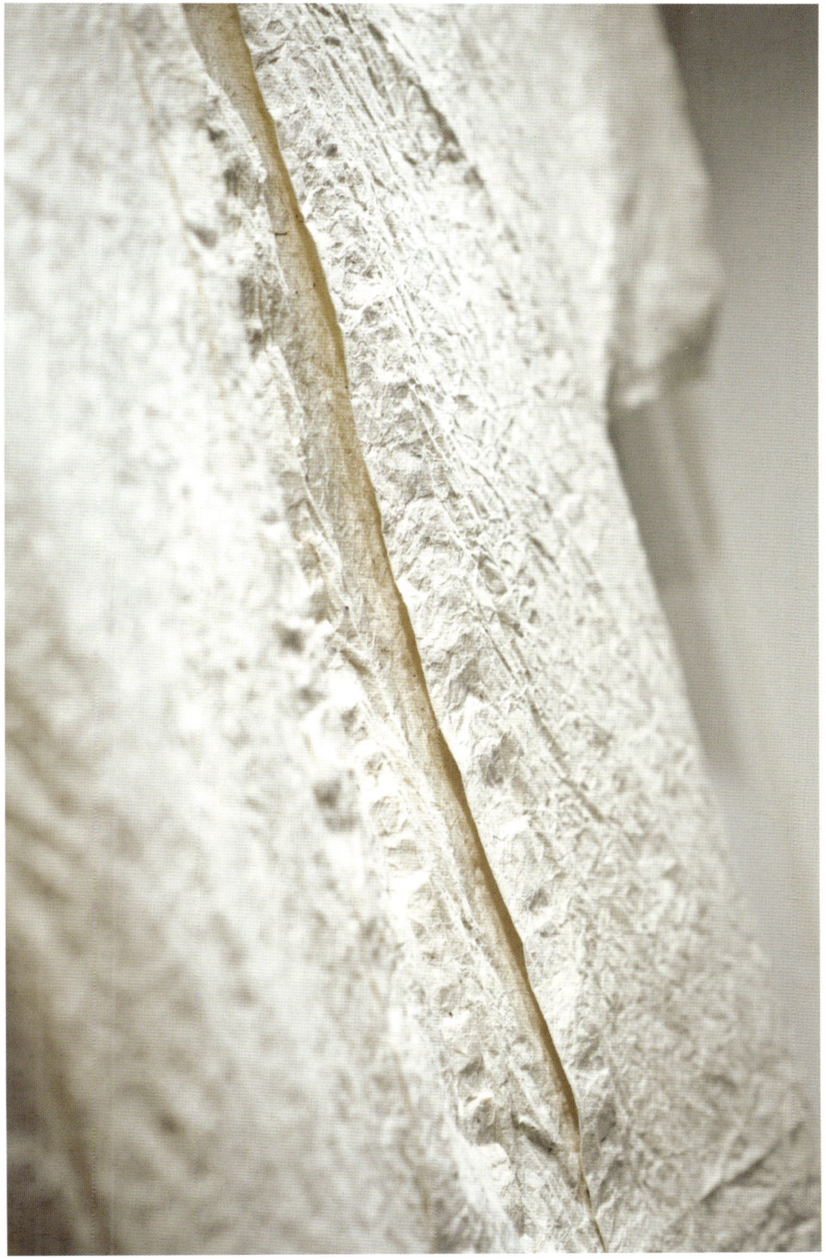

*The Mulberry Coat* (detail)

# RICHARD SKELTON

**40. *I Know Not Where***

2014

Text on paper

51 x 33 cm (x 2)

**41. *Still Glides the Stream***

2014

Text on paper

51 x 33 cm (x 2)

Many of Dorothy Wordsworth's entries from her Alfoxden journals start with the word 'walked', before departing, linguistically and geographically. Richard Skelton's 'I Know Not Where' is a distillation of Dorothy's texts, inviting the reader to wander through two hundred of her words, to find their own routes and, in so doing, to write their own topographical narratives. This work is accompanied by ten *haiku*-like fragments composed by the artist using the same process.

'Still Glides the Stream' takes an elliptical path through William Wordsworth's 'River Duddon' sonnets, atomising the original texts by revealing their constituent elements and drawing attention to the presence of ancient 'water-words' within their composition. These words, in the Germanic and Celtic language families, would have been spoken in the British Isles long before Wordsworth's time.

The new poem can be thought of as a series of eddies within a river's main stream. The first part collates all thirty three original sonnets into a single text and erases each occurrence of a water-word. These gaps in the text, which in many cases render it meaningless, enact the process of language loss—the poem appears to decay before our eyes. Language, like a river, is fluid, ever changing, and 'meaning' itself is uncertain; it cannot be guaranteed in perpetuity.

The second part of the new poem is a negative image of the first, reclaiming the lost water-words and presenting them extant. In so doing it reimagines Wordsworth's text as a landscape through which the River Duddon itself flows —eroding the softer sediment to reveal fragments of older, obdurate material.

*I Know Not Where* (opposite page)

a dog-violet more solitary
action enveloped morning song
adders-tongue evening moss cups songs
advances eyes motion sound
after fanned moved source
air feathery multitudes spinning
alone ferns murmur spring
along firs nearly staring
an flat neither stitchwort
and flowers network strange
are followed noise streaked
beautiful form nor stream
became found oaks strewed
beeches fringed obscured stripped
berries from of sun
between furze once sunshine
black gaunt one that
blackened glittering opened the
blossom gloss overshadowed their
blue grand palest thick
blue-grey great periwinkles thin
boughs green perpetual thready
breeze grey pink through
brighter ground pleasant to
bristled half plentiful tops
brook half-marked primroses tracks
brown-red hanging rapidly trees
by hard return twisting
called hazels returned under
ceaseless hollow returning unmarked
clear horizon ridges upon
cold hues road upper
coloured immense roads vapour
commotion in rose veil
coombe invisible sea very
cowslips ivy sea-green view
crescent know serpents violent
crimson laden shadows walked
current land sharp warm
damp lark sheep waterfall
dark leaves sheep-bells where
dead life shelter which
deeper like shore white
dell line shower wind
dew-drops lines silvery winding
dim low skeletons with
dimmer makes skirting withered
distances mist sky wood
distant moon small woods
dividing moonlight sober yellow

where
noise flowers
in multitudes

plentiful

the twisting tracks
the hollow roads:

fringed
with small life

with ivy
twisting
bristled serpents:

dark laden

by the black brook:

the veil of life
obscured
morning and evening

the invisible veil:

the shadows of oaks
a blackened murmur

WALKED

the palest current:

a half-marked
glittering
crescent stream

alone:

adders-tongue
low ferns
advances of stitchwort
found under trees

until dark returned:

found under
gaunt flowers

by furze spinning
a thin, strange brook:

perpetual murmur

through air:

a ceaselessdark winding
green songs of the dead

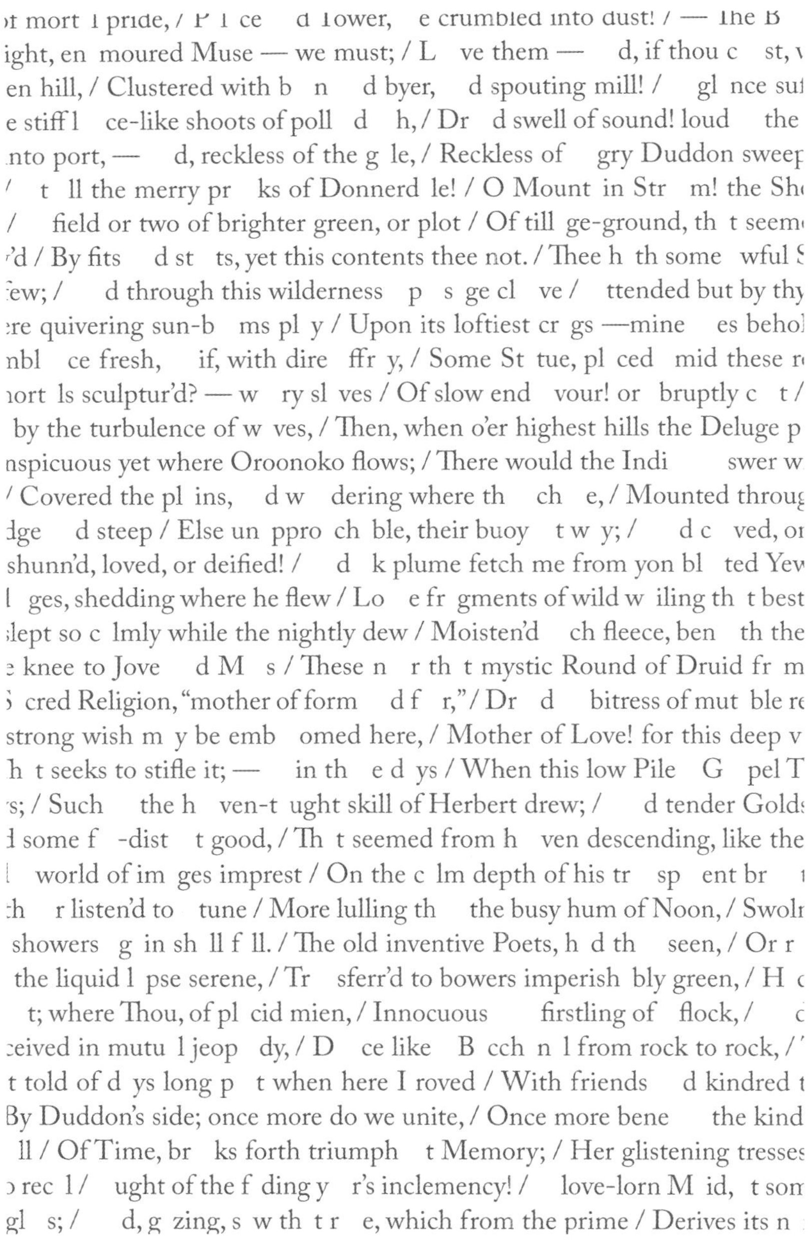


*Still Glides the Stream* (detail, left and right)

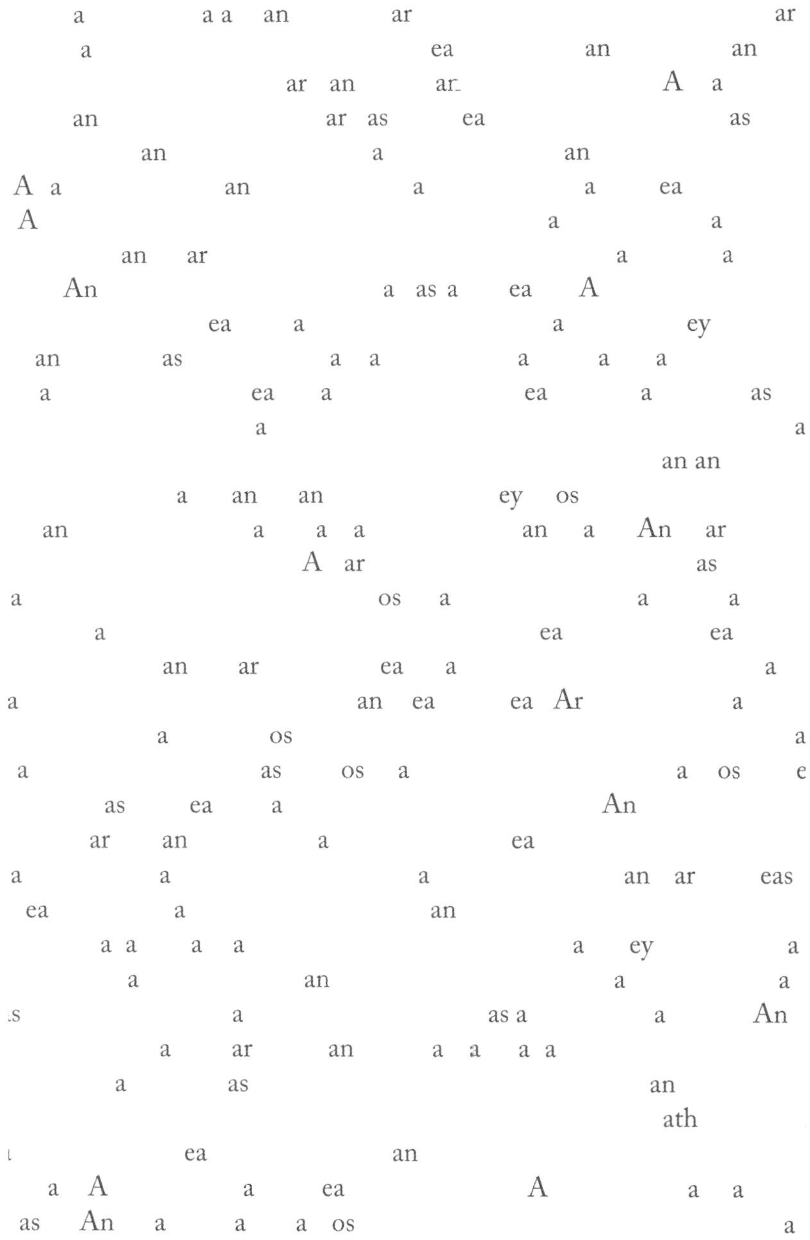


*Still Glides the Stream* (opposite page)

Not envying sh des which h ply yet m y throw / gr teful coolness round th t rocky spring, / B ndusi , once responsive to the string / Of the Hor ti n lyre with b bbling flow; / C mless of flowers th t in perenni l blow / Round the moist m rge of Persi n fount ins cling; / Heedless of lpine torrents thundering / Through icy port ls r d nt h ven's bow; / I seek the birth-pl ce of n tive Str m.— / ll h il ye mount ins, h il thou morning light! / Better to br the upon this ery height / Th p s in needless sleep from dr m to dr m. / Pure flow the verse, pure, vigorous, free, d bright, / For Duddon, long lov'd Duddon, is my theme! / Child of the clouds! remote from every t int / Of sordid industry thy lot is c st; / Thine re the honors of the lofty w te; / Not seldom, when with h t the v ll s f int, / Thy h d-m ed Fr s with sp gled tissue qu int / Thy cr dle decks;— to ch unt thy birth, thou h t / No m ner Poet th the whistling Bl t, / d Desol tion is thy P tron-s int! / She gu ds thee, ruthless Power! who would not sp e / Th e mighty forests, once the bison's screen, / Where st lk'd the huge deer to his sh ggy l ir / Through p ths nd l s roofed with sombre green, / Thous d of y rs before the silent ir / W pierced by whizzing sh ft of hunter keen! / How sh ll I p int thee? — Be this n ked stone / My s t while I give w y to such intent; / Pl ed could my verse, sp king monument, / M ke to the es of men thy f tures known. / But of ll th e tripping l mbs not one / Outruns his fellows, so h n ture lent / To thy beginning nought th t doth present / Peculi r grounds for hope to build upon. / To dignify the spot th t gives thee birth, / No sign of ho tiquity's esteem: ppe s, d none of modern Fortune's c e; / Yet thou thyself h t round thee shed gl m / Of brilli t m , instinct with freshness r e; / Prompt offering to thy F ter-mother, E th! / T ke, cr dled Nursling of the mount in, t ke / This p ting gl ce, no negligent dieu! / Prot n ch ge seems wrought while I pursue / The curves, lo ely-sc tered ch in doth m ke; / Or r ther thou ppe st glistering sn ke, / Silent, d to the g zer's e untrue, / Thridding with sinuous l pse the rushes, through / Dw f willows gliding, d by ferny br ke / St ts from dizzy steep the und unted Rill / Rob'd inst dy in g b of snow-white fo m; / d l ughing d es the dventurer, who h clomb / So high, riv purp e to fulfil; / Else let the D d h clow d wend, d ro m, / Seeking less bold chievement, where he will! / Sole listener, Duddon! to the breeze th t pl y'd / With thy cl r voice, I c ught the fitful sound / W fted o'er sullen m d cr ggy mound, / Unfruitful solitudes, th t seem'd to upbr id / The sun in h ven! — but now, to form sh de / For Thee, green lders h ve together wound / Their foli ge; hes flung their ms ound; / nd birch-trees risen in silver colonn de. / d thou h t lso tempted here to rise, 'Mid sheltering pines, this Cott ge rude d gr ; / Wh e ruddy children, by the mother's es / C elessly w tch'd, sport through the summer d y, / Thy pl d sociates: — light endless M y / On inf b ms lonely N ture lies. / Ere yet our course w gr ced with soci l trees / It l cked not old rem ins of h wthorn bowers, / Where sm ll birds w bled to their p amours; / e ier still, w he d the hum of bees; / I s w them ply their h mless robberies, / d c ught the fr gr ce which the sundry flowers, / Fed by the str m with soft perpetu showers, / Plenteously yielded to the v g t breeze. / There bloomed the str wberry of the wilderness; / The trembling e-brigh t showed her s pphire blue, / The thyme her purple like the blush of even, / d, if the he th of some to no c ess / Invited, forth th peeped so f ir to view, / ll kinds like seemed f vourites of H ven. / "Ch ge me, some God, into th t br thing r e!" / The love-sick Stripling f cifully sighs. / The envied flower beholding, it lies / On L ura's br t, in exquisite rep e; / Or he would p s into her Bird, th t throws / The d ts of song from out its wiry c ge; / Enr ptured, — could he for himself eng ge / The thous dth p t of wh t the Nymph bestows, / d wh t the little c eless Innocent / Ungr ciously receives. Too d ing choice! / There e wh e c lmer mind it would content / To be uncull'd flow'ret of the glen, / Fe less of plough d sythe, or d lking wren. / Th t tunes on Duddon's b ks her slender voice. / Wh t pect bore the M who roved or fled, / First of his tribe, to this d k dell — who first / In this pellucid Current sl ked his thirst? / Wh t hopes c me with him? wh t designs were spr d / long his p th? His unprotected bed / Wh t dr ms encomp ss'd? W the Intruder nurs'd / In hideous us ges, d rites accurs'd, / Th t thinned the living d disturbed the d d? / No voice replies; — the rth, the ir is mute; d Thou, blue Str mlet, murmuring yield'st no more / Th soft record th t wh tever fruit / Of ignor ce thou might'st witness heretofore, / Thy function w to h l d to restore. / To soothe d cl nse, not m dden d pollute! / The struggling Rill insensibly is grown / Into Brook of loud d st tely m ch, / Cr d ever d on by pl k d ch; / d, for like use, lo! wh t might seem zone / Ch en for orn ment; stone m tch'd with stone / In studied symmetry, with interp ce / For the cl r w ters to pursue their r ce / Without restr int. — How swiftly h ve th flown! / Succeeding — still succeeding! Here the Child / Puts, when the high-swoln Flood runs fierce d wild, / His budding cour ge to the proof; — d here / Declining M hood l rns to note the sly / d sure encro chments of infirmity, / Thinking how f st time runs, life's end how n r! / Not so th t P ir wh e youthful spirits d nce / With prompt emotion, urging them to p s; / sweet confusion checks the Shepherd-l s; / Blushing she es the dizzy flood k ce, — / To stop hamed — too timid to dv ce; / She ventures once g in — other p use! / His outstretched h d He t untingly withdr ws — / She sues for help with piteous utter ce! / Chidden she chides g in; the thrilling touch / Both fee when he renews the wish'd-for id. / h! if their fluttering h rts should stir too much, / Should b t too strongly, both m y be betr yed. / The frolic Loves who, from yon high rock, see / The struggle, cl p their wings for victory! / No fiction w it of the tique ge; / sky-blue stone, within this sunless cleft, Is of the very foot-m rks unbereft / Which tiny Elves impressed; — on th t smooth st ge / D cing with ll their brilli t equip ge / In secret revels — h ply fter theft / Of some sweet b be, flower stolen, d co se weed left, / For the distr cted mother to ssu ge / Her grief with, she might! — But, where, oh where / Is tr ce ble vestige of the notes Th t ruled th e d ces, wild in ch cter? / — Deep underground? — Or in the upper ir, / On the shrill wind of midnight? or where flo ts / O'er twilight fields the utumn l g s mer? / On, loitering Muse! — The swift Str m chides us— on! / lbeit his deep-worn ch nel doth immure / Objects immense, portr y'd in mini ture, / Wild sh pes for m y str ge comp ison! / Ni g as, lpine p ses, d on / bodies of N i ds, c lm byss es pure, / Bright liquid m sions, f hion'd to endure / When the bro d O k drops, l fless skeleton, / d the solidities of mort l pride, / P l ce d Tower, e crumbled into dust! / — The B d who w lks with Duddon for his guide, / Sh ll find such toys of F cy thickly set. — / Turn from the sight, en moured Muse — we must; / L ve them — d, if thou c st, without regret! / H il to the fields — with Dwellings sprinkled o'er, / d one sm ll H mlet, under green hill, / Clustered with b n d byer, d spouting mill! / gl nce suffices. — should we wish for more, / G y June would scorn us; — but when bl k winds ro r / Through the stiff l ce-like shoots of poll d sh, / Dr d swell of sound! loud the gusts th t l h / The m tted forests of Ont io's shore / By w teful steel unsmitten, then would I / Turn into port, — d, reckless of the g le, / Reckless of gry Duddon sweeping by, / While the w m h rth ex lts the m tling le, / L ugh with the generous household h rtily, / t ll the merry pr ks of Donnerd le! / O Mount in Str m! the Shepherd d his Cot / e privileged Inm tes of deep solitude; / Nor would the nicest chorite exclude / field or two of brighter green, or plot / Of till ge-ground, th t seemeth like spot / Of st tion y sunshine: — thou h t view'd / These only, Duddon! with their p ths renew'd / By fits d st ts, yet this contents thee not. / Thee h th some wful Spirit impelled to l ve, / Utterly to desert, the h unts of men, / Though simple thy comp ions were d few; / d through this wilderness p s ge cl ve / ttended but by thy own voice, s ve when / The Clouds d Fowls of the ir thy w y pursue! / From this deep ch m — where quivering sun-b ms pl y / Upon its loftiest cr gs — mine es behold / gloomy Niche, c p cious, bl k, d cold; / conc ve free from shrubs d m es gr ; / In semb ce fresh, if, with dire ffr y, / Some St tue, pl ced mid these regions old / For tutel y service, thence h d rolled, / St tling the flight of timid Yesterd y! / W s it by mort ls sculptur'd? — w ry sl ves / Of slow end vour! or bruptly c t / Into rude sh pe by fire, with ro ing bl t / Tempestuously let lo e from centr l c ves? / Or f hioned by the turbulence of w ves, / Then, when o'er highest hills the Deluge p t? / Such fruitless questions m y not long beguile / Or pl gue the f cy, mid the sculptured shows / Conspicuous yet where Oroonoko flows; / There would the Indi swer with smile / imld t the White M 's ignor ce, the while, / Of the Gr t W ters telling, how th r e, / Covered the pl ins, d w dering where th ch e, / Mounted through every intric te defile, / Triumph t, — Inund tion wide d deep, / O'er which his F thers urged, to ridge d steep / Else un ppro ch ble, their buoy t w y; / d c ved, on mur l cliff's undr ded side, / Sun, moon, d st s, d b t of ch e or pr ; / Wh tsoe'er th sought, shunn'd, loved, or deified! / d k plume fetch me from yon bl ted Yew / Perched on wh e top the D ish R ven cro ks; / loft the imperi l Bird of Rome invokes / Dep ted ges, shedding where he flew / Lo e fr gments of wild w iling th t bestrew / The clouds, d thrill the ch mbers of the rocks, / c int silence hush the timorous flocks, / Th t slept so c lmly while the nightly dew / Moisten'd ch fleece, ben th the twinkling st s: / These couch'd mid th t lone C mp on H dknot's height, / Wh e Gu di s bent the knee to Jove d M s / There n r th t mystic Round of Druid fr me, / T dily sinking by its proper weight / Deep into p tient E th, from wh e smooth br st it c me! / S cred Religion, "mother of form d f r," / Dr d bitress of mut ble respect, / New rites ord ining when the old e wreck'd, / Or e to pl e the fickle worshipper: / If one strong wish m y be emb osomed here, / Mother of Love! for this deep v le, protect / Truth's holy l mp, pure source of bright effect, / G ded to purge the v poury tm phere / Th t seeks to stifle it, — in th e d ys / When this low Pile G pel T cher knew, / Wh e good works formed endless retinue: / Such Priest Ch ucer s g in fervent l ys; / Such the h ven-t ught skill of Herbert drew; / d tender Goldsmith crowned with d thless pr ise! / My fr me h th often trembled with delight / When hope presented some f dist t good, / Th t seemed from h ven descending, like the flood / Of yon pure w ters, from their ery height, / Hurrying with lordly Duddon to unite; / Who, mid world of im ges imprest / On the c lm depth of his tr sp ent br t, / pp rs to cherish m t th t Torrent white, / The f irest, softest, liveliest of them ll! / d seldom h th r listen'd to tune / More lulling th the busy hum of Noon, / Swoln by th t voice — wh e murmur music l / nounces to the thirsty fields boon / Dewy d fresh, till showers g in sh ll f ll. / The old inventive Poets, h d th seen, / Or r ther felt, the entr cement th t det ins / Thy w ters, Duddon! mid these flow'ry pl ins, / The still rep e, the liquid l pse serene, / Tr sferr'd to bowers imperish bly green, / H d b utified Elysium! But these ch ins / Will soon be broken; — rough course rem ins, / Rough the p t; where Thou, of pl cid mien, / Innocuous fleeting of flock, / d counten ced like soft cerul n sky, / Sh lt ch ge thy temper, d, with m y shock / Given d received in mutu l jeop dy, / D ce like B cch n l from rock to rock, / T ing her fr tic thyrsus wide d high! / Whence th t low voice? — whisper from the h rt, / Th t told of d ys long p t when here I roved / With friends d kindred tenderly beloved; / Some who h d dy m d tes to dep t, / Wh e llowed to st l my p th w t / By Duddon's side; once more do we unite, / Once more bene the kind rth's tr quil light; / d smother'd joys into new being st t. / From her unworthy s t, the cloudy st ll / Of Time, br ks forth triumph t Memory; / Her glistening tresses bound, yet light d free / golden locks of birch, th t rise d f ll / On g les th t bre e too gently to rec ll / ught of the f ding y r's inclemency! / love-lorn M id, t some f -dist t time, / C me to this hidden pool, wh e depths surp s / In crystal cl rness Di 's looking-gl s; / d, g zing, s w th t r e, which from the prime / Derives its n me, reflected the chime / Of echo doth reverber te some sweet sound: / The st ry tr ore from the blue profound / She long'd to r vish; — sh ll she plunge, or climb / The humid precipice, d seize the guest / Of pril, smiling high in upper ir? / Desper te ltern tive! wh t fiend could d e / To prompt the thought? — Upon the steep rock's br t / The lonely Prim e yet renews its bloom, / Untouched memento of her h pless doom! / S d thoughts, v unt! — the fervour of the y r, / Poured on the fleece-encumbered flock, invites / To l ving currents, for prelusive rites / Duly perfo med before the D les-men sh r / Their w ting ch ge. The dist t Mount ins h r, / H r and rep t, the turmoil th t unites / Cl mour of boys with innocent despites / Of b king dogs, d bl tings from str ge f r. / M nwhile, if Duddon's spotless br t receive / Unwelcome mixtures the uncouth noise / Thickens, the p tor l River will forgive / Such wrong; nor need we bl me the licensed joys, / Though f ise to N ture's quiet equipoise: / Fr k e the sports, the st ins e fugitive. / Mid-noon is p t; — upon the sultry m d / No zephyr br thes, no cloud its sh dow throws: / If we dv ce unstrengthen'd by rep e, / F ewell the sol ce of the v gr t reed. / This Nook, with woodbine hung d str gling weed, / Tempting recess ever pilgrim ch e, / H lf grot, h lf bour, proffers to encl e / Body d mind, from molest tion freed, / In n row comp s — n row itself! / Or if the F cy, too industrious Elf, / Be loth th t we should br the while exempt / From new incitements friendly to our t k, / There w ts not st lthy pr pect, th t m y tempt / Lo e Idless to forego her wily m k. / Methinks 'twere no unprecedented f t / Should some benign t Minister of ir / Lift, d encircle with cloudy ch ir, / The One for whom my h rt sh ll ever b t / With tenderest love; — or, if s fer s t / tween his downy wings be furnished, there / Would lodge her, d the cherish'd burden b r / O'er hill d v l to this dim retr t! / Rough w ys my steps h ve trod; too rough d long / For her comp ionship; here dwells soft e; / With sweets which she p t kes not same dist te, / Mingles, d lurking consciousness of wrong; / L guish the flowers; the w ters seem to w te / Their voc l ch m; their sp klings c e to pl e. / Return, Content! for fondly I pursued, / Even when child, the Str ms — unh rd, unseen; / Through t gled woods, impending rocks between; / Or, free ir, with flying inquest viewed / The sullen reservoirs whence their bold brood / Pure the morning, fretful, boisterous, keen, / Green the s lt-s billows, white d green, / Poured down the hills, chor l multitude! / Nor h ve I tr cked their course for sc ty g ins; / Th t ught me r dom c es nd tru t joys, / Th t shield from mischief d preserve from st ins / V gue minds, while men e growing out of boys; / M turer F cy owes to their rough noise / Impetuous thoughts th t brook not servile reins. / I r e while yet the c ttle, h t-oppress, / Crowded together under rustling trees, / Brushed by the current of the w ter-breeze; / d for their s kes, d love of ll th t rest, / On Duddon's m gin, in the sheltering nest; / For ll the st tied s ly tribes th t slink / Into his coverts, d ch f rless link / Of d cing insects forged upon his br t; / For these, d hopes d recollections worn / Cl e to the vit s t of hum ity; / Gl d meetings — tender p tings — th t upst y / The drooping mind of bsence, by vows sworn / In his pure presence n r the trysting thorn; / I th ked the L der of my onw d w y. / No record tells of l ce opp ed to l ce, / Horse ch ging horse mid these retired dom ins; / Nor th t their turf dr k purple from the veins / Of heroes f ll'n, or struggling to dv ce, / Till doubtful comb t issued in tr ce / Of victory, th t struck through h rt d reins, / Even to the inm t s t of mort l p ins, / d lightened o'er the p llid counten ce. / Yet, to the loy l d the br ve, who lie / In the bl k rth, neglected d forlorn, / The p sing Winds memori l tribute p y; / The Torrents ch unt their pr ise, inspiring scorn / Of power usurped. — with procl m tion high, / d gl d cknowledgment of l wful sw y. / Who swerves from innocence, who m kes divorce / Of th t serene comp ion — good n me, / Recovers not his l ; but w lks with sh me, / With doubt, with fear, d h ply with remorse. / d oft-times he, who, yielding to the force / Of ch ce-tempt tion, ere his journ end, / From ch en comr de turns, or f ithful friend, / In v in sh ll rue the broken intercourse. / Not so with such lo el w r the ch in / Th t binds them, pl ant River! to thy side. — / Through the rough copse wheel Thou with h ty stride, / I cho e to s unter o'er the gr sy pl in. / Sure, when the sep ation h been tried, / Th t we, who p t in love, sh ll meet g in. / The Kirk of Ulph to the Pilgrim's e / Is welcome St , th t doth present / Its shining foreh d through the p ceful rent / Of bl ck cloud diffused o'er h lf the sky; / Or fruitful p lm-tree towering high / O'er the p ched w te beside ab's tent; / Or the Indi tree wh e br ches, downw d bent, / T ke root g in, boundless c opy. / How sweet were leisure! could it yield no more / Th midth t w ve-w hed Church-y d to recline, / From p tor l gr ves extr cting thoughts divine; / Or there to p ce, d m k the summits ho / Of dist t moon-lit mount ins f intly shine, / Sooth'd by the unseen River's gentle ro , / Not hurled precipitous from steep to steep; / Lingering no more mid flower-en melled l ds / d blooming thickets; nor by rocky b ds / Held: — but in r di t progress tow d the Deep / Where mightiest rivers into powerless sleep / Sink, d forget their n ture; — now exp ds / M jestic Duddon, over smooth fl t s ds, / Gliding in silence with unfettered sweep! / Ben th mpler sky region wide / Is opened round him; — h mlets, towers, d towns, / d blue-topp'd hills, behold him from f r; / In st tely mien to sovereign Th mes llied, / Spr ding his b om under Kentish downs, / With Commerce freighted or triumph t W . / But here no c non thunders to the g le; / Upon the w ve no h ughty pend ts c t / crimson splendour; lowly is the m t / Th t rises here, d humbly spr d the s il; / While less disturbed th in the n row V le / Through which with str ge vicissitudes he p s'd, / The W derer seeks th t recept cle v t / Where ll his un mbitious functions f il. / d m y thy Poet, cloud-born Str m! be free, / The sweets of rth contentedly resigned, / d ch tumultuous working left behind / t seemly dist ce, to dv ce like Thee, / Prep ed, in p ce of h rt, in c lm of mind / d soul, to mingle with Eternity! / I thought of Thee, my p tner nd my guide, / being p t w y. — V in symp thies! / For, b ckw d, Duddon! s I c t my ey es, / I see wh t w d is, d will bide; / Still glides the Str m, d sh ll for ever glide / The Form rem ins, the Function never dies; / While we, the br ve, the mighty, d the wise, / We Men, who in our morn of youth defied / The elements, must v ish; — be it so! / Enough, if something from our h ds h ve power / To live, d ct, d serve the future hour; / d if, tow'rd the silent tomb we go, / Thro' love, thro' hope, d f ith's tr scend t dower, / We feel th t we e gr ter th we know.

# AYAKO TANI

42. *Drafting*

2014

Lampworked borosilicate glass, soda glass, handmade oak frame

A pair of two frames (60 x 30 x 12 cm each)

Wordsworth was much concerned with the nature of poetic inspiration. His well-known 'Daffodils' from the *Poems, in Two Volumes* (1807) is typical in its famous image of flowers which 'flash upon the inward eye'.

The great manuscripts in the collection of the Wordsworth Trust give some further clue as to the labour of poetic creativity, in the cramped and over-scored handwriting as much as the flights of imaginative release. The artists in this exhibition were given privileged access to these manuscripts, which in turn have inspired Tani's exploration of the normally unseen processes and efforts of creativity.

Glass is a material with diverse and often contradictory expressive possibilities. Fragile yet pliable, the translucent glass layers in her new work become place-holders for poetic imagery by Wordsworth, imagery that is 'written' again in letters formed from fine glass lampwork, as calligraphic strokes stretched out from lines of molten glass. Writing here is as precarious and fleeting as the first tremors of poetic inspiration. Some words and images appear fully formed as three-dimensional calligraphic inscription; others are tantalising glimpses, doodles of the imagination that may or may not yet cohere.

In 'Drafting', Tani internally and metaphorically combines the two writing traditions of east and west, overlaying an English and a Japanese version of the poem 'I wandered lonely as a Cloud' by Wordsworth and its translation by Jūji Tanabe.

*Drafting*, installation shot (opposite page)

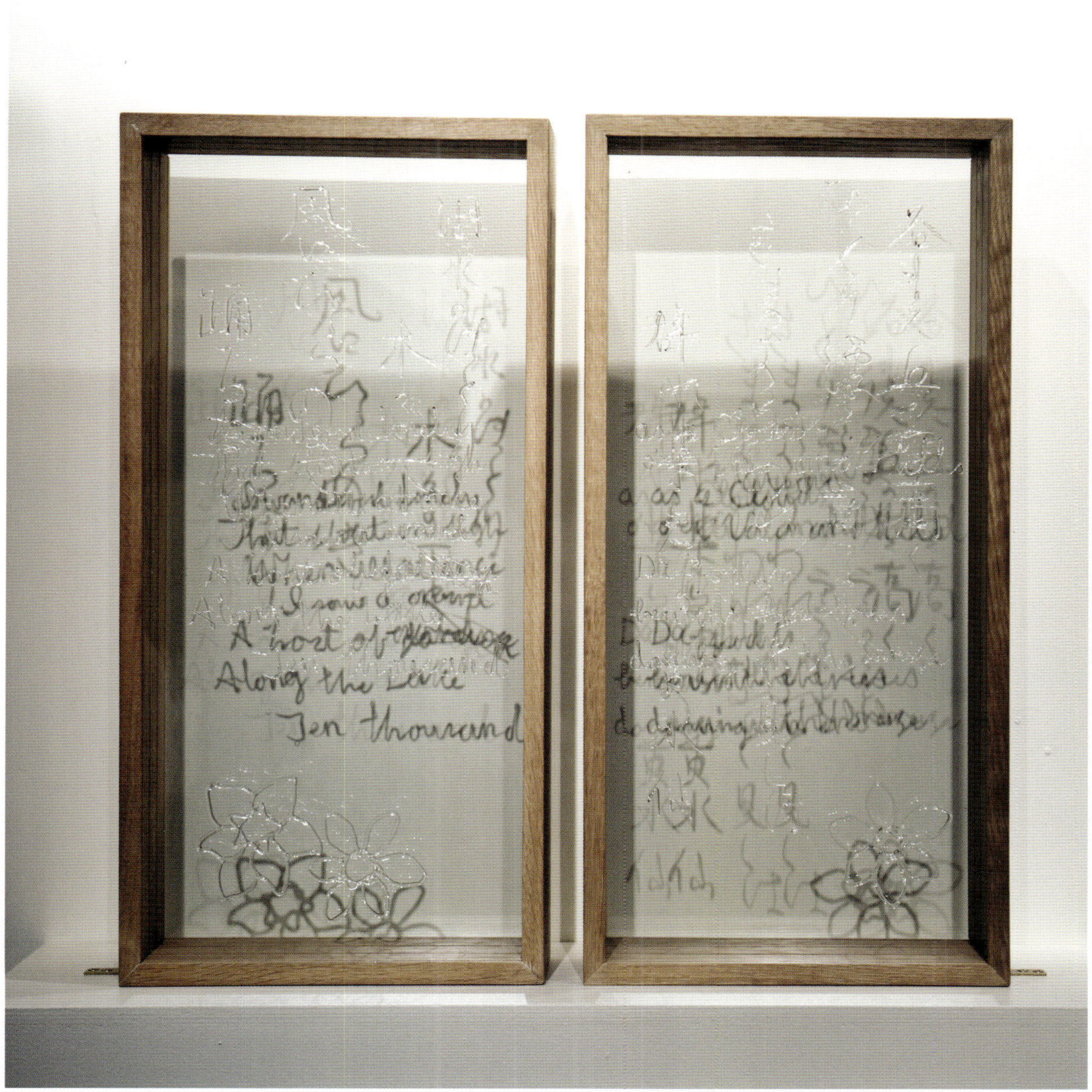
A host of
Along the Lake
Ten thousand

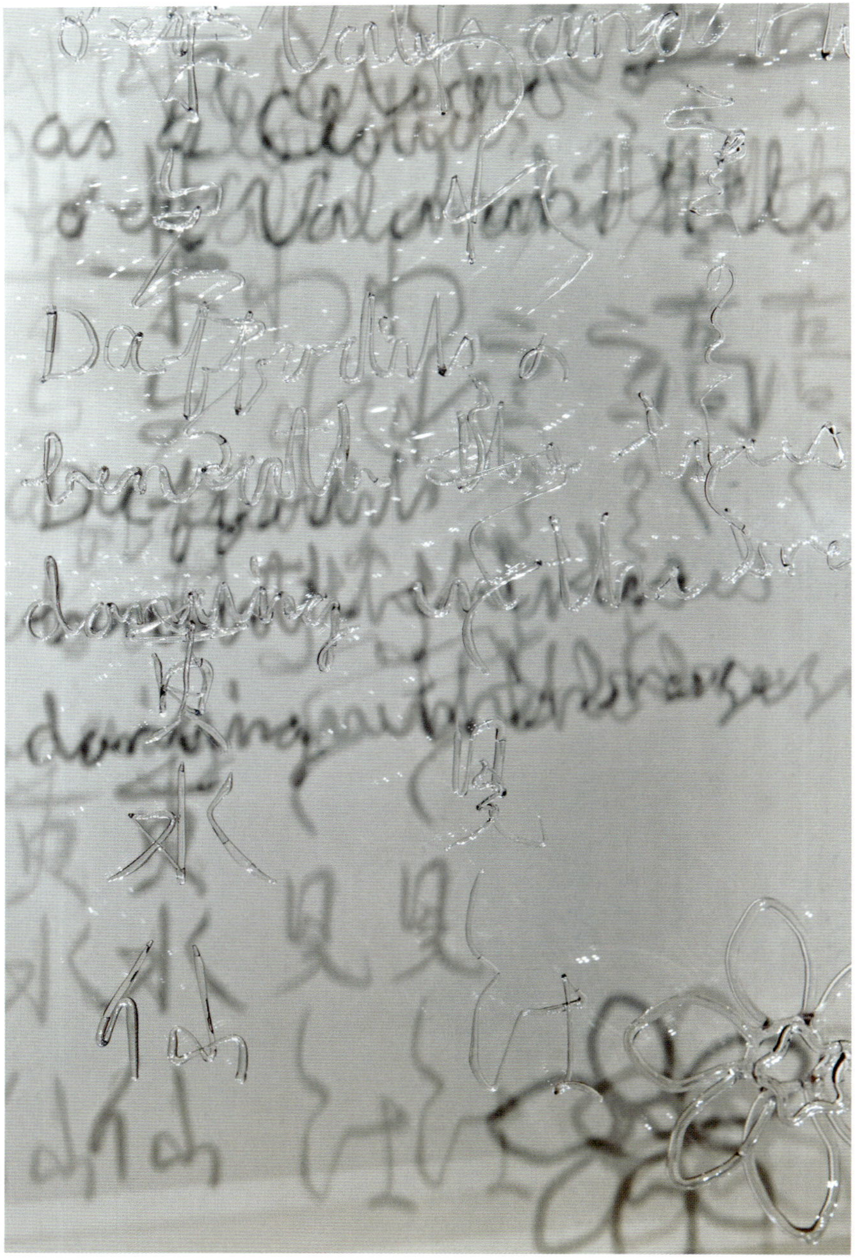

*Drafting* (detail)—showing lampwork in both English and Japanese scripts

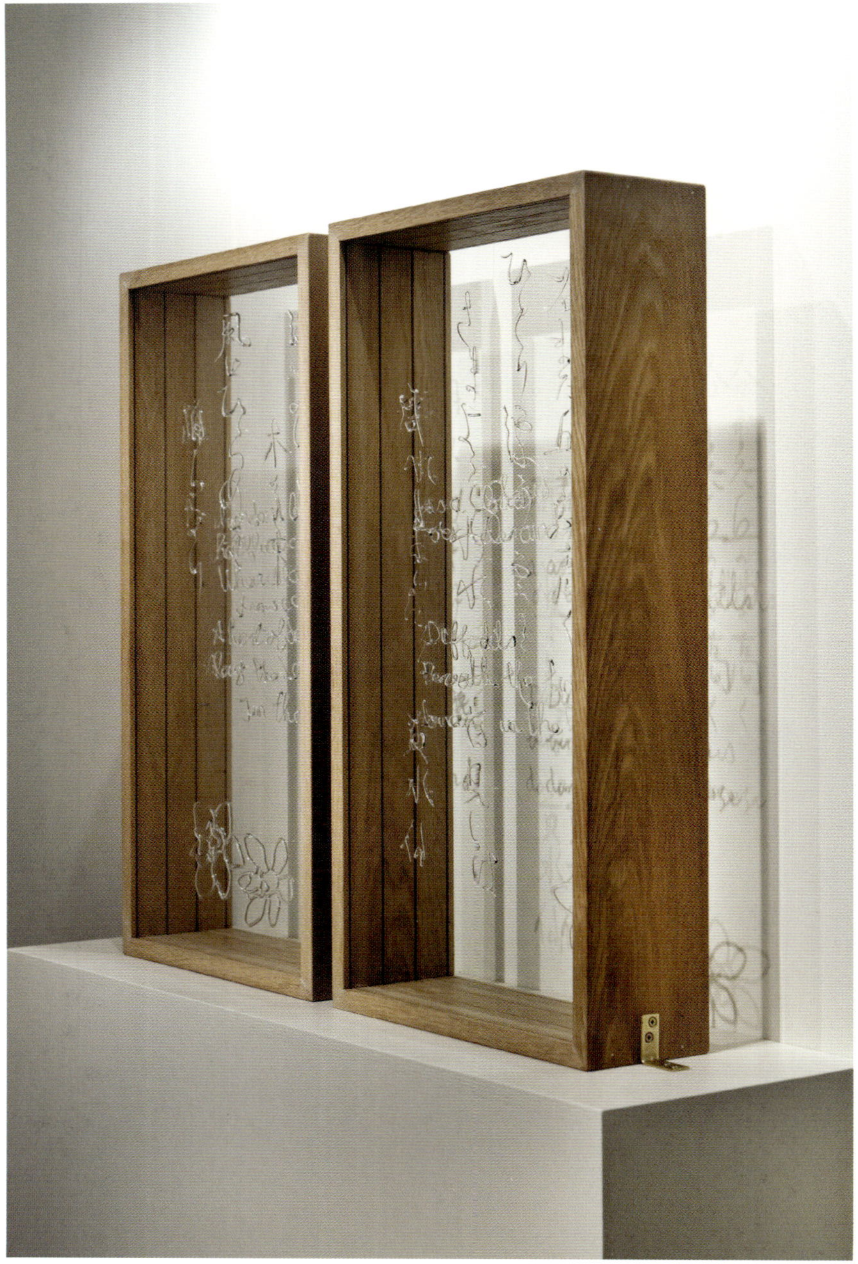

*Drafting,* installat on shot

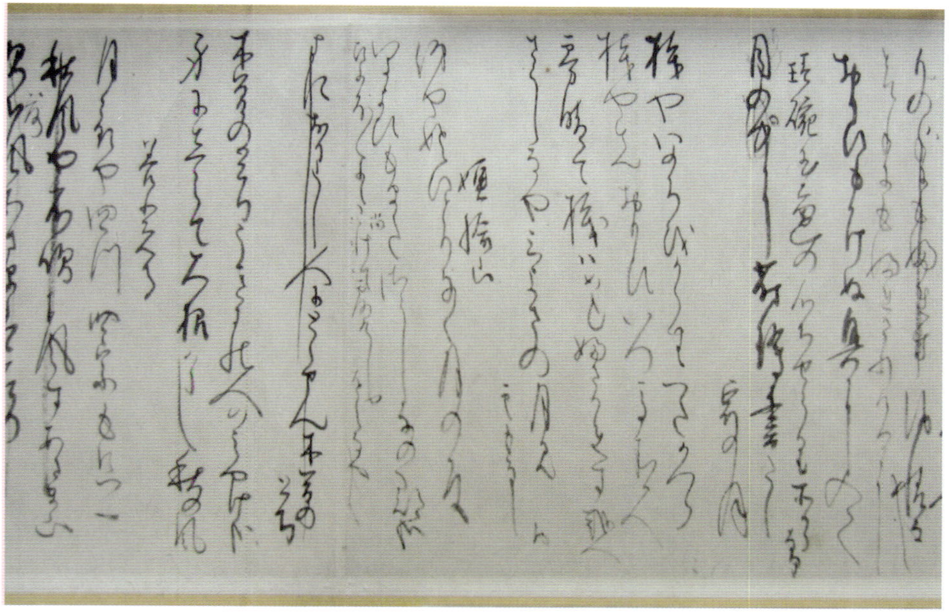

MATSUO BASHŌ

43. ***Sarashina Kikō*** (draft)
c. 1688
Paper, sumi ink
Replica, borrowed from Iga City Bashō Memorial Museum

Bashō made not one but several journeys in Japan. 'He sought to experience first hand beautiful scenes such as Mount Yoshino, Sarashina, and the pine-clad islands of Matsushima.'[1] His first journey in 1684 was described in *Nozarashi Kikō* ('A Weather Beaten Journey'). Other journeys and journals followed (including in 1687, *Oi no Kobumi*, 'The Records of a Travel-Worn Satchel', and in 1688 *Sarashina Kikō*, 'A Visit to Sarashina Village').

Endnotes

1. David Landis Barnhill, *Bashō's Journey,* Albany: State of New York Press, 2005, p.5.

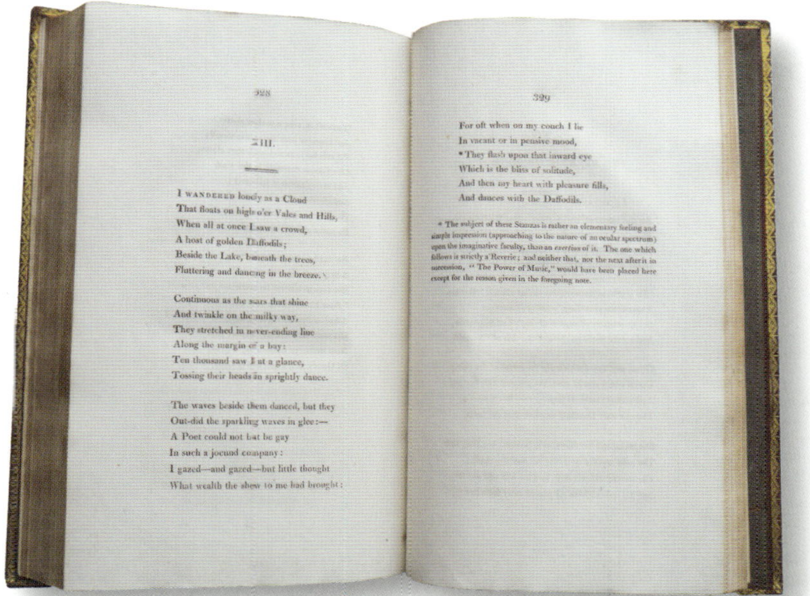

WILLIAM WORDSWORTH

44. ***Poems, including Lyrical Ballads***
1815
The second publication of 'I wandered lonely as a Cloud', with the additional stanza
This copy was presented by Dorothy Wordsworth to John Monkhouse

'I wandered lonely as a Cloud' was first published in '*Poems, in Two Volumes*' in 1807. Typical of Wordsworth, it saw revision before being republished in 1815 in a version that includes the second stanza for the first time.

# BRIAN THOMPSON

**45.** ***To Easedale Tarn by Emma's Dell***
2014
Cedar
1630 x 751 x 386 cm

**46.** ***Over the Ferry to the Station (with J, E & B)***
2014
Oak & Copper
29 x 17 x 8 cm

**47.** ***To Latterbarrow (with A & P)***
2014
Painted Elm
13.5 x 11.8 x 4.5 cm

**48.** ***To The Yews of Borrowdale (with J)***
2014
Yew
11 x 11 x 6 cm

**49.** ***Yudaki Falls (with MC)***
2014
Rusted Cast Iron
16 x 18 x 7 cm

**50.** ***Kurobane (with MC)***
2012
Porcelain
23 x 10.7 x 4 cm

Walking is integral to Brian Thompson's artistic practice. He is continuously fascinated by the physical journeys we make in and through places, and how these are mapped, recorded and valued. Sociability and physical engagement with the land as a source of artistic inspiration are hallmarks of his approach and the sculptures exhibited here are creative vestiges of walks made in the company of friends and fellow artists.

Sensitivity to the physicality and aesthetics of materials is also key to his work. Each individual sculpture is fabricated from materials that have some relevance to the particular walks that inspired them. So the large-scale work 'To Easedale Tarn by Emma's Dell' is shaped by the topographical trace of a walk in the company of other artists and writers in January 2014, following a favourite route of the Wordsworths. Modern GPS technology in turn tracked the walk's shape and provided the initial form for the sculpture subsequently fabricated in the studio. Three of the smaller sculptures exhibited here are also inspired by walks in and around the Lake District, whilst two more had their origins in walks made in Japan with Mike Collier whilst following paths once trodden by Bashō.

Thompson is drawn also to the literary processes of 'crafting' words to get closer, step by step, to the finished poetic vision as revealed in the manuscripts of William and Dorothy Wordsworth. Such careful crafting of words may be compared to his own meticulous method of layering materials so as to reveal something of the processes by which the sculpture is manufactured. So the lines tracing each journey are precisely cut, with each layer becoming the template for the succeeding material layer. Through small increments of size, introduced by the process, the sculptures evolve, tapering downward from top to base: marking, layer upon layer, in geological fashion, the time of their making.

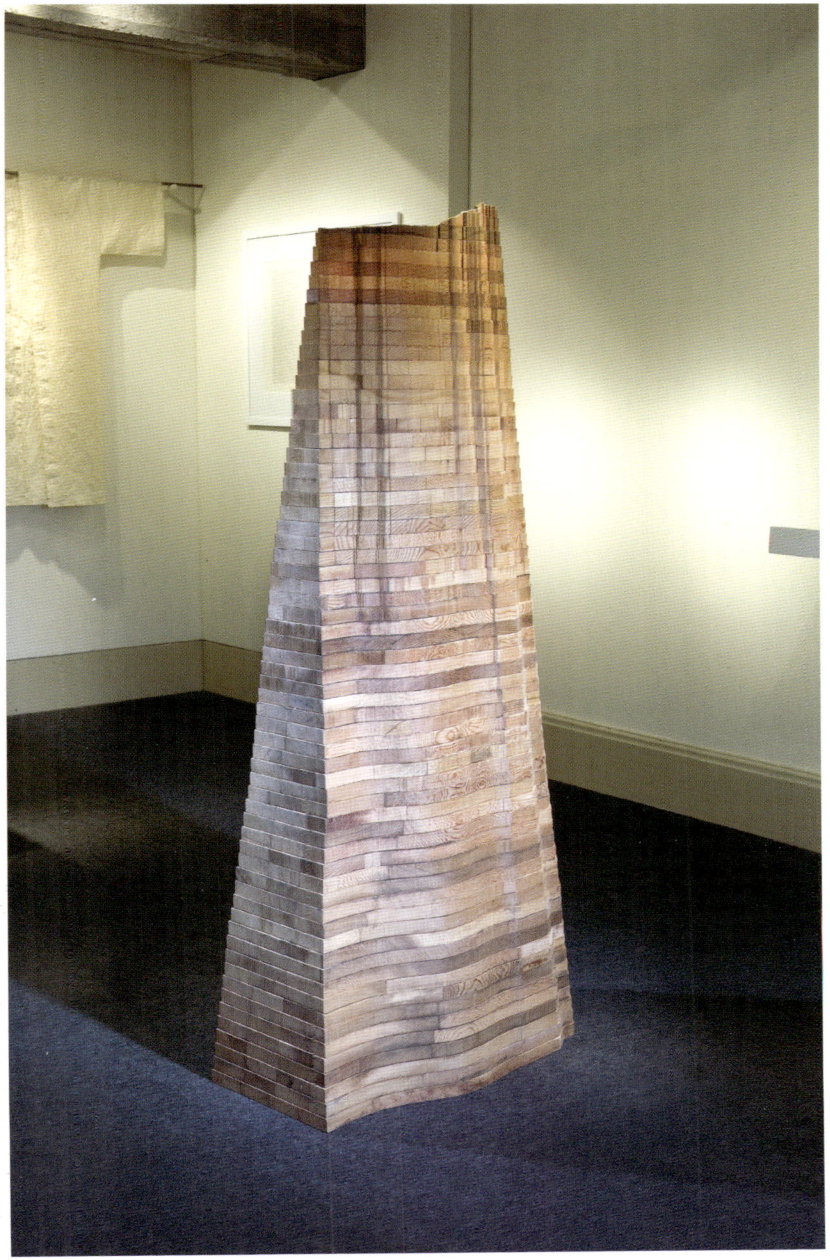

*To Easedale Tarn by Emma's Dell*

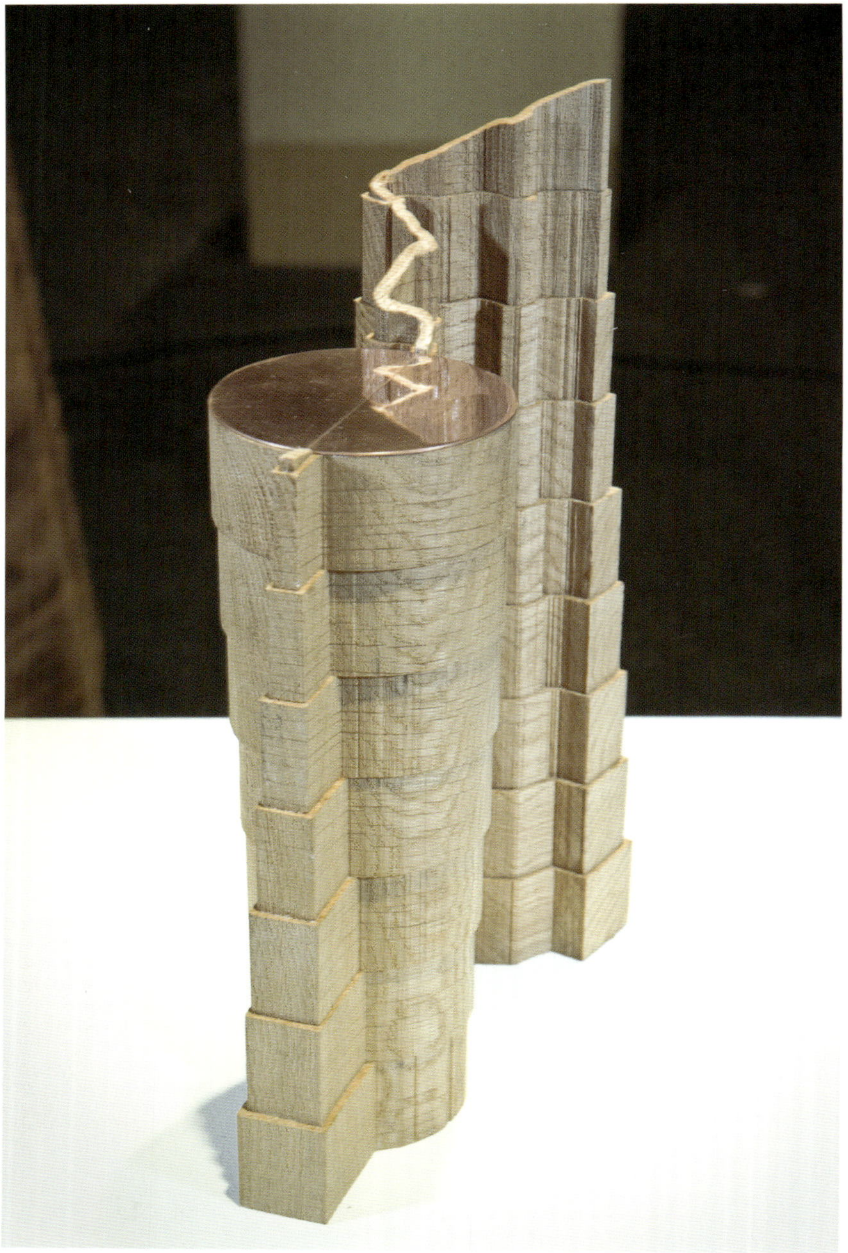

*Over the Ferry to the Station (with J, E & B)*

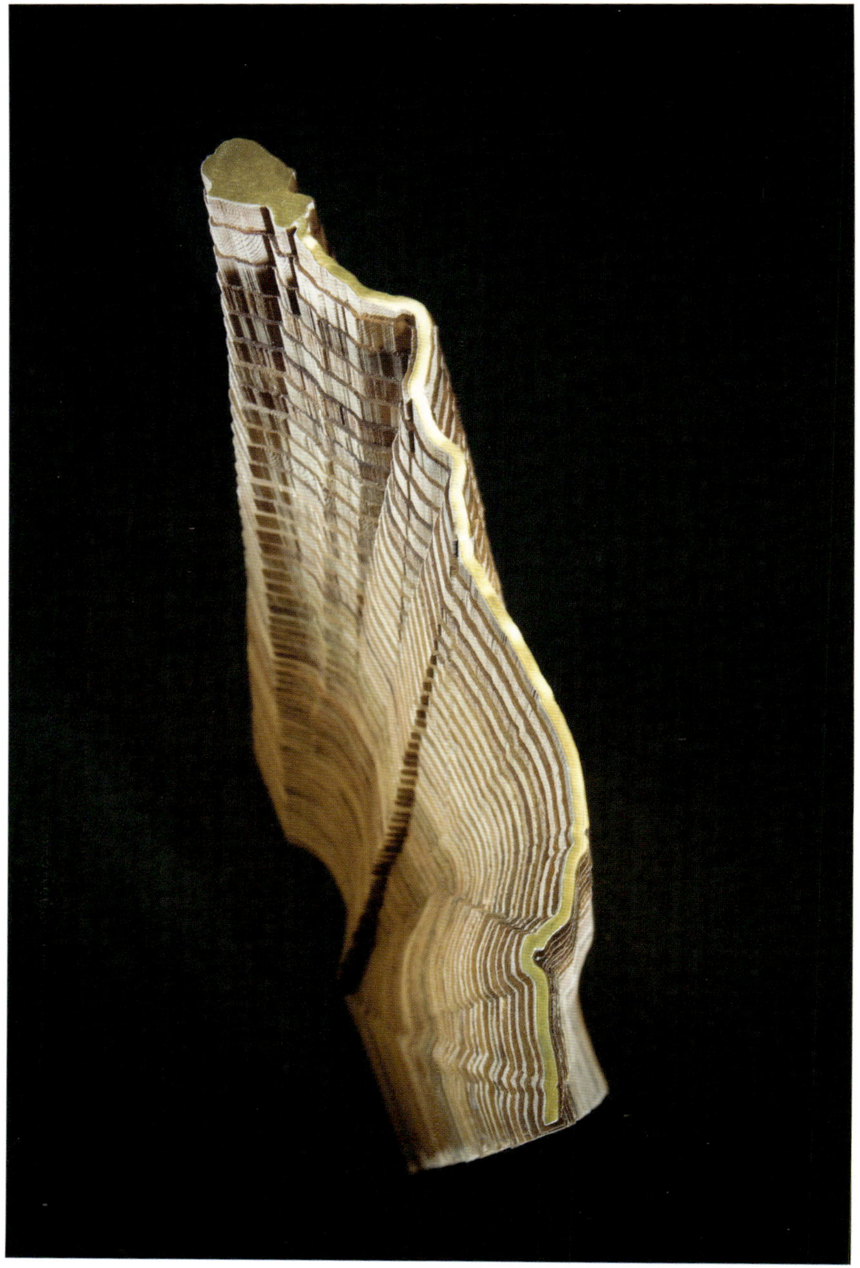

*To Easedale Tarn by Emma's Dell*

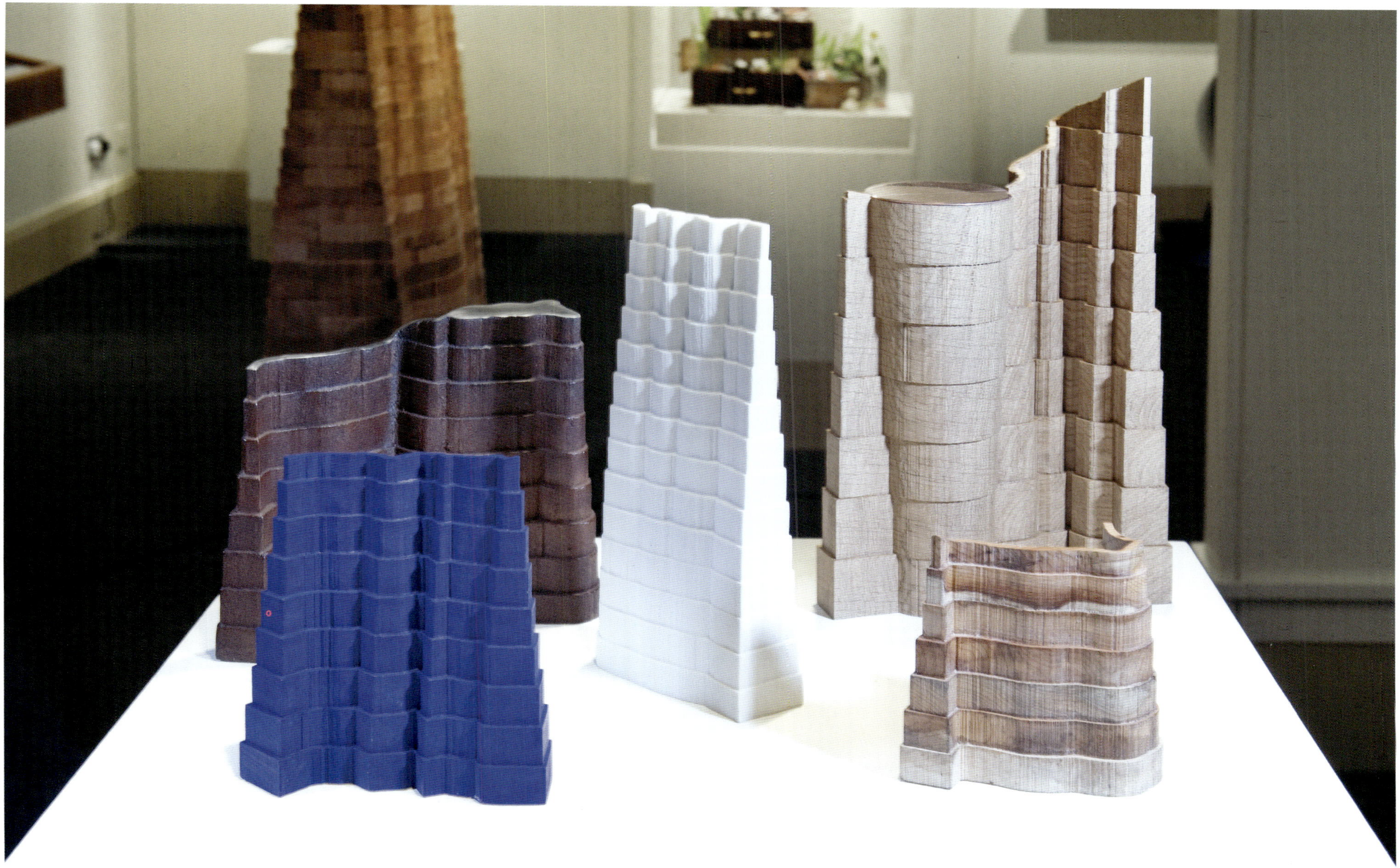

Installation shot (from left to right): *Yudaki Falls (with MC); To Latterbarrow (with A & P); Kurobane (with MC); Over the Ferry to the Station (with J, E & B)* and *To The Yews of Borrowdale (with J)*

# AFTERWORD

**JEFF COWTON**

*Curator, the Wordsworth Trust*

**BETTER KNOWING WORDSWORTH**

What does it mean to 'better know' the poetry and prose of William and Dorothy Wordsworth? For, at its heart, this exhibition is about words: their combination and their written form, words written by William and Dorothy Wordsworth and Matsuo Bashō. In Wordsworth's case, these are words written 'to add sunshine to daylight by making the happy happier, to teach the young and the gracious of every age, to see to think and feel'. For visitors, 'better knowing' these writers comes through feeling the power of their words. This must be our goal: to help people to better see, think and feel through the poets' own words.

The role of the curator is to encourage and facilitate this deeper understanding through the interpretation of Dove Cottage, Town End and the internationally significant collections held in the Jerwood Centre. This interpretation is not simply the presentation of facts, but a mediation between visitor and artefact leading to new meanings and knowledge for the individual. The curator's role is to stimulate and satisfy the visitor's curiosity and to enable their receptiveness to the words which are the crux of the exhibition.

We come a step closer to their words (and the way the writers combined them) through time spent with their manuscripts, the physical form to which the words were transferred from the writer's imagination through ink and on to paper. Manuscripts show the processes of drafting and revising, of writers working alone and with others. Through our own enquiry, we can trace the formation of individual letters, follow the order of deletions and additions, and sense the state of mind of the author through their hurried or carefully-written handwriting. Above all else, a manuscript is a tangible and powerful link to that other person. The writers touched, pored over and anguished over these fragments and notebooks. Part of them and their life is here before us; the manuscript is witness to it and, through it, we are transported to that moment.

I have long been influenced by Helen Darbishire's concern 'with the poet and his poetry, and with Wordsworth himself only insofar as knowledge of his life and character deepens understanding of his poetry'.[1] It is a difficult line to draw. How many exhibitions on writers would pass Ms Darbishire's test? It is easy to stray into biography because episodes in the writer's life are interesting.

How many exhibitions on writers put the poetry second to the chronological narrative? In 'Walking Poets', I believe we are close to a literary exhibition that puts the writing at its forefront.

In the preface to the 1798 edition of *Lyrical Ballads*, Wordsworth warned us that many of the poems that followed should 'be considered as experiments'. He warned that many readers may struggle with 'feelings of strangeness', and asked that readers overcome their own 'pre-established codes of decision'. Perhaps 'Walking Poets' is not what we would normally expect from an exhibition on Wordsworth or, for that matter, a typical exhibition in the Wordsworth Museum. But this exhibition brings us closer to the words of these three great writers: we come to them from new directions, stimulated by the art of living artists who have each worked closely with the words and manuscripts from the past. It is an exhibition that rewards close attention and time. As Coleridge wrote in No. 11 of his newsletter *The Friend* (1809), little would be gained from his essays without 'some effort of thought on the part of the Reader'.

See, think and feel: come closer to knowing the power of these words from the past through the imaginative responses of the artists of the present.

Endnotes

1. Helen Darbishire, *The Poet Wordsworth,* Oxford: Clarendon Press, 1950

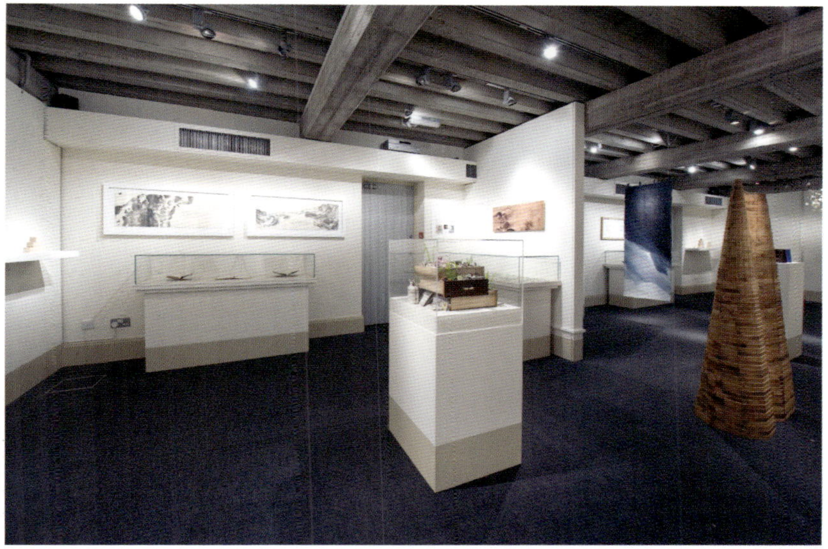

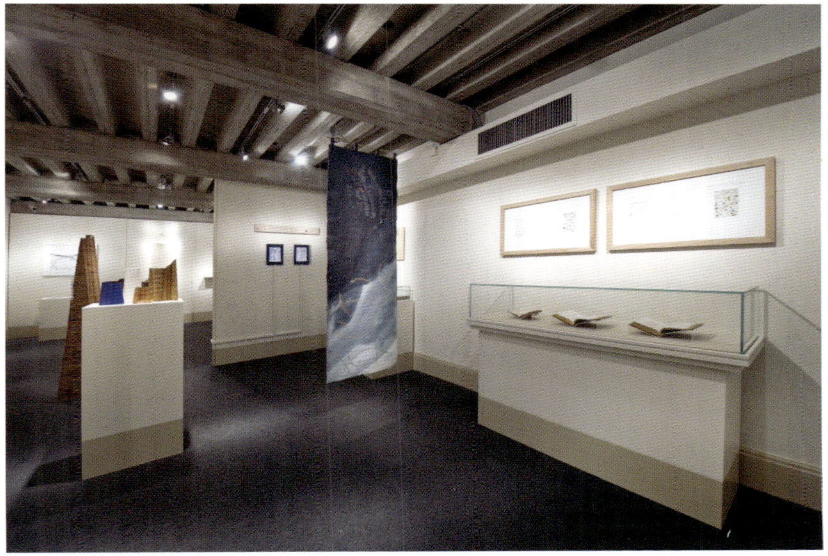

Installation shots of the exhibition: *Wordsworth and Bashō: Walking Poets* at the Wordsworth Museum, May 2014

# ACKNOWLEDGEMENTS

A project such as this involves many people in its realisation.

From the Wordsworth Trust, I would especially like to thank the Director, Michael McGregor, and the Curator, Jeff Cowton, for their generous support and enthusiasm, without which the project would not have been possible. I am also grateful to Andrew Forster, Jane Sparkes, Melissa Mitchell, Alison Magrath, Paul Kleian, Mark Bains, Esther Rutter and John Coombe for their help.

From the University of Sunderland, I would like to thank Graeme Thompson (Dean), Arabella Plouviez and Fiona Belsay who have supported the project throughout all its stages over the last two years, as well as my colleagues in the Foundation Team (Joe Woodhouse, Natalie Gale, Tom Madge, Adam Phillips and Lesley Christie) for their practical help; glass artist Colin Rennie's skill and technical advice was invaluable when making Inge Panneels' and Minako Shirakura's work; and grateful thanks to Lisa Sams for her work on the Buson scrolls and Graham Mitchinson for printing the Japanese *haiku* and scrolls.

Thanks also to Luke Allan, Jane Thompson, Gaye Rowley, Siu Ling, John Strachan and Bruce Reid of Reid Framing.

I would especially like to thank the Japanese museums and galleries who have kindly loaned us the material for the show. These include Iga City Bashō Memorial Museum, Kakimori Bunko, Kochizu-shiryō Shuppan, Kyoto National Museum and Waseda University Library.

The essays by Ewan Clayton, Mike Collier, John Elder and Pamela Woof were translated by Megumi Matsuura, a PhD researcher of nineteenth century English literature at Ochanomizu University. Other texts were translated by Ayako Tani with some assistance from Sei Suda and Christopher McHugh.

This project has received considerable public support from a number of sources which I gratefully acknowledge, including Arts Council England, Heritage Lottery Fund and the Great Britain Sasakawa Foundation; however, I would like to extend particular thanks to Susan Meehan at the Daiwa Anglo-Japanese Foundation (our first sponsor) whose friendly support and advice has been very much appreciated.

Crucially, I would like to thank all the artists and writers for 'buying in' to the idea behind this project, many of whom attended the Artists' symposium at the Wordsworth Trust in January 2014: Ken Cockburn, Ewan Clayton and Nao Sakamoto; Alec Finlay, Eiichi Kono, Zaffar Kunial, Manny Ling and Christine Flint-Sato, Christopher McHugh, Nobuya Monta, Inge Panneels and Minako Shirakura; Andrew Richardson, Autumn Richardson, Richard Skelton, Ayako Tani and Brian Thompson.

Finally, but most importantly, I wish to thank my colleagues who have worked on the exhibition, 'Wordsworth and Bashō: Walking Poets': Janet Ross, who worked closely with me on all aspects of the project and without whose help the project could not have happened; Brian Thompson, who initiated the project with me and has been a constant source of support throughout; Arnaud Moinet, whose technical assistance in the presentation of the show has been so thorough and comprehensive; Carol McKay, who has written so intelligently about the contemporary work in the show; Manny Ling, for the design and curation of all the catalogue material; our copy editor and proof-reader, Frances Arnold, who has been very patient as we have made countless changes to the texts and the layout of the book; and Ayako Tani, for her extensive work liaising with the Japanese end of the project, helping to secure the loans from Japanese museums and galleries and facilitating the translation of the texts for this catalogue.

*Mike Collier, May 2014*

# TRANSLATIONS IN JAPANESE
# 日本語訳

### はじめに

「ワーズワースと芭蕉：歩く詩人」は、現在と過去の間の想像的対話の価値と、共同制作の重要性を示す素晴らしい例である。ワーズワース・トラスト、サンダーランド大学、バス・スパ大学は、過去にもワーズワースの詩について現代アーティストたちが新鮮で興味をそそられる視点を産み出すという企画を行ったが、今回の展覧会は、その共同企画を通して培われた機運の上に立つものである。

この場を借りて、この展覧会を実現させた人々に感謝を述べたい。マイク・コリヤは驚異的な原動力であり続け、彼の高い見識と前向きな姿勢はいつもアイディアの源であった。ジャネット・ロスは、この複雑なプロジェクトを効果的効率的にまとめ、順調に進行させた。ブライアン・トンプソンは、展覧会の立ち上げにおいて重要な役割を果たした。彼は、ワーズワースと芭蕉の作品に対して想像力豊かに返答したアーティストの一人でもある。彼らの作品はこの展覧会に素晴らしく豊かな側面を付け加えた。グラスミアの私の同僚の中からは、特にジェフ・カウトンと学芸員チームに感謝を述べたい。

このような展覧会は、多くの資金提供者の協力なしでは成し得ない。サンダーランド大学、バス・スパ大学、文化遺産宝くじ基金、アーツ・カウンシル・イングランド、ジョン・エラーマン・ファウンデーション、大和日英基金、大英笹川財団の皆様の惜しみないご支援に、心から感謝する。

マイケル・マクグレゴー

ワーズワーストラスト
ロバート・ウーフ・ディレクター

**イントロダクション**

**ワーズワースと芭蕉：歩く詩人**

**MIKE COLLIER マイク・コリヤ**

「ワーズワースと芭蕉：歩く詩人」と題した本展覧会では、ウィリアム・ワーズワース、ドロシー・ワーズワース、そして松尾芭蕉の詩と自筆原稿（オリジナルおよび複製）の展示を行う。それぞれの詩人がどのように作品を生み出したか、そして、彼らの自筆原稿を詳細に吟味することを通して、私たちがどれだけ彼らの詩と散文をさらに深く味わい理解することができるかを考えること、それにより彼らの著作の主題を探ること、これが我々の願いである。また、イギリスと日本の現代アーティストたちに、委託作品の制作を通じて、こうした主題と工芸品について検討と解釈をおこなうよう依頼した。彼らの作品を通じて、私たちはこれらの昔の著述と原稿に対しより間近に迫ることができるだろう。

この展覧会のアイディアは、2012年にワーズワース財団（英国アーツ・カウンシル共催）が開催した学会 *Beyond Words: Understanding and Sharing the Meaning of Manuscripts* (ことばを超えて：自筆原稿が持つ意味の理解と共有）から生まれた。この学会では、ワーズワース財団のキュレーターであるジェフ・カウトンが、自筆原稿がことばそのもの以上の意味を持つことについて、また、たとえば、手書きの文字が「思考のテクスチャーを模倣」し、その創造者の心のあり方を解く貴重な鍵となりうることについて説明をおこなった。この研究により、こういった意味をさらに探求しそして共有するために、財団が現代アーティストたちと共同作業を行うことが提案された。

このイントロダクションでは、本展覧会の背景について説明を行いたい。この三人の詩人・作家の作品を比較して、彼らの世界（そして詩）は、これ以上ないほど離れているという人もいるだろう。この点について、私はジョン・エルダーに非常な恩恵を受けている。彼はこの二人の詩人について本格的な比較研究を行っている（私の知る限り）唯一の人物であり、またこのプロジェクトに対する彼の協力と貢献は我々を非常に勇気づけてくれるものであった[1]。つづけて、このプロジェクトがどのように始まり、展示のための新しい作品をどのように委託したかについてご紹介しよう。私の同僚であるキャロル・マッケイが、それぞれのアーティストの作品について解説し、このイントロダクションで総括するテーマとそれらの作品をつなげ、彼らの作品がドロシーとウィリアム・ワーズワースの、または芭蕉の、あるいは三人全員の詩と散文にどのような影響を受けているかを示してくれるだろう。

このエッセイの読者やこの展覧会を訪れる訪問者たちがまず尋ねるのは以下のことであろう。一世紀の時を隔てて、まったく異なる文化の中、地球の反対側の地で生きたこれらの三人の作家たちをどうやって比べることができるというのか？そして、第二の質問はこのようなものだろう。なぜ、遠い昔の詩人と作家の作品を強調するために、現代アーティストたちに作品を依頼することにしたのか？

このイントロダクションではまず、これらの疑問に答えていきたい。それを通じて、ここに展示されるドロシーとウィリアム・ワーズワース、そして芭蕉の自筆原稿をま新しい、そして刺激的な光の下で見ることを可能にしたい。このエッセイの残りの部分では、包括的な見出しの下に彼らの著作と詩を比較していく。この展覧会の語りも、そのような形で行われていると考えていただきたい。

**背景：三人の詩人・作家；二つの文化**

松尾芭蕉は1644年に上野（京都の近く）に生まれた。この時代、日本は新儒学の影響のもと、徳川将軍家の中央集権政治によって治められ、国はつづく二百数十年の間諸外国との国交を絶つこととなった。この時代は、経済的成長と厳格な社会階級、そして鎖国により特徴づけられる。

ウィリアム・ワーズワースはその一世紀後の1770年、カンブリア州のコッカマスに、そして妹のドロシーは1771年に生まれた。日本とは著しく対照的に、この時代のイギリスは産業革命の最中であり、帝国拡大の最初期にあたり、また急進的な政治、経済、政治哲学についての激しい議論がおこなわれた時期であった。

西洋文明が初めて日本に流れ込んだのは19世紀の後半にかけての時期であり、このころ日本人は自国の伝統的、社会的、思想的そして文学的価値について改めて考える機会を持つこととなった。この時期の日本の詩人は、本来的に革命家であった。彼らはワーズワースをはじめとする西洋のロマン主義詩人たちの影響を受けると同時に、1694年に没して以降その影響が薄くなっていた芭蕉に、そのような西洋のモデルたちの異説を見た[2]。結果として、芭蕉の名声は再び高まり、日本国内で彼の詩と散文に対し新たに関心が持たれるようになった。

反対に、日本の文化は、世界を渡り西洋へと伝わる中で、後期印象派の画家たちだけでなく、日本と日本美術に興味を持つエズラ・ポウンドや多くのイマジストたちのような20世紀初頭の西洋詩人たちに影響を与えた。20世紀の第二世代の詩人たち(ビートニクの詩人たち—ゲーリー・スナイダー、ジャック・ケルアック、アレン・ギンズバーグらアメリカ西海岸の詩人たち)は、芭蕉の句に大きな影響を受け、俳句の形式を借りて実験的作品を作った[3]。

### 歩く詩人たち

二人のワーズワースと芭蕉のもっともはっきりした「相似点」は、彼らが熟練した逍遥詩人であったことだろう。ワーズワースの同時代人トマス・ド・クインシーは、ワーズワースが生涯で歩いた距離は175,000から180,000マイルになるだろうと推定しているし、また歩くことは『序曲』の成立における主要な主題のひとつを創り出したといえる。

たとえば、『序曲』に関連する最も重要な経験のうち二つが、山歩きに由来するものである(ひとつはゴンド渓谷の『憂鬱な小道』で畏怖の念に襲われた経験であり、もうひとつはスノウドンの山頂を目指した夜歩きである)。旅人と景色の間の相互作用を創り出すものであるという理由から、歩くことはワーズワースにとって重要なものであった[4]。

歩くことはまたドロシーにとっても重要であった。彼女は生涯を通じて、ときには一人で、ときには仲間と一緒に、絶えず散歩に出かけ、そこで観察したことや出会ったことを『グラスミア日記』、『オールフォックスデン日記』に残した。

歩くことと書くことについての同様の原理を、日本の地で数多くの旅に出た芭蕉にも等しくあてはめることができるだろう。「彼は、吉野山、更科、松島の松林に覆われた島々などの美しい風景を自分で経験することを求めた」[5]。彼が1684年に行った最初の旅の様子は『野ざらし紀行』に収められている。それに続いて彼はまた旅に出、紀行を残した。(1687年の『笈の小文』、1688年の『更科紀行』。本展覧会には後者の紀行のレプリカが展示される)。1689年の傑作『奥の細道』で、彼の芸術は最高の形式に達した。この句集/旅行記で、—彼は、1689年5月に始まり、弟子の曾良とともに 1200マイルを5カ月以上かけて歩いた最後の旅について物語っている。日本語の「奥」は、日本の本州の東北奥地を指すとともに、内面という意味における「深部」、たとえば山の奥や精神的内奥をも意味する[6]。この紀行を一種類だけでなく二つの版にわたって展示できることは我々の喜びである。ひとつは芭蕉の真蹟の複製である。もう一つは与謝蕪村(1716–1784)による写本で、こちらは一世紀以上のちの1778年にその書と画が描かれた。蕪村は芭蕉を敬愛した江戸時代の俳人であり画家である。芭蕉の独創的な作品の写本を作るにとどまらず、蕪村は自分自身も師の足跡を追って「奥地」を目指し旅に出た。

この展覧会の紹介文の中で、最近の研究によりワーズワースと芭蕉が直観的に認識していたことが証明されたことに触れておくのは興味深いことであろう。すなわち、歩くことが創造的霊感を促進するという事実である。スタンフォード大学の研究者たちが、人々の創造力のレベルを歩いている状態と座っている状態で比較した結果、歩いているときのほうが人間の創造的生産量は平均60パーセント増加することを発見したのである[7]。

### ワーズワースと芭蕉:環境学の先駆者?

芭蕉にとってもワーズワースにとっても、「人間」と自然は大地の大いなる全体性へ向かって—そして天上の全体性へ向かって——つに織り合っていくものであった。ワーズワースの著述には汎神論の要素がみられるし、芭蕉のそれには禅の要素がある。ダヴ・コテージでの展示では、これに関連する二つの文章を紹介している(ひとつはワーズワースのもので、『序曲』第14章のスノウドン登山の記述からの抜粋である。もうひとつは芭蕉による月山への登山についての記述である)。ここには自然の力に包摂される人間という感覚がよく表現されている。

> 天空に高々と昇った月が
> 私の頭上に大きく輝いていた
> そして自分が、巨大な霧の海の岸辺に立っているのに気づいた
> この霧の海は穏やかに静まり返って私の足元に横たわっていた
> そして何百という峰々が、この静寂の海原のいたるところに
> その黒々とした背をもたげていた。

そして遠く遠くはるかかなたでは
霧が岬のような格好になって乗り出し
海、本物の海に向かって突っ込んでいき
本物の海のほうは少なくとも人の目に届く限りでは
お株を奪われて縮こまり、威厳を失ってしまっているようだった。[8]

ふたつ目は芭蕉の『奥の細道』からの抜粋である。

八日、月山に登る。…雲霧山気の中に氷雪を踏みて登ること八里、さらに日月行道の雲関に入るかと怪しまれ、息絶え身凍えて、頂上に至れば、日没して月顕はる。笹を敷き、篠を枕として、臥して明くるを待つ。日出でて雲消ゆれば、湯殿に下る。[9]

ワーズワースと芭蕉両者の詩と散文の支えとなっているのは、確かに、単なる自然の「観察」以上のものである。日本の著述家の白谷はこう述べている。「芭蕉は自然を自らの内に取り込み、自分自身を自然の最奥へ、すべての音が静寂と永遠の世界へと溶け去るところへと運び去った」[10]。同様に、ウィリアムとドロシー・ワーズワースも、風景とは単に「目に見えるもの以上のもの」であり、それらが「その要素、大地、大気、水」[11]へと凝縮されていると感じ、理解していた。例を挙げれば、ドロシーの散文は、異常なまでの感情的鋭敏さによって捉えられた多くの瞬間に彩られている。1802年4月15日の、「風が私たちの息を捕まえた」[12]といった記述や、その後の1802年5月7日の夜についての、「イーズデイルにかかる夕暮れの恐ろしいまでの不気味な輝き」[13]といった記述などがその例である。

ドロシーとウィリアム・ワーズワース、そして芭蕉の詩と散文は、直接的で何ものにも媒介されない自然との経験─私たちの活発な想像力によって可能となるような自然との経験─の重要性を強調している。ロマン主義の詩人たちの作品は、啓蒙主義以降、経験の測定と記録により重点を置き、自然世界に対する感情的創造的反応の価値を切り下げてきた世界の捉え方に対し、バランスを取るよう主張してきたのだと私は考えている。彼らのそうした態度は、環境汚染と気候変動という二つの災難に直面している現代世界に生きる私たちにとって、より関連性を持つものだといえるだろう。

**ワーズワースと芭蕉の詩と散文の中の人々**

二人のワーズワースと芭蕉は「自然詩人」とみなされているが、これはおそらくは誤解を招くものでもあるだろう。というのは、彼らはまた人々や「文明化された自然」[14]といったものにも大いに関心を持っていたからだ。たとえば、芭蕉の散文には彼が「旅の道中で」出会った実に様々な人々が登場する。その一人ひとりが、非常に異なった、独自の人物である。ワーズワースのいくつかの詩の主題に目を向ければ(『船乗りの母』、『乞食』、『除隊兵』、『蛭取る人』)、彼が歩くなかで出会った人々に興味を向けていたことがわかるだろう。同様に、ドロシーの日記には、地元の友人、知人、文学者の友人について彼女がしきりに意見を述べている様を見ることができる。

**過去から現在への連続性**

ワーズワースと芭蕉の作品は、過去につながると同時に現在へとつづく、創造的な省察と活動の継続的な連続体の一部である。ロマン主義の詩は、急進的で特別なものだった。会話的なことばが使われ、自然に対する直接的な観察が行われた。一方ワーズワースは、あらゆる人に理解されるようなより直接的な詩の形式を求めて、「過去を探索した」[15] - つまり民俗文学やバラッドを収集した。こうして生まれたのが『抒情民謡集 』である。

芭蕉の著述(句および散文)は「時の経過やあらゆるものの無常といった感覚に深く染め抜かれており、また過去と現在の連続性についてしばしば言及している」[16]。ロマン主義と同様、彼の著作も直接の先人のそれとは完全に異なるものだった。彼は洗練された宮廷の人為的な機知ではなく、日常生活と自然世界についての自分の知識と省察に、そして中国古典詩の知識(若いころに京都で5年間学んだもの)に依って句作をおこなった。

芭蕉は、簡潔ではあるが深遠で厳粛な句作の形式を作り上げた。彼は中国の李白や杜甫、日本の宗祇や西行と言った漂泊の詩人を崇拝していた。人為的なものはなにもなく、地口や洗練された技巧の試みなどもない。ドロシー、ウィリアム・ワーズワースと同じく、芭蕉も自然と直接に深くかかわることについて書いている。本展覧会では、このような姿勢を強調する芭蕉の鍵となる三つの絵入りの句を展示している。

枯枝に烏のとまりたるや秋の暮[17]

古池や蛙飛びこむ水の音[18]

荒海や佐渡に横たふ天河[19]

我々はまた、このカタログと展覧会で展示される幅広い新たな作品たちにより、読者と訪問者たちが自筆原稿を新しい目で見ることを、つまりそれらを刺激的な生きた記録として、過去から現在へと延びる創造的な連続体の一部として見ることになってくれればと願っている。

**協同的実践**

しばしば孤独な天才として描かれるワーズワースが、実は創作において協同制作を好んだというのは、驚くべき事実だろう。彼のもっとも有名な詩の題名『わたしは雲のようにひとり孤独にさまよい』は、このようなワーズワースのよく知られた受容を促すものである。一方で、彼はコールリッジとの密接な協同作業から彼(ら)の最初の重要な作品である「抒情民謡集」を出版しているし、また彼のほかの著作はドロシーの大きな協力の下に成り立っている。彼女は、彼の詩の主題となった経験を共有し、彼が記憶の助けとして読み返すこととなった日記にそれらの経験を記録し、また一日のうちの何時間もの時間をかけて、詩を実際に書きあげ、また書き直したのである。

芭蕉もまた、仲間とともに旅を行うなど、創造的協同作業の恩恵を受けている。たとえば『奥の細道』には彼の旅の仲間である曾良のことば(ときには彼の句)が差し挟まれている。

このような協同作業の精神に従い、我々はこの展示に共同で出品するよう多くのアーティストを招待した。そしてまた、文化交流の精神の下に、イギリスと日本のアーティストに協同作業をおこなってもらった。

**手紙の応答**

芭蕉は200通ほどの手紙を書いたといわれている。その多くが彼の出版された散文と同じ形式で書かれており、なかには俳句を含むものもある。ワーズワースは何千通もの手紙を書いた。手紙はもっとも純粋で直接的な著述であり、しばしば彼らの感情がさらけだされる場でもある。当然のことながら、芭蕉の散文や詩には直接的な感情の発露は見られないが、手紙の中には束の間の感情の高まりがみられる—たとえば、酒堂という名の弟子が仲間の弟子と仲たがいをした後に大阪に分門を開こうとしていることを聞いた際、芭蕉はこのような手紙を書いている。「お前にはいくぶん自分勝手なところがあるようだ。私の言うことを聞かないならば、お前との縁は切るつもりだ」。

ワーズワースにとって、手紙のやり取りは日常生活の重要な部分を占めていた。手紙は家族や友人と連絡を取る唯一の手段だった。たとえば、コールリッジからの手紙がとどくと、それはワーズワース家の雰囲気に大きく影響をおよぼした。配達の代金は受取人が支払うことになっており、また紙や郵便代は費用がかかった。二枚目の紙を使うのを避けるために、隅の1インチまで文字が書かれることがしばしばだった。手書きの文字、訂正箇所の数、手紙のレイアウトなどから、送り手と受け取り手の関係が礼儀正しいものであったのか、あるいは親しいものであったのかを詳しく知ることができる。

**手稿をフレーミングする**

本展覧会では、幾人かのアーティストがコールリッジやワーズワースによって展開された以下のような観念について探求をおこなっている。すなわち、ある対象や事物を描写するのに使われることばと対象そのもの間には、ある特殊な関係—詩的な、具象化された関係—があるという考えである。ウィリアム・ゴドウィンへの手紙[20]の中で、コールリッジは「言葉は物事を具象化しているのだ。単にある考えや事物の代理をしているのではなく」と述べている。また、彼は、「言葉は『生命あるもの』—植物や生命体のように—であるという言語的信念」[21]を抱いていた。そして、このように続けている。

> 「思考」は、恣意的な記号なしには為しえないものだろうか?そして、「恣意的」という言葉はどの程度呼び誤りであるだろうか?言葉やその他の種々のものは、植物の器官であり芽生えなのだろうか。それが成長する法則とはどのようなものだろうか?—この法則の内にあるものを使って、僕は「言葉と事物」という古臭い対立項を壊して、それを、いわば、「事物と生きる事物」といった言葉へと高めたいのだ[22]

本展覧会に出展するアーティストの多くが、ワーズワースと芭蕉(そしてその信奉者の蕪村)のテクストの印刷した版だけでなく手稿にも焦点を当てている。ロマン主義詩人の一個人として表現の力はもちろん印刷されたことばの中にもはっきりとあらわれるが、ここに展示された手書きの原稿ではその力はさらに大きく強められている。同様に、私たちが芭蕉の俳句を理解する時には、たいてい高度に審美的でそぎ落とされた現代的な形態(活字を組み、紙の上に印刷された俳句という形)をとおしておこなうが、一方で、実際の芭蕉と蕪村の書は、なお美しく抑制され省略された形であるにせよ、本来はずっと個人的力にあふれ、素晴らしく、表現に富むものである。

こうして、ウィリアムとドロシー・ワーズワースの手稿と、芭蕉と蕪村の書を並べてみると、これらの詩人たちは私たちが最初に思っていたよりかけ離れてはいないと考えられるであろう。この展覧会に参加した現代アーティストのうちの数人は、まさにこのような表現に富む姿勢を発展させた。また、ほかのアーティストたちは、広い意味で芭蕉から影響を受けた20世紀の西洋詩人たちの作品の、非一自意識的な活字組みの詩に焦点を当てている。

**二人のワーズワース、芭蕉、禅:智への旅**

ここまで、このイントロダクションでは、ワーズワースと芭蕉の直接的な、そしてどちらかと言えば前例のない比較をおこなってきた。しかし、私がこのプロジェクトを始めるにあたって、探求するに値すると直観的に「感じた」ある別の領域がある。それは、これらの著述家たちのより深遠な、「精神的な」関連である。これを、ワーズワースと芭蕉のもうひとつのつながりだと言うことは可能だろうか、そして、もしそうできないとしたら、この三人の著述家たちの姿勢の異なりは、彼らについて、そして彼らを生み出したそれぞれの文化について何を語るのだろうか?

たとえばキーツが言ったような、ワーズワースの「自己に焦点を当てている」という性質とは反対に、ワーズワースの記述の中には詩人の自我が世界の中に包摂されるような部分が多くあるように私には感じられた。そして、この感覚はジョン・G・ルディの魅力的な書物「ワーズワースと禅の精神」を読んでますます強まった。序文でルディはこのように述べている。「彼の詩全体にわたって、ワーズワースは忘我の瞬間を記録に残しているが、これは禅において自己忘却の正式な手順を踏んで経験される宇宙の流入の経験と、その過程および姿勢において驚くほど類似している。禅の修行僧の場合と同じく、このような自己忘却の機会こそ、彼の芸術の精神的基礎であり、また彼の想像力の背後にある推進力でもある」[23]。

われ高められし思想の喜びもて
わが心を動かす一つの存在を感得せり
そは落日の光の中と、円き大洋と、生ける大気と
はた蒼き空と人間の心とを住家として
遥かに深く浸透せるあるものの崇高なる感じなり[24]

ルディはこう続ける。「ワーズワースの正典からの詩のうちのあるものと、禅の文学および哲学の主要な書を比べることで、ワーズワースの芸術の中の自意識的でも自己中心的でもない傾向を確立し、この詩人の神秘的合一という観念への傾倒についてよりよく理解し、彼の作品に対しイデオロギー的というより普遍的な文脈を打ち立てることができるだろう」[25]。

私は普遍的な事物を探し求めた
天地のありふれた表情を丹念に観察し
同時に、目を精神の内部に向け、じっとそこに注意をそそぎ
見つめ、期待し、耳を澄ませた
そして自分の思想を広げた
つる草がはびこり広がるように、私は自分の思想を四方に広めた
そして襟を正したくなるような、ひときわ厳粛な使命
人間のあらゆる感動の底にしっかりと生き続けている
あの冷静な魂を高揚させるもの、そういうものの訪れを
私は体験した[26]

そして、私にとって最も興味深いのは(というのも、私はドロシー・ワーズワースの作品を非常に高く評価しているからなのだが)、ルディは、この「領域」に関する彼女の著述こそ、ワーズワースの思想に重大な影響を及ぼすものであったと述べている。「物事の神秘を受容する彼女の力、物事の背後に知的な規則や、いわば分離したロゴスといったものを必要とせずに、ものを見、聞き、感じることのできた彼女の能力こそ、彼女が宇宙と合一を果たすための手段であった」[27]。彼によれば、ドロシーの著作には以下のようなものがある。

「自らを超えた何かを探し求めるのではなく、すべてを自由に受け入れ、自然の与える衝撃—月の輝き、『霧に煙る山々の風』の戯れ—を書きとめる精神[28]

…ドロシーは、自然の眼そのものとなり、そこにあるものだけを読み取り、物事の表面を超えて何かを探し求めたりはしないのだ」[29]

二人のワーズワースと芭蕉についてのこのような読みは、幾分推論的な比較だといえるだろう(実際ある同僚には、理由のないことではないが、危険な読みだと言われた)。しかし、このようなものこそ、私がこのプロジェクトを進めていく力となったものだし、またこの展覧会にかかわった多くのアーティストが作品を作る上で意識下で取り組んできたことだと私は信じている。この展覧会で展示されているドロシーとウィリアム・ワーズワース、そして芭蕉の詩や自筆原稿を読み、または現代アーティストたちの作品を見て、彼らの作品の間により深い関係を見出すかどうかは、このエッセイの読者と展覧会の訪問者の方々自身のご判断に任せるとしよう。

**展覧会を準備するにあたって**

この展覧会の「序曲」として、2014年1月、ダヴ・コテージのジャーウッド・センターで、ワーズワース財団主催のシンポジウムが、本展覧会に参加したアーティストたち出席のもと開かれた。これは、皆が集まって意見を交わすユニークな機会となっただけでなく、ワーズワースの詩の原稿の原本(その90パーセントが財団の所有である)と、寛大にも京都国立博物館と早稲田大学図書館より貸借した芭蕉の作品の複製に触れるという特権に預かる機会ともなった。こういった自筆原稿に触れられる機会というのは、もちろん、稀である。だから、このような非常に文化的価値の高い素材を手にできることは、冬の「ワーズワースの湖水地方」の景色に刺激を受けるのと同様に、素晴らしいことであった。マニー・リン、クリスティン・フリント＝サト、ナオ・サカモト、ユアン・クレイトンらによる水墨画と日本の伝統的な和紙を使った本の装丁のワークショップがシンポジウムを彩り、またアーティストの多くが、彫刻家のブライアン・トンプソンの先導の下、イーズデイルの小道を歩いた。

この三日間(2014年1月20日から22日)の我々の目的は、オリジナルの自筆原稿の持つ美とパワーを引き出すことにより、視覚的に驚きを与えるような展覧会を創り出すこと、そして、現代アート作品に触れることを通して訪問者が自筆原稿を新鮮な目で見られるようになる方法を見つけることだった。そのため、シンポジウムの期間中、これらの文書をどのように扱うかが、展示会のための新しい作品を創造する過程において、決定的な部分を担うこととなった。

この数日間は非常に生産的で濃密なものだった。アーティスト全員がグラスミアのソーニー・ハウ・ユースホステルに滞在し、日中は財団図書館の豊富なテキストや原稿に目を通し、夕食をとりながらアイディアを共有した。シンポジウムは大きな成功をおさめ、このカタログや展覧会で展示されている作品へと結実することとなった。

この展覧会に参加してくれたアーティストに多大な感謝を申し上げる。ユアン・クレイトン、ケン・コバーン、アレック・フィンリー、クリスティン・フリント＝サト、ザファー・クニアル(2014年ワーズワース財団駐在詩人)、エイイチ・コウノ、マニー・リン、クリス・マキュー、ノブヤ・モンタ、インガ・パニールズ、アンドリュー・リチャードソン、オータム・リチャードソン、ナオ・サカモト、ミナコ・シラクラ、リチャード・スケルトン、アヤコ・タニ、そしてブライアン・トンプソン。彼らはこのプロジェクトが提示する挑戦に立ちあがり、そして最高度に卓越した、かつ驚くほど多様な作品(詩、ガラス、カリグラフィー、彫刻、絵画、デザイン、陶磁器、そして音楽／音)を創り出した。

そして最後に—注意書きとして—私自身は第一にアーティストであり、折に触れてキュレーターとして活動しているが、けっしてワーズワースまたは芭蕉のどちらの作品にも詳細な知識を持った大学人ではないことを付け加えておこう。このような立場が有用な場合もあるだろうが、しかしこのような情熱で可能になることにも限りがある。そのため、ワーズワース財団のキュレーターであるジェフ・カウトンには大変お世話になった。このプロジェクトを通して、彼の協力、助言、そして情熱は非常に大きなものであった。また、このカタログのためにより詳細なエッセイを書いてほしいという私の依頼に快く答えてくださった文筆家の方々にもお礼を申し上げたい。

ジョン・エルダー名誉教授：アメリカ、ミドルベリー大学、東聖子教授：十文字学園女子大学、大石和欣准教授：東京大学、ユアン・クレイトン教授：サンダーランド大学、パメラ・ウーフ氏：フーズワース財団会長、キャロル・マッケイ博士：サンダーランド大学 。

私は彼ら一人ひとりに恐る恐る近づき、率直に言って不可能な仕事をお願いした—ワーズワースと芭蕉の作品について、たった1000語で何か書いてほしいと言ったのだ。彼らもまた、別種の、しかし困難な挑戦に、敢然と立ち向かった。私はまた、彼らによって読者がワーズワースと芭蕉の作品に対しより深い洞察を得ることを望む。また、キャロル・マッケイによる個々のアーティストと作品の紹介は、この展覧会とカタログで示される新しい作品が、ワーズワースと芭蕉の作品を新しい目で見ることをどのように助けてくれるかを明らかに示すものとなるだろう。また、ジェフリー・ウィルキンソンに、このプロジェクトのあらゆる段階で、心のこもった貴重な支援を授けてくれたことを感謝したい。ジェフリーが最近発表した魅力的なエッセイは、『西の諸島への細道—キーツが芭蕉と旅をしたら』と題されている[30]。

それにしても、なぜ今この展覧会が時宜を得ていると言えるのだろう?ウィリアムとドロシー・ワーズワースの詩、そして芭蕉の句は、自然をありのままで価値あるものと考えるように、そして、(21世紀において我々が政治的理由からそうするように)議論を組み替え、経済的合理主義者たちの言語を使ったりしないように、私たちに促してくれるように思える。認識言語学者のレイコフはこう言っている。「敵の言語と価値観を採用すれば負けだ。それは彼らの枠組みを強化することになるから」[31](ジョージ・モンビオットによれば)自然の価値を算定すれば、「明らかになるのは以下のことだ。そこには何の内在的価値もないこと、それが保護に値するのは、それが我々に対し有用である場合のみであること、それは代用可能であること。そして、自然を愛する人々を堕落させ疎外する一方で、自然に興味のない人々の価値観を強化することになる」[32]。経済的合理主義者たちの「枠組み」を採用することで自然を守ることができると信じている人々は、彼らの敵が仕掛けた罠に入り込んでいっているのだ。敵が仕掛ける(モンビオットによれば)最も強い主張—価値を問う主張—は、今は聞かないことにしよう。そしてこれこそが、いつにも増して今こそ、ドロシーとウィリアム・ワーズワースの、そして芭蕉の詩と散文が聞かれ理解されるべきであり、そして、私たちが日本と東洋の自然に対する態度から多くを学ぶべき理由である。

(翻訳　松浦恵美)

**注**

1. John Elder, *Imagining the Earth: Poetry and the Vision of Nature,* Urbana, IL: University of Illinois Press, 1985, pp.93–115 (Chapter 4, 'The Footpath of Tradition').

2. Makoto Ueda, *Matsuo Bashō; The Master Haiku Poet,* Tokyo: Kodansha International, 1982, pp.176–7.

3. Jeffrey Johnson, *Haiku Poetics in Twentieth-Century Avant-Garde Poetry,* Lanham, MD: Lexington Books, 2011, pp.61–3.

4. David McCracken, *Wordsworth and the Lake District: A Guide to the Poems and their Places*, Oxford: Oxford University Press, 1988, p.3.

5. David Landis Barnhill (trans.), *Bashō's Journey,* Albany, NY: SUNY Press, 2005, p.5.

6. *Ibid*. p.4.

7. May Wong, 'Stanford study finds walking improves creativity', *Stanford News,* 24 April 2014.

8. *The Prelude* (1805), XIV. 40–49.(岡三郎訳、『ワーズワス・序曲』国文社、1991年)

9. Matsuo Bashō, *The Narrow Road to the Deep North and Other Travel Sketches,* London: Penguin, 1996, trans. N. Yuasa, p.125.(英訳)

10. Yoshinobu Hakutani, *Haiku and Modernist Poetics,* New York: Palgrave Macmillan, 2009, p.17.

11. Pamela Woof, 'Wordsworth and Dorothy Wordsworth: Walkers' in Collier, M. (ed.), *Wordsworth and Bashō: Walking Poets*, Sunderland: Art Editions North, 2014.

12. Pamela Woof (ed.), *Dorothy Wordsworth: The Grasmere and Alfoxden Journals,* Oxford: Oxford University Press, 2008, p.85.

13. *Ibid*. p.97.

14. Donald Keene, *Appreciations of Japanese Culture,* Tokyo: Kodansha International, 1982, p.124.

15. Henry Hitchings, *The Secret Life of Words: How English Became English,* London: John Murray, 2008, pp. 265–6.

16. David Landis Barnhill (trans), *Bashō's Journey,* Albany, NY: SUNY Press, 2005, p.5.

17. Robert Hass, *The Essential Haiku,* Tarset: Bloodaxe Books, 2013, p.30.(英訳)

18. *Ibid*. p.35.

19. *Ibid*. p.53.

20. William Keach, 'Romanticism and Language', in Curran, S. (ed.), *The Cambridge Companion to British Romanticism,* Cambridge: Cambridge University Press, 1993, p.111.

21. *Ibid.*

22. Samuel Taylor Coleridge, *Letters—Collected Letters of Samuel Taylor Coleridge.* Griggs, E. L. (ed.), 6 vols., Oxford: Clarendon Press, 1956–71 (Letters I, pp.625–6).

23. John G. Rudy, *Wordsworth and the Zen Mind: The Poetry of Self-Emptying,* Albany, NY: SUNY Press, 1996, p.16.

24. *Lines written a few miles above Tintern Abbey,* 93–99. 田部重治訳、『ワーズワース詩集』岩波書店、1938年)

25. *Ibid* p.17.

26. *The Prelude* (1805), III. 110–18. (岡三郎訳、『ワーズワス・序曲』国文社、1991年)

27. *Ibid* p.9.

28. *Lines written a few miles above Tintern Abbey*, 134–36.

29. *Ibid.*

30. Geoffrey Wilkinson, 'The Narrow Road to the Western Isles – if Keats had journeyed with Bashō' in *The Keats-Shelley Review,* Vol. 28 No. 1, April 2014, 49–57.

31. George Monbiot, 'Can you put a price on the beauty of Smithy Wood?', *Guardian,* 22 April 2014, p.27.

32. *Ibid.*

**マイク・コリヤ**

教師、作家、キュレーターならびにアーティスト。ゴールドスミス・カレッジ(ロンドン)でファインアートを学び、ICA(ロンドン)でギャラリーマネジャーになる。フリーのキュレーター、アートオーガナイザーとして、イギリス国内外にて活動。1985年レイン・アートギャラリー(ニューカッスル)にて芸術開発戦略を運営するためにニューカッスルに拠点を移し、同ギャラリーにてタイン州国際現代美術展を立ち上げた。2004年から、サンダーランド大学にて教鞭を執る。継続して自身の制作活動を行っており、多くの作品において「歩くこと」は主要テーマ。2010年に博士号を取得(サンダーランド大学)後、文化活動の担い手が歩くことを通じてどう世界とつながりを持つか、を研究する機関WALK(Walking歩き、Artアート、Landskip風景、Knowledge知識)を立ち上げた。

## 境界にある者たち

**JOHN ELDER ジョン・エルダー**

生物学者は、二つの生態系の間にある境界域を、移行帯、すなわち縁(ふち)と呼ぶ。「際縁効果」により、境界地域はしばしば特別な豊かさを持つことになる。そこには隣接するそれぞれの生息域の固有種や、あるいはその移行帯に独自の種がやどるのだが、その場ではたいてい並はずれて高い密度の生物量がみられる。縁もまた、潮流帯の変動のなかで、あるいは人の手の入らなくなった牧草地に森林が進出する遷移線において、変化していく。だから、この移動する縁にやどる豊かな資源に引き寄せられる生物にとって、用心深さが何より重要な条件となる。えさを求めてやってきた彼らが、ほかの生き物の昼食ともなりかねない。

この展覧会に参加する芸術家や文筆家は、この危険な、しかし可能性豊かな縁に乗り出した。危険な、というのは、ワーズワースと芭蕉の詩的世界には劇的な隔たりがあるからだ。どちらもお互いの国を訪れたことはなかったし、ワーズワースはこの日本人の先達の書物を、読むことはおろか、聞いたことすらなかった。ひとりは禅仏教の伝統に修練し、もうひとりはキリスト教世界にそだったという事実にくわえて、両者とももう一方が読んでいた書物にはほんのすこし触れることすらなかった。芭蕉は杜甫や西行の伝統から影響を受け、ワーズワースはシェイクスピア、スペンサー、ミルトンに連なる。しかし、なににもまして印象深いのは、二人の詩人の間の深い共鳴である。それによって、芭蕉は今日の西洋の詩人に重大な影響を与えることとなり、ワーズワースは日本で非常に愛好されている。

今回の展示への出品作品を制作するにあたって、ケン・コバーンは、『序曲』の第二巻にある「従順な精神にとっては/なんの親交もないような物事のなかにある/親和性を注視すること」という一節に引き込まれた。芭蕉とワーズワースの親和性(affinity)について考える上で、この語がラテン語の*affinis* (*ad* + *finis*)、つまり「境界上にある」ということばに由来することに触れておくのは、妥当なことであろう。社会の周縁や、自然と文化の変わり続ける縁という、そこでこそ洞察が生まれる場所を、二人ともが自らの生業としていたという点で、彼らは同じ種類の作家である。芭蕉の東北奥地へとつづく細い旅路を記した『奥の細道』は、*Michael*の冒頭やそのほかでみられるワーズワースの「人間の領域」からの出立という選択の先鞭をつけるものであった。

ワーズワースも芭蕉も、社会の本流からの精神的な、そして身体的な離脱を求めた。困難な旅をつづけた芭蕉は、人里離れた地へとたどり着く。そこは女性たちが歌いながら地を耕し、農耕という古代の共同体の律動へと詩が立ち戻る場所であった。

「風流の初やおくの田植うた」
芭蕉は、裕福な風流人のつどう人為的に儀式化された茶室に背を向け、真の簡素さを求めて田園の奥へと分け入っていった。おなじようにワーズワースも、「多くの現代作家たちの華美で愚かしい文体」を拒絶し、「つつましい田舎の生活」を求めた。その地でこそ、「心の本質的な感情は、成熟を遂げるためのよりよい土壌を見出すのだ…」(『抒情民謡集』の第二版に寄せられた1800年のワーズワースの序文より)

芭蕉が女性の田植え唄に霊感を受けたのと同じように、ワーズワースも、また別の縁で聞いた『麦を刈る乙女』の歌に、想像力を膨らませ、心を掻きたてられた。「彼女が何を歌っているのか、誰か教えてはくれないか」という詩人の問いかけは、この女性の孤独な労働だけでなく、彼女が話す言葉—スコットランドのゲール語—も、古代の遠く離れた地のもののように彼には感じられたことを示している。いくぶんはこのような隔たりのために、この出会いは詩人の記憶と想像力の源泉として残り続けたのであろう。

「それが聞こえなくなってずっとのちもなお／わたしが心に抱きつづけるその調べ」
芭蕉とワーズワースが、社会からの因習的で物質主義的な要請に背を向けるという選択をとったのは、より深い認識を求める思いからであった。このような両者の本質的な類似性を指摘した最初の学者の一人に、R・H・ブライスがいる。彼は、1936年から亡くなる1964年まで、日本で生活し、英語を教え、禅と俳句をまなんだ。戦時中に抑留されている間も、彼は教鞭をとり、研究を続けた。彼の壮大で奇矯さに富んだ数多くの書物の中には、*Zen in English Literature and Oriental Classics*(禅と英文学)や、ふんだんに図説を取り入れ、簡潔に*Haiku*(俳句)と題された4巻本の研究書などが含まれる。後者の傑作(1949年出版)の第一巻で、彼はこう述べている。「俳句は、ワーズワースが『時の諸点』と呼ぶものを記録する。それは、何か非常に神秘的な理由から特別な意義を持つような瞬間、…一種の悟り、あるいは啓蒙であり、その瞬間に、私たちは物事の生を覗き見るのである」

『奥の細道』と『序曲』を比べるとき、ブライスのこのような対比は特に印象深い。繰り返し言っておくが、まずは両者の大きな隔たりを認めておくことが重要である。芭蕉の作品はずっと短いものだし、ワーズワースの語りに比べると、その表現にあからさまに自伝的なところはずっと少ない。『序曲』にあるような、ケンブリッジやロンドンでの生活や、あるいは革命期フランスの旅に関する政治的記述のような長々しいくだりは、そこには見られない。そうではあるが、しかし、彼らが世界の文学の中で歩くことについてもっとも共鳴する意見を示した二人であり、さらに両者の作品が、突然訪れる凝縮された認識の瞬間にもっとも鋭い焦点を当てていることは、十分に認められるだろう。

芭蕉は、しばしば旅の途中で出会った現象や出来事を書きとめ、それから立ち止まってその瞬間の持つ意味を俳句にまとめ上げる。その一例として、俳人が山形地方を訪れたときの記述が挙げられる。芭蕉はこう記している。「岩上の院々扉を閉ぢて物の音聞こえず。岸を巡り、岩を這ひて、仏閣を排し、佳景寂寞として心澄みゆくのみおぼゆ」。それに続いて句が詠まれる。「古池や蛙飛びこむ水の音」

『序曲』のなかでも、これと似たような言い回しやことばの強度の変化が、くり返し見られる。ただし、ワーズワースの場合、それはしばしば先行する経験からの後退であったり、あるいはその凝縮であったりする。第六巻で、それと知らぬうちにすでにアルプスを越えていたことに気づき、詩人は「憂うつな沈滞」に襲われる。しかし、そのような気持ちは次のような視覚的経験に突然取って代わる。「澄みわたる青空から降りしきる奔流／まるでおのがじし内に声を持つように／われわれの耳のすぐそばで唸りをたてる岩々／道ばたにて語る黒い雨にぬれた岩山」。ワーズワースが通常使う様式は、散文ではなく無韻詩であり、また、駆り立てられた彼が突然ある経験について語りだすとき、そのことばは芭蕉の俳句ほどには独立したものでもなければ、簡潔でもない。しかしそれでも、このふたつの詩は同じ本質的なリズムを共有しており、その語りを捉え、照らし出しているのは、ある洞察の閃きである。そのような瞬間に、読者たちも社会の要請から解放され、生命に満ちた縁で起こる直観的認識という経験へと向かうのである。

(翻訳:松浦恵美)

**ジョン・エルダー**

ポモナ・カレッジとイェール大学に学んだ後、ミドルベリー大学（米バーモント州）にて37年間、英語と環境学を教えた。イギリスのロマン主義、アメリカのネイチャーライティング、そして日本の俳句に特に関心を持っている。近年の著作*Reading the Mountains of Home, The Frog Run, Pilgrimage to Vallombrosa*は、文学論とバーモントの風景描写と回顧録とを織り交ぜたものである。最新作*Picking up the Flute*はウェブサイトで公開され、木製の横笛でアイルランド伝統音楽を吹いたことが、その笛の調べとともに回想されている。妻リタとともに、米バーモント州ブリストルのグリーンマウンテン国有林の中に住み、州の環境保護や気候問題に取り組み、また、夕暮れに横笛やコンサーティーナを演奏することを楽しみとしている。

## ワーズワースとドロシー・ワーズワース　逍遥者

**PAMELA WOOF パメラ・ウーフ**

> 私はよく一人で歩いたものだ、
> 嵐や暴風雨の中を、また星明りの夜に
> 　　　　　…そして私はよく立っていたものだ
> 岩々の陰に、そして
> 大昔の大地の、霊妙な言葉や
> 遠くを吹きわたる風に宿る物音に耳をすませていた[1]

20代後半のワーズワースは、13歳、14歳の少年であった頃の自分、まだ学校に通う若者であった頃の自分を思い出していた。時々、彼は飼い犬と散歩をし、その犬は、

> 私が立ち止まると、うんざりして、不安がっていた[2]

というのも若きワーズワースは、「詩の創作に苦心」していたからである。ぴったりのイメージが浮かんだ時には、犬は心のこもった愛撫を受けた。また、見知らぬ者が創作にふける詩人に近づいてきたときには、彼に「時機のよい警告」を与えたりした。このときワーズワースは、その後生涯続けることになった、歩きながら詩行を大きな声で口ずさむ癖を身につけているところであった。そうやってことばの響きを聞き、より洗練させようとしたのだ。彼は時折、夏の朝に「そのとき熱烈に愛情を抱いていた友人」と二人で歩いた、

> 霞の立ち込める湖の、穏やかな縁のそばを
> お気に入りの詩を、声をそろえて繰り返し
> あるいはさらに多くをそらんじた
> 私たちの周りで歌う鳥たちほど幸せに[3]

これらの散歩は、ホークスヘッド・スクールの授業が始まる午前6時半よりもずいぶん早い、まだ夜明けごろにおこなわれたのだろう。

このようにして、ワーズワースは早くから多才で創造力豊かな散歩者となることを学んだ。

彼は一人でも、仲間と一緒にも歩いた。昼でも夜でも、どんな天候であっても歩いた。動くことも、じっと立っていることも好きだった。大地の音が語りかけてくるのを聴き、また歩くにつれて自分自身の声がリズミカルに出てくるのを聴いた。これらすべては、彼の成人期においてずっと、彼にとってもっとも近しく、もっとも深い共感を寄せてくれる散歩仲間であり友人となった妹に、彼が再会する以前の出来事であった。

ドロシー・ワーズワースは、6歳の時、母親の死後間もなく、4人の兄弟から切り離されていた。兄弟たちと再会するまでには、父親もすでに亡くなっており、この時ワーズワースは17歳、ドロシーは15歳であった。それからさらに9年以上の時を経て、彼らはペンリスの祖父母の家で再会し、すぐに打ち解けたが、ドロシーが23歳になるまで長い時間を一緒に過ごすことはほとんどなかった。

ワーズワースは早いうちから、散歩とそれに伴う生き生きとした思考を楽しむようになり、学生時代や青年期には、川沿いや山岳地帯を通る長い徒歩旅行を続けた。ドロシーはどのように遠いヨークシャーまで旅をしたのだろうか。彼女は、ハリファックスでの子供時代の生活や、自分を育ててくれたやさしい母の従妹、地元の友人や学校を、愛していた。15歳でハリファックスから引き離された彼女は、友人との手紙の中で、彼女がもう得ることのできない喜びを言葉に残している。

> ああ！どれほどあなたの居間に飛び込みたいことか。…ああ！あの暖炉はどれくらい幸せな子どもたちの集まりに囲まれていたことでしょう…店の裏道から続く坂の上を横切る私を、あなたが見つけることはあるかしら[4]

ドロシーは友人たちと食器洗い場や菜園、そのほかお気に入りのたまり場でよく遊んだ。彼女は、またジェーン・ポラードと一緒に「気持ちのよいコルダー川の土手沿い」を「歩き回りたい」と思っていた。そして、ジェーンのについてこう記している。

> ホワイトリーの森？それとも古い小道やバークスウッドかしら？昔の楽しみを思い返すと、黒い小皿を手に持って苔桃の実を探してその辺りをさまよったものね。[5]

そんな活動的な一日が終わると、ドロシーはぐっすりと眠ったものだった。30代前半の1803年、兄と長く骨の折れる散歩をし、ケタリン湖へついた後に、その日々を思い出している。

> わたしは、子どものころ、夏休みのある日に一日中遊んだ後そうしたように、わらのベッドでぐっすりと眠った[6]

私たちのほとんどは、同じようなことを経験しているだろう。それは、ワーズワースが山で過ごした少年時代に経験したものの強烈さからはほど遠い。

> 孤独な山々の間で
> 私のあとをかすかな息遣いが追いかけてきて
> 得体の知れないものの動く音がした
> まるでそれらが芝生の上を歩いてくるかのような
> 静かな歩みが聞こえてきた[7]

あるいは、彼の眠っているあいだ、あるいは起きているあいだに忍び込んできた恐ろしい空白について考えてみよう。無断で小船に乗り、少年ワーズワースは山中の湖を照らす月光の中、オールを漕いで見つけたのだった、

> 生きている人間の姿とは似つかない、
> 力強く、巨大な形をしたものを
> それが日中、私の心をゆっくりと動き
> 夜には夢の苦しみの種となった[8]

ドロシーはまだ山のなかでそんな力を発見してはいなかった。ひょっとすると私たちのように、彼女はおもに自分の想像力やワーズワース自身の詩から、そのような力に気づくに至ったのかもしれない。これらの詩をとおして、彼女は、ワーズワースが青年期の孤独な散歩をとおして知り、気づくようになった力を理解したのだ。

しかしながら、ドロシー自身も非凡な若い女性であった。17歳から22歳にかけて、彼女は叔父のウィリアムとその若い家族と一緒に、ノーフォークの平坦な田舎にあるフォーンセットの教区司祭館で暮らしていた。その地で、彼女は散歩することの価値をいくらか理解するようになった。最初の散歩は、1790年から91年にかけてのクリスマスが終わってから6週間、叔父のもとに滞在していた兄と一緒におこなった。彼はその夏、学部の友人とともに、刺激的な革命期のフランスから、スイスの崇高なるアルプス山脈、そしてイタリアを、まるで進

軍するかのように歩いた。さて、イングランドの教区司祭館にいたころのワーズワースは、妹のことをもっとよく知るようになった。彼女は彼らがたどった道をジェーンにこう語っている。

> わたしたちは毎朝2時間ほど歩き、夕方には4時か4時半に庭へ出て、6時まで行ったり来たりしながら歩いていたものです。[9]

散歩がしやすく、つまずくような石もない、ごく狭い範囲の小道や野原、道路や台地といった場所を行ったり来たりするお決まりの散歩は、ワーズワースにとって思考し、会話し、さらにとりわけ詩作をおこなうのに最適な機会となった。散歩しているときの体の途切れることのないリズムは、無韻詩の流れを手助けし、また思考が必要なだけ、時には１段落分、時には１ページ分も、その動きが邪魔されずに続くのを助けた。後に、ワーズワースが丘の多い湖水地方の庭にテラスを建てたとき、中世の修道院のように、瞑想を促す平らな小道を作った。グラスミアの美しい山や森、谷に囲まれるなかを、ワーズワースは、ときには一人で、ときにはドロシーと、歩いて回った。

ドロシーがフォーンセットで学んだふたつ目の散歩の仕方は、たったひとりで長い道のりを歩くことだった。19歳の若い女性であり、教区司祭の姪である彼女が、ひとりで友人の家まで歩いていくのは適切だとは思われなかった。その友人である「すてきなミス・バロウズ姉妹」[10]の住む村までは、たった３マイルしか離れていないにもかかわらず、である。「私は一人でいくの。私って大胆じゃないかしら？」[11]と、ドロシーはハリファックスに住む友人ジェーンに打ち明けている。そして、彼女はまた歩いて家まで帰った。確かに、同時代の小説であるジェーン・オースティンの「高慢と偏見」に登場するミス・ビングリーのような人物なら、ドロシーを不作法と判断したであろう。

しかし、こうしたことのおかげで、彼女とワーズワースがグラスミアに家を建てた1799年の終わりごろには、ドロシーは詩人ワーズワースにとって完璧な散歩仲間となっていた。兄妹は連れ立って歩くことを楽しんだ。彼らは、言葉を交わしたり沈黙したり、創作したり何かに言及したり、その辺を歩き回ったり、または谷の周辺まで足を伸ばしたりもした。二人一緒に、または友人たちと、あるいは一人で、日夜いつでも、どんな季節でも散歩をした。グラスミアと湖水地方を歩き回り、その経験を書き記すことで、二人はこの地を自分たちのものとした。

幾年も同じ土地に暮らし、自分たち自身と同じく谷間の風景も変化していくのを見つめることは、彼らが空間と場所のなかを散歩しているというだけでなく、時間の中を歩いているということをも意味した。そのような意味が、たとえば、彼らが日常歩く土地の道沿いの木にもまとわりついていた。航海中に二人のところへ滞在していた弟ジョンは、1800年、木々の密生する森に小道を開いた。兄である詩人は、のちにその小道を発見し、そこを歩きながら、弟の少年時代と海での生活、「ある遠い場所で／船の甲板の上」を歩き回るときに彼が抱いた気持ちの変化、そして彼が歩きながら故郷の丘の「消えることのない思い出」とそれらの丘についての兄の詩を思い描く様を書いた。その兄は、「海のような音」[12]をたててざわめく木立を通って、「彼の」道を、詩作をしながら歩いたのだった。そして彼らの妹は、すでにすばらしく豊かなこの連想に付け加えて、「ジョンの木立」への幾度にもわたる訪問について、日記にこのように書き記している。

> 頭上の木々の間では、海のような心地よい音がしていた。わたしたちは行ったり来たりしながら、ジョンを偲んだ。[13]

ここで、自然と海、そして3人の兄弟の愛は、思いと感情、言語が共有されるなか、空間と時をこえて、ひとつになっている。

グラスミアの散歩はなぜそれほどに特別なのだろう。ワーズワースはかつて、フランスとアルプスはもちろん、北ウェールズを歩き、夜明けを見るつもりが月をつかまえたスノウドン登山もした。ソールズベリ平原を一人でこえ、ワイ渓谷を上って北ウェールズを歩いた。ケンダルからケスウィックまではドロシーと歩いた。彼らはグラスミアまで18マイル歩き、そこで一晩滞在し、もう15マイル歩いてケズウィックまで進んだと、ドロシーは1794年に自信を持って、しかし不正確に、述べている。ドーセットにあるレイスダウンのあたりはドロシーと、サマセットのカントックではコウルリッジとドロシーとともに歩いた。ドイツのゴスラーはドロシーと歩いたが、彼ら二人ともが寒さをしのぐため毛皮に身を包まなければならなかった。北西部のソックバーン・オン・ティーズから湖水地方へは、コウルリッジと航海から帰っていたジョンとともに歩いた。そして最後に、1799年12月暮れの寒い雪の三日間、ふたたびソックバーンからヨークシャーをこえてウェストモアランドへ至り、そしてグラスミアに帰るまでをドロシーと歩いた。この最後の旅の終わりはダヴ・コテージで、この旅の道中すべてから詩が生まれたのだった。

しかし、グラスミアはさらに歩くことを高め、詩を高めた。ワーズワースと妹はこの地に暮らしていた。この場所が彼らの故郷だった。彼らはそこを単に歩いて過ぎただけではない。その地に踏み入り、深く踏み入り、そしてその場所について永遠の知識を得たのだ。彼らの著作には、故郷である場所を歩くことで得られる豊かな反応が刻まれている。彼らの創作は一時のものという以上であった。感情、イメージ、言葉が永遠に残る記憶になった。

イメージや観察は、概して詩人よりも日記の書き手のほうがすばやく書き留めるものである。ワーズワースは確かに屋外に出て、時折はすばやく頭の中で創作したが、いつも即座にアイデアをつかみとっていたわけではない。そしてまた、創作の後には、紙の上での修正を行う時間も必要だった。それは時間のかかる過程であっただろう。

ドロシーは、後で省略した日について書き足すことがあったにせよ、その日の出来事についての自分の考えをその夜のうちに書いた。彼女は自分の周りの空と大地を見わたした。歩いた。湖水地方に着くと間もなく、ワーズワースと離れているあいだに、彼女はある夜アンブルサイドからグラスミアに至るまでの4マイルを、途中は郵便局長のニコルソン夫人に付き添われて歩いた。ドロシーは以下のように記している。

> この方はとても優しい。でも申し訳ないことに、月の光のそそぐ湖のそばを誰かと一緒に歩きたくはない。[14]

それが彼女の気持ちだったのだろう。彼女は「水面にニシンの群れのように輝く月の光」[15]を見た。あるいは違う季節には、「一日中土砂降りの雨が降」っているため、お茶が終わるまで出かける気にならなかったけれども、「果樹園のように満開の、山腹のサンザシ」[16]を見て、このようなありふれた雨の日、荒涼とした山腹に、太陽の光を浴びた春の果樹園にあるような、強烈なみずみずしさと色、香りという突然の予期せぬ存在がもたらされるのを発見した。しかしながら、彼女のイメージの繊細な美とともにあるのは、その儚さへの悲しみである。そのたった一週間後、彼女はもはや楽しげな比較をすることなく、ただ事実だけを現実的に記している。

> 下方のサンザシの花が消え、山の上にはかすかな白の花が咲いている

実際、ハウスマンが100年ほど経ってからと述べているように、50回春を迎える間に桜が雪に飾られる様を見られる可能性はほとんどない。

もちろん家のなかにはやらなければいけない仕事がたくさんあった。たくさんのダイオウの花を処理し、パンを焼き、服の修繕をし、読書し、客を迎え、お茶を飲み、アイロンをかけ、手紙を書き、詩を複写し、庭仕事をした。家を出て外を歩き、谷の様子の変化のよく目につく細かな点に夢中になる時、ドロシーはしばしば興奮して比喩を用いた。出版のための執筆ではなかったため、日記はすばらしい自由に満ちており、現実の詳細と具体性からのはるかな跳躍とが混じり合っている。果樹園のように咲く満開のサンザシはその一例である。また、ワーズワースとドロシーはジョンの木立へ出かけ、しばらく座って聞き耳を立て、「お互いに見えないように」横になり、「大地の平和な音」に耳を澄ませ、鳥のさえずりだけでなく滝の音を聞いた。

> 滝の上にまた別の滝があるのではないが―空中で水の音がしていた―空気の声のようなものである。[17]

大地に横たわり、大気中の水の音を聞く。単に目に見えるものを超えた知覚である。ワーズワースは、実際に目を閉じていた。ここでは風景が要素に、大地や空気や水に圧縮されている。その力はすべての基礎であり、「空気の声」という概念は魔術的なものである。

ときには歩くのさえ速すぎることがある。ワーズワース兄妹は、しばしば散歩中に立ち止まって座り、横になり、聞き耳を立て、そして見つめた。

> わたしたちは長い時間、塀の下で休んでいた。羊と子羊が野にいた。小屋は煙を出していた。芝生の上に横になっているとき、私は羊の背骨が輝く銀色の線になるのを見た。羊のいる場所に日の光が当たるからだった。それが羊を美しく見せていたが、別の種の動物のような、どこか奇妙な感じを与えていた。まるでもっと輝かしい世界に属しているかのように。[18]

歩くことと止まることを繰り返すことで、とても自然に物事に気づき、目にする事物に心を留め、幻想の世界まで心を連れ去ることが可能になる。

また、ワーズワース兄妹は、散歩の途中でじっとしていることを選ばないこともあった。たとえば、彼らは風や天候のせいでとどまることを強いられることがあった。アルズウォーター下流から出発し、湖の全長を歩き、グラスミアまで高い山の峠を越すとき、「猛り狂った」風が

吹いていた。彼らは二度休息を取らなくてはならず、一度は「大きなボート小屋で、それからハリエニシダのやぶの下で…その風は我々の呼吸を奪った」

この強制的な休息は、彼らが物事に気付くだけでなくそれを思い出すことも意味している。ドロシーは、2日後に日記を書いたなかで、小枝の多様な色彩まで思い出している。湖岸にどんな花が生育しているか書き、後になってさらに思いだしたものをリストに付け加えている。また、どうして水辺に水仙が少ししか咲いていないのかと考えているうちに、それが「どんどん増えていき、最後には—…」、そして彼女の言葉は「なんとも美しい水仙」の勝ち誇るような描写へと高まっていく。その喜びにより、彼女の文章は、ドロシーの場合には珍しいことなのだが、動詞に動詞を重ねて長くなっていき、祝福にあふれた光景の充溢を表現する。

> 水仙は周囲にある苔むした石の間で育ち、疲れた時枕に頭をのせるように、自らの頭を石の上に置いて休んでいるものがある。また、他のものは頭を持ち上げてゆらめいたり踊ったり、まるで湖中で吹き付ける風と一緒になって本当に笑っているかのようにしていたりする。水仙はとても陽気に、たえず輝き、変化しているように見える。[19]

ワーズワースは、1802年の4月のこの日、ドロシーと一緒に歩いていた。我々は当時の彼の反応を知ることはない、というのも、それが記憶の波となって彼に押し寄せるのはそれから二年後のことだからである。1802年のその散歩は、二年後に記憶から呼び戻され、そして変化していた。それは言わば、詩人の心の中で眠っていたのであり、ひとりでに鮮やかにあらわれ出た。しかしその鮮やかさは、ドロシーの描写よりも穏やかな、かつ劇的なものだった。ただ時間と記憶を経ることによって、その経験は完全に詩人自身のものとなったのである。それゆえに、『私は雲のように孤独にさまよい』という詩の中で、より適切なことに彼は孤独であり、妹とともにいるのではない。風は今や「猛り狂って」おらず、花々をもっとやさしく「ゆらめかせ踊らせる」そよ風となっている。詩人は、ドロシーのように、ふたつ、三つと徐々に、そして「どんどん増えていき、最後には—…」というふうに花々に出会うのではない。彼の認識は劇的である。「とつぜん、私は群れを見た」。あてどなく「さまよった」あと、詩人が求めたのは啓示の力である。そのようなものは存在しなかったのだが、彼はそれを創りだした。ワーズワースの最も広く知られている詩について、これ以上ここで語る必要はないが、一緒におこなった散歩がこの二人の作家に違った影響を与えたのを見ておくことは重要である。ドロシーはそこから、花々と激しい風両方への生き生きとした、明るい共感を持った記述を生み出した。一方ワーズワースにとっては、その散歩は想像力に満ちた再創作であり、本能的な喜びの回帰として、ついには踊る水仙の豊かさとして、心の中にあるからこそ永遠となった豊かさとして、再び蘇る記憶となったのである。

彼は、現実では必ずしもそうではなかったが、詩の中ではよく一人で歩いた。彼の隣を精神的な意味でともに歩くよういざなわれるのは、読者である。

> もし公道から、歩みを
> グリーン・ヘッド渓谷の騒々しい小川の方へ向けるなら
> 足は険しい小道に苦しむことになるだろう…

しかし小川沿いには、「人目に隠された谷」があり、そこには

> 数頭の羊、岩や石、頭上を空高く航海する鳶がいる

そして読者は気づくことになる、

> 谷川のほとりには
> 自然石の散らかった堆積がある。

『マイケル』という詩は、近くに住んでいた羊飼いのある老人にとってのその石の意味、悲劇的な意味についての作品である。ワーズワースの興味を引いたのは、その場所の情景そのものではなく、谷と野原、山の高さとそこを吹く風、小川のほとりの未完成の羊の囲いに用いる石、それらと人間との関係であった。1800年10月のある晴れた日、ワーズワースは妹とともに「羊の囲いを探して、グリーン・ヘッド渓谷を登っていた」[20]。ドロシーは日記の中でこの場所について、山には橙色のシダ、丘の頂上には草を食む家畜、空には舞う鳶、ふぞろいに分離した心臓に近い形の、崩れ落ちた羊の囲い、小川での水の分岐や小さな滝のきらめきを記している。彼女の残した一節はありのままの場所の描写である。

この同じ散歩が彼を記憶の中へと、記憶の層へと突き進ませている。少年だったとき、彼は

本には無頓着だったが、自然の力を感じ取っていた

また彼は、グラスミアの羊飼いの老人について、ホークスヘッドの家の夫人が語った物語の力をも感じ取っていた。その夫人、アン・タイソンがその話を聞いたのは少女のころだったので、小川のそばの羊の囲いを作り終えられなかったその羊飼いはずっと前に亡くなっていたことになる。『マイケル』という詩は、大いなる愛と喪失、そして喪失に耐えることについての探求であるが、そこで語られるのは「何千もの霧」、「これらの野や丘」、嵐や山々、

感情や放射物、
太陽にとっての光、風にとっての音楽であるような事物

と切り離すこともできない。

ワーズワースが描いた羊飼いの老人の情熱が実に真に迫っているのは、山々が彼にどんな生活を与えてくれたか彼自身よく知っていたからである。彼は霧や風について知り、学生のときには雑木林をぶらつき、青年期にはそこを歩いて抜け、今や毎日それを目にしながら生活していた。10月のある朝、彼は歩きながら、記憶と想像力の中で、これらの人気のない山々の間に、人間の愛と強さがいかに終わりのない責めと苦しみに対処できるのかについての祝福があることを、見出したのだった[21]。

ワーズワースとドロシーは、グラスミア渓谷の林の中だけでなく、道を歩き、立ち止まっては話し、あるいは話を聞いた―ドロシーはとりわけ話を聞くのが得意だった―貧しい人々、たくさんの道のりを歩かざるをえない社会の周縁にいるような人々、たとえば乞食や除隊兵、みすぼらしい人、年取った船乗り、捨てられた女、未亡人、犬と泣く赤ん坊を連れた家族らの悲しい物語を聞いた。ワーズワースと妹が歩いたのは楽しみのためであり、彼らが会った旅人のほとんどがそうであったように、必要に迫られてのことではなかった。二人はそうした人々に、パンやわずかの金を与えた(ドロシーはかつて1シリングほども渡したことがあり、後になって6ペンス払えばすんだかもしれないと思ったりもした)。しかし、何よりも二人は彼らに注意を向けた。二人は彼らの話に耳をかたむけた。ドロシーは時折、放浪者が彼女に話した物語を書き留めたが、結局その説明は物語詩人としてのワーズワースの役に立っていたはずである。彼は情熱にあふれた急進派であり理想主義者であって、フランス革命の初期からより平等な社会を望んでいた。あの驚くほど独創的な、1798年にコウルリッジと共同で出版した『抒情民謡集』には、貧しい人々の哀愁や回復の力についての詩が含まれた。彼が、というより彼ら二人ともが、詩の有用性についてよく考えていた(このことは1800年の『抒情民謡集』第二版の序文で語られている)ことから、これはきっと兄の役に立つと考えてのことだったと思われるが、ドロシーはその前の週に彼らが出会った老人について記録している。この老人は物乞いで生活しており、「信心の本をいくらか」売ろうとしていた。彼はかつて蛭取りだったが、「蛭がめっきりいなくなってしまった」。ドロシーはその男の様子、服装や持ち物、そして彼が語ったこと、たとえば妻と9人の子どもの死、ひとり生きている船乗りの息子の全くの不在、季節ごとにおこる問題と蛭の不足、荷馬車を運転しているとき頭蓋骨にひびが入った事故について詳細に語っている。[22]

ワーズワースは実際のところその散歩や当時のドロシーの出会いについての記述を詩作に生かしたわけではなかったが、二年後に一人で詩人としてまた別の孤独な散歩をしていたとき、いわば自分自身の詩の中を散歩していたときに、その想像の散歩の中で、二年前の老人のことを思い出した。その男は詩の中ではまさに蛭取りであって、そして実際に「小さな池や沼地」のそばに立っていた。「老人は雲のように静止して立ち」、詩人は彼との会話にふけっている。読者である我々は、詩のこの時点で詩人とともに歩き、夜雨のあとの太陽を楽しみ、鳥の声を聞き、「川の心地よい音に満ちた」空気を吸いこむ。空や芝生、野うさぎ、木々や遠くの川のように、「沼地を旅する人」のように―その人は我々を散歩へと案内してくれる詩人自身なのだが―我々は様々な喜びを感じ取る。旅人は「少年のように幸せで」ある。しかしながら孤独に散歩するうちに詩人は考えにふけり始め、詩人の気分は不安になったり憂鬱になったりと、幸せの真逆なものへと変化する。我々の案内人である詩人が、そして彼と共に歩んでいた我々が、蛭取りの男に出会うのは、彼がこの落胆の思いに苦しんでいたまさにその時である。さてこのとき、ワーズワースは確かに、その男に遭遇したときの彼自身の記憶にくわえて、二年前のドロシーの詳細な描写を利用したであろう。老人は圧倒的な苦難に瀕したときの人間の強さや忍耐力の一例として、彼ら二人の心を打っていた。そしてワーズワースは、詩の最初の草稿を書き終えたとき、詩の数連をその老人が直接言った言葉と彼の特徴についての詳細、ドロシーが日記の中で挙げていたような具体的な事実などに捧げた。このすべては、それを最初に読んだサラとメアリー・ハチンソンにとって手に負えないものであった。事実、彼女たちは老人の言葉を「長すぎる」と言った。はじめ、ワーズワースは激高し誤解されたと感じたが、後に詩のその部分のほとんどを抹消し、大地の輝ける朝と詩人の幸せではじまった散歩に焦点を当て直して詩を書き終えた。彼の詩は、彼の精

神のより暗い部分へと移っていったのである。蛭取りは彼自身の悲劇的な歴史からは切り離され、湖水地方のあちこちに見られる、氷河によって過去に長い年月をかけて運ばれ、様々な時代の岩石層の間に堆積する迷子石のひとつのような、疎外された世界における忍耐力の象徴となっている。あるいは、その蛭取りは、束の間日の光の中で休息を取るため海の深部から這い出てきた、古き時代の、今や死に瀕した海の獣であると、ワーズワースは述べている。こうした比較により、蛭取りは歴史の中において彼に特有の人生の具体的な詳細のほとんどを失ってしまった。彼はほとんど神話的であり、驚くべき忍耐力の象徴である。詩人は池のそばでじっとしている老人のところまで歩いていき、彼の「危険で面倒な仕事」について、彼の「多くの困難」について、そしてどのようにして

池から池へ、沼から沼へと歩き回った

のかを聞く。詩人は、その前に感じていた落胆やほとんど恐怖に近い気持ち、そして「悲惨な死を遂げた偉大なる詩人たち」を思い出しながら、老人のことを「私が夢の中で会ったことのある人」であるように感じる。蛭取りは、自分の仕事を辛抱強く続け、詩人にまた語りかける。

蛭を集めながら、遠く広く、
彼は旅をした。このようにして自分の足元の、
蛭たちの生息する池の水をかき回しながら

詩人はこの詩を「その時沼地にいた旅人」、つまり散歩者として始めている。蛭取りもまた旅を続けて来て、今やかなり年を取っているが、なお池から池へと歩き、立ち止まり、水をかき回してはまた歩いている。詩人の歩みと老人の歩みは、詩人の意識のなかで入り混じっているようである。老人の旅、老齢にあってもなお続く忍耐、人生全体にわたる彼の辛抱強い歩みは、ワーズワースにとって力強いイメージとなり、彼の一部となった。

私の心の目に、映ったように思われた
もの憂げな沼地の周りをたえず
ひとりで静かにさまよっていた彼の姿が

ワーズワースはこの詩を「決意と独立」と呼んでいた。蛭取りはある目的とともに歩いており、そして詩人に出会ったが、それは詩人も同じであった。

グラスミアの谷を歩くことは、人生の一部だった。それは体や心、精神を回復させた。

わたしはあまり体の具合が良くないので、散歩はせず輝く太陽は沈むに任せていた。今、ひどい雨が降ってきたので、今日はもう歩かないだろうと思う。

と、ドロシーは1802年4月の終わりに日記に不満を漏らしている。それでも彼らはそう遠くはないが十分なところまで歩いた。

わたしたちは我が家とオリッフ家の間を行ったり来たりし、話をした。・・・ウィリアムはわたしを石の上にほったらかしにして行ってしまった。

ワーズワースはおそらく自分の歩みを進めたのだろう。ドロシーはよく戸外に座っていた。そして明らかに、彼女の気分は回復したようだ。

わたしたちは帰宅した後、チョーサーの訳文を訂正した[23]

この時と同じように、老齢に差し掛かり病を患うようになると、ドロシーは外へ出て、回復をもたらす(と彼女が言う)自然という存在に近づきたいと願った。家に閉じこもっている時のことを、このように記している。

太陽がとても明るく輝き、鳥もたいそう心地よく歌うので、わたしは心が痛ましくなるほど戸外へ出たいと思った。そして言いつけを破って庭へ出ていきたい気持ちに半ばさせられた。[24]

1804年までには、家にはよちよち歩きの幼児がおり、もうひとり赤ん坊が生まれる予定だった。ワーズワースが戸外で詩作をする習慣を身につけたのは、このことに加えて、ダヴ・コテージに住みだしたからかもしれない。ドロシーはキャサリン・クラークソンに1804年2月にこう言っている。

・・・彼は毎朝外を歩いています。たいていはひとりで行きますが、そのたびにごちそうを持ってきてくれます。心地よく穏やかな天候は、概してひどく雨が降るので、彼は傘を持って出かけます。彼はその傘の下で、雨降りの時間の多くは、道や野のただ中にじっと立っています。[25]

ワーズワースは、自分の幼少期についての詩(『序曲』)を創作しているのだとドロシーは説明している。そして彼は5月の終わりまで同じ場所に座り続け、雨もまた降り続いていた。ドロシーは新しい文通仲間のビューモント夫人にこう書き送っている。

・・・彼は今歩いていて、この二時間屋外にいます。朝の間中ひどく雨が降っているのに。雨降りのとき、彼は傘を持って出て、一番の隠れ場所を選んで、そこで行ったり来たりしています。彼の散歩は、時々4分の1マイルもしくは半マイル程度になることがあり、選ばれた境界の中で、まるで牢獄の壁によってきつく足を縛られているかのようです。彼はふつう、詩を屋外で創作します。詩の創作にとても熱中している間は、時がどのように過ぎるのか知ることはめったになく、雨降りなのか晴れているのかどうかも気づきません。[26]

この二種類の散歩—瞑想的な歩みと、遠くにまで及ぶ歩み—は、ワーズワースと妹にとって生涯を通じて絶えず続いたものであった。ドロシーにとっては、1830年代始めに重い病に陥るまで(その後1855年まで生きた)、ワーズワースにとっては1850年に亡くなる直前までのことである。湖水地方でのこの毎日の散歩—アンブルサイド、ケスウィック、アルズウォーター、ラングデール渓谷までの—のあいだには数十回の挑戦的な徒歩旅行がおこなわれたが、ワーズワースはまたこれらの材料のうちに詩を見出した。散歩することは彼の生命であり、不可欠なものだった。ワーズワースはそのことを分かっており、1805年版の「序曲」においてその必要性を論じている。街の中にいくらか美徳を見つけ出すことはできたが、彼が心を向けていたのは、

ああ、小道よ、孤独な道よ、
おまえたちを探していた、おまえたちは私が大切にするものすべて、
人間らしい親切や自然の喜びに満ちている

彼はつづけて、「自分たちの愛する乙女とともに野や森を」散歩する幸福を、妹と「二人にとっての故郷」であるグラスミアで散歩したときのことを述べている。

毎日歩きまわるという比べようのない喜び
その喜びを、私は平穏に瞑想することができ、
私の愛する知恵を見いだすことができた
詩人の音楽を、見知らぬ野や森に教え
人々と語り合うことができた。もし人に会えば、
そこで我々は一人の友人と出会うことになる

私は公道がとても好きだ。私の目をもっと喜ばせてくれる光景はほとんどない
そのようなものには私の想像力を超える力があった
幼年期の始まりから
私の足がこれまでに歩いてきた境界を超えた
あるむき出しの崖の上の消えゆく線
その線を毎日見ていると、
永遠への案内のようであった

・・・孤独な道は私にとっての学校である
そこで私は毎日、最高の喜びの気持ちで読み取った
人間の情熱を
そして人間の魂の深淵を見た[27]

ワーズワースの詩はこれらすべてを証明している。彼らが歩いた大地の一部を歩くことは、ワーズワースにとっても妹のドロシーにとっても取るに足らないことではなかった。散歩は詩の創造的な音楽のための背景であった。散歩は、人間が出会い、互いに共感する場所であった。また、より多くのことを、恐らくは永遠を、発見するための招待であった。悲惨さだけでなく悲しみ、喜び、威厳、美をも含んでいた。散歩は歩く者を生かし、思いがけないものへの注意を呼び起こした。グラスミアのよく知っている道はワーズワース兄妹にとって深い美をたたえており、そして世界の未知の道は人間の美しさをたたえ、詩人の心と一緒になって

私の前にある果てない道に横たわる
世界を通って旅をする思いへと[28]

溶け合っていくものだった。

(翻訳　松浦恵美)

**注**

1. See the whole passage, *Prel.,* II, 321–41.
2. *Ibid.,* IV, 90–120.
3. *Ibid.*, V, 587–91.
4. *Letter*, 16 June 1793.
5. *Letter,* 10 and 12 July 1793.
6. *Journals*, I, 377–78.
7. *Prel.*, I, 329–32
8. *Prel.*, I, 424–26.
9. *Letter,* 23 May 1791.
10. *Letter,* 26 June 1791.
11. *Letter,* 5 June 1793.
12. See the poem, 'When first I journeyed hither'.
13. GJ, 23 Feb 1802.
14. GJ, 2 June 1800.
15. GJ, 31 Oct 1800.
16. GJ, 9 June 1802.
17. GJ, 29 April 1802.
18. GJ, 29 April 1802.
19. GJ, 15 April 1802.
20. GJ, 11 Oct 1800.
21. See the poem 'Michael'.
22. GJ, 3 Oct 1800.
23. GJ, 28 April 1802.
24. Letter, 12–17April 1834, in *The Letters of William and Dorothy Wordsworth: The Later Years, 1821–53*, ed. Ernest De Selincourt, rev. Alan G. Hill, 4 vols., Oxford: Oxford University Press, 1978–88.
25. *Letter,* 13 Feb 1804.
26. *Letter,* 25 May 1804.
27. *Prel.,* XII, 126–65.
28. See the poem 'Stepping Westward'.

『序曲』(Prel.)については以下を参照。*The 1805 text in William Wordsworth, The Major Works,* ed. Stephen Gill, Oxford: Oxford University Press, 1984.

手紙は以下を参照。*The Letters of William and Dorothy Wordsworth: The Early Years, 1787–1805*, ed. Ernest De Selincourt, rev. Chester L. Shaver, Oxford: Oxford University Press, 1967.

引用文は以下を参照。*The Tour Made in Scotland are from Recollections of that Tour, A.D. 1803.* また、日記は以下を参照。*Journals of Dorothy Wordsworth,* ed. Ernest De Selincourt, 2 vols., London: Macmillan, 1941

ドロシーのグラスミア日記(GJ, 日付)は以下を参照。*The Grasmere and Alfoxden Journals,* ed. Pamela Woof, Oxford: Oxford University Press, 2002.

日本語訳は以下を参照。岡三郎訳、『ワーズワス・序曲』国文社、1991年。田部重治訳、『ワーズワース詩集』岩波書店、1938年。藤井綏子訳『ドロシー・ワーズワスの日記』海鳥社、1989年。

**パメラ・ウーフ**

ニューカッスル大学生涯学習課文学講座元講師。長年にわたりワーズワーストラストの理事を務め、現在は名誉会長。夫ロバート・ウーフ博士と共に、ワーズワースとロマン派に関する論文を多数発表し、また展覧会への貢献をしてきた。2013年にワーズワーストラストにて開催された『ドロシー・ワーズワース、すばらしき日常』展は、女性としてまた作家としてドロシー・ワーズワースに初めて焦点を当てた展覧会であった。同題の著書(ワーズワーストラストにて入手可能)にて、ドロシー・ワーズワースの独創的な素晴らしい文学についてさらに議論をすすめている。また、彼女の編集したドロシー・ワーズワースの『グラスミア日記』『アルフォックスデン日記』は定評を得ている。

## 北への想起の旅路—芭蕉とワーズワス

KAZ OISHI 大石和欣

松尾芭蕉がしのぶの里にたどり着いたのは元禄2年（西暦1689年）旧暦5月2日のことであった。東北に向けて江戸深川の家を出発してから36日目にあたる。徒歩での長い旅路をへて福島にほど近いこの村を訪れたのは、「しのぶもぢ摺り」として知られるこの地の布地染めに用いられたと伝えられる著名な岩を一目見たいがためであった。

「しのぶもぢ摺り」は古来より使われている和歌の歌枕である。「しのぶ（信夫、忍ぶ）」という地名は忍ぶ草といわれるシダ類の植物から派生したものであるという説もあるが、「ひそかに想い焦がれる」あるいは「昔を追懐する」という意味の動詞「偲ぶ」と発音が同じであるために、「よじれた模様」を石の上で摺りこむ「もぢ摺り」という言葉と一緒に使われることで「人知れぬ恋に心をかき乱される」あるいは「浮き立つような想い出」を含意するものとして用いられていた。しかし、しのぶの里で芭蕉が見つけた石は、忘れ去られたように田のなかで地面に半分埋まっていた。近くの田圃では早乙女たちが田植えをしている。そんな風景を前にして芭蕉は一句詠む。

早苗とる手もとや昔しのふ摺[1]

早乙女たちが田植えをする腕の動きが、かつて石の上で伝統的なもぢ摺りを染めていたとされる人びとの手つきを芭蕉の心に想起させ、同時に「しのぶもぢ摺り」という歌枕を通してひそかに恋心を伝えあった古の時代を想像したのである。歌枕といういわば人為的に情緒を喚起する「場（トポス）＝常套的表現（トポス）」を借用しながらも、想起というプロセスを通して新たな意味と情感を織りこんだのである。東北への旅路は芭蕉にとってそうした古来からの文学的トポスへの巡礼の旅であった。

上述の一句はイギリスのロマン派詩人ウィリアム・ワーズワスの『麦刈る乙女』の俳句版とも言えよう。1803年にスコットランドへ旅行した際に見た風景を後に回想しながら書いた詩である。穀物を刈り、束ねながら歌を口ずさんでいる「孤独なハイランドの乙女」（2）が詩人の想像力を膨らませ、「悲しい、遠い昔のことごと、古の戦争」、そして現在および未来の「褻事（けごと）」へと誘うのである（19-20行，21行）。[2] ワーズワスにとってのスコットランド旅行は東北へと向かった芭蕉の旅路と似ている。[3] 記憶に残された過去の声を来訪し、想像し、そして追憶する旅なのである。

しのぶ村を出立すること6日目、芭蕉は今度は多賀城跡に「壺碑（つぼのいしぶみ）」を発見し狂喜する（30）。当時すでに跡形もない砦が築かれたことを記念して神亀元年（西暦724年）に聖武天皇が建てた石碑であり、古来より「遠すぎるもの」あるいは「見ることがかなわぬもの」の喩えとして詠みこまれてきたやはり歌枕の一つである。碑に刻まれた文字は厚い苔で覆われていたが、読めないわけではなかった。じつは見つけた石碑が「壺碑（つぼのいしぶみ）」と同一のものかどうかは定かではないが、芭蕉はそれと信じ、「山崩川流て道あらたまり石は埋て土にかくれ木は老いて若木にかは」る不易流行のこの世において、千年ものあいだ石碑が古代の人びと記憶のかたちとして生き残っていたことに感動したのである（31）。この記念碑のわきに立った芭蕉は、歴史の流れのなかで自らの詩人としてのアイデンティティを再吟味し、再確認したのである。芭蕉の旅はそうしたワーズワス的な「時場」（"spots of time"）、つまり内省的な自己検証を行う瞬間が、文学的記憶や集合的記憶と遭遇することで喚起される文学的観光旅行の一種であったとも言えよう。

ワーズワスの場合と同じように、俳人としての芭蕉の生涯において「放浪」は重要な部分を占めている。日本各地を流離った12世紀の詩人西行の足跡を訪ねて東北へとおもむく前にも、東海・近畿地方を中心に3回ほどの徒歩旅行をし、そこで詠んだ俳句とともに紀行文を出版している。俳人の感性と自然との美しい調和がそこにはある。芭蕉の自然描写は、ワーズワスの『叙景素描』や『序曲』の詩行とおなじく絵画的であり、想像力を刺激し、同時に内省的である。一方で、これまでの伝統とは異なる新しい俳句を確立しようと苦闘している形跡があることもたしかである。芭蕉の最後の旅の記録であり、死後元禄15年（西暦1702年）になって出版された『奥の細道』には、自意識や無駄な言葉を極限までそぎ落とし、高度に洗練された俳句の美学が、飾り気のない散文とともに提示されている。「月日は百代の過客にして」（9）ではじまるこの紀行文には、不易流行という芭蕉の世界観が凝縮されていると言ってよい。この感性に基づいて芭蕉は時の流れのなかで不変のまま留まっているもの、古来より歌人たちによって讃えられ、受け継がれてきた文学的名跡や集合的記憶の「場」を見極めることができたのである。そんな「場（トポス）＝常套的表現（トポス）」のひとつひとつを訪れ、そこで句を詠むことで、芭蕉は地霊として過去の歌人たち、そこに生きた人びとの魂と記憶を想起し、新しい時代の言葉で永遠化したのである。

ワーズワスの詩において、旅はより内省的な自己の記憶への遡及となっていることが多い。しかし、数度にわたる彼のスコットランド旅行に際して書かれた詩は、芭蕉の『奥の細道』と比肩しうるものである。スコットランドの農民詩人ロバート・バーンズや英雄ロブ・ロイらの墓、オシアン伝説ゆかりのフィンガル洞窟、廃墟となった城など文学的名跡や史跡を訪ねる集合的記憶に向かう旅の記録だからである。芭蕉が「壺碑」で詩人としてのアイデンティティを再確認したように、ワーズワスは1803年にバーンズの墓を訪れた際に、彼の詩が「野卑な真実の上に／立派な詩の玉座を打ちたてる方法」(「バーンズの墓にて」35-36行)を教えてくれたことを想い出し、詩人としての自らのあり方を再確認している。[4]　1814年の旅行の際に見た名高いヤローの実際の風景には失望したものの、1831年に再訪した折に書かれた『ヤロー再訪』は、時の流れに対する鋭敏な感性と歴史感覚に満ちている。「私たちが変化し、変わり続けてきたけれど」、蛇行するこの川は「過去、現在、未来を／すべて調和的に」つなぎ合わせている(36行、29－30行)。[5]　そこには、「心温まる愛情に導かれて／なかには遠路はるばるやってくる人を含めて客たちが一同に会するように」(31-32行)、古の人びとと今生きている人びとの記憶をともに蘇生させ未来へとつなぐ絵画的な川の風景が広がっている。また、「過去を偲ぶ時の支配」のもとで「穏やかに鎮められ、／静寂につつまれた」キルフーン城の廃墟では、無常観がよりはっきりと浮びあがっている(『オー湖キルフーン城への辞』21行、41-42行)。[6]　1803年にロブ・ロイの墓を訪れた際の詩や、1831年にボスウェル城と廃墟となったブレッドベイン伯の館と一家の墓を訪問した際の詩では、スコットランドの英雄を想起することで、人びとの集合的記憶とアイデンティティを確かめようと試みている。たとえば『廃墟の田舎屋』のような他の詩でもワーズワスは人間の運命と自然の推移を謳っているが、スコットランド旅行に際しての詩は、芭蕉の俳句と同じように墓や廃墟などに埋もれてしまった集合的記憶をたどり、蘇生しようとすることにより強い動機が働いている。

芭蕉の俳句のなかで英雄を集合的記憶として地霊化する声が聞こえるのは、文治5年(西暦1189年)に平泉で非業の最期を遂げた源義経と郎党たちのために詠んだ一句であろう。

夏艸(なつくさ)や兵共(つわものども)が夢の跡(40)

命を落とした英雄たちの生き様を想起し、讃えることで時の流れに抗うように永遠化されたもうひとつの「時場」がこの句には詠まれている。

日英二人の詩人たちによるこうした詩的想起を考察してみると、いずれも意図的な記録の操作や創作的要素を作品に織りまぜていることに気づかされて、実に興味深い。旅の後に回想しながら創作している過程で、ワーズワスは実際の状況を脚色したりしているが、同じように芭蕉も俳句紀行文の芸術的効果を高めるために旅程の順序を頻繁に操作し、変更している。彼の自筆稿には流れるような筆で旅の様子が記されているが、推敲の過程で新たな白紙が切り貼りされて修正された人為的形跡が残っている。歌枕に凝集された過去を追想し、讃える文学的記念という彼の旅の目的を示唆しているだけではなく、万物の無上さを意識し、その時の流れのなかに生きている感覚を研ぎ澄ませた詩人の回想と自省が言語化の過程で集合的記憶のなかに再構築されていったのが垣間見えるのである。[7]

**注**

1. 松尾芭蕉『芭蕉自筆　奥の細道』上野洋三・櫻井武次郎編(岩波書店、1997年)24頁。芭蕉の『奥の細道』からの引用はすべて本書に基づき、引用頁は本文中にカッコ内にて示すこととする。

2. William Wordsworth, *Poems, in Two Volumes, and Other Poems*, 1800–1807 ed. Jared Curtis (Ithaca: Cornell UP, 1983), 184-85.

3.　芭蕉とワーズワスを「旅」というテーマで正面から比較・分析した研究は意外なことに稀である。ジョン・エルダーは、芭蕉の『奥の細道』およびワーズワスの『序曲』のいずれにおいても、自我と自然、過去と現在との融合が「歩くという過程を媒介として詩的に表現されている」と論じている。John Elder, *Imagining the Earth: Poetry and the Vision of Nature* (1985; Athens: U of Georgia P, 1996) 107. しかし、「北」への旅行においては、「過去」は個人の記憶ではなくむしろ「集合的記憶」により密接に結びついている点に注意する必要があろう。

4. William Wordsworth, *Last Poems*, 1821–1850, ed. Jared Curtis (Ithaca: Cornell UP, 1999) 308.

5. William Wordsworth, *Sonnet Series and Itinerary Poems*, 1820–1845, ed. Geoffrey Jackson (Ithaca: Cornell UP, 2004) 491.

6. William Wordsworth, *The Poems of William Wordsworth: Collected Reading Texts from the Cornell Wordsworth Series*, ed., Jared Curtis, 3 vols. (Penrith: Humanities EBook, 2009) 3. 605.

7.　『奥の細道』には4つの原本がある。弟子素龍(そりゅう)が清書した柿衛本・西村本に加えて、1996年に発見された野坂本(中尾本)は、20世紀初頭に再発見された芭蕉の弟子の曾良による曾良本と同じく推敲の跡が多い。原稿のうえに白い紙を切り貼りして新たに加筆・修正がされている。注1で挙げた『芭蕉自筆—奥の細道』では原本の修正部分を写真で確認できる。

**大石 和欣**

東京大学大学院総合文化研究科言語情報科学科准教授。東京大学卒業、オックスフォード大学にて博士号を取得。日本学術振興会研究員を経て、放送大学、名古屋大学にて教鞭を執った。著書に、*Coleridge, Romanticism, and the Orient: Cultural Negotiations*, (David Vallins, Seamus Perryと共著、2013年)、'POETICA', vol.76, Special Issue: *Cross-Cultural Negotiations: Romanticism, Mobility and the Orient* (Felicity Jamesと共編、2011年)、*An Ideological Map of (Mis)reading: William Blake and Yanagi Muneyoshi in Early-Twentieth-Century Japan* (in Steve Clark and Masashi Suzuki (eds.)), *The Reception of Blake in the Orient* (2006年)など、イギリスロマン主義に関する論文を多数発表している。

## 筆跡と原稿—場所と社会に内包・体現される関係

**EWAN CLAYTON ユアン・クレイトン**

日本の俳人松尾芭蕉の洗練された書と、イギリスのロマン派詩人ウィリアム・ワーズワースの簡素で遊びのない筆跡を比較するのは、奇妙なことに思えるかもしれない。しかし、この比較により、二つの対照的な文化の中で書くことが果たした役割が明らかになるばかりでなく、ヨーロッパにおける書くことの歴史において重要な一時期が明らかになるという意味で、これは啓示的である。ワーズワースの存命中に、筆跡の受容に変化が起こった。それは、階級やジェンダーや職業を示すしるしではなくなり、個人の性格や出来事を映し出すものと考えられるようになったのである。このような洞察により、最終的にはグラフィックな記号の生産行為は20世紀芸術のひとつに連なることとなり、西洋においてカリグラフィーは芸術形態のひとつとして再生し、そして西洋における筆記は東アジアの伝統に接近することとなった。

しかし、この二つの世界について、短い紙幅のなかでどう語ろうか?おそらく、詩的な方法をとり、対象たち自身に文脈に沿って語らせるほかないだろう。

***

二つの書台がある。芭蕉のそれは低く、床に座って書くようにできている。その上には書道の道具が置かれている。硯は、触るとひんやりと冷たく、その漆黒の表面のくぼみには水がたまっていて、隣におかれた黒い墨を擦るのに使われる。ほんのりと香りが付けられたこの墨の棒は、炎のエッセンスである煙を固めた煤の粉から作られている。そのすぐ横には芭蕉の筆が置かれている。武士階級の一員であり、書道の教授を収入の足しにしていた父が、彼にこれらの道具の使い方を教えた。そして、若き君主であり友人でもあった藤堂良忠の館で、彼は初めてそれらを用い、句を詠んだ。

良忠が25歳で突然の死を遂げたのち、芭蕉は良忠の遺髪を奉納するため高野山に赴く。転がる岩々、霧、そびえたつ杉林の中で、彼は往古のこの社の開祖であり、日本密教の伝統の創始者である空海、すなわち弘法大師(774-835)の影響を感得する。能書家であった空海の影響は、芭蕉の初期の作風の中にうかがうことができる。時代を経るにつれて、芭蕉の作風は彼の詩的理解の発展を反映して変化し、乾いた平明さへと移っていった。芭蕉は、孤独な道程で旅の記録を残すためだけでなく、彼の周囲に集まった友人、庇護者、弟子への贈り物となる献詞を作るためにも書を残した。彼と書との関係とは、このように気易いものであった。

芭蕉がなぞった文字は、中国の殷の後期に行われた占いの儀式に遠く由来する。儀礼の供物として納められた骨を焼いてできたひびは、宇宙のなかでうごめく現出力のしるしとして読まれた。幾世代にもわたり、占い師たちはこうした「答え」をあらわす形を予言として読み解くようになっていった。その初めより、東アジアの書記体系における文字は、現出しつつある現実を象徴するものになぞらえられた。紀元1世紀より以降、中国において書は表現力に富む伝達手段と考えられ、8世紀までには書の美学に関する批評文学が発展した。

***

ワーズワースの書き物机の上には、筆記のための道具がひとそろい置かれている。真鍮のトレイの上にガラスのインク壺がふたつ、そこに羽ペンがたててある。ガラスと真鍮の光沢は、その上におかれたペンとは対照的だ。ペンはがちょうの風切り羽根からつくられる。ものを書くためには、その羽根を手で切り取って裂け目を入れ、さらにはひんぱんに整形しなおさなければならない。そうしなければ、ワーズワースのノートや紙片の表面にはペン先が引っ掛かり、インクがあふれて飛び散ることになるだろう。ワーズワースは彼が選ぶノートに関してはちょっとした鑑識眼を示していて、赤いモロッコ革で装丁したものや、カレーで買った青い紙の表紙がついたものを使っていた。しかしペンにはあまり関心が払われなかった。鉄塩とタンニン酸で作られたインクは希薄で渋みを含んでおり、時間が経過すると黒から灰色へ、そして茶色へと退色していった。しかしこれについてはワーズワースも当時のご多分にもれなかった。筆記具に鑑識眼を示すこと自体が稀だったのだ。

ワーズワースが8歳になるころには、はるか南の海峡の向こう、アルプスの近く(のちにワーズワースがたどることになる道だが)で、スイスの牧師ヨハン・カスパー・ラヴァーター(1741-1801)が、当時広く読まれることとなった『観相学断片』(1775－8)を出版していた。その第二版では「筆跡に見られる性格」の章が追加され、またゲーテが序文を寄せた。ラヴァーターは当時の「時代精神」のなにものかをとらえて、このように書いている。「我われがそれぞれに自分だけの、独特で模倣を許さないような筆跡を持っているということは十分に考えられることである…このような筆跡の比類のない多様さが、道徳的性格の実質上の相違にもとづいているとは考えられないだろうか?」[1]

印刷技術がヨーロッパの地方の町にまで広がっていたその当時、筆跡が個々人の特質を伝えるものと考えられるようになったのは、人々が活字の画一性に慣れたことへの反動からであった。[2]ワーズワースが30歳になる18世紀末には、書くことは個人の本質的な力や精力から生じると捉えなおされ、まもなく自筆書の収集が始まり、そしてラヴァーターの研究は筆跡にあらわれる個性についてのはっきりとした認識へと発展していた。筆跡学研究の基礎が置かれたのだ。[3]

ワーズワース自身はこの本を読んだことはなかっただろうが、想像力と感情にかかわる世界における進化についてはつねに先導者であった彼は、17歳のころまでには、筆跡と筆記道具に精神—肉体の関係を対応させる論を展開していた—これに類するものとしては記録に残る最初のものであろう。彼の漠然とした想像の中では、書くことは明らかに心理的内容の投影を伝えるものだった。彼が詩的想像力の活動に没頭するようになったころ、ワーズワースの手はそれを書き記すのに苦しみを伴うようになっていた。筋肉が動きにくくなり、体の左側、心臓のあたりに痛みが起こるようになったのだ。「本当ならこの5倍も書いていなければいけなかったのだけれど、体の片側の不安さと心臓のあたりの鈍い痛みでそれができなかった—痛みといったけれど、不安と熱という言葉のほうが僕の気持をより正確に表しているだろうね。とにかく、これのせいで書くことがいやなものになっている」(ワーズワースからコールリッジへの手紙、ゴスラーにて、1798年12月)。この症状はこの後一生彼についてまわった。

右利きの人間が体の左側に負荷を感じることには、身体的理由を見いだせない。これは心情的な苦痛によるものだっただろう。ワーズワースの痛みは、彼個人の場合のみならず彼の生きた時代において、手と心臓が一旦分離され、その後また新しい形で結びつくということが起こった可能性があることを示唆するものである。この出来事は、西洋の書にまつわる物語の中のある重要な転機を示すものである。それは、たんに文字の形状についてだけではなく、書くという行為そのものについての真正性がはっきりと求められるようになったことを示している。[4]ここに、西洋で初めての心のカリグラフィーへの発展へと繋がりうる瞬間があらわれたのだ。しかし、ああ、それが一巡りするには幾世代を経なければならないだろう。

（翻訳：松浦恵美）

**注**

1.　以上に述べられた芭蕉の三つの時期のうち、中期に関するさらなる例については、展示会カタログ「芭蕉：『奥の細道』からの贈りもの」（東京、出光美術館、平成21年、2009年）を参照。

2. ワーズワース財団はこうしたペントレイを収蔵している。

3. Lavater, J. K. *Physiognomische Fragmente zur Beförderung der Menschenkenntnis und Menschenliebe*, Leipzig: 1775–1778.

4. Lavater, J.K. *Essays on Physiognomy*, trans. C. Moore. London: 1797, Vol. 4, p.200.

5.個人間の筆跡の相違がイギリスの法的状況において物証として認められた最初の例は、イギリスの裁判官ジェフリー・ギルバートが残した1726年の記録に記されている。Thornton, T.P. *Handwriting in America*, New Haven: Yale 1996, p.35を参照。

6.　自筆書に対する関心の高まりの最初の証拠となるもののひとつが、ジョン・テーヌによる1788年の*British Autography, a collection of the Facsimiles of Royal and Illustrious Personages with their Authentic Portraits*の出版である。テーヌは269人の肖像画を筆跡と署名の上に掲載しているが、これはあたかも筆跡が肖像の別の一面を構成しているようである。

7.　ラヴァーターの本が1806年に医師ジャック＝ルイ・モローによってフランス語に翻訳されたとき、モローは筆跡についての部分を拡充した。イギリスの著作 John Holt Schooling の*Handwriting and Expression.* London: Kegan Paul, Trench, Trübner & Co. 1892, p.6, には、「M.　モロー氏の記録によれば、筆跡学は1806年以降幾人かによって真剣に実践されている」とある。

8. Wordsworth, W. *The Letters of William and Dorothy Wordsworth*. Vol 1. Eds. Ernest de Selincourt and Chester Shaver. Oxford: Clarendon, 1967, p.236.

9.心についての想像的象徴主義に関するさらなる議論についてはHillman, J. *The Thought of the Heart*, Ascona: Eranos 1981.を参照。

**ユアン・クレイトン**

サンダーランド大学デザイン学科教授。同大学で、マニー・リンと共に国際カリグラフィー研究センター(IRCC)を運営。サセックス州ブライトンに自らのカリグラフィーワークショップを構えている。サセックス州ディッチリング村に近いところに育ち、エリック・ギルによって設立された工芸組合へ親子三代にわたり勤めた。長年、パロアルト研究所(PARC)のコンサルタントを務め、生活様式の形成に文書がどう利用されるかを研究してきた。2013年、書くということの歴史について、著書 *The Golden Thread* を Atlantic Books より出版。南・中央アジア、アフリカ、ヨーロッパ、北アメリカなど世界中で講義、作品の展示をおこなっている。

## 西洋と東洋の旅の詩人――ワーズワースと芭蕉から新しい創造へ――

**SHŌKO AZUMA 東　聖子**

今年は芭蕉没後３２０年、生誕３７０年である。このようなメモリアルイヤーに、英国の美しい湖水地方にあるワーズワース博物館において、比較文化的な視野で、また創造力にあふれる新しい試みの展覧会を開催されることは、まことに嬉しいことである。

### Ｉ芭蕉

＜文学・藝術にとって旅とは何か？＞

松尾芭蕉といえば漂泊の詩人として有名だが、芭蕉は中国の旅の詩人杜甫を尊敬し、また日本の旅の歌人である西行を敬慕していた。中世の兼好法師の随筆『徒然草』のなかにこうある。

　いづくにもあれ、しばし旅だちたるこそ、目さむる心地すれ　（第１５段）

兼好はどこであろうと、しばらく旅へ出ることは、目が覚めるように新鮮な気持ちがするものだと言っている。つまり旅は日常生活からはなれて、人間のみずみずしい感性を取り戻させてくれるものだ。たしかに、私どもが旅でであうひとつひとつのものは、どれも輝いてみえる。

　さて、芭蕉はといえば、旅についてこんなことを言っている。

　東海道の一筋もしらぬ人、風雅におぼつかなし、ともいへり（土芳（どほう）『三冊子（さんぞうし）』）

芭蕉が弟子に「東海道の一筋も知らない人が俳諧をたしなむのはたよりないことだ」と言ったというのは有名な話である。俳諧を作ろうと志すならば、江戸時代の五街道の第一である東海道ぐらいは旅をしておきなさいと語り、藝術にとって旅の体験を重要視している。

芭蕉は、４０代になって５つの紀行文を書いた旅をしている。江戸時代は街道もあまり整備されず、徒歩や駕籠や馬をつかった旅はさぞ辛いことも多かったことだろう。『野ざらし紀行』『鹿島詣（かしまもうで）』『笈（おい）の小文（のこぶみ）』『更科紀行』『おくのほそ道』・・・満４０歳から４５歳まで、行脚の日々は芭蕉の体を疲れさせた。５０歳、大坂で亡くなった時は、最後の旅である九州・四国への旅の途中だった。

＜天地の変化は藝術の種＞

師芭蕉のことばとして、また、こんなことも伝えている。

　師の曰く「乾坤の変は風雅の種なり」といへり。（『三冊子』）

師の芭蕉は「天然自然の変化は、すべて俳諧の材料である」といわれたと言う。「風雅」とは広義では藝術、狭義では俳諧のことである。四季のある日本の風土の中では、天地の変化を心にとめて、なにかを感じた時は、その光が消えないうち言い留めなさいとも語っている。そして芭蕉は常に古びをきらって、「新しみをせめよ」とも語っており、オリジナリティのたえざる深化を目指していた。旅へ出ることは、天地の中を歩いてゆき、新しい発見をめざすことであった。

### Ⅱワーズワース

＜夏目漱石の「英国詩人の天地山川に対する観念」の論＞

英国のワーズワースは１９世紀のロマン主義を代表する最も優れた自然詩人である。近代日本の代表的小説家であり英文学者でもある夏目漱石は、この論の中で、ワーズワースの自然主義は、＜智＞よりなるもの、あるいは＜哲理的直観＞よりなるものであり、また「玄の玄なるもの、万化と冥合し宇宙を包含して余りあり。ワーズワースの自然主義是なり」と述べている。

＜ワーズワースと芭蕉＞

芭蕉（1644-1694）は、日本の江戸時代前期を生きた詩人である。ワーズワース（1770-1850）は、日本で言えば江戸時代の後期にあたる。両者とも国民的詩人であり、自然と対峙した詩人である。旅を愛して、哲学的な理論を背景としている。１３歳頃に、同じように父を亡くしている。異なるのは、ワーズワースは家庭人であり、芭蕉は生涯独身であった。しかし、芭蕉は多くの門弟と親しく交流していた。ともかくも、１７世紀東洋の詩人と、１８世紀後半から１９世紀前半の西洋の詩人である。

**Ⅲ両者の「水仙」の詩**

ワーズワースの「水仙」の詩はこころひかれる名作だが、芭蕉にも「水仙」を詠んだ俳句がある。

ワーズワース　　　「水仙」(原題:『私は独りさまよった、浮雲のように』)

谷また丘のうえ高く漂う雲のごと、
われひとりさ迷い行けば、
折しも見出でたる一群の
黄金色に輝やく水仙の花、
湖のほとり、木立の下に、
微風に翻えりつつ、はた、躍りつつ、

天の河に輝やきまたたく
星のごとくに打ちつづき、
彼らは入江の岸に沿うて、
はてしなき一列となりてのびぬ。
一目にはいる百千の花は、
たのしげなる躍りに頭をふる 。
……(略)……
わが心は喜びに満ちあふれ、
水仙とともにおどる。

芭蕉
水仙やしろき障子のとも移り
(水仙の白い花がいけてある。白い障子と映りあって清楚で美しい)

其にほひ桃より白し水仙花
(水仙の花は、その匂いも色も白桃よりずっと白くて優雅であるよ)

水仙は冬の季語で、日本の水仙は白くて清楚なイメージがある。西洋の黄色いラッパ水仙とは、異なっている。また、日本の古典和歌では音読みのために作品に詠むことはなかった。近世の俳諧になって初めて詠まれた素材である。芭蕉は白い美しさを好み、彼の俳句には水仙が大切に詠まれている。また、江戸時代の浮世絵でも室内や、水辺の水仙が描かれている。他に、ワーズワースと芭蕉は郭公・胡蝶・雛菊その他の共通の素材を扱っている。

**Ⅳ新しい挑戦へ**

＜歩くことと創作／筆蹟からの再構築＞

今回の展覧会のコンセプトは、かなり新しい試みである。第一には、詩人・文学者・藝術家にとって「歩く」という行為は何をもたらすのかという、大変にシンプルだが、人間にとって本質的なテーマとなっている。新しい視座が開けてくるかもしれない。第二には、藝術家の「筆跡」から、それを受容して、さらにそこから新たな創作をこころみるということである。これも興味深いことだ。ただし、拠るべき「筆跡」は複製でも真蹟であるべきだ。そして、この二つのテーマは、現代において創造的読者の出現を期待させる。

最後になったが、現在、グローバル化のなかで、国際HAIKUが活況を呈しており、一説には世界約５０か国で、多くの人々が各国言語で俳句を創作しているといわれている。ここ英国でも、英国俳句協会がすばらしい活動をしている。私もデーヴィッド・コブ元会長からその活動をうかがった。俳句は世界で最も小さい短詩型文学で、その＜瞬間の美＞に世界の詩人たちは魅力を感じている。

今回の英国におけるワーズワース博物館での芭蕉とコラボレートした斬新な展覧会に対して、感謝と期待を申し上げる。そして、ご来館の皆様には日本にある芭蕉記念館(東京都江東区)・芭蕉翁記念館(三重県伊賀市)や芭蕉ゆかりの資料館にも、いつかぜひ訪れていただきたい。ワーズワースと芭蕉についての今回の展覧会を、企画された関係者の方々に敬意を表したい。そして、皆様にはどうぞ自由な発想を感じながら新しい創作を楽しく鑑賞していただきたい。

**東　聖子**

十文字学園女子大学教授。日本女子大学文学部国文学科卒業、お茶の水女子大学大学院人間文化研究科比較文化学専攻(博士課程)。人文科学博士(お茶の水女子大学)。専門は日本近世文学・比較詩学で、芭蕉の俳諧に関する著作多数。『蕉風俳諧における＜季語・季題＞の研究』(明治書院、2003年)で山本健吉賞受賞。『おくのほそ道』を題材として、東洋と西洋の文学における旅の描写の比較研究も手がけている。

## アーティスト紹介

### KEN COCKBURN
**ケン・コバーン**

*While yet we may*
2014年
本
13 cm x 18 cm

*While yet we may*
2014年
カード一式
10 cm x 9 cm x 3.3 cm

ケン・コバーンは、エディンバラ在住のフリー作家、翻訳者、編集者、ライティングチューター。彼はかねてより俳句に関心を持ち、共同制作を取り入れ、媒体に固執しない活動を行っている。アレック・フィンレーとの共作 *The Road North* 北の道)は、芭蕉による17世紀の東北日本の旅のスコットランド版である。

この旅の展覧会におけるコバーンの作品は、地理的歴史的に離れた詩人たちの言葉を寄せ合わせ、詩的に連結するという、共同制作の手法としては一見シンプルなものである。*While yet we may* と題された、詩の冊子と箱入りのカードの作品は、芭蕉の『おくのほそ道』からの引用17語と、ワーズワースの『序曲』と、『ティンターン修道院上流数マイルの地で』からの引用51語とで構成されている。

この作品のアイディアは、詩人ガエル・ターンブル(1928-2004)の'Variable Construction'(可変的構築)から来ている。それは、二セットのカードから成り、一セット目の28枚のカードは1枚ごとにひとつの名詞が、その他の112枚のカードにはそれぞれ修飾語が与えられている。ターンブルの言うように、112の修飾語のいずれが、どの名詞と結びついてもよい。

出版されたバージョンではそれぞれの修飾語がひとつの名詞とペアにされているが、彼は、このバージョンも他のバージョンに劣らず完成形であると記している。コバーンの冊子 *While yet we may*にも同様のことが言える。

ルーク・アラン、アレック・フィンレー、ローナ・アーヴィン、ライラ・マツモトに感謝をこめて。

### MIKE COLLIER
**マイク・コリヤ**

*The Texture of Thought: Fairfield*
ドロシー・ワーズワースの日記より、1801年10月23、24日
デジタルプリント、パステル彩色
2014年
35 cm x 65 cm

*The Texture of Thought: Helvellyn*
ドロシーワーズワースの日記より、1801年10月25日
デジタルプリント、パステル彩色
2014年
35 cm x 65 cm

マイク・コリヤの作品は、芭蕉やワーズワースを含む先人の「足跡」を歩くことに関連していることが多い。彼は、ドロシー・ワーズワースが日記の中に描いた湖水地方の数々の丘歩きのルートを辿り、そういったウォーキングからインスピレーションや、特定の地方の現象的理解と作品の間の関係を模索する製作の題材を得る。

この展覧会に出品する作品は、ドロシーが気に入った丘歩きのルートや行こうとしたルートを記述している『グラスミア日記』(1801年)から、引用箇所をスキャニングし、ユニゾン社

製のハンドメイドパステルで彩色したものである。

魅惑的なほど繊細なドロシーの日記帳は、職人の手のあともついており、
手書きの文字ともども含蓄があり、苦心の跡を見せている。取り消し線や書き直しによって不明瞭になっているため、デジタル画面や印刷物の文字に慣れている現代の読者には、この日記の判読は難しい。コリヤは彼独自の直感的な色彩表記で、この日記の内容に呼応するように即興的に色を塗り、視覚的策略の層を添える。

コリヤは、この創造的な再加工の題材として、ドロシーが好んだ、そして彼自身も何度も歩いたルートの描写箇所を選択した。フェアフィールドの峰に登ろうとしたが天候により失敗した記述と、その二日後、ヘルベリン山の上で見た荘厳な風景の記述である。これらの二作を通して、コリヤは再度ドロシーの言葉と彼女の空想、彼女の自然描写における特徴的に斬新な才能に焦点を当てている。

### EWAN CLAYTON and NAO SAKAMOTO
**ユアン・クレイトン、坂本直昭**

*Infinite Imagination: two poets at night, the moon on Mount Snowdon; the Milky Way over Sado Island*
2014
藍染楮和紙、墨、金銀箔
180 cm x 66 cm

英国在住のカリグラファー、ユアン・クレイトンと、日本で和紙の製作を手がける坂本直昭の共同制作は、ワーズワースと芭蕉の詩的世界観が呼応しあう、心揺さぶる美しいインスタレーションを作り上げた。

掛軸のように下げられ、大きさは手ごろでありつつ広がりを持ち、両面に書いてある文字は見えながらもわかりにくい。*Infinite Imagination*（尽きない想像力）と題されたこの作品は、芭蕉の一見シンプルな書と、ワーズワースの文字を詰め行が重なり合った原稿に語りかける。ワーズワースと芭蕉を改めて書くという過程において、クレイトンと坂本は、書かれた文字の美と外見的特徴に注目した。原稿の保全作業でよく使われるように、坂本の楮和紙は藍で染められ、染めの重なった上部はより不透明に、下部はより透けて見えるようになっており、これがクレイトンがカリグラフィーを書き重ねるベースとなる。この、ほぼ無制限の紙面は、カリグラフィーの探検への挑戦である。このような共同制作には、互いの材料だけでなく、世界観、美観、哲学を合わせるという脆弱性もはらんでいる。

クレイトンと坂本は、芭蕉やワーズワースの作品の裏側にあるより深い思惑に魅了されている。二人の作品は、ワーズワースの『序曲』1805年版のスノードンに上る箇所、ならびに天の川を詠んだ『荒海や』の俳句、これら月明かりの注ぐ空間や自然の世界に陶酔する瞬間を捉えた詩を基としている。

### ALEC FINDLEY
**アレック・フィンレー**

*word-mntn* (羽黒山)、2014、カエデ材の立方体、各 4 x 4 cm
*word-mntn* (小倉) 、2014、カエデ材の立方体、各 4 x 4 cm
*word-mntn* (シハリオン) 、2014、カエデ材の立方体、各 4 x 4 cm
*word-mntn* (スクール・ナン・ギレン) 、2014、カエデ材の立方体、各 4 x 4 cm
*word-mntn* (スライオッホ) 、2014、カエデ材の立方体、各 4 x 4 cm
*word-mntn* (日光)、2014、カエデ材の立方体、各 4 x 4 cm

*a-ga: on mountains*, 2014, 本, 13 cm x 18 cm.

アレック·フィンレーの美しくシンプルな木製のキューブを積んだ作品は、あるレベルでは子供の積み木を連想させる。一見遊び心に満ちた作品であるが、その実、折り重なった文学的、芸術的、哲学的関連性を秘めている。この作品を含め、フィンレーはよく芭蕉の俳句の影響を受けた作品を作り、また、風景における人間の関わりに関心を寄せている。この積み木型の作品は、もともとスコットランドのスカイ島から望める山々の名前を使ったプロジェクトで生まれた。フィンレーはこれをさらに発展させ、今回の作品はスコットランドと日本の両

方の山の名前を用いて構成されている。見る者に、ブロックを動かして好きな山の名前を作る遊びを空想させる斬新な試みである。

様々な媒体を使用するフィンレーの作品の多くは共同制作であり、社会環境に一体化させたりデジタル形式で共有されたりして、創作とは本質的に共同で行われるものという信念を表している。

作品 *word-mntn* は、我々の山への個人的・集団的感性に関するフィンレーの興味を、名称の語源的ルーツから、詩と行為遂行的な芸術的研究を通して拡大させた。また、山を見る、歩く、歩かないことへの考えを収めた最新の著書 *a-ga: on mountains* も、今回あわせて展示されている。

**EIICHI KONO**
**河野英一**

*Homage to Bash*
37 cm x 140 cm
2014
毛筆、手漉き楮和紙、犂耕体

芭蕉の作品を通して、河野は自身の青年時代の文化を振り返っている。成人後の人生の半分をイギリスで過ごした河野にとって、芭蕉に立ち返ることは、日本語や幼少時の言葉を思い出すことでもある。芭蕉も行った書くという行為そのものによって、芭蕉に敬意を示し、『おくのほそ道』の全文を紙の両面にわたり一筋に連なるように配した。句読点という印刷字体のしきたりを排した構造は、河野の言う ‘texture of walking narrative’ (歩きの物語の感触)を作り出した。

河野は芭蕉という日本の重要な詩人についてよく見聞きして育ち、俳句という簡明な的確さにも親しんでいたが、この長大なたびの日誌を読み、書写することで、彼はまた違った芭蕉に出会った。芭蕉は突如、知らない土地と時代の知らないものとなり、文字を書くという行為だけで精一杯だった。

河野はこのように語った。書くということは労力を要する。時には退屈であり、時には爽快であり、集中力を要する。だが、その肉体的苦痛にも関わらず、私は繰り返しこの物語に取り組み完遂せざるを得なかった。時間とともに、私の小さな文字で書写するリズムと感覚が、旅する芭蕉に重なり彼の思いに寄り添うように感じたのだ。

**MANNY LING and CHRISTINE FLINT SATO**
**マニー・リン、クリスティーン・フリント・里**

*Mountain Lines, Water Lines*
各46 cm x 106 cm(額装含む)
2014
墨、和紙

西洋と東洋(ワーズワースと芭蕉)の出会いは、マニー・リンとクリスティーン・フリント・里による共同制作によく集約されている。フリント・里は日本に住むイギリス人の墨絵アーティストで、リンは香港出身でイギリスに住み、西洋のカリグラフィーから中国式の書まで幅広く手がけている。

両者の書の伝統の中核にあるのは、既に存在する言葉に、創造的に再度意味を持たせ解釈するということである。画と言葉の組み合わせは東アジアの美術の伝統においてよく見られる。芭蕉自身も、彼の俳句や日記の側に絵を残すことがよくあった。リンはまずワーズワースの「ティンターン修道院上流数マイルの地で」の一節を選び、この共同再解釈作品の基礎とした。フリント・里はこれをさらに進め、山と水と自然の潜在能力の解放—東アジアの墨絵の伝統において、彼女がもっとも良く可視的に表現できる要素—に関する節を加えた。

その結果できた作品は、幾重もの工程と連想の重なりを明示している。ワーズワースの一節は、フリント・里の墨絵の上に書かれたリンの文字によって再度描写された。書という最も伝統的な芸術への、リンの実験的なアプローチが、彼の使う、植物や自然の動きに視覚的に呼応する筆運びの中に見て取れる。フリント・里の山々と水の描写は、東アジア絵画において重視される淡い塗り、線、点々などの抽象的な要素を個人的に再解釈し、伝統と現代の活動とに同時に結びつける。この作業によって、イングランド詩人の象徴たるワーズワースが、東アジアの材料と書の視点をもって描き直される。和紙と墨は、即興性や偶然の幸運と事故をも受け入れる身体的工程と結びついている。

**CHRISTOPHER MCHUGH**
**クリストファー・マキュー**

*Flotsam and Jetsam (Portmanteau)*
2014
磁器、テラコッタ、ソーダガラス、ミクストメディア
約120 x 60 x 50 cm

クリストファー・マキューの作品は、芭蕉とワーズワース双方に見られる世の儚さや人の記憶といったテーマに呼応するものである。『奥の細道』の中で芭蕉はよく歴史的な遺跡を訪れ、古に想いを馳せる句を詠んだ。ワーズワースは、人間の産み出した建造物も書物もやがては崩壊し、自然が取って代わるであろうことを危惧していた。そして、両人とも、旅の途中で出会った無名の人々の生活を記録することに関心を持っていた。

マキュー自身も同様に、ともすると見過ごされ失われてしまう物語を呼び覚まし、焼き物の作品として物質化している。この作品 *Flotsam and Jetsam (Portmanteau)*—「がらくた(旅行かばん)」の意—はスリップキャスト法と型押し法で作られた何百もの焼き物の小片から成っている。恒久的な焼き物の部品を、展覧会ごとに期間的に盛り合わせるという展示方法、また傷だらけの磁器のかけらによって、無と有の間の二面的な立場に立ち、永遠の喪失感と憂鬱さを表している。焼き物の山を貫くソーダガラスで作られた草は、文明を越えて永続する自然を示唆している。

作品のタイトルは、ダヴ・コテージに展示してあるワーズワースの旅行かばんと、芭蕉の作品名『笈の小文』に起因している。'Portmanteau'という単語には、旅行かばんという意味の他に、二つ以上の語を合わせてできる新しい意味の言葉、という意味もある。『奥の細道』で、芭蕉は藤原三代の栄華のち荒れて草原となった平泉を訪れ、世の無常を詠んでいる。これは、ワーズワースが『廃屋』に描写している、人の儚さと悠久の自然とも呼応する。マキューは、この二人の詩人の言葉を組み合わせて新たな作品へと統合した。

**NOBUYA MONTA**
**門田展弥**

*An Imaginary Dialogue*
ヴィオラ: 古味 亜紀
ギター: 濱田 圭
全19分

もし芭蕉とワーズワースが出会ったら、もし芭蕉が湖水地方を歩いたら、もしワーズワースが日本の山野を歩いたら、どのような反応をしただろうか、という空想を広げて、門田は4楽章から成るこの曲を作曲した。この想像上の会話は旋律となり、旅し、さすらい、遠く離れた者に思いを募らせるといったテーマが響き渡る。

門田の作品を裏打ちする音楽と詩の関係について、もう少し探ってみよう。ワーズワースと芭蕉は、自然の音に調和していた。ワーズワースの詩において景色の描写は音となり歌い、古池や蛙飛び込む「水の音」は芭蕉の最もよく知られた句のひとつである。より哲学的な意味においては、ワーズワースの詩は音楽の隠喩で満たされ、音楽の調和は基本思想である。このような音楽と詩のつながりや美意識は、調性音楽において国際的方向性を示してきた音楽家・作曲家の門田にとって大変重要である。

門田は大阪に生まれ、日本とヨーロッパで作曲を学んだ。現在、国際的に第一線の音楽家たちと共に演奏活動を続けている。

## INGE PANNEELS and MINAKO SHIRAKURA
**インガ・パニールズ、白倉美奈子**

*Wanderers of the Earth: the Milky Way Above*
2014年
ガラス、紙
不定形（ガラスの地図約20 x 20 mm、封筒11.4 x 16.2 cm、円形のカード直径4–5 cm）

*Wanderers of the Earth: Walk*
2014年
ガラス
25 x 75 x 4 cm

*Wanderers of the Earth: the Milky Way Above*（さすらう者たち：天の川を見上げて）は、英国に拠点置くアーティスト、インガ・パニールズと日本に拠点を置く白倉美奈子による共同作品である。二人はこの共同作業を、物理的に遠距離にいる両者を引き合わせることの可能な現代の通信機器（Eメールとスカイプ）を使って完成させた。

まさしく、彼らの新しい作品は「文通」に基づきまたその結果としてできたもので、それは世紀を越えて我々にもたらされた詩人たちの原稿や手紙から影響を受けてもいる。2014年の春、パニールズと白倉は、このアイディアを形にするためにサンダーランドの国立ガラスセンターに集まった。芭蕉とワーズワースが星と星座について言及しているところから着想を得て、彼らは世界地図をあしらったガラスの小片を作った。それらは和紙に包まれて、世界中の友人知人へと贈られた。円形の和紙カードと、それに各々の言語で「星」と書き、送り返してもらうように誘う手紙が同封されていた。このようにしてプレゼントを贈り合い集めた「星」が、インスタレーションの一部となっている。このインスタレーションに付随したもうひとつの作品、*Wanderers of the Earth: Walk*（さすらう者たち：歩）と題されたガラスパネルは、ワーズワースと芭蕉の星に関する詩が、それぞれパニールズと白倉の筆跡によってしたためられている。パネルの色は、時間の変化と空間的な間隔（東西）を示唆している。このインスタレーションは、ワーズワースと芭蕉が彼らの詩を通じて伝えた無限と不可思議な感覚に関連して、宇宙を体現してみようというアーティスト達の試みである。

## ANDREW RICHARDSON
**アンドリュー・リチャードソン**

*The ghostly language of ancient earth*
2014
対話型地図とデジタルプリント
23インチ型モニター（1280 x 720 ピクセル）

リチャードソンの作品は旧来と新世代の地勢描写を融合する。ワーズワースの『序曲』から引用した言葉を、グラスミアとその周辺の三次元対話型地図にあてはめた。スクリーン上で操作できる地図で、文字の地勢を色々な角度から眺めたり、「言葉の道」を辿ったりすることができる。この「言葉の道」は、詩の一行ごとの言葉の数と長さによって、道の方向が変わるというふうに、ワーズワースの詩と直接関係している。一方、併せて展示されているプリント版では、この地図を静止画として、より落ち着いてじっくりと見ることもできる。

ワーズワースが記した風景の輪郭を再度描写するにあたり、リチャードソンは、この詩人の元々の言葉に立ち戻り、そして比喩的に地図へ表した。それにより、鑑賞者はタッチスクリーンパネルにより、地図の中の道と、ワーズワースのもっとも有名な傑作の詩の行を同時に辿ることができる。我々鑑賞者の指は、文学的そして空想的な散歩につれて行くのである。このようにしてリチャードソンは、タッチパネルでデジタル式に繋がった我々の世界の視点から、ワーズワースの詩に対して現代的反応を返している。地表に散らばったワーズワースの言葉は、鑑賞者それぞれの手によってまた読解が可能なように再形成されるのである。

AUTUMN RICHARDSON

**オータム・リチャードソン**

*The Mulberry Coat*
2014
楮和紙、縫製
123 cm x 128 cm

*Go To The Pine*
2014
紙に印刷された文字
29.7 cm x 42 cm

オータム・リチャードソンは、生態学、特に植生態に注目し、自然風景を生かした作品を様々な媒体で制作している。芭蕉もまた、身近で小さな物事に注意を払い、周囲にある草や木について書き、詠った。

作品 *Go To The Pine* は、芭蕉が奥の細道の旅において言及した木々を列挙し、それを通じて仮想の北への旅路を辿ろうとした。

芭蕉は、旅に出るにあたり、手製の衣、笠、履物を必要とした。これらは全て植物性であり、彼の書に影響を与えた。

芭蕉はこのように記している。「草の扉に独りわびて、秋風のさびしきおりおり、妙観が刀を借、竹取の巧を得て、竹をさき竹を枉げて、自笠作りの翁と名乗る。」

*The Mulberry Coat* とは、芭蕉が着ていたかもしれないという想像上の着物で、生成りの楮和紙を綿糸で縫い合わせて作られた。紙製の衣類に注目した時、リチャードソンは、身を包み守ることができ、考えを書き留めることができ、そして景色に直接触れられるといった紙の価値と、芭蕉の書における物質性を強調する。

RICHARD SKELTON

**リチャード・スケルトン**

*I Know Not Where*
2014年
紙
33 cm x 50.8 cm (二点)

*Still Glides the Stream*
2014年
紙
33 cm x 50.8 cm (二点)

ドロシー・ワーズワースがつけた『アルフォックスデン日記』は、'walked' (歩いた)で始まるものが多い。リチャード・スケルトンの作品 *I Know Not Where* は、ドロシーの言葉を精製したもので、200ほどの彼女の言葉の間をさすらいながら自分の道を見つけ、地形的な物語を書くことに読者をいざなう。また作品には、俳句を思わせる十の言葉のかけらが添えられている。

*Still Glides the Stream* は、ワーズワースのソネット作品『ダッドン河』において、「水」に関する古い単語がどのように表れているかに着目した作品である。それらの単語は、ゲルマン語、ケルト語属族に属し、おそらくワーズワースの時代よりはるか以前にブリティッシュ諸島で話されていたらしい。

この新しい詩は、川の中にある渦のようなものと捉えることができる。はじめに、原文の33のソネットを全てひとつの文として並べ、そして「水」に関する言葉が出てきたらそれを消去する。こうして文章に穴が開き、意味を成さなくなることで、言語が失われる過程を示してみせる。川のように、言葉は流動的で絶えず変化し、意味もさえも不確かで、永続を約束されたものではないのである。

詩の後半は、初めの部分とは反対のイメージである。失われた「水」の単語を再生し、現存する言葉として提示する。これは、ワーズワースの言葉を景色のように想像してみることである。そこには、澱みを溶き流し、古くて硬い石のかけらを掘り起こす、ダッドン河の流れがある。

**AYAKO TANI**

**谷　綾子**

*Drafting*
2014
二対のフレーム（各 60 x 30 x 12 cm）
ランプワーク技法、ガラス、オーク材

ワーズワースは、詩のインスピレーションの本質について大変関心を寄せていた。『二巻組詩集』(1807年)に収められたかの有名な「水仙」の詩が詠うように、花は「脳裏に鮮やかに蘇る」。

ワーズワーストラストに保管されている原稿をよく観察すると、びっしりと詰めて書かれた文字、斜線を引かれた文字などが見られ、詩を書き上げるのに払われる労力を窺い知ることができる。この展覧会に参加したアーティストたちは、これらの原稿を手に取れるという恩恵に与った。その中で谷は、普段は目に触れないこうした創作過程の労力について探究心を得たのであった。

ガラスは、多様で、相反する表現力を秘める素材である。脆弱であるも柔軟で、何重かに用意された板ガラスの層は、ワーズワースによる詩的描写を書きとめる場である。谷はそこへ、ランプワーク技法を用いて、溶けたやわらかいガラスから毛筆で書くように線を引き出し、文字を「書いた」。これらの線は、詩の初めのインスピレーションのように、少しおぼろげで儚い。いくつかの言葉は立体的な毛筆線としてはっきりと見えるが、その他の文字はちらちらと見えるだけであったり、言葉になるかならないかもわからない夢想的ないたずら書きであったりする。作品中の日本語は田部重治による訳を引用。

**BRIAN THOMPSON**

**ブライアン・トンプソン**

*To Easedale Tarn by Emma's Dell*
2014
ヒマラヤスギ
1630 x 751 x 386 cms

*Over the Ferry to the Station (with J, E & B)*
2014
オーク、銅
29 x 17 x 8 cms

*To Latterbarrow (with A & P)*
2014
ニレ、塗料
13.5 x 11.8 x 4.5 cms

*To The Yews of Borrowdale (with J)*
2014
イチイ
11 x 11 x 6 cms

*Yudaki Falls (with MC)*
2014
鋳鉄
16 x 18 x 7 cms

*Kurobane (with MC)*
2012
ポーセリン
23 x 10.7 x 4 cms

ブライアン・トンプソンの芸術的活動において、ウォーキングは欠かせない要素である。ある土地へ、そして土地から土地へ、実際に旅をすること、そしてそれがどのように記録され評価されるかということに常に興味をそそられている。トンプソンにとって土地は芸術的なインスピレーションの源である。土地との付き合い・身体的関与が彼のアプローチの特質であり、展示作品は彼が同僚のアーティスト達と歩いた旅の足跡である。

肉体の敏感さと素材への審美眼もまた、彼の作品の鍵である。各彫刻は、それぞれのウォーキングに関連した素材で作られている。*To Easedale Tarn by Emma's Dell* イーズデールターン湖へ、エマの谷より）と題した大型の彫刻は、2014年1月に、この展覧会に参加している他のアーティストや作家たちと共にワーズワースが好んだ丘歩きのルートを歩いたときの、地形的軌跡によって形作られている。現代のGPS技術により、ウォーキングの軌跡が記録され、スタジオに戻ってからそれを彫刻にするのである。小型の作品は、うち三点が湖水地方でのウォーキングからインスピレーションを得た作品で、残り二点は日本において、かつて芭蕉が通った道を辿ったウォーキングを基にしている。

トンプソンはまた、ウィリアムとドロシー・ワーズワース兄妹の原稿に見られる、詩の一語一語を仕上げてゆく言葉の「手工業」とも言うべき文学的プロセスに心を惹かれている。そのような最新の注意を払う言葉の創作は、作品を作る過程を垣間見せるように素材の層を重ねていくトンプソンの緻密な手法と比較できる。材料の板をその旅の軌跡の形に正確にカットし、カットされたその板を次のテンプレートとしてさらに下の層を作ってゆく。この方法によって、層が増えるごとに外周が一回りずつ太くなり、地層のように層が重なり、広がった裾野から細い先端へと立ち上がるような彫刻ができるのである。

## あとがき
## ワーズワースをより良く知る

ウィリアムとドロシー・ワーズワースの詩と散文を「より良く知る」とは如何なることであろうか。この展覧会においては本質的に言葉のこと、つまりウィリアムとドロシー・ワーズワース、そして松尾芭蕉によって書かれた言葉と文書についてのことである。ワーズワースにおいて、それは「幸福者をさらに幸福にして昼光に日光を注ぎ、いつの時にも若者と風流者に、見て、考えて、感じることを教えるために書かれた」言葉である。訪れる者は、詩人たちの言葉の力を感じとることにより、彼らを「より良く知る」。詩人の言葉を通じて、人々がより良くものを見、考え、感じることの一助となること、それが我々の目指すところに違いない。

学芸員の役割は、ダヴ・コテージとジャーウッド・センターが保有する世界的に重要な文献のコレクションとを通じて、人々のより深い理解を促し、支援することである。この解説というのは、単なる事実の提示ではなく、個々人に新たな意味と知見をもたらすような、来訪者と作品との仲介である。学芸員の仕事は、来訪者の好奇心を刺激し、満たし、展覧会の核心である言葉というものに対する受容力を持たせることである。

作家の想像の中から言葉がインクを通じて紙の上に移された、手稿というものを取り扱う中で、我々は、彼らの言葉と創作に一歩近づく。手稿には、作家単独や共同作業の下書きや推敲の跡がある。手稿を調べれば、文字のかたち、削除と追加の順番を辿ることができるし、急いで書いたか丁寧に書いたかによって書き手の心理状態を窺い知ることもできる。そして何にもまして、手稿は、他者との有形かつ強いつながりである。書き手は、その紙切れやノートを手で触れ、目で見つめ、創作の苦労をした。いま我々の目前にあるのは、作家と彼らの人生の一部なのである。手稿はその目撃者であり、それを介して、我々は創作の瞬間へ連れて行かれるのだ。

私は長らく、ヘレン・ダービシャーの「ワーズワースの人生や人柄についての知識が、彼の詩の理解を助ける場合にのみ」[1]という、詩人自身に対する関心の向け方に影響を受けている。詩人自身と詩の間の線引きは難しい。どれだけの展覧会が、ダービシャー氏のテストに合格するだろうか。人生のエピソードは面白いから、作家の伝記へと話しを逸らすことは簡単にできる。どれだけの展覧会が、詩そのものをさておいて、時系列の説明ばかりしてきただろうか。しかし「歩く詩人」展は、書くということを前面に押し出した展覧会に近づいたものだと信じている。

1798年の『抒情民謡集』の序文でワーズワースは、多くの詩は「実験と捉えられるべき」と注意している。彼は、多くの読者が違和感を持つかもしれないと警告し、予め決められた判断基準を乗り越えるよう読者に呼びかけている。おそらく「歩く詩人」展は、ワーズワースに関する展覧会やワーズワース博物館における展覧会として、通常予想されるような類のものではない。しかしこの展覧会は、三人の偉大な作家の言葉に、我々を近づけるものである。過去の手稿と言葉をじっくり研究した現代のアーティストたちの作品によって、我々は言葉と原稿に新しい角度から向き合う。細やかな注意と掛ける時間に報いる展覧会である。コールリッジが1809年の便り『フレンド』第11号に、彼のエッセイから何かを得るには「読者側のいくらかの思考の努力」が必要だと書いているように。

見て、考え、感じるべし—現代のアーティストたちの想像たくましい返答を通して、過去の言葉の力を知ることに近づいてもらいたい。

ジェフ・カウトン
ワーズワース・トラスト 学芸員

1. Helen Darbishire, *The Poet Wordsworth,* Oxford: Clarendon Press, 1950